Doris Lessing

# Doris Lessing

## The Poetics of Change

Gayle Greene

*Ann Arbor*

THE UNIVERSITY OF MICHIGAN PRESS

Published in the United States of America by
The University of Michigan Press
Manufactured in the United States of America
♾ Printed on acid-free paper
1997 1996 1995 1994 4 3 2 1

*A CIP catalogue record for this book is available from the British Library.*

Library of Congress Cataloging-in-Publication Data

Greene, Gayle, 1943–
Doris Lessing : the poetics of change / Gayle Greene.
p. cm.
Includes bibliographical references and index.
ISBN 0-472-10568-X (alk. paper)
1. Lessing, Doris May, 1919– —Criticism and interpretation.
2. Literature and society—England—History—20th century.
I. Title.
PR6023.E833Z68 1994
823′.914—dc20 94-33418
CIP

*To Doris Lessing*

*. . . a wild dedication . . . to unpathed waters, undreamed shores*

*and to my students at Scripps College*

# Contents

# Acknowledgments

First, I wish to thank Jean Wyatt, whose sensitive and helpful reading of this book and whose friendship through the years facilitated this and many other projects. Thanks also to Rena Fraden, who read much of the manuscript, and to Mike Zeller, who not only read it but went so far as to check quotes; to Vicki Ratner, Janet Adelman, Elizabeth Abel, and Elizabeth Minnich, whose friendship and advice have been mainstays; and to Margaret Drabble, for her generous encouragement and personal support. To Keith Webber for endless patient hours of computer help and LeAnn Fields of the University of Michigan Press for her unfailing assistance. Thanks to the Doris Lessing Society, for all its good work publishing the *Doris Lessing Newsletter* and putting together the yearly Lessing MLA sessions—these, taken together, comprise an invaluable compendium of information on Lessing. I wish also to acknowledge Scripps College for several research grants to work on this book. And as always and ever, to my mother, Agnes Greene, and my aunt, Lydia Greenspoon, who have given me examples of spirited and intelligent and long-lived women.

This book is dedicated to my students, many of whom came to love Lessing as I did and who helped me immeasurably in the process of reading and understanding the novels. Finally the book is a kind of homage to Doris Lessing, the writer who mattered to me most—more even, in the end, than Shakespeare. She not only provides an example of change in her own life and works, she has been the inspiration of change to others, certainly to me. One of the advantages of working on a living writer is that you get to say thanks.

## Chapter 1

# Introduction

> Although she was born in a country of ample skies and capacious landscapes, she was afflicted, and from her earliest years, with feelings of being confined. . . . The society around her seemed petty, piffling, to the point of caricature. As a child she could not believe that the adults were serious in the games they played. Everything done and said seemed a repetition, or a recycling, as if they were puppets in a play being staged over and over again. Afflicted by an enormous claustrophobia, she . . . as soon as she was self-supporting left her family and that society.
>
> —Doris Lessing, *Shikasta*

Doris Lessing is quite simply the most extraordinary woman writer of our time, and one of the most controversial. She is—as Margaret Drabble says—"one of the very few novelists who have refused to believe that the contemporary world is too complicated to understand"; by contrast with her, Drabble adds, most others seem like magazine writers.[1] Bursting in on the quiescent postwar literary scene with *The Grass Is Singing,* Lessing articulated connections in the early fifties—between sex, race, and class—that would not be understood for decades. She is, as Drabble says, "not afraid of ideas."[2] Nor is she afraid of bending the shape of the novel to explore ideas, and in the course of her career she's taken on the big ones: the end of imperialism, the hope and failure of communism, the threat of nuclear disaster and ecocide, madness, terrorism, freedom, faith.

Where did Lessing come from? How to account for the appearance of this anomalous radical voice on the conservative literary scene of the fifties?

### Dispossessions

She was born in Persia, October 22, 1919. Her father, Alfred Cook Tayler, had taken a job managing the Imperial Bank of Persia in Kermanshah because he couldn't stand the prospect of being a bank clerk in England. But the defining event of this man's life was World War I: "I think the best of my father died in that war, that his spirit was crippled by it."[3] "I do not know exactly how long he was in the trenches," Lessing writes in 1984, "but altogether it was months. He said he was lucky not to have been killed a dozen times over." Once, his appendix kept him from being killed with his entire company in the Battle of the Somme. On a second occasion,

> shrapnel in the leg—prevent[ed] him from being killed with every other man in the company, at Passchendaele . . . . But the war did him in nevertheless: he lost his leg, and was psychologically damaged. He went into the fighting active and optimistic, and came out with what they then called shell shock.[4]

Tayler married the woman who tended him through convalescence, Emily Maude McVeagh, born in London—"she was essentially urban, this woman who would find herself on a farm in the veld" (*G*, 1, 54). "My mother nursed him . . . a handsome man, but minus a leg and inwardly in torment." "It took her a long time to decide [whether to marry], and she became ill with the strain of it all": "As a nurse she should have known what she had to face in a man so damaged." They married in 1919 and had Doris in 1919: "It was on the wedding night, they joked, that my mother must have got pregnant, though they were armed with the works of Marie Stopes, and had decided not to have a baby yet, if at all" (58). Thus Lessing would see herself as child and heir to the war and would generalize this, making "children of violence" her metaphor for all of us living in the twentieth century, all of us begotten, born, and bred in the aftermath or preparation for war.[5] "He was still so low in spirits: he simply did not seem able to pull himself out of his ugly state of mind. And she was ill, and did not know why" (58).

That same year, 1919, they emigrated to Persia. "He had to leave England—he couldn't stand it—so why not Persia?" He hated banking,

> but at least he was getting out of England, where he knew he could never live again. Coming back from the trenches he felt as all the soldiers of the war did: betrayed by the politicians who had lied to them and did not keep promises; betrayed by the civilians who talked patriotic nonsense and had no idea of what the trenches were like; betrayed by the jingoistic newspapers. (*G*, 1:58–59)[6]

He liked life in Kermanshah, where he was managing a bank and "was not at anybody's beck and call." But Lessing's mother "was having a difficult pregnancy. . . . She was expecting a son . . . did not even consider the possibility of a daughter" (60). "The birth was difficult" and "above all, I was a girl. When the doctor wanted to know my name, and heard that none had been prepared, he looked down at the cradle and said softly, 'Doris?'" Her mother complained "that to have a girl was a disappointment that nearly did her in altogether, after that long labour; . . . that I was an impossibly difficult baby, and then a tiresome child, quite unlike my little brother Harry who was always so good." So began the "resentment" that would mark this mother-daughter relationship for the duration (61).

Doris's father was transferred to Tehran, where he was unhappy because he was no longer a manager but "had to work under someone else," though her mother loved the social life they had there. After they had been in Persia five years they returned to England, and Lessing remembers those six months in England as "of cold, damp, dreariness, ugliness," her father wanting "only to leave England." Visiting the Southern Rhodesia stand at the 1924 British Empire Exhibition at Wembley—"the Southern Rhodesia stand had maize cobs eighteen inches long, and the posters, yards high, claimed that anyone could make his fortune in maize-farming within five years"—he decided, "on impulse," "which is how he ran his whole life," to take his family to Rhodesia to start a farm.

> Where did they imagine they were going to? Certainly they expected a social life not unlike that in Tehran, for my mother had trunks full of clothes from Harrod's. Also curtains and hangings from Liberty's, and visiting cards. Also a governess. (*G,* 1:64)

They bought 1,500 acres, at ten dollars an acre, in Southern Rhodesia, a few hundred miles south of the Zambesi River, a hundred miles from Mozambique, seventy miles from Salisbury, the capital of Rhodesia (today part of Zimbabwe). "It was still a wilderness that my parents were taking on. Not one acre had been cleared for planting." Lessing describes the terrain: "It was virgin bush. . . . Every kind of animal lived there: sable, eland, kudu, bushbuck, duiker, anteaters, wild cats, wild pigs, snakes . . . all day birds shrilled and cooed and hammered and chattered" (65).

The mud and thatch hut they built was "expected to last only a year or so" but it remained their home for nearly twenty years:

> Its walls were of mud smeared over poles and whitewashed, the roof thatch cut from the grass in the vleis, the floor stamped of mud and dung. All the floors

> were covered with black linoleum, and furniture was made from petrol and paraffin boxes stained black and curtained with flour sacks that were dyed and embroidered by my mother. In the front room . . . were Persian rugs, Liberty curtains, a piano and the heavy display silver of the period. (*G,* 1:66)

Tayler's attempts to grow maize failed—he knew nothing about farming; and besides, "the slump had begun"—"Long past were the days when farmers made sudden fortunes out of maize":

> Things were against my father, but his own nature was worse. He did not really care. . . . Left to himself, my father would dream his life away, content, contemplating the African night sky, sunsets, ants at work in a log, fires burning their slow way across the mountains in the dry season, the changing colours of the veld . . . and the fascinating improbabilities of human behaviour.[7]

As time passed, Lessing's father's "dreams of getting rich in five years . . . . [became] a brave family joke," and his get-rich-quick schemes, which included developing a rod for divining for gold, became more desperate. Lessing describes him as "ill, irritable, abstracted, hypochondriac," though she also notes that everyone who knew him from before the war remembered him for his "high spirits, his energy. . . . Also . . . his kindness, his compassion and—a word that keeps recurring—his wisdom. I do not think these people would have easily recognized the ill, irritable, abstracted, hypochondriac man I knew" ("My Father," 86).

Emily Tayler had periods of illness from which she would pull herself together and be "brave and resourceful" ("My Father," 91):

> About a year after the arrival in Africa, my mother became ill and took to her bed and stayed there . . . . It is clear now that she was . . . having a breakdown . . . . The worst for her was the isolation. What my father reveled in—for he had at last found the life that suited him—was destroying her. (*G,* 1: 66–67)

Lessing describes her mother's illnesses as "a way of denying what she knew she had to face" (68):

> She never saw that her husband was not living in a real world . . . We were always about to 'get off the farm.' A miracle would do it—a sweepstake, a gold mine, a legacy. And then? What a question! We would go to England where life would be normal. ("My Father," 91)

Lessing sees her "childhood in the old thatched mud house in the bush" as "a miracle of good luck!": "We were surrounded by every kind of wild animal and bird, free to wander as we wanted over thousands of acres, solitude, the most precious of our gifts"; but meanwhile "our mother lay awake at night, ill with grief because her children were deprived, because they were not good middle-class children in some London suburb" (*G,* 2: 235). She was difficult with "the servants" and with her children. She pushed ladylike proprieties on her daughter, which were violently resisted: "She never freed her judgments from thoughts of class, but then she did not see why she should" (*G,* 1:52). "Poor woman, for the twenty years we were on the farm, she waited for when life would begin for her and for her children, for she never understood that what was a calamity for her was for them a blessing" ("My Father," 91).

"I am not as sorry for [my father] as I am for her," Lessing writes; "She never understood what was happening to her" (*G,* 1:68). "Quite simply, he had a dimension that she lacked"; "he had always been contemplative and philosophical . . . but there was something detached in him which was hard to take" (57). "I believe that his nature so different from hers, was why my mother married him," but that "scope" was "always overwhelming her best self, which was a magnificent common sense" (57).[8] Lessing recalls how at night he would take his chair outside "to watch the sky and the mountains, smoking, silent . . . makes you think—there are so many worlds up there, wouldn't really matter if we did blow ourselves up—plenty more where we came from" ("My Father," 93): "Is it any wonder I turned to space fiction?"[9]

Readers of Lessing's novels will recognize many of these details, for she will spend the rest of her life writing them through in her fictional characters and situations. She has only recently begun to write of them in the first-person singular, however. Most of the above quotes are taken from two autobiographical essays published in *Granta* in the mid eighties, "My Mother's Life," parts 1 and 2, where she attempts to confront the grim truth of her mother's life. "Writing about my mother is difficult," she says; "I keep coming up against barriers, and they are not much different now from what they were [years ago]" (*G,* 1:68).

On the one hand, Lessing is generous in her account of her:

> She was endlessly adaptable and inventive. She had too much energy, capacity, for her situation. Her fate should have been to run a large organization, hospital or even an industry. On the farm she burned herself out. (*G,* 2:228)

And again, in a 1992 radio interview:

> My mother was a very remarkable woman, very tough, very brave, and I remember seeing her with the 1914–18 army revolver, . . . my father's, holding it to the head of a cobra that had emerged from the flower bed. (Bookshelf)

On the other hand, she is frank about the "antagonism" they locked into:

> Better say, and be done with it: my memories of her are all of antagonism, and fighting, and feeling shut out; of pain because the baby born two and a half years after me was so much loved when I was not . . . . She didn't like me—that was the point. It was not her fault: I cannot think of a person less likely than myself to please her. (*G*, 1:61)

This antagonism peaked during her adolescence:

> I was critical about what I saw around me, the poverty of the blacks, the attitudes of the whites, but in a confused, uninstructed way, and this left me vulnerable to her. But what was really making her ill was that she needed to project all her energies and talents into her daughter, who would live, for her, the life she had been prevented from living. But the girl had become a sullen, angry wall of rejection, usually silent, then cracking into rudeness and derision. (*G*, 2:237)

"I had no defense," Lessing recalls, "except to become cold and indifferent . . . . I was the apotheosis of a difficult adolescent. Now I am appalled at how I treated them both—though I could not have done differently. For them it must have been intolerable. For me it was intolerable" (*G*, 2:237–38).

When she was seven Lessing was sent to school at the Roman Catholic Convent in Salisbury, and at thirteen she transferred to the Girls High School, also in Salisbury, but withdrew at fourteen, on account of "eye trouble"—supposedly. Of the convent school in Salisbury she said in a 1992 radio interview, "It was awful, it was a horrible place"—and one could hear the shudder in her tones: "I'm sure it was the worst time in my life, it was horrible." The nuns "were peasant girls from Germany who had become nuns because of the economic conditions in Europe" and who were "very cruel, not meaning to be, and it was very very bad for me, the whole thing was terrible . . . . It was very bad" (Bookshelf). This experience seems to have stamped her with a horror of formal education.[10] She was delighted to be allowed to withdraw from school and return home, partly because the experience was so terrible but partly because, since her mother wanted her to be formally educated, it was kind of a triumph to opt out: "I could have been educated—formally, that is—but I felt some neurotic rebellion against my parents who wanted me to be brilliantly academic. I simply contracted out of the whole thing and educated myself" (Newquist, 49).

Returned to the farm, she read voraciously: "I read a great deal. There was no one to talk to, so I read. What did I read? The best—the classics of European and American literature. One of the advantages of not being educated was that I didn't have to waste time on the second-best" (Newquist, 49). During this time, she wrote and tore up "two bad novels" and then returned to Salisbury, to a job in the Central Telephone Exchange: "My mother experienced this as a final defeat: her daughter was a common telephone operator. The life she was leading . . . was 'fast,' cheap and nasty" (*G,* 2:237–38). Shortly thereafter her father's health became so bad that her parents moved into Salisbury. "My mother moved him into a pretty little suburban house in town near the hospitals, where he took to his bed and a couple of years later died. For the most part he was unconscious under drugs. When awake he talked obsessively about 'the old war'" ("My Father," 93).

At the beginning of World War II, Lessing was nineteen and working in Salisbury, when she met and married a man named Frank Wisdom—it was, as she says, "an utterly wrongheaded marriage." They had two children, John and Jean, who were to stay in Africa when she left for England. She divorced Wisdom in 1943.

In the course of time she became involved in more serious work, as a typist for the official Parliament record and on various government commissions such as the Kariba Dam Project. Between 1942 and 1948 she became active in a Marxist group, drawn to the Communist party because "it was the only people I'd ever met who fought the color bar"—though, as she later said, "We really believed in ten years time the world would be Communist, which made us certifiable." She left the Party in 1956, the year of the Hungarian revolt, along with many others who were disaffected with the Soviet Union and Stalinism.

Through her work with the Communist party she met Gottfried Lessing, a refugee from Hitler's Germany, whom she married in 1945; they had a son, Peter, in 1947, and divorced in 1949. "Let's put it this way," she said in an interview, "I do not think that marriage is one of my talents. I've been much happier unmarried than married" (Newquist, 1963, 46).

She arrived in London in 1949. The war was just over and what struck her most was the ruined landscape, the austerity, the mood of self-righteousness and nostalgia, that she describes in *The Four-Gated City* and *In Pursuit of the English*. She had her son Peter with her and the manuscript for *The Grass Is Singing,* which was accepted by Michael Joseph in London and was an instant success; "I had very good reviews, and I had enough money to keep me going for a bit, but I certainly was extremely short of money, quite often" (Bookshelf). In the ten years after leaving Africa she wrote four more novels, dozens of short stories, reviews, articles, essays, and plays. She was on the board of the *New Left Review,* which was formed by English leftists after the break with the Party. In the fifties she helped organize the First Aldermaston March and other antinuclear activities. She was a friend of R. D. Laing, radical psychologist, and Clancy Sigal, American blacklisted writer (Saul Green in *The Golden Notebook*). In 1956 she returned to Rhodesia and South Africa, where she had been declared a "prohibited immigrant" because of her Communist affiliations, and wrote of this trip in *Going Home* (1957); she did not return to Africa for twenty-five years. She has been back several times since then and has recently written about Zimbabwe in *African Laughter*.

Lessing has published twenty novels, eleven volumes of short stories, six works of nonfiction, five plays, and a volume of poetry, and is at work on her autobiography. Since she was thirty-five she has been living exclusively from her writing—"I've made my living as a professional writer ever since, which is really very hard to do. I had a rather hard going." But it has kept her free, this writer who cares so deeply about freedom: "In England you don't have to 'go commercial' if you don't mind being poor" (Newquist, 47). Her advice to young writers is "don't review, don't go on television, try to keep out of all that" (53). Of politics she says, "I have never thought that politics resolved anything, nor have I ever defended any definite political position";[11] yet she also said, in 1989, "I remain a socialist."[12]

One son, Peter, lives in London, John in Zimbabwe, and her daughter, Jean, in South Africa.

## Deconstructions and Reconstructions

It seems astonishing that Lessing came from Southern Rhodesia, though it is perhaps not so astonishing when one realizes that colonial societies make glaringly apparent the structures of oppression that are more masked elsewhere. As a female and a "colonial," Lessing was "doubly dispossessed." Besides this, she was doubly exiled:[13] she spent her childhood among people who were longing to return to England, and then, when she moved to England, she found herself longing for Africa—and she was *literally* exiled when she was declared "prohibited."

On the one hand were long hours spent in a solitary and spectacular natural landscape: "From my point of view the most important thing was the space, you know, there was practically nobody around, and I used to spend hours by myself in the bush"; "I did things that no girl of that time would have done in Britain or in Europe. We had a kind of freedom and independence that now I marvel at, I was so lucky to have had it" (Bookshelf). On the other hand was an emotionally fraught family life, rife with unspoken tensions and disappointments, that imbued her with claustrophobia about the family and a wariness of human relations.

Lessing assesses the effects of this "very difficult family situation" in a 1980 interview:

> My position in the family was such that I was very critical, and fairly early on. I had to be, because my mother and father were both in complicated emotional states. I was under terrible pressure as a child, which is true of every child, mind you, but I think it was slightly worse in my case. And then I was in this social set-up, which I disliked, this white-black thing. I can't remember a time when it didn't make me uneasy. . . .

When the interviewer suggests, "So you were able to see clearly the dynamic between white settlers and the black population?" Lessing responds,

> I wasn't clearly seeing it at all. It took many years for me to see it. I think it had far more to do with the family set-up. I had to fight every inch of the way against a very difficult family situation.[14]

She reiterates this in the 1992 radio interview:

> People become writers because they've had a very pressured childhood, and that doesn't necessarily mean a bad childhood. I don't think "unhappy childhood makes writer," but I think a child that has been forced to become conscious of what's going on very early—they often become writers.

She describes herself as developing "this extremely clear, critical eye about what goes on—which is not always a good thing . . . You tend to be somewhat bleak, which I am" (Bikman). But from this came an acuity and sensitivity to subtext. "I became an expert in emotional blackmail by the time I was five," she recalls. "The way [my mother] saw it was that her childhood had been cold and loveless, and she would make sure that her children were governed by love. Love was always being invoked" (*G,* 1:61). To Mr. Quest's admonishment that her mother is a good woman who loves her, Martha retorts, "'Good?' . . . What do you mean by 'good'? . . . 'Love'? What's love got to do with it? . . . You just use words and—it's got nothing to do with what actually goes on . . . " (ellipses in original).[15] This distrust of official versions, this sense that "listening to the words people use is the longest way around to an understanding of what is going on,"[16] is what makes Lessing the de-masker, the dismantler of systems, that she is.[17]

One of the things that most drew me to Lessing is her ability to penetrate the surfaces. When I first read *The Golden Notebook* it was not only its analysis of sexual politics, its articulation of the problems of women and men in our times in relation to the times, that fascinated me; it was passages like this:

> Anna, watching, thought amusedly: If I said to Molly you stopped Richard talking simply by making fun of him with your hands, she wouldn't know what I meant. (*GN,* 25)

And this:

> Anna thought, I wish I hadn't become so conscious of everything, every little nuance. Once I wouldn't have noticed: now every conversation, every encounter with a person seems like crossing a mined field; and why can't I accept that one's closest friends at moments stick a knife in, deep, between the ribs? (43)

For all the words she has written, for all her amazing literary productivity, there is often in Lessing's work a strong sense of the unreliability of language—a sense that the most important conversation going on at a given time may not be the one that is being verbalized, that "you have to deduce a person's real feelings about a thing by a smile she does not know is on her face, by the way bitterness tightens muscles at a mouth's corner."[18]

This is something she taught me, at a time when I very badly needed to know it: that if I was hearing another conversation, inhabiting "another room" (to use one of her recurrent metaphors), so too were others.[19] I think this is one reason her works continue to appeal to feminists, whatever her disavowals of feminism may be. This demystification of verbal and ideological systems resonated powerfully with women were who just then developing, in the fifties and sixties, a sense that they inhabited a different reality from that articulated by the dominant culture.

Yet at the same time that she unmasks current orthodoxies, she also pushes us to imagine "something new"—and the term *something new* recurs in her fiction.[20] In her 1957 essay, "A Small Personal Voice," Lessing asserts that "literature should be committed."[21] Early in the *Children of Violence* she describes Martha as being "of that generation who, having found nothing in religion, had formed themselves by literature":

> It is of no use for artists to insist, with such nervous disinclination for responsibility, that their productions are only "a reflection from the creative fires of irony," etc., etc., while the Marthas of this world read and search with the craving thought, What does this say about my life?[22]

Lessing insisted that the artist has a social responsibility at a time when the New Criticism, with its Ivory Tower aesthetics, made such a view unfashionable, and she analyzed these aesthetics as a function of cold war politics.[23] She believes in the "responsibility" of the artist "as a human being, for the other human beings he influences," describing "him" as "an instrument of change for good or for bad" —as "an architect of the soul" ("SPV," 6,7).

"But if one is going to be an architect, one must have a vision to build towards" ("SPV," 7). It is the purpose of this book to understand that vision.

*Chapter 2*

# Efforts of Imagination

There are only two choices: that we force ourselves into the effort of imagination necessary to become what we are capable of being; or that we . . . blow ourselves up.

—Doris Lessing, "The Small Personal Voice"

Why is it that writers, who by definition operate by the use of their imaginations, are given so little credit for it. We "make things up." This is our trade.

—Doris Lessing, *The Sirian Experiments,* Preface

For nearly half a century, Doris Lessing has been a chronicler of our time. At the beginning and end of the sixties, her epic works *The Golden Notebook* and *The Four-Gated City* render the "ideological 'feel' of our mid century" (as she describes her intent),[1] taking us from the cold war of the fifties through the social revolutions of the sixties, the retrenchments of the seventies and eighties, and finally to Armageddon at the end of the century—when she moves "off into fantasy" (as she says) at the end of *The Four-Gated City.*[2] At the end of the sixties, she was predicting ecological and political disaster, in the poisoning of the planet and "Britain's version of a Fascist phase," which occur at the end of *The Four-Gated City;*[3] and in the early seventies, in *Memoirs of a Survivor,* she was depicting the sort of devastated urban scene that has long since become familiar in inner cities in the United States and England. So accurate have been her readings of contemporary social movements that she has come to be viewed by many as a sage, seer, prophetess—a Cassandra.[4] I've no doubt that if there is a future, Lessing will be one of the writers by whom we'll be remembered—one of the writers who will be seen as expressing what we were about.[5]

Lessing is a complex and prolific writer, always restless, moving, probing, testing the limits of the possible and seeking new possibilities—searching for "something new" against the "nightmare repetition" of the past.[6] A study of her forty-odd-year writing career does not yield easy generalizations, for she is not easy in any sense—not easy to characterize and not always easy to take. In her feminism, her politics, her narrative forms, she is impossible to "place"; at home neither on the Left nor the Right, an exile, both metaphorically and actually, she continues to baffle critics who would claim her or categorize her,[7] remaining what Mona Knapp terms "an outsider on principle, in voluntary exile from all collectives and movements."[8] In her long and varied career her fiction has progressed through dramatically different stages, passing from realism through postmodernism, fantasy and "space fiction," and back to realism—formal moves that correspond to philosophical shifts from Marxism and feminism through Sufism and that have bewildered, alienated, and at times even lost her readers. When she feels trapped by readers' expectations or by her own earlier practices, she invents a new form or springs for a new identity, always describing such moves as liberating, always in search of "freedom."[9]

Though *The Golden Notebook* remains the single most important work of feminist fiction in this century, Lessing has refused to be classified as a feminist writer, distancing herself not only from the women's movement but from political movements generally. Yet she has continued to write fiction that focuses on women and that celebrates women as the center and source of value in the modern world, and she has continued to write politically and to portray "the individual conscience in its relations with the collective" (as she describes *Children of Violence,* "SPV," 14). And she has—or at least until recently—used the novel as "an instrument of change" ("SPV," 6) and a means to "something new."

## "Something New"

Given the ideological and political constraints of the fifties, the publication of *The Grass Is Singing,* Lessing's first novel, in 1950, was remarkable indeed. She was immediately hailed as a bright new talent and grouped with the "Angry Young Men"—an association she did her best to deny, since she saw their work as characterized by the "pettiness and narrowness" it decried and as "extremely provincial," not in the sense that "they come from or write about the provinces" but that "their horizons are bounded by their immediate experience of British life and standards" ("SPV," 15).

After *The Grass Is Singing,* Lessing began publishing the five-volume epic that takes Martha Quest from her childhood in southern Africa through the end of the world, the *Children of Violence*. She published its first three novels—*Martha Quest* (1952), *A Proper Marriage* (1954), *A Ripple from the Storm* (1958)—in close succession; she then interrupted the series with *The Golden Notebook* (1962) and returned to it in the mid sixties, completing it with *Landlocked* (1965) and *The Four-Gated City* (1969). In the context of postwar retreat—political, intellectual, literary—the *Children of Violence* was "something new" indeed: there was nothing like Lessing's radical critique of Anglo culture, nor was there anything like her satire of nostalgia in a postwar fiction that was saturated with nostalgia.[10] In writing a series that chronicled the life of her times, she did what male series writers C. P. Snow and Anthony Powell were doing, though her portrayal of English society was far less genial than theirs;[11] and in voicing protest, she made common cause with the Angry Young Men, though her protest had an ideological edge that theirs lacked. Her fiction invaded male territory but went beyond what male writers were doing, in combining protest with ideology with a scathing critique of Anglo society.

Yet her fiction was also, from the beginning, a "women's writing," centering on women's consciousness and concerns. It resembled, in its exploration of female interiority, the "feminine" sensibility of postwar writers such as Elizabeth Bowen, Sylvia Plath, and Penelope Mortimer, but it went beyond what these novelists were doing, not only in dramatizing the malaise that produced the second wave of feminism, but also in presenting it in political terms. Anna's realization, doing door-to-door canvassing for the Communist party, that "this country's full of women going mad all by themselves," all thinking "there must be something wrong with me" (*GN*, 167), articulated early on, before any other English novelist, that "the personal is political." In fact *The Golden Notebook* and the *Children of Violence* are dramatizations of the worlds described by Simone de Beauvoir and by Betty Friedan: *The Second Sex* was published in 1949, the year before *The Grass Is Singing* (though it was not translated into English until 1953), and *The Feminine Mystique* was published the year after *The Golden Notebook*.

From the start Lessing's understanding of sexism was informed by an awareness of racism gained by coming of age in colonial Southern Rhodesia and by an awareness of class gleaned from Marxism: from the start she understood that the oppression of one group is linked to the oppression of all. Even in her first novel, the small-scale and conventionally well-made *Grass Is Singing,* she criticizes the protagonist, Mary Turner, for her shortsighted targeting of men as the enemy, her ignorance of the relation of sexual and racial oppression—her "arid feminism": "How could she know? She understood nothing of conditions in other countries, had no measuring rod to assess herself with."[12] No writer I know of was making these sorts of connections in the early fifties. Only much later, in the late sixties, when women in the New Left began to look to Socialist theory for a radical theoretical framework that could explain the oppression of women in relation to that of other groups, would white feminists begin to understand the connections Lessing was seeing decades before, connections that African-American feminists would describe as "the intersection of multiple structures of domination."[13]

It would be difficult to overstate the impact *The Golden Notebook* had on women of my generation, the direct and immediate identification we felt with it, the thrill of recognition. We found ourselves in the pages of that novel—it offered validation, corroboration of who we were: "The shock of recognition of oneself, the sense of 'Yes, someone is writing about *my* life exactly as it is' is overwhelming."[14] Anna describes herself as "the position of women in our time" (*GN,* 579), and for many of us this was no exaggeration. Here was a literary protagonist living the kind of life a woman had never lived before, struggling with commitments to herself, work, children, relationships, politics; no one had ever spoken to us and of us and for us as Lessing did. "After years of our attempts to identify ourselves with Quentin Compson, Augie March, and the Invisible Man, not to mention Lolita and Franny Glass, we were presented with a novel whose persona was an intellectual, a political activist, an artist, as well as a lover, a mother—a woman."[15] Marilyn Webb writes, "These were the first novels I'd read about women I might know, not mythical characters I'd never meet."[16] "It was the first book I'd read, apart from Simone de Beauvoir's *Second Sex,* which seemed to be really addressing the problems of women in the contemporary world," says Margaret Drabble: "Nobody seemed to have written about them in the way that we were experiencing them."[17] Laurie Stone writes, "her truculent, anxious, hungry heroines . . . this band I knew. It was the early 1970s and meeting myself in literature felt like a confirmation of reality."[18] Jean McCrindle describes *The Golden Notebook* "as a way of finding out about the world and who I was and where we stood in the world and what love and emotions were all about."[19] Jenny Taylor writes, "For women who found reading and discussing novels an important reference-point, often a crucial form of self-perception and analysis, Doris Lessing loomed up—wherever one looked, she seemed to be waiting" (Taylor, 5). Kate Millett describes the importance of *The Golden Notebook* "to the thousands of women who read it";[20] Wilson describes *The Golden Notebook* as "a manual of womanly experience" (in Taylor, 71); Annette Kolodny says she used it as a way of interviewing prospective lovers (pers. comm., Oct. 1989).

Conversations I've had with friends (Lillian Robinson, Elizabeth Abel, Myra Goldberg, Ann Rosalind Jones, Annette Kolodny, Tania Modleski, Dorothy Kaufman, Molly Hite, Helene Keyssar, Carol Turbin, Catherine Davis) corroborate my sense of *The Golden Notebook* as a transformative work and a touchstone for a generation. Rachel Blau DuPlessis begins her autobiographical-experimental meditation "For the Etruscans": "Frankly, it was *The Golden Notebook.* Which pierced my heart." DuPlessis expresses the sense of being haunted by *The Golden Notebook* and needing to return to it again and again:

> A self-questioning, the writer built into the center of the work, the questions at the center of the writer, the discourses doubling, retelling the same, differently . . . .

Of course I am describing *The Golden Notebook* again. Again.[21] So, too, did *The Golden Notebook* draw me back year after year: it made me a feminist, then made me a feminist scholar, and finally I reorganized my professional life around it, changing my area of study from Renaissance to contemporary fiction. Drabble's description of *The Golden Notebook* as "a transforming work. There is nothing at all like it"[22] is not hyperbolic. Lisa Alther says "any number of my friends speak of the crisis of self-examination that accompanied their first reading of *The Golden Notebook* and the *Children of Violence* series, unabashedly admitting these books 'changed their lives.'"[23] Jane Marcus says "I never would have gone [to graduate school] if it hadn't been for Elaine Shinbrot, who gave me Doris Lessing's *The Golden Notebook.*"[24] (It's not surprising that Lessing describes writing *The Golden Notebook* as having changed her: "Writing *The Golden Notebook* completely changed me. When I started it I was a Marxist and a materialist . . . [but] I suddenly found myself writing easily about things with which I had no personal acquaintance.")[25]

Annis Pratt calls it "one of those novels that seemed to speak directly to a whole generation's experience" (*DL,* viii). Susan Lardner calls it "a feminist gospel, a representative of Modern Woman."[26] Margaret Drabble hails it as "a document in the history of liberation."[27] Susan Lydon describes it as "almost . . . a Little Red Book" of "women's liberationists," "probably the most widely read and deeply appreciated book on the women's liberation reading list, Simone de Beauvoir's *The Second Sex* and Betty Friedan's *The Feminine Mystique* notwithstanding" (*Ramparts,* 48). Drabble similarly pairs Lessing with de Beauvoir,[28] as does Elizabeth Wilson: "In the strange cultural landscape of 1960 [Lessing and de Beauvoir] loomed up, Cassandras of women's experience."[29] Ellen Brooks describes Lessing's depiction of women as "the most thorough and accurate of any in literature";[30] Elayne Antler Rapping calls the novel "a nearly pure expression of feminine consciousness . . . honestly reflecting the truths of feminine experience."[31] It is true that some women readers found Anna problematic as a "role model" and saw the novel as "alienated from the authentic female perspective" and "apart from 'the feminine' and from feminism,"[32] but I think these disappointments derive from the narrowly prescriptive criteria of early feminist criticism, the expectation that literature should provide role models and "authentic female perspective." (The way men read *The Golden Notebook* is a whole other story, which I tell in chapter 4: in fact to see the difference between the way men and women read the novel is to understand why a feminist critical approach was necessary.)

Lessing's work also had enormous influence on women writers. Lisa Alther says, "I could never have started writing novels without having read Doris Lessing's books";[33] "almost every woman writer I know acknowledges a debt to Doris Lessing" (*WRB,* 243), a debt that is abundantly clear in her own novel *Other Women.* Drabble describes Lessing as a "touchstone" and "a mother and seer,"[34] and her *Waterfall* draws on *The Golden Notebook,* as her *Middle Ground* does on *The Summer Before the Dark* and *The Radiant Way* draws on *The Four-Gated City.*[35] Lessing also had demonstrable influence on works such as Lois Gould's *Final Analysis,* Valerie Miner's *Movement,* Erica Jong's *Fear of Flying,* Anne Oakley's *The Men's Room,*[36] and Dorothy Bryant's *Ella Price's Journal.* In *Ella Price's Journal,* Ella recognizes deep affinities with Anna, despite their differences:

> I don't know anything about women like this—free, independent women who earn their own living, raise their own children, sleep with whoever they want, make their own rules. But in some strange way their lives don't seem to be much different from mine.[37]

Even in works where Lessing's influence is not immediately apparent, the feminist quest she articulated in *The Golden Notebook* and *The Children of Violence* entered the culture with the force of a new myth: as Jenny Taylor says, Martha's quest became "the epic, archetypal story of our times."[38]

*The Golden Notebook* was published within a year of Betty Friedan's *Feminine Mystique,* Plath's *Bell Jar,* and *The Report of the Commission on American Women*—all appeared in 1962–63. It took the rest of the sixties for the women's movement to emerge with the ideology and visibility of an international movement. The visibility (or notoriety) came with the picketing of the 1968 Miss America contest in Atlanta, when the crowning of a sheep and alleged bra burning—which never actually took place—drew national press coverage.[39] One could argue (as I have in *Changing the Story*) that Lessing's novels played a crucial role in the consolidation of the movement that took place in the course of the decade—that her works, along with Betty Friedan's, Simone de Beauvoir's, Germaine Greer's, Shulamith Firestone's, Juliet Mitchell's, and the numerous "mad housewife" novels published during the sixties,[40] helped make the second wave of feminism.

Jean McCrindle describes *The Golden Notebook* as "prophetic" because it "prefigure[s] all sorts of things that were actually to happen in the next ten years—to me personally, and in the external world. I think I even felt that I wouldn't fully understand it until I had actually lived another ten years of my life. I can still pick it up now and say, 'God, *now* I know what she is saying about that'" (in Taylor, 55–56). Lessing herself felt that *The Golden Notebook* had "skipped a stage of opinion, assume[d] a crystallization of information in society which has not yet taken place," which was why it was misunderstood: "This book was written as if the attitudes that have been created by the Women's Liberation movements already existed. . . . If it were coming out now for the first time, it might be read, and not merely reacted to" (*GN,* ix–x). Lessing sees fiction as intuiting the future, as "com[ing] out of that part of the human consciousness which is always trying to understand itself, to come into the light,"[41] and she describes the novelist as "almost like an organism, which has been evolved by society as a means of examining itself":[42] "At times, when I write, my obsessiveness seems to me to be madness, but when I finish a book, it's already almost a common situation" (Torrents, 13). She sees herself as intuiting something new in the world—"Some terrible new thing is happening. Maybe it'll be marvelous. Who knows?" for "we live in dreadful and marvellous times where the certainties of yesterday dissolve as we live."[43]

## The Poetics of Change

Difficult though Lessing is to categorize, she is always concerned with change. "What interests me more than anything is how our minds are changing," she says ("SPV," 65–66). She urges "a new imaginative comprehension" (*GN,* 61), "a new kind of knowledge" (*LL,* 157), "a new sort of understanding" (*FGC,* 357) against the nightmare of history and the repetitive cycles of behavior—psychological, social, historical—that lock us into the patterns of the past. No writer speaks so urgently of the necessity of change and uses her fiction so compellingly as "an instrument of change" ("SPV," 6), and few writers have had so great an effect on so many; she is, as Drabble calls her, "the kind of writer who changes peoples' lives" ("Cassandra," 50).[44]

Though Lessing dissociated herself at an early age from formal systems of education, always she is concerned with education. The *Children of Violence* is, as she terms it, a *Bildungsroman* ("Author's Notes," *FGC,* 615). Martha vows that she would *"not* be like her mother" or like any of the older woman she knows, though this leaves her wondering "Who was she going to be like?" (*MQ,* 10). Finding herself "named" as "British," "adolescent," "twentieth-century," "female," and "doomed," she is overcome by a weariness that *"it had all been done and said already"* (*PM,* 34) and protests, "If this has all been said, why do I have to go through with it? . . . it was time to move in to something new" (*MQ,* 8–9). But "go through it" she must, and the *Children of Violence* shows her living through the conventional roles allotted women—"woman in love," wife, mother—and needing to play each one out thoroughly, exhaustively, before she can "move in to something new." This series provides a kind of anatomy of change, an investigation of what enables it and what prevents it. It explores the means to change—memory, imagination, and "growing points": "In every life there is a curve of growth, or a falling away from it; there is a central pressure, like sap forcing up a trunk" (*FGC,* 192). It also explores the impediments to change—the tendency to divide, deny, forget.

Always Lessing is concerned with getting us to "step outside what we are" ("SPV," 8) and stretch our imaginations to conceive of "another order of world altogether."[45] Her fiction is visionary and revisionary in getting us to see that our reality is not the whole of reality and to imagine an elsewhere. She describes literature (together with anthropology) as "one of the most useful ways we have of achieving this 'other eye,' this detached manner of seeing ourselves" (*Prisons,* 8). In her early works her protagonists are ethnologists like herself, students of their own, alien cultures; in later works she, and they, assume the perspective of visitors from outer space. This "other eye" is instrumental to change, for if we can see our culture as conventional rather than inevitable, then we can imagine it as capable of being changed. It is also instrumental to freedom, for "to imagine free man, . . . is to step outside what we are" ("SPV," 8).

Most of Lessing's fiction is a search for the "four-gated city," an effort to guide us to a better society—to get us to create it or to imagine it: for the means to the city is the imagination. Early in the *Children of Violence* Martha is entranced by a vision of an ordered and harmonious society, "a noble city, set foursquare and colonnaded along its falling, flower-bordered terraces," a "fabulous and ancient city" whose "citizens moved, grave and beautiful, black and white and brown . . . the blue-eyed, fair-skinned children of the North playing hand in hand with the bronze-skinned, dark-eyed children of the South" (*MQ*, 11), all living together in "generous and freely exchanged emotion" (*MQ*, 79). This utopia is the antithesis of her actual world, where people are pitted against one another in a mad scramble for profit and power, and all Martha's actions are efforts to get to it, however misguided and dead-ended most of them turn out to be.

Martha's journey begins as she makes "the effort of imagination" that takes her beyond the conventional divisions and barriers that fragment her society—beyond the confines of gender, race, class, and nationality. It is an effort that "exhausts" her:

> She could not remember a time when she had not thought of people in terms of groups, nations, or colour of skin first, and as people afterwards . . . the natives . . . the Afrikaans . . . the British, with their innumerable subgroupings. . . . And each group, community, clan, colour strove and fought away from the other, in a sickness of dissolution; . . . a fever of self-assertion . . . when nothing but a sober mutual trust could save them. Martha could feel the striving forces in her own substance; the effort of imagination needed to destroy the words *black, white, nation, race,* exhausted her, her head ached. (*MQ*, 47)

She is aided by her visionary moments on the veld, when she senses herself as "one" with the universe, enduring "a slow integration" with "the great wheels of movement." Such moments teach her "futility," but they also give her the knowledge of unity that becomes elaborated in Lessing's belief, in the later novels, in the oneness of each with all—an intuition Lessing found verified in Sufism.[46] And these moments also teach Martha that "something new was demanding conception, with her flesh as host" (*MQ*, 52–53), a sense that is fulfilled at the end of *The Four-Gated City,* when she brings forth the "new children" that represent "a future for our race" (604).

It is imagination that points the way to something new because imagination counters the deadly tendency to divide and compartmentalize and acquiesce to what is. Imagination is the access to wonder, which Lessing (like Aristotle) places at the origin of human inquiry.[47] But Lessing is not interested in imagination as it relates to personal genius or artistic inspiration; to her it is the sympathetic imagination that matters, imagination as empathy, connectedness, the "sober mutual trust" that might save us—for it is the failure of this faculty that has laid our world waste. Imagination is the means of fulfilling our best selves and social responsibility: it is the means to freedom and to creating a world where all can be free. This is why, when the band of survivors sets forth to make a new world at the end of *Four-Gated City,* they "quoted to each other Blake's 'What now exists was once only imagined'" (586).

What Martha is seeking, finally, is freedom—freedom conceived not as freedom from the claims of others but as living responsibly and acknowledging interdependence. Though Lessing sees independence as important, particularly for women, for whom it is particularly difficult, she values connectedness as much as she does autonomy. And so, paradoxically, freedom comes from encumbrances, from taking others on, seeing others through—and opportunities present themselves in strange places. Often what looks like a burden turns out to be a blessing, as, for example, when, taking on Mark Coldridge's family, Martha develops intuitive powers that save the saving remnant of the human race; here, as elsewhere in Lessing's fiction, surrogate relationships allow room for learning and growing that biological relationships do not. In *Memoirs* it is the narrator's taking responsibility for Emily and Emily's taking responsibility for Hugo and Hugo's guarding Emily and Gerald's taking on the gangs of children that develop saving strengths in all. In *The Diary of a Good Neighbor* Jane Somers takes on the ninety-two-year-old Maudie and thereby "delivers" not only Maudie, but herself. In *Shikasta* Johor tells a series of cautionary tales about people who, had they realized their potentials, would have been there to save others—tales that illustrate the relation between individual self-fulfillment and social responsibility (174–89).

This means that human relations provide "growing points"—and again, opportunities turn up in unexpected places. Female friendships—Martha's and Lynda's, Al·Ith's and Dabeeb's, Jane's and Maudie's—allow growth, but so too do doomed passions and love affairs (Martha's for Thomas, in *Landlocked;* Mark's for Lynda, in *Four-Gated City;* Julia Barr's for Jon Brod, in *Retreat to Innocence*). Sometimes a relationship that seems a calamity turns out to be an opportunity, "operating to bring some individual nearer to self-knowledge, understanding," as Johor says in *Shikasta* (175). Such relationships may involve a clash of cultures, as in *Marriages,* where the differences between Al.Ith and Ben Ata generate growth both for the individuals and for their cultures. In *The Sirian Experiments* Ambien of Sirius is jolted out of complacency by the Canopean Klorathy, though in this novel the education is all one way and the lesson is foreknown: Canopus instructs Sirius, male instructs female, and this static pattern is quite unlike the dynamic interchange of *Marriages,* where each is changed by the other. So, too, in *Retreat to Innocence,* the love affair of Julia Barr, provincial English schoolgirl, with the Czech Communist Jon Brod brings her up against her limits and enlarges her perspective, but again, the education is one way, with male instructing female. These novels tend to be somewhat schematic, programmatic, predictable; I find them less interesting than those which I have chosen to focus on, where Lessing uses the writing as a "growing point" and a probe, as an "instrument of change."[48]

But freedom is not easy. Lessing's characters often assume that they can attain it by cutting loose from the claims of others or stepping off a cycle, but they learn that it requires long, arduous processes, not only of "working it through" but of seeing others through. This is why "very few people really care about freedom or liberty," as Anna says, or about the efforts required to make a free society: "Very few people have guts, the kind of guts on which a real democracy has to depend. Without that sort of guts a free society dies or cannot be born" (*GN,* 567). For just as the oppression of one incurs the oppression of all—an understanding that goes back to *The Grass Is Singing*—so too does the freedom of one require the freedom of all: " 'Free! What's the use of us being free if they aren't?' " (*GN,* 458).[49] Lessing's characters do not travel alone; theirs is not the solitary journey of the mystic—which is why her mysticism is not, as is sometimes claimed, escapist.[50] Always it is the life of the society that she cares about.

I am particularly interested in those novels which not only portray characters who change but which also enlist the reader's imagination in processes that transform our consciousness and understanding. *The Golden Notebook, The Four-Gated City, Landlocked, Memoirs,* and *Shikasta* are what Roland Barthes calls "writerly" texts, open and processive and participatory works that require us to piece together patterns and relationships.[51] Reading *The Golden Notebook* teaches us to "look at things as a whole and in relation to each other," as Lessing says in the introduction (*GN,* xiv), and so counters the tendency to divide and compartmentalize, which is a major obstacle to growth; reading *The Four-Gated City*—and *Memoirs* and *Shikasta*—is, similarly, an exercise in making connections that strengthens the sympathetic imagination. But the imaginative participation they require has a special meaning in Lessing's philosophy: reading these novels becomes an act of re-creation, an exercise of the moral faculty that can repair the ruination of the world.

This writerly dimension of her fiction puts Lessing in a complex relation to realism, for she is simultaneously one of the great realist writers of our century and a writer who chafes against the assumptions of realism. Both *The Golden Notebook* and *The Children of Violence* dramatize the dynamics of historical change in a way that fulfills Georg Lukács's ideal of a socially responsible and transformative "realist literature";[52] both fulfill Anna's (and Lukács's) ideal of "a book powered with an intellectual or moral passion strong enough to create order, to create a new way of looking at life" (61). *The Golden Notebook* focuses on an exceptional individual whose subjectivity is felt to matter and whose world is richly specified in relation to social and historical circumstances; it gives us a protagonist who is strikingly singular at the same time that she is representative—for Anna is as representative of her age as Julien Sorel is of his. Yet *The Golden Notebook* also unmasks the conventions of realism, challenging the assumption that literary and linguistic forms are innocent "reflections" of reality, and this tension between the form and its deconstruction is part of the novel's fascination. Actually, as my readings demonstrate, even those early works that are usually seen as straightforward mimetic realism, the first *Children of Violence* novels, critique realism in terms that resemble Barthes's;[53] and ultimately this dissatisfaction with realism pushes Lessing "off into fantasy" (as she says of the end of *The Four-Gated City*), for "I could no longer say what I wanted to say inside the old form" (*DLN*, 3).

## Female Identity and the Possibilities of Change

Lessing's relation to feminism is as problematic as her relation to realism. Whether or not she is a "feminist" writer, it is clear that her sense of possibilities is integrally bound up with her sense of female identity: hope about one is hope about the other. Lessing has always had a strong sense of what Nancy Chodorow calls woman's "tendency toward . . . boundary confusion and lack of separateness from the world," her tendency to define and experience herself as "continuous with others";[54] and, like Chodorow, she sees female boundary fluidity as originating in the mother-daughter relationship. Generally, when she is bleak about female identity she is also bleak about the possibilities of change, and when she is hopeful about female identity she is optimistic about change: for the sympathetic imagination that is the means to something new is that empathy, relatedness, and openness that she, like Chodorow, associates with women.[55] Thus whatever her reservations about feminism, her view of woman is at the center of her sense of possibilities, informing everything else.

In her first novel, *The Grass Is Singing,* the protagonist relives the life of the mother and dies for it, and the circular structure—final scene returning to first scene—is the narrative correlative of the grim view of female identity in this work, of protagonist's (and author's) matrophobia—and the word *matrophobia* was actually coined in an essay on Lessing.[56] Similarly, in *A Proper Marriage,* where Martha reenacts the life of her mother in an unwanted pregnancy and unhappy marriage, circular forms (like the Ferris wheel that spins outside her bedroom window) symbolize "the nightmare repetition." But in *The Golden Notebook* female identity is re-envisioned as the means to change: it is her female boundary fluidity, her ability to leave herself "open for something" (473), that allows the protagonist to accomplish something new—as it enables the author herself to achieve something new. Similarly, in *The Four-Gated City* the intuitive powers Martha develops by becoming surrogate mother to Mark's children, telepathic powers that allow her to enter the experiences of others, put her on "the main line of evolution" and assure "a future for our race" (*FGC,* 497, 624).[57] The formal and structural correlative of this shift is the transformation of closed, vicious circles to open and liberatory structures that accommodate change—to processive and participatory forms that render "something . . . worked through."

But the trajectory of Lessing's development is not simple, for in *The Summer Before the Dark,* published four years after *The Four-Gated City* (1973), Lessing again envisions female identity as a trap, as Kate Brown feels herself diminished and debilitated by the qualities of empathy and relatedness that she has had to develop to raise four children. At the end she can only say "no"[58]—a statement confined, however, to her hair, for she has no choice but to return to the home that is the source of her unhappiness, in a closed, circular structure that, if not so hopeless as that of *Grass Is Singing,* severely constrains future possibilities. Against this grim determinism one can understand Lessing's turn to fantasy.

In *Memoirs of a Survivor,* published a year after *Summer,* it is those same qualities of compassionate receptivity that were repudiated as a cage in *Summer* that free the protagonist and her world from the nightmare repetition. Though the protagonist does little more than observe and enter imaginatively into the experiences she observes, this exercise of the sympathetic imagination enables her to step off "this merry-go-round" (94) and lead the characters of her world "into another order of world altogether" (217). The way forward to the new dimension is also the way back, through Eastern and Western mystical traditions: the move from history to myth takes Lessing back to the oldest knowledge of the race, to those ancient repositories of wisdom, the Bible, the Koran, and Sufic lore.

The protagonist of *Memoirs*—like Martha in *The Four-Gated City* and Al.Ith in *Marriages*—emerges as the savior of the race, a kind of female Christ or "cosmic mother." The means to salvation in these novels are Christian virtues of sacrifice, patience, endurance, compassion; for as Martha's lover Thomas Stern tells her, when he urges her to "feel the stars and their time and their spaces," it is "the householders . . . who are nearest to being—what's needed." Though the cosmic perspective, the "new kind of knowledge" that Thomas describes, makes "the house with the tree outside" obsolete, the "householder" is still, paradoxically, more than ever, what is needed (*LL,* 193, 116–17). Thus Martha performs a "holding operation" that holds the Radlett Street house together and the protagonist of *Memoirs* performs a holding operation for the world of her novel, and in both novels such efforts are redemptive. Even in *Shikasta* the saving graces are embodied by a householder who is, again, female: Suzannah, who represents the qualities of constancy, self-effacement, and steadfastness necessary to hold things together.

In *The Marriages Between Zones Three, Four, and Five* Lessing constructs a fantasy situation in which female identity is knowledge and power: indeed, the unity of one with all that is the moral basis of the universe is envisioned as a kind of cosmic boundary fluidity. As elsewhere in Lessing's fiction, it is the protagonist's ability to remain open and to cross boundaries—boundaries between Zone Three and Zone Four as well as boundaries within herself—that enables her to redeem her world. Al.Ith must break down in order to break through (as Martha and Anna do), and she must descend to Zone Four before she can ascend to Zone Two; and, as elsewhere, the way forward is the way back, for she is guided to Zone Two by old knowledge which is preserved by the Memories and chroniclers.

Thus in *Memoirs, The Four-Gated City, Shikasta,* and *Marriages* women save the world. But these are not "real" worlds that they save: in order to empower female virtues, Lessing requires a framework of fantasy, for when she returns to realism her sense of possibilities diminishes. Interestingly, she makes the transition back from Canopus to London under the guise of "Jane Somers": while Doris Lessing is still—officially, publicly—charting the rise and fall of galactic empires, she returns, under cover of a pseudonym, to focus in on the life and death of a ninety-two-year-old woman, Maudie Fowler, whose physical decrepitude she delineates in a social realism more graphic than any she uses elsewhere. Yet the pseudonym may be seen as a kind of fantasy framework, and so too may the situation Lessing constructs in *Diary of a Good Neighbor,* which allows the protagonist to atone for former failures of sympathy by caring for Maudie, to become mother to the mother and "deliver" her from life. As Jane develops the sympathetic imagination that enables her to enter into Maudie's experience, she is herself liberated from her bounded, defended ego, in an interaction that exemplifies a right relation of youth and age and delivers her from the "nightmare repetition."

But when Lessing returns to social realism as Doris Lessing, her vision turns bleak indeed. In *The Good Terrorist* Alice has the compassionate, nurturing capacities that would have been saving graces in Lessing's earlier fiction but that, here, come to nothing: for Alice is a figure so desperately at odds with herself that, though she directs her considerable energies to a "holding operation" like that of Lessing's earlier protagonists, all she manages to do is to bring together a bunch of dangerous children long enough to allow them to explode a bomb in a crowded downtown street, killing five and injuring twenty-three innocent people. If most of Lessing's works are *Bildungsromane, The Good Terrorist* is a kind of anti-*Bildungsroman,* for this is a protagonist who can neither connect nor remember. In this novel, as in *The Fifth Child,* Lessing is no longer asking us to imagine better worlds.

Lessing's sense of possibilities is thus bound up with her sense of female identity: happy endings derive from female power and unhappy endings from female disempowerment. But female empowerment requires a structure of fantasy. These generic variations are not unlike those in Shakespeare's plays, where happy endings are similarly associated with female empowerment and female empowerment similarly requires the elaborate constructs of the comedies and romances—and it says something about the progress of women from the 1590s to the 1990s, that female efficacy is still so fantastic. Only in *The Golden Notebook* is female identity equivalent to female power and redemption envisioned in the here and now, which is one reason this novel is so extraordinary.

## A Feminist Novelist

I think I know why Lessing never became involved with organized feminism. In the late sixties, when the women's movement emerged as a social and political force, Lessing was in her late forties. She had lived through a period of intense political involvement in her twenties and thirties, the kind of engagement difficult to repeat in one's forties. She had charted feminist quest throughout the fifties, in the Martha Quest novels, and had revolutionized female literary expression in the early sixties, with *The Golden Notebook*. By the time feminism consolidated itself into a movement, in the late sixties, Lessing had moved on to other things: by then she was "off into fantasy," into a global, cataclysmic perspective from which "the aims of Women's Liberation . . . look very small and quaint," as she says in the 1971 introduction to *The Golden Notebook* (ix).

In lectures, interviews, and introductions, Lessing reiterates her refusal to be classified as a feminist writer,[59] and most feminists I know have taken her at her word by now and have given her up as a lost cause. Obviously she is not a feminist writer in any simple way, yet I persist in believing that she is deeply feminist—feminist not in offering strong female models who climb to the top of existing social structures (which I, like Adrienne Rich, see as "tokenism" rather than feminism), but, rather, in envisioning (and indeed, helping to bring about) what Rich terms "a profound transformation of world society and of human relationships."[60] I'd go so far as to say that her works *require* a feminist reading. For one thing, Lessing interrogates Western values—individualism, competition, materialism—in terms like those developed by feminism. For another thing, Anna, Martha, Al.Ith, and the narrator of *Memoirs* are the saviors of civilization because their boundary fluidity makes them capable of exercising sympathetic imagination; they are also further along "the main line of evolution" than men are. This valorization of the feminine is not the same thing as feminism, of course, and it could be argued that the qualities Lessing values—patience, endurance, self-sacrifice—are the old womanly virtues, traditionally valued by men because they serve patriarchal interests. But Lessing envisions these qualities not as affirming the status quo, but as transforming it, as capable of seeing civilization through to new forms that allow freedom for all. Most significantly, in getting us to view culture from without, to read it as a set of conventions, her works perform the reconstructing and demystifying work of feminism: they provide what Teresa de Lauretis terms "a view from elsewhere."[61] Her textual practices are a kind of "textual feminism" that is not only deconstructive but reconstructive, participatory in a way that is also liberatory.

Besides, Lessing's evolution—from the matrophobic *The Grass Is Singing, Martha Quest,* and *A Proper Marriage* through the more optimistic sense of female identity in *The Golden Notebook, The Four-Gated City,* and *Memoirs*—intuits a major movement within feminism: the reconceptualization of "difference" that characterized a second stage of feminism in France, England, and the United States (so described by Julia Kristeva and Wendy Kaminer, for example).[62] Whereas early feminist efforts set out to prove women's similarity with men,[63] a second stage of feminist thought has emphasized "difference": that women conceive of themselves in terms of relationship and have more fluid ego boundaries than men came to be reenvisioned as a strength rather than a weakness. This shift was corroborated by revisionist analyses in the social sciences: Nancy Chodorow, Dorothy Dinnerstein, Jane Flax, Jean Baker Miller, Carol Gilligan, and Sara Ruddick redefined female identity in positive terms.[64] Lessing's evolution from a view of the self as socially-constructed to a conception of selfhood as essential and trans-social also corresponds to a development within feminism, for the shift from an emphasis on equality to an emphasis on difference entailed a shift from a view of gender as socially constructed to a view of it in quasi-essentialist terms.

But it is above all the power of Lessing's novels to change peoples' lives and the effect she has had raising the consciousness of a generation of women readers that make her a feminist writer. Each time I teach her and see the effect she has on readers, I learn something about her power to change minds. It matters less whether Anna or Martha are heroic role models than that they think and change and that their developments give women a sense of possibilities. Students see the world differently after reading Doris Lessing: reading her helps them develop critical and analytical tools, to discover their authority against the weight of tradition—to "see things differently" (*Shikasta,* 254).

I was teaching a semester-long course in the novels of Doris Lessing during "the last war"—during the early months of 1991, when the attentions and energies of the United States were cranked up to bombing a small country of dark-skinned people we had no particular reason to hate, a country that we had, in fact, been plying with military aid not so long before. Lessing's analysis of the intoxication of wartime in *A Proper Marriage* assumed particular poignance, as did her analysis of "enemy-making," the way the human mind splits off what it finds unacceptable in itself and scapegoats its own projections. But most striking were the connections students saw between the conventions that enmesh Lessing's characters and the propaganda machine being created to convince us that this was a just war.

"She taught me how to think," my best senior told me, as she gave me a paper on media manipulations of the war. Lessing teaches people how to think not because she indoctrinates them with a particular philosophy, but because she teaches them to stand outside their culture and to realize that since culture is a set of conventional arrangements, it may be changed.[65] She gives us a way of imagining otherwise, a way of entertaining other possible perspectives on our lives—and irony, the capacity to tolerate a multiplicity of views, emerges as a saving grace in her fiction.[66] There is no better teaching device than the novels of Doris Lessing—they inspire idealism at the same time that they activate critical judgment. I could see her books awaken students' outrage at the waste of human potential by our present social arrangements. I could see her works engage their sense of wonder and evoke their sympathetic imagination. I could see them becoming for my students—as they have been for me—growing points.

It is this empowering of women that makes her a feminist writer, whatever her reservations about organized feminism: her effect on readers today is as revolutionary as it was when women of my generation first discovered her. Lessing develops the kind of students rare these days or in any day, but especially in these days of fear and backlash and reaction and cynicism. What Anna says in *The Golden Notebook,* that very few people really care about freedom, is even truer thirty years later, as we rapidly sink into "the new ice age of tyranny and terror" that Anna foresaw in her worst moments (343). But Lessing's fiction helps free peoples' minds and helps make the kind of person who might be capable of freedom and making a free world. Her works have a yeastlike effect that continues beyond the end of the novel, which is why they are, as Drabble calls *The Golden Notebook,* "territory gained forever" ("Cassandra," 52).

Having discussed the dim view Lessing takes of critics and literary criticism, my students and I speculated about what she would think of us for spending a semester reading her work. Though some thought she'd think us absurd, others did not: they thought (and I agreed) that we had become the readers she laments the lack of in the introduction to *The Golden Notebook* (xvi–xvii). Such readers are rare because it takes time and commitment to become one. Her works are not easy, and to take a class through *The Golden Notebook, The Four-Gated City, Memoirs of a Survivor,* and *Shikasta* is to take students through areas most have barely dreamed of. Interestingly, young readers, lacking the prejudices of their elders, often follow her through these areas more readily than many critics do.

## Critical Abuses

In a sense Doris Lessing would hardly seem to need justifying, since she has so long been recognized as a "great author." But I think it's outrageous that she has never received the Nobel Prize, given her brilliant literary career. And I've found, reading through reviews of her work and discussing her with people (many of whom have entrenched opinions on the basis of reading one or two of her novels), that she does need some defending. It's not that I expect everyone to love her—she's far too strong-minded and idiosyncratic for that—but I'm dismayed by certain prejudices that get expressed again and again. Part of the impulse behind this book is to counteract these prejudices—that her turn to mysticism and science fiction is a sort of "spacing out" (in John Leonard's term);[67] that she has no sense of humor; that she is not a "stylist"; that she's "depressing."

I think that Lessing has never been forgiven for writing *The Golden Notebook*—everything she wrote thereafter would be seen as a falling off, and male critics especially would take glee in noting this, since that novel had been fairly critical of men. As she says in the preface to the Jane Somers novels, "most reviewers and readers want you to go on writing the same book" (xi); and indeed, reviewers do show amazing unimaginativeness in approaching her works, a reluctance, a refusal, to grant her her premises. But it is not only her mysticism that puts people off: so too does her realism. The pseudonymous *Diary of a Good Neighbor* was rejected by one publisher because it addressed a subject no one wants to think about, old age, and the Jane Somers hoax—which she concocted to expose the whole process of publishing and reviewing as promoting only that which has already succeeded—put a lot of noses out of joint. She is not afraid to look at things that no one else dares to and to say things that no one else dares to.

People often refer to her in terms like those used for George Eliot—formidably intelligent, important, serious, but not much fun.[68] Like Eliot, she is assumed to have no sense of humor and to be an awkward stylist: *turgid, prolix, polemical, preachy,* and *flat-footed* are terms one often encounters. Gore Vidal characterizes her prose as, "at best," "solid and slow and a bit flat-footed";[69] according to William Pritchard, "She has cultivated (or made the best of) a singularly unlovely prose, rhythmically pedestrian."[70]

Here's Richard Jones (whoever he is): "Doris Lessing says that writing *The Diaries of Jane Somers* enabled her to write in ways that she normally cannot. But Jane Somers is every bit as prolix and dowdy as Doris Lessing"; he refers to "510 pages of humourless Somerish realism."[71] Rosemary Dinnage refers to "the very flat-footedness of her style."[72] What books are they reading? I wonder.

One need only read her sentences aloud (as one does often in teaching) to realize that they bristle with irony, with a humor the more potent for being understated. Much of it is dark comedy, admittedly, and perhaps not everyone will even see the humor in passages like this: "in fact so far behind them was the age of Joe McCarthy, enormous numbers of people could not remember it, and were saying it never had happened. One thing was certain, no one would believe that it might happen again" (*FGC,* 325). Or like this:

> *Scene of the time:* A room full of middle-aged people eating hard, preoccupied half the time about weight problems, always on diets of one sort or another, most of them smoking . . . most of them on sleeping pills and sedatives, all of them drinkers and all of them drunk—talking about the youth.
>
> The youth took drugs. They were irresponsible. They were selfish. They were dirty. They were self-indulgent. (*FGC,* 518)

These are not riotously funny, to be sure, but I find their acerbic wit quite wonderful. About irony Lessing has recently written, "Well—the pleasures of irony, one sometimes has to think, are the only consolation when contemplating the human story" (*Prisons,* p.14).

Reading her sentences aloud, one also realizes that many of them are quite beautiful. And it's not only the isolated image or sentence that dazzles; the patterns of repetition and revision that she elaborates throughout long and complex fictional structures are as powerful as anything one finds in the plays of Shakespeare. Lessing is an innovative writer who has had to teach readers how to read her, for her fiction offers startling and original forms that stretch our imaginations to conceive of something new, forms that have been missed or misconstrued by many reviewers and critics.[73] In her introduction to *The Golden Notebook,* published nearly a decade after the novel itself (in 1971), she pointed out aspects of the novel's structure that critics still, nine years after its publication, had not noticed. As my readings demonstrate, other of her works have been similarly misread.

One reason I give these novels close readings is that not many other critics have. I'm fascinated by what she does with circles: I trace an evolution from the closed, vicious circular structures of the early, matrophobic texts to the open, liberatory forms of the later texts, and I see a relation between the breaking of circles and the interrogation of convention. I'm intrigued by her play with endings, the ways she finds of resisting narrative closure and devising open, nonteleological forms that render processes of working through and point a way beyond teleology. I'm struck by images and metaphors that intimate the existence of another world glimmering just beyond this one, beyond our senses and perceptions, a world attainable through wonder.[74] In the chapters that follow I try to convey some of the texture of her prose, the intricacy of her structures, the rich resonances of her intertextuality. Still, I'm amazed at how little I've managed to render of the whole.

As for the idea that she's depressing, I find Lessing's energy and feistiness, her passionate plea for imaginative sympathy and the examined life, anything but depressing. When Anna Wulf leaves therapy she realizes that she has internalized that wise, maternal, witchlike woman, her therapist, Mrs. Marks, and that she will always be able to summon her in herself. For me Doris Lessing is that strong, wizardly presence. You can return to these books again and again and realize that they not only grow with you but that they are the cause of growth in you. They allow the confidence that things make a kind of sense; they offer (and, like Johor, I use the word cautiously), a kind of faith: "I am putting the word *faith* here. After thought. With caution. With an exact and hopeful respect" (*Shikasta,* 203).

*Chapter 3*

# *Children of Violence:* "Something Worked Through"

> Yes, forgetting, forgetting again and again, life brings one back to points in oneself . . . over and over again in different ways, saying without words: This is a place where you could learn if you wanted to. Are you going to learn this time or not? No? Very well then, I'll wait for you. If you're not ready now, too bad! I'll find ways of bringing you back to it again. When you are ready, then.
>
> . . . that feeling of something having been got over, done with, worked through . . . To have worked through . . . was, after all, to have been made free.
>
> —Doris Lessing, *The Four-Gated City*

The *Children of Violence* explores change as a subject and dramatizes change as a process.[1] A *Bildungsroman* (as Lessing calls it), it focuses on a specific education, Martha's "difficult, painful process of educating herself" (*MQ,* 12), while also addressing generalized questions relating to learning—remembering, forgetting, repressing, envisioning, imagining.[2] In the nearly two decades Lessing took to write the series—between 1952, when *Martha Quest* was published, and 1969, when *The Four-Gated City* appeared—Lessing herself changed, evolving from a view of the self as socially constructed to belief in an essential self that is linked to a transsocial collective reality, and from a belief in the adequacy of language to a mystical sense of its inadequacy.[3] These shifts correspond to her evolution from socialism to Sufism, history to myth, and they dictate formal developments away from the realism of the first three novels to the lyric and mythic forms of the last two, *Landlocked* and *The Four-Gated City,* both written after the radically innovative *Golden Notebook.*

Lessing is initially drawn to realism because it is the mode best suited to express "the individual conscience in its relations with the collective," and her remarks in "The Small Personal Voice" suggest that she agrees with Georg Lukács's analysis of realism as depicting man as "a social being inseparable from social and historical environment."[4] The *Children of Violence* is usually read as straightforward mimetic realism. The style seems to offer itself as a transparent reflection of a preexistent reality; the action centers on a single protagonist; events unfold chronologically in a tangibly rendered social setting and tend to be episodic, "haphazard, resembling the course of life itself," as Sydney Janet Kaplan describes it.[5] But in the course of the series Lessing encounters a contradiction between the conservative tendencies of realist narrative convention and her radical reevaluations of social convention: the problem she confronts writing The *Children of Violence* is how to use the novel to say something new when the discourses from which the novelist creates are inscribed within the ideologies she repudiates—an impasse she confronts in the third volume, *A Ripple from the Storm.* In order to break this impasse she interrupts the series with *The Golden Notebook,* and when she returns to complete it, it is with the altered forms of the final volumes, the lyrical-mythic *Landlocked* and the strange hybrid *Four-Gated City,* which moves "off into fantasy," as she says, its form "shot to hell," for "I could no longer say what I wanted to say inside the old form."[6]

As important as this move beyond realism is Lessing's evolving sense of female identity, and it too has implications for her formal developments. From viewing it as a liability, she comes to see it as a strength and salvation, associated with the imaginative sympathy that is the hope of humanity. In her first novel, *The Grass Is Singing,* the protagonist Mary Turner repeats the errors of her mother and dies, and the novel's circular structure is the narrative correlative to matrophobia. In *Children of Violence* Martha's mother, Mrs. Quest, though a more menacing figure than Mrs. Turner, evokes a more complex response. Martha is torn between her desire to resist her mother, her determination "*not* [to] be . . . like her" or like any of the other older women she meets—"I won't give in, I won't" (*MQ,* 10, 19)—and her desire to give in, which she calls a "female compliance," a "need to say yes, to comply, to melt into situations" (*LL,* 14, 15). She reaches (as she later says) "for anything as a weapon in the fight for survival," banishing pity as "an enemy" that could "destroy her" (*FGC,* 218, 222) and building "bastions of defence" (*PM,* 94). However all her defenses only lock her into "cycles of guilt and defiance" (201) and leave her caught in the same repetitive patterns—biological, social, historical—that determined the life of her mother;

and the circle imagery that pervades the early *Children of Violence* novels—like the circular structure of *Grass Is Singing*—represents the triumph of the past and "the nightmare repetition" (*PM,* 77, 95). But in the course of the series, as Martha works through and beyond these cycles and Lessing re-envisions "female compliance" as a source of something new, the formal correlative to this shift is the transformation of closed, vicious circles to open, liberatory structures that accommodate change.

Though the style of the *Children of Violence* has disappointed even devoted Lessing readers—Roberta Rubenstein, for example, finds the early novels "prolix, cumbersome," "rather pedestrian in style and conception," "plodding in pace and commonplace in incident"[7]—Lessing is thwarting expectations (Martha's, the reader's) that have been formed from the fiction of "men or men-women" (*PM,* 62) with a processive form that renders "something . . . worked through" (*FGC,* 427). Martha wonders what really happens after Nora slams the door of the doll's house (*PM,* 274) and after Natasha settles down to motherhood (*PM,* 205–6), and the series allows Lessing to investigate the "ever-after" excluded by the well-made novel—to write beyond endings. It allows an unfolding obedient to the imperatives of "women's time," a process like the gestation Martha intuited in her illumination on the veld when she sensed that "what was demanded of her was that she should accept something quite different: it was as if something new was demanding conception, with her flesh as host" (*MQ,* 52–53). What is "demanded" of her is a seventy-year gestation during which she develops qualities that enable her to bring forth "the new children" at the end of *The Four-Gated City,* the hope and "future for our race" (*FGC,* 608, 604).

Thus what looks like passivity in Martha, an infuriatingly "female" tendency to drift, is actually a necessary part of the process of growth.[8] What is required of Martha is the capacity to endure each stage until it has worked itself out in her, a slow, painful process whereby she can work herself free, a "working through" like that which occurs in psychoanalysis. Since "this business of charting the new territory meant a continual painful effort of discovery, of trying to understand, to link, to make sense, and then falling back again, 'forgetting'; and then an effort forward again—a baby trying to walk" (*FGC,* 473)—learning requires repetition. The series' gradual unfolding and repetition and circling back over material allow Martha to return to places in herself and know them for the first time—and my echo of T.S. Eliot is deliberate, since *The Four Quartets* haunts *The Four-Gated City,* as *The Waste Land* does *Landlocked.*[9] Thus repetition is not only a structural device but also a deliberate teaching device, and it is reconceptualized in the course of the series from the "nightmare repetition" of the early novels to release in *The Four-Gated City*[10]—in the course of which the closed, vicious cycles of the past are transformed to liberatory forms that allow "something new."

## Working It Out, Working It Through

The first three novels, *Martha Quest, A Proper Marriage,* and *A Ripple from the Storm,* explore the ways a developing mind is circumscribed by convention; and appropriately, those novels that portray the individual as most determined by the collective are also the most formally conventional. "The experts" young Martha reads, though "in doubt as to how she should see herself," "all had in common" the message "of fate, or doom . . . that it was much too late to change" (*MQ,* 9). Conceived in the aftermath of World War I by parents who "were both having severe nervous breakdowns" (*MQ,* 239), Martha is born into a family that is itself overdetermined. Both mother and father represent the sum total of social and historical processes: Mrs. Quest, trapped by her reproductive system and ground down by the social system; Mr. Quest, a man broken, like so many men, by the wars of this century—an age appropriately termed "no man's land":[11] he "lost his health, and perhaps something more important than health in the war" (*MQ,* 20). Both parents are representative of processes that threaten Martha, and the problem she faces is like that confronted by Joyce's Stephen Dedalus, of extricating herself from the entangling "nets" of nationality, religion, language, and family—except that the "nets" that enmesh her are more insidious, more endangering, because she has so thoroughly internalized them. As a female trained in compliance, her consciousness is awash in "social currents flowing through . . . devious channels" (*MQ,* 115).

As one who has been "formed by literature" (*MQ,* 166), Martha "see[s] herself . . . through literature" (*MQ,* 7). She turns to books as "guides" in her "journey of discovery" (*MQ,* 199–200) and reads with the question, "What does this say about my life?" (*PM,* 62). But the books that shape her consciousness are a complicated legacy. They enable her to imagine "something better," to envision an "ideal landscape of white cities and noble people" (*MQ,* 27), but they give her no clue how she can attain this ideal. She turns to them for "some pattern of words" (*PM,* 204) that will help her understand her situation: "Books. Words. There must surely be some pattern of words which would neatly and safely cage what she felt—isolate her emotions so that she could look at them from outside" (*PM,* 61).

But since books are written from inside the system she is trying to understand, they cannot help her see it "from outside"; rather, they entrench her more firmly within it.

Besides, "novels from earlier times" (*MQ,* 7) entextualize her in the tradition of romantic love,[12] teaching her to expect that a man will provide shape and "end" to her life, that her life will be marked by definitive turning points, endings and beginnings. Lessing describes her as "always waiting for these 'moments,' these exquisite turning points where everything is clear, the past lying finished, completed, in one's shadow, the future lying clear and sunlit before!" (*MQ,* 241). But Martha discovers "a gap between herself and the past," a distance between her experience and that of "the heroines she had been offered" (*MQ,* 10): "Is it really conceivable that [women] should have turned into something quite different in the space of about fifty years? Or do you suppose they didn't tell the truth, the novelists?" (*PM,* 205). When her own marriage fails to provide a happily-ever-after resolution, she marvels at the transformation of Tolstoy's Natasha: "In the books, the young and idealistic girl gets married, has a baby—she at once turns into something quite different; and she is perfectly happy to spend her whole life bringing up children with a tedious husband" (*PM,* 205–6). Martha concludes that "women in literature were still what men, or the men-women, wished they were" (*PM,* 62).

Lessing's characterization of Martha as a novel-reader whose relation to life is mediated by fiction implies a more sophisticated awareness of the ideological complicity of narrative forms than is generally attributed to the author of these early, supposedly unselfconscious works. It implies an understanding of fiction at odds with the traditional view of realism as a neutral or innocent reflection of a preexistent reality; in fact it implies a view of it more like Roland Barthes's than Georg Lukács's. According to Barthes and others, realism produces meaning by evoking and combining cultural codes that are the received ideas of the culture, and it appears "realistic" because it draws on familiar systems that reaffirm our sense of the familiar. Moreover, since each invocation of a code is also its reinforcement or reinscription, realist narrative does more than encode ideology: it actually creates it. Thus to invoke resolutions like Natasha's is in some sense to necessitate them, to perpetuate them as the myths of the culture: this is why realism is criticized as a conservative form that counters tendencies toward change.[13] How, then, is it possible to write something new and oppositional using narrative conventions that are complicit with the system the novelist is opposing? How can books written from within a system point a way out? Such questions are vital to anyone seeking change against a sense of social determinism, but they are especially central to feminist debate. They are versions of Audre Lorde's question: How can we dismantle the master's house using the master's tools?[14]

The first three novels show Martha repeatedly imagining that she has just taken the step that has put a definitive end to the past—to life on the farm, in the town, to marriage, motherhood, politics—and made a glorious new beginning. She believes that she has just found the "key," "door," or "gate" to some new dimension, always conceived of in terms related to her ideal city, in romantic love, sex, Marxism. But each time her hope is disappointed, in a pattern of elation and deflation like that which occurs from episode to episode of *Portrait of the Artist as a Young Man* and between the end of *Portrait* and beginning of *Ulysses*. The city informs her quest in ways she barely realizes, for she seeks it everywhere—in the young people in the town, in marriage, in the political group. But what she finds always turns out to be some ironically debased version of what she seeks: the "magic circle" of the club (*MQ,* 137–38, 163, 169), the "circle of women" in *A Proper Marriage,* the circle of political activity in *Ripple,* are not open, inclusive, groups offering "generous and freely exchanged emotion" (*MQ,* 79), but exclusive social circles that deliver her over to repetition and entrapment. Repeatedly in the course of the novels, Martha exchanges (as Rubenstein says) "one enclosure for another," or, to borrow a term from D. H. Lawrence's *Women in Love* (a novel Lessing alludes to in *A Proper Marriage* and that suggests a similar sense of a civilization on the "death slopes"), what looks like a way out only turns out to be "a way in again."[15] Each attempt at the new entrenches her more firmly in the old, leaving her trapped in cycles—biological, psychological, social, political, historical—that reduce people to "mere pawns in the hands of an old fatality"; "nothing could alter the pattern" (*PM,* 94–95): *"It had all been done and said already"* (*PM,* 34).

Moreover, the entrenchment in society is also an entrapment in mortality, a loss and "forgetting" of the transcendental reality of which Martha had intimations on the veld. The long, lyrical description of October just after she returns to her mother's house from school, having failed to take the matric supposedly because an eye infection has impaired her vision, orchestrates her "passage" into the "sleep and forgetting" that is the condition of mortal life. "One cannot remember" is repeated three times, like a threefold incantation or a spell, suggesting the loss that leaves Martha "in a shock of shuddering nostalgia": "But nostalgia for what?" (*MQ,* 21–22). October is the month Martha was born (*MQ,* 197)—and it is also the month Lessing was born—and the October described here is another sort of birthday, a descent into the cave of the world, into a darkness and somnolence that impair Martha's vision in ways she only later understands.

Martha's forgetting is rendered imagistically as an exile from light. *Martha Quest* begins with Martha in the sun, positioned in opposition to her mother and her mother's friend, Mrs. Van Rensberg ("a fat and earthy housekeeping woman" [10]), both of whom are "screened from the sun by a golden shower creeper," gossiping and knitting wool; Martha is reading in the sun, defiantly, determinedly, though the light hurts her eyes. The two elderly ladies knitting in the shade offer an image of what de Beauvoir calls "immanence," female entrapment in the "narrow round of uncreative and repetitious duties" traditionally associated with women:[16] "Everything was the same; intolerable that they should have been saying the same things ever since she could remember" (*MQ,* 2). Martha's defiance suggests that she is resisting the fate being spun for her, refusing the destiny represented by the women in the shade—"the eternal mother, holding sleep and death in her twin hands like a sweet and poisonous cloud of forgetfulness" (24)—though by the end of the novel, she will have succumbed to it.

The first novel, *Martha Quest,* has the most conventional form because this is the only form the protagonist is capable of making for her life at this point: Martha breaks with her parents, leaves the farm for the town, becomes accomplished in the ways of the town, and ends with "a proper marriage." Though she is astute about the "lies, evasions, compromises" (*MQ,* 7) in her mother's language and finds her "conventionality" contemptible (*MQ,* 88, 125, 180, 221), she lacks the resources to construct an alternative because her means of interpreting the world—the wisdom of elders, bits of popular culture from magazine and film (*MQ,* 42, 185), and books loaned her by the Cohen brothers—have all been provided by that world.

Martha later refers to her sexuality and books as her most important "weapons" against her mother (*FGC,* 230), but both weapons have been forged by the society she is trying to resist. In fact the former has been forged by the latter: her sexuality has been constructed by her reading, for reading is the conduit for the "social currents" (*MQ,* 115) that reach her even on the solitary veld (42, 185), so that, when she arrives in the town, she instantly acquires the "new skilled vivacity which was part of her equipment as a girl about town . . . together with a new vocabulary" (111). She shapes her appearance to "the tall, broad-shouldered, slim-hipped, long-legged" image of woman in magazines "just before the war" (141), as she tailors her sexual and emotional responses to the "romantic tradition of love" that books leave her "heir to" (*MQ,* 184). She imagines that each man she meets will rescue her, surrounds him with illusions, and "submits . . . with a demure, childish compliance, as if she were under a spell" (149)—first to Billy, then to Donovan, Adolphe, and finally to Douglas. When she marries at the end of *Martha Quest,* she is, like Mary Turner, repeating the life of her mother, and the engagement ring her mother forces on her "like a chain" (235) is the first of the many rings that pervade the imagery of the next novel. But the closure is not complete, for though "she would marry . . . she also heard a voice remarking calmly that she would not stay married" (243). The point of view angles oddly, as it does at the end of all these novels, to the sardonic perspective of Magistrate Maynard: "Four more weddings to get through. Well, he thought cynically, that would be four divorces for him to deal with in due time"; and it angles out more widely to register the distant rumblings Martha dimly hears—"She remembered that someone had been saying that Hitler had seized Bohemia and Moravia" (246–47).

In *A Proper Marriage,* Martha becomes so deeply immersed in marriage and motherhood that she is blocked off entirely from the hope of anything better, though at the end of this novel her intimation of "an ideal to live for" revives when her reading about the Russian Revolution enables her to conceive, once again, of the possibility of something new: "it was as if her eyes had been opened and her ears made to hear, like a rebirth" (285–86). In the next novel, *A Ripple from the Storm,* she imagines that political activity will provide something oppositional, but it too disappoints, yielding only recycled versions of the old because human beings are too deeply entrenched in the structures of the past to create anything new. By this time in the series, Martha has lived through the most important myths of her society—romantic love, motherhood, belief in the efficacy of political action—and has revealed that nothing new can come from them or from the institutions and ideology that express them. The nightmare she has in *A Ripple from the Storm,* of a monstrous reptile embedded in bedrock, ancient and extinct but still powerful and alive—"alive after so many centuries" (*RS,* 85)—symbolizes the stalemate she encounters, the "nightmare repetition," the "great bourgeois monster" (*PM,* 77). And indeed, the narrative quality of *Ripple*—flat, stale, unalleviated by the brilliant flashes of poetic imagination that animate most of Lessing's fiction—in itself suggests stalemate.

Martha will find her way to something new in the course of the series, not as she thought she would, through the dramatic crises and resolutions she has come to expect from fiction, but by means of a slow, painful process through each stage. She—like the reader—must relinquish her desire for definitive ends and dramatic new beginnings and learn that the way to the "new" is by living *through* each stage of the process, by working it through; for as she later realizes, "If you start something, get on a wavelength of something, then there's no getting off, getting free, unless you've learned everything there is to be learned—have had your nose rubbed in it" (*FGC*, 106).

Working it through for Lessing requires not only writing beyond endings but in some sense dispensing with endings, doing away with the imperative of the ending and the crises and resolutions that it imposes. Each novel makes gestures toward closure (the "proper marriage" at the end of *Martha Quest,* the end of that marriage at the end of *A Proper Marriage,* the end of "the group" at the end of *Ripple,* the deaths of father and lover and even another "proper marriage," Anton's, at the end of *Landlocked*), while each ending also introduces new material, allowing "loose ends" that work against closure (the formation of the political group at the end of *A Proper Marriage,* the Dobie and Johnson trial at the end of *Ripple,* the strike at the end of *Landlocked*) and suggest the existence of ongoing processes that cannot be contained by the literary frame. That Lessing well knows how to use endings to conventional effect is clear from *The Grass Is Singing,* a well-made novel that begins with a murder and proceeds back through an investigation of "causes"—causes that widen to encompass the whole system of racial and sexual exploitation of colonial southern Africa—while also moving forward to conclude with the murder; but she makes no concession to such principles in the *Children of Violence* series.[17] Since the sense of an ending is a major source of tension, its absence makes for a certain slackness and shapelessness. Making one's way through the *Children of Violence* has struck more than one reader as "having one's nose rubbed in it," but Lessing has devised a form that takes the reader through the process of change; and if this process seems painful, at times tedious, this only bears out the point that change is not easy; nor can it be contained within neat, well-made forms.

## Sex, Death, and *A Proper Marriage*

In *A Proper Marriage* Martha is so sunk in the dark cave of the world, so caught in repetitive cycles of behavior, that all intimation of anything better "vanishes": "As for that other, deeper knowledge, the pulse that really moved her, a knowledge that amounted to a vision of mankind as nobility bound and betrayed—that was vanishing entirely" (69). This novel, like the first, begins with a description of two women screened from a blinding and oppressive sun; but whereas in the first novel Martha was positioned defiantly in the sunlight against the two women in the shade, here Martha has become one of the women in the shade:

> Two young women were loitering down the pavement in the shade of the sunblinds that screened the shopwindows. . . . It was impossible to look outwards towards the sun-filled street, and unpleasant to look in towards the mingling reflections in the window glass. They walked, therefore, with lowered gaze. (1)

Having married with the expectation that marriage will be "a door . . . closing on her past" (*MQ,* 241, 228), Martha discovers that marriage only entrenches her more firmly in the society she had hoped to escape, leaving her "caged and trapped" (*PM,* 28). Rather than providing access to "something new and rare" (*MQ,* 216), marriage locks her in interconnected "social circles" (*PM,* 49) and rounds of meaningless social activities. Even before she discovers she is pregnant, she is mesmerized by the Ferris wheel spinning outside her bedroom window, "the great dragging circle of lights" "like a warning," "like a damned wedding ring" (29–30), "dragging its glittering load of cars in its circle" (68). The Ferris wheel is at the center of a cluster of images relating to circles and cycles—"cycles of guilt and defiance" (201), "the cycle of procreation" (152), "the cycle of birth" (251), the circles of friends and of women (36, 249, 255, 272)—which work together with imagery of nets, webs, cages, bonds, traps (28, 81, 91, 95, 99, 137, 201, 202, 250, 266, 337) to suggest (as such images do in *The Oresteia*) a "sense of appalling fatality" (34).

Martha is in the shade throughout this novel, her eyes averted from light.[18] Insofar as her imagination is working, it apprehends only nightmare. She is haunted by a vision of "an unalterable sequence of events" extending back to the past and forward to the future:

> She saw her mother, a prim-faced Edwardian schoolgirl, confronting . . . the Victorian father, the patriarchal father, with rebellion. She saw herself sitting where her mother now sat, a woman horribly metamorphosed, entirely dependent on her children for any interest in life, resented by them, and resenting them; opposite her, a young woman of whom she could distinguish nothing clearly but a set, obstinate face; and beside these women, a series of shadowy dependent men, broken-willed and sick with compelled diseases. This the nightmare, the nightmare of a class and generation: repetition. (94–95)

The same process that transformed her mother from a spirited young woman into a representative of the convention Martha now loathes must inevitably transform Martha herself into a representative of that same convention and so, too, transform her own daughter. The nightmare seems to obliterate all possibility of change, for what appears to be new only turns out to be "part of the inevitable process she was doomed to" (77); it permits neither beginning nor end, only eternal recurrence, reducing people to "mere pawns in the hands of an old fatality" (94). Actually, this vision of "unalterable events" does admit alteration, though Martha does not see it, for the strong nineteenth-century patriarchs have been replaced by the "shadowy dependent men" shattered by twentieth-century wars. This decimation of the male population by twentieth-century is not in obvious ways hopeful, but it does break the hold of the past.[19]

The nightmare repetition takes the form of the "cycle of procreation" for women and the cycle of war for men—"love and death" (182). These cycles feed one another, generating mutually reinforcing fantasies; as Martha's lover Thomas Stern says, "war has given us back the pure essence of romance" (*LL,* 89). The connection is expressed comically in the overcrowding of the nursing home where Martha has her baby—"we're so full—it's the war" (*PM,* 142); and there is more truth than Martha suspects in her glib reply to Mr. Maynard that she married "because there's going to be a war" (59), since the war affects her in ways she barely understands. Romance captivates the imaginations of women as war captures the imaginations of men, and both promise something new and real, pregnancy enticing women with the idea of "a new creature . . . new and extraordinary" (252) and war promising men "climax," "real living," "real experience" (223). But while promising the new, both deliver repetition, romantic love consigning women to a "cycle of procreation" (152) in which they become mothers and then become *their* mothers, and war fixing men in a historical cycle that dooms them to become their fathers in a second world war reminiscent of the first. Martha understands the power of both myths and resents their hold on her; she understands that "that phrase, 'having a baby,' which was every *girl's* way of thinking of a first child, was nothing but a mask" concealing a banal repetition (274), and she "resents very much that her emotions were being roused by flags, music, and solemnity against her will" (121), sensing also that such emotions are complicit with nostalgia and forgetting (25).

So appalling is her sense of "the nets tightening around her" that she consoles herself that "the war will break it up, it won't survive the war" (49), turning to war for the sense of an end that will give her life meaning. The nearness of death, "exquisite knowledge of loss and impending change" (66), enhances experience in the same way that writing for the end provides shape and significance in fictional form. As Thomas Stern says, "what war fosters . . . is . . . the frustrations of romance . . . Partings and broken hearts . . . just enough frustration to keep love alive"—and that he derives this "analysis" "from novels" (*LL,* 89) suggests a relation of narrative endings to the longing for death like that described by Peter Brooks: "We seek in narrative fictions . . . that knowledge of death which . . . writes *finis* to the life and therefore confers on it its meaning."[20] It is this "unhealthy, feverish illicit excitement of wartime, a lying nostalgia, a longing for licence" that Anna Wulf repudiates in her successful first novel *Frontiers of War,* associating it with a "nihilism" that is "one of the strongest reasons why wars continue" (*GN,* 63–64).

The emotion that infects the young people of the town is a longing to be "swallowed up in something bigger," a version of the desire to participate in the collective:

> By midnight they were dancing as if they formed one soul; they danced and sang, mindless, in a half-light, they were swallowed up in the sharp, exquisite knowledge of loss and impending change . . . and underneath it all, a rising tide of excitement that was like a poison . . . They were all longing to be swallowed up in something bigger than themselves; they were, in fact, already swallowed up . . . Their days . . . were nothing but a preparation for that moment when hundreds of them stamped and shouted in great circles to the thudding drums . . . this was the culmination of the day, the real meaning of it, the moment of surrender. (66–67)

Despite her determination to act rationally, Martha finds herself caught up in "that grand emotional culmination at midnight, when she joined the swinging circle of intoxicated dancers controlled by the thudding of the drums" (69). This "moon-drugged city given over to dancing, love, and death" (182) is, like the moon-crazed city in *Briefing for a Descent into Hell,* a perversion of the ideal city, a shadow city governed by "nostalgia for something doomed" (81).

Though war holds out the chimera of relationship, promising men "the comradeship of men" (224) and women "the community of women" (150, 155), what it actually delivers is the division of women from men and the destruction of relationship. It drives men and women to assume regressive and aggressive postures toward one another:

> For, just as [Douglas] was playing a role . . . the young hero off to the wars for adventure—so [Martha] began to speak in the ancient female voice which he found utterly irritating . . . a small, obstinate, ugly voice remarked that there would be wars so long as men were such babies. (68)

The men "band together against the impositions of the women," "escaping their wives" (133) and "sigh[ing] after lost freedom" (83). The women are appalled when they come upon their husbands playing war, "scrambling and fighting . . . yelling and whooping" "with savage joy" (132) before they even know who the enemy is; but they, too, resort to ancient roles and "female ruses" (83) and an "armoury of weapons against men"—Stella rushes home to her mother's "like the heroine of a music-hall joke" (82), Alice gets herself pregnant, and Martha assumes the tones of a "conventional jailer wife" (120). Though the idea of war feeds the fantasy of romance, what war actually does is decimate the male population and leave women alone to live out their days with the ghostly images of their "true" but dead loves, images enshrined in the hearts and faded photographs of Mrs. Quest, Mrs. Talbot, Mrs. Maynard, Elaine, Jasmine, Maisie, and finally Martha, who is left mourning a dead lover of her own, Thomas Stern.[21] While fueling romantic illusions, war renders such illusions the more futile for being bound to dead men.

Determined to "cut the cycle" (95) by not having a child, Martha discovers that she is pregnant, a wartime statistic, victim of biology and history. Though at first she imagines that she can control her pregnancy "if she were determined enough" (112), she is soon made to realize its inexorability: "claimed by that other time" (113, 123), she "sinks in the development of the creature, appallingly slow, frighteningly inevitable, a process which she could not alter or hasten." Pregnancy drags her back to "the dark blind sea," "the impersonal blind urges of creation" (127), compelling her to relive the evolution of the species with the developing embryo, and she emerges at the end of each day "dazed": "Inside her stomach the human race had fought and raised its way through another million years of its history" (113). The process of giving birth makes her regress in yet another way, when "the ancient being in her . . . cried out to God [and] Mother" (145); whatever illusion of control she retains at this point is shattered when pain stuns her into forgetfulness, leaving her incapable of remembering what it is like not to feel pain or to connect the state of pain with painlessness. After the birth she finds herself subjected to the further humiliation of postpartum depression, yet another "predictable chemical process" (152). This account of the physical processes of pregnancy—which is altogether unprecedented in fiction—suggests a sense like de Beauvoir's that woman's participation in procreation is "a process of self-destruction and self-narrowing" (245).[22]

At two crucial points in the novel, when Martha is deciding whether to go through with her pregnancy and when she is deciding whether to embark on a second pregnancy, she seeks advice from her mother. In the first conversation she asks directly, "You didn't want to have me . . . What did you *feel*?" But "Mrs. Quest had forgotten how she had felt. She was no longer interested" (97). Later, after Mrs. Quest has intervened by discussing with Douglas whether Martha should have a second child, thereby precipitating the crisis that ends her marriage, Martha again tries to "have a sensible talk with her" (259). She reminds her that she once needed to oppose her own mother, to which Mrs. Quest replies that she was "very fond" of her mother: "How can you say such a thing?" (260). Mrs. Quest has not only forgotten her own past, she is so awash in platitude that the best she can offer is the advice that maternity is a woman's "deepest satisfaction in life and that Martha must sacrifice herself to her children as she had" (127).

On the collective, as on the individual level, conventional formulations take the place of understanding. The political opinions of the Zambesian youth consist of "the phrases they had read that morning in the *Zambesia News*," and "the fact that this newspaper was contradicting itself . . . from day to day did not matter in the least" (67). A similar collective amnesia is evident in attitudes toward the Soviet Union: Martha can find "no connection" between the headlines of two years ago and today (278). Only Mr. Maynard seems to remember the last war and draw the (not very original) moral that "the more things change, the more they remain the same" (56); and though his nihilism frightens Martha, she will remember, years later, his analysis of the English and their "evasions":

> The working classes were undoubtedly just where they used to be, but everyone of my "class" seemed concerned only to prove not only that they were entitled to a good life, but that they had already achieved it. Further, it was almost impossible to hold a conversation . . . because . . . speech was full of gaps, pauses, and circumlocutions where words used to be. (56)

Yet even as Martha is caught up in these bleakly repetitive cycles, change is occurring, a process invisible to her but evident to us when we contrast a day in the life of Martha before Caroline is born and a day in her life afterward. On the first day (60–81) Martha's hours are passed in a meaningless drifting; on the second day (200–211) each hour is governed by Caroline's needs, as Martha builds "a life of her own, with obligations and responsibilities" (243). When Douglas returns and invades the "lonely, proud, self-contained life she had made for herself" (239), she has difficulty reconstructing her "determined self-deception" with regard to him (102)—though reconstruct it she does, and allows herself to be drawn into the "circle of women" that comes with the house on the avenue. When she emerges from her daughter Caroline's first few years to wonder what to do with the rest of her life, everyone—mother, husband, doctor—urges her to have a second child; and though her own amnesia conspires with their advice, "she did not altogether forget. And she did *not* choose to begin again" (252).

Martha finds a way out of her marriage partly because she develops new faculties —most important, her memory—and partly because she is propelled out (as she was propelled in) by historical forces beyond her control: in this case, by the changed attitude toward the Soviet Union and the formation of "the group," which holds out the promise of significant political action. Beginning and end of *A Proper Marriage* are marked by conversations with Mr. Maynard and Dr. Stern, magistrate and "archpriest" (274), secular and spiritual authorities (for Dr. Stern is as much a "priest" as a doctor, his practice consisting mainly of women patients seeking emotional support). The difference in the way Martha responds on her first visit to Dr. Stern and the way she responds on her final visit provides measure of change: whereas in the first encounter she was completely vulnerable to his manipulations, in their final meeting she is critically aware of the way he is working her. The end of *A Proper Marriage,* like the beginning (and like the end of *Martha Quest*), widens, as Martha, on her way out of her marriage, confronts Magistrate Maynard, acknowledging his sardonic comment—"I suppose with the French Revolution for a father and the Russian Revolution for a mother, you can very well dispense with a family"—to be "a very intelligent remark" (345). Again, the repetition draws attention to change, for whereas when they met at the beginning of the novel she nearly broke down into pleading with him to dissolve her marriage, here she has found a way out on her own. Also, as in *Martha Quest,* where Martha's reservations about her marriage left a loose end, so too in this novel does Martha have reservations: "There's something so damned *vieux jeu* . . . in leaving like Nora, to live differently! . . . One is bound to fall in love with the junior partner, and the whole thing will begin all over again" (*PM,* 274). In the next novel—in a movement familiar by this time in the series—Martha does begin again, making a second marriage (with Anton) as disastrous as the first.

## "Alive After So Many Centuries": *A Ripple from the Storm*

In 1956, when Khrushchev denounced Stalin at the Twentieth Congress and later that year invaded Hungary, Lessing (and several thousand others) left the Communist party. *A Ripple from the Storm,* published in 1958, reflects that disillusionment. This novel concerns the impossibility of change through political action, and the stalemate that is its subject is reflected in the narrative itself. In this case I agree with Rubenstein's characterization of the writing as "flat and undynamic," of the novel as a "somewhat tedious chronicling of the political activity" that "seems like one endless Communist party meeting" (*Novelistic Vision,* 57). The style is as bloodless and disembodied as the Communist party is abstracted from the real problems of Zambesia; it lacks anything like the October "passage" in *Martha Quest,* the resonant circle imagery of *A Proper Marriage* or the stunning lyrical effects in *Landlocked* and *Four-Gated City,* and is almost entirely without symbolism—except for the striking image in Martha's dream, of the saurian embedded in Mr. McFarline's "gold-eating pit," ancient, extinct, yet "alive after so many centuries." But *Ripple* is also a brilliant study of the sexual politics of men and women in politics. It exposes the disjunction between radical politics and the interests of women that women activists in the United States were soon to discover—it anticipates that moment in 1964 when women in SNCC (Student Nonviolent Coordinating Committee) who had been told that their "only position" in the movement was "prone," realized they needed their own movement.[23]

*A Ripple from the Storm* opens with high hopes for new beginnings. Public enthusiasm for the Soviet Union combines with Martha's personal exhilaration at leaving her marriage to produce a "yeasty new mood" (38), and Martha's ideal of a better world, which had receded in *A Proper Marriage,* revives, brought to life by the idealism Anton so movingly voices: "Comrades, this is the dawn of human history . . . Upon us, upon people like us . . . depend the future of mankind, the future of our species" (53). Anton's words seem to voice Martha's deepest intimations, for his terms are her own—he promises a "key," a "light," "sunlight," "dawn," and an end to "the ugly past" (53–54). Again, the sense of an end provides definition, but whereas in *A Proper Marriage* the war was the promised end, here everyone is looking forward to a time "after the war" when "a fresh phase of the Revolution would begin" (37–38).

Against the prevailing optimism, Tommy's lament—"But it's so hard to change"—is a lone but significant voice: "Half the things I feel seem to be wrong but I feel them. I know they are wrong but I can't help it" (70). Tommy's admission that it is difficult for anyone raised in South Africa to really change their feelings about black people is a statement of the power of conditioning: "I don't think any people brought up here, white people, can ever be good Communists . . . I don't think we can change ourselves" (72). Jasmine tries to reform him by having him read *War and Peace,* but Tommy responds, "All the time I'm reading this, I feel—mixed up in it. I mean to say, if I were there, I'd be thinking just what all these generals and old ladies think. I'd be the same as them. And that makes me confused. Because they were all a bunch of reactionaries, weren't they?" (71)

From the start, the obstacles to change, both personal and political, are glaringly apparent. The group is cut off from the life of the colony, at odds with the Trotskyists, and divided within itself, having defined a new pecking order that is, like the old one, based on class—though its new hierarchy privileges the working class. Martha finds, instead of the harmony she had hoped for, "gulfs" and "gaps" of the sort she has always known (35). Completely cut off from the real proletariat of this country, the black workers, the group cannot even agree on their relation to the "coloreds" with whom they do have some contact: Anton orders them not to become involved with "personal" problems in the colored community, in response to which the Royal Air Force members pull out, accusing the group of "white-settler ideology" (151); Anton responds, as he always does, by "making an analysis" of the situation (81). Though the group cherishes illusions about its effectiveness, drawing up a long document making racial prejudice illegal and delineating how the colony will be governed under communism, and voting this manifesto in clause by clause (175), the most accurate commentary comes from the women: from Martha—"We talk and talk and analyze and make formulations, but what are we doing? what are we changing?" (88); and from Maisie—"I mean . . . what's the point? . . . there's no chance of putting any of it into practice . . . So why go to all this trouble?" (176). Maisie even doubts that the end of the war will make a difference, even doubts that the war will end—"'After the war. It might be years and years. Sometimes I think there'll be a hundred years war" (176).

On a personal level, people are unable to make new beginnings because their conditioning turns out to be stronger than their consciously held beliefs. Throughout, it is "their temperaments, and not their politics" (*LL,* 267) that determine their deepest responses, and temperament is part of the system they are trying to change—they are "mixed up in it," in Tommy's phrase. Martha is uncomfortably aware of the power of conditioning:

> How do I know what I feel and what I don't? I've only to hear a boy scouts brass band on Sunday afternoon and tears come into my eyes. Anton has only to call me "little one" and a lump comes into my throat . . . It's as if somewhere inside me there was a big sack of greasy tears and if a pin were stuck into me they'd spill out. (226)

The force of conditioning is most unpleasantly driven home to her on the occasion when she responds with girlish confusion to the rapacious Mr. McFarline, "a lover of woman, a woman lover, eyeing her": "it was one of those moments she was made to learn something about herself . . . she felt exposed" (163–64). Her marriage to Anton, the most glaring instance of "the nightmare repetition," reveals the power of her romantic fantasies: it is her longing to be "created" by a man that first draws her to him (38), though this desire is at odds with her commitment as a Communist and though she criticizes herself for behaving "like a silly clinging vine" (122); still, his phrase *"my little one* . . . filled her with repose" (156). She wonders "why? Is it because he's the leader of the group?" (97); "it was simply luck, or some kind of choice I don't understand. But not *my* choice" (172).

Men's responses to women are similarly determined by vestigial emotions that have nothing to do with their political convictions. Jimmy's sentimentality about his working-class mother leads him to glorify the sacrifices of women in a way so maudlin as to prompt Martha's suggestion that men prefer to keep women where they are so they can continue being sentimental about them; and his real reason for criticizing his female comrades for their attention to appearance is that they have snubbed him (87, 88, 93, 121). Most of the men in the group display attitudes that corroborate Marjorie's claim, "when we get socialism we'll have to fight another revolution against men'" (247). Though the group intends to transform the society that has produced women like Martha's mother and her landlady, Mrs. Carson (described as "a variety of psychological dinosaur" [20]), in fact, it only reduplicates the male-female dynamics of the world outside: "This question of women's rights is a complicated one," as Marie says (186).

The central problem confronting the group, the fact of Maisie's pregnancy, is not something their doctrine equips them to deal with, though the baby represents "the future of mankind" that is supposedly their responsibility. The men respond to this problem—as they respond to the women—according to their characters, "who they are." Anton is sympathetic in theory and suggests that the group devote an evening to the subject—"The problems of women, in my opinion, have not been given sufficient thought in the movement" (48–49)—but he is unsympathetic in actuality, remarking that Maisie "should have thought of that before, instead of getting pregnant and then feeling sorry for herself" (112). That his terms echo Magistrate Maynard's reprimand of the poor woman in court—"But my dear lady, you should have thought of all that before running yourself into debt" (107)—demonstrates the consistency of "the pompous, hypocritical, essentially male fabric of society" (19) and the irrelevance of political convictions to gut responses. Piet's attitude toward his wife Marie is sexist and condescending (81, 117), though his politics are radical, and her analysis of the assumption of male supremacy that cuts across politics, class, and color, is scathingly accurate:

> Men! If there's one thing that teaches me there's no such thing as colour is that men are men, black and white . . . There you sit . . . every man jack of you with a little woman at home running after you like great boobies with your food and your comforts, and out you come, lords and masters, to sit talking, making decisions, and when you get back home you'll say: Is the supper ready! (186)[24]

Athen articulates the same doctrine as Anton—"This is a time which is difficult for women" (171)—but he, unlike Anton, behaves generously to Maisie because it is his nature to be generous. Andrew acts heroically in marrying Maisie and assuming responsibility for another man's child, but reverts, upon the return of the "rightful" father, to the most narrow possessiveness and prudishness, capitulating entirely to convention. The failure of this relationship is the most disappointing in the novel because it held out the most promise.

This novel demonstrates fascinating disjunctions between peoples' politics and actions. Jasmine is torn between sexual attraction to Jackie Bolton and intellectual disapproval of his political style (12, 16). Anton is split between his radical political convictions and conventional attitudes toward property, and between his bold politics and timid sexuality, as Martha discovers: "There was something essentially contradictory between the image of the revolutionary, essentially masculine, powerful and brave, and how Anton had behaved with her in bed" (155). Anton and Andrew, though agreeing on doctrine, differ in styles and personalities and have little affection for one another (177). Mr. Maynard and Mrs. Talbot, pillars of the community, continue their lifelong adultery, whereas Marjorie and Colin, "reds" who believe in free love, make a good "solid" marriage (76). The most striking disjunction of this sort is in the contrast between Mrs Maynard and Mrs. Van der Blyt:

> For here was Mrs. Van, radical by conviction, known to everyone as "a Kaffir-lover," a socialist and a libertarian. And yet surely she was deeply conservative by nature and by temperament? The pattern of her life showed it, with its ranks of solid, unradical children, its complement of well-brought-up grandchildren, its comfort and its order. And here was Mrs. Maynard, conservative by conviction, unegalitarian, aristocratic. Yet surely there was something romantically anarchistic in her that was shown by her cabinet of wire-pulling ladies, and her passion for intrigue and even her handsome husband with his discreet but of course gossiped-about liaisons . . . Then there was the one son in contrast to Mrs. Van's well-founded family, the unsatisfactory Binkie. And no grandchildren at all. (196)

Mrs. Van may be "conservative by nature and temperament," but she is also a socialist and atheist, self-educated and self-sufficient, who represents the triumph of individual will and intelligence over conditioning. "There had been two great illuminations in this woman's life": the first was when reading *The Story of an African Farm* made "an intellectual revolution in her . . . she . . . got hold of suffragist and socialist newspapers and . . . came to a conclusion. It was that she had been brought up in a backward part of a country whose ideas were decades behind the times" (192–93); the second, that "she was superior to her husband," is no less revolutionary, for

> she did not do what nearly all women do when they understand they have made a bad bargain—create an image and fight a losing battle, sometimes for years, in the no-man's land between image and truth. She told herself that her development must depend on her own efforts and that they must be secret efforts. (193)

Her battle wins her "herself" (205), though it costs her "emotion": "Emotion was dangerous. It could destroy her" (194). Significantly, Mrs. Van is the only woman in these novels who does not have a "dead lover," since she has no need of illusion. It is she who is the guide Martha is seeking, though Martha does not yet realize it, and she and Martha miss each other (as

Stephen and Bloom do in *Ulysses*); but in *The Four-Gated City,* Mrs. Van's coat will protect Martha on her night walks through London, and still later Martha will grow into this mantle, assuming herself the role of formidable matron.

Such disjunctions between "temperament and politics" call into question what people say and mark the beginning of a change in Martha's (and Lessing's) attitude toward language that becomes significant in the next novels. Martha has come to realize that "listening to the words people use is the longest way around to an understanding of what is going on" (*RS,* 7) and, having ceased to believe that words provide a "key," has stopped seeking "some pattern of words" that will provide access to new knowledge. Though in this novel such disjunctions are not particularly promising, since "temperament" usually pulls backward to the bedrock of conditioning, in the next novels they become hopeful, as the bedrock is blasted away to reveal an "essential self" that eludes social structuring. As Thomas puts it in *Landlocked,* "It is, after all, a question of what people are, and about this we know very little" (118).

Martha's dream life, which had receded in the previous novel, returns here, most strikingly in her nightmare of "an extinct saurian that had been imprisoned a thousand ages ago" in McFarline's "gold-eating pit." Martha finds this immense, half-fossilized but living creature embedded in bedrock, layered with the dust of ages, "landlocked" but still powerful and alive—"It's alive after so many centuries. And it will take centuries more to die" (84–85). The lizard represents "history" as Mr. Maynard has described it, "a record of misery, brutality, stupidity," the accumulated error of the past, and though Martha once dismissed him for this view as a "specimen of horror from a dead epoch" (46–47), by the end of the novel she has come to share it. Associated with the predatory McFarline, the monster signifies white male European exploitation—of women, workers, Africa, nature—and it represents Martha's complicity with McFarline as well, evidenced in that moment when she responds to his flirtation. Martha's question "perhaps I can dig it out?" (5) echoes Tommy's question about the possibility of change.

This novel which began with such high hopes for new harmony concludes with fragmentation, splintering, dispersal, "futility" (262): Maisie and Andrew are "at an end" (240); the group is "at an end" (259); "the Left such as it was, was fragmented" (261); and Mrs. Van's political career is in ruins. The splintering of the Left occurs in a particularly vicious way, as McFarline bludgeons Mrs. Van with the most primitive of weapons: "If Mrs. Van were the last woman alive in the world he couldn't bring himself to f—— her"

(247). Anton reads the situation as proof of the need to "make a fresh analysis," though, as Martha points out, "there are only three of us left." She is left "examining two very clear convictions that existed simultaneously in her mind":

> One, it was inevitable that everything should have happened in exactly the way it had happened: no one could have behaved differently. Two, that everything that had happened was unreal, grotesque, and irrelevant . . . But it's not possible that both can be true, Martha thought. (261–62)

Both are in fact true: everything that has happened is inevitable according to the laws of causation that govern history, and everything that has happened is also "irrelevant" to Lessing's new sense of what is real and important. History may still hurt, but it is ceasing to matter.[25]

What is also at an end for Lessing, at least for now, is the narrative mode suited to expressing the historical and to reiterating the familiar, the mode that assumes that the social reality we inhabit is the whole of reality. Realism is part of the impasse reached at this point in the series, complicit with the conditioning that prevents the creation of anything new. Lessing will find means of breaking through—of blasting the reptile out of the bedrock—formally, in the narrative innovations of *The Golden Notebook, Landlocked,* and *The Four-Gated City,* and philosophically, in the Sufism that becomes pronounced in the final volumes of the *Children of Violence*.

## Chapter 4

# *Landlocked:* "A New Kind of Knowledge"

Though all in this novel seem locked into stasis, "landlocked," *Landlocked* is the first novel in the *Children of Violence* in which real change occurs.[1] The novel begins in the shadow of the end, with everyone waiting for the end of the war and Martha waiting for her father's death and her divorce from Anton so that she can leave for England. The war does end, early on, its poignantly hollow "Victory Day" observed from the perspective of Mrs. Quest, but it makes no difference in the lives of these characters, providing neither the demarcation nor the release they had anticipated, since the cold war and fear of the Soviet Union enforce another kind of stasis: "The only thing was to sit tight and wait."[2] After the end of the war, the characters remain immobilized, "Thomas, waiting to go to Israel, Martha waiting to go to England—they felt like people filling in time before trains on a station platform" (174). Besides, in some sense the war never ends, for (as Thomas asserts) the twentieth century remains a "time of war" (230).

Yet change is occurring, though it is, in its initial stages, destructive: the cataclysmic destruction of the Second World War, the fact of forty-four million dead, so alters the world as to render irrelevant the systems—moral, philosophical, epistemological, linguistic, literary—that ordered experience in the past. But in accordance with the Sufism that from here on becomes pronounced in Lessing's thought, the destruction of the old allows for the emergence of the new. The destruction that has so altered the world that we cannot think or talk about it in customary ways is rendered hauntingly, powerfully, by a lyrical mode that strains against the limits of language to express the inexpressible horrors of the century as well as something new emerging from them. Language is no longer adequate to the central questions of Martha's existence—her relation with Thomas or the war's forty-four million dead—it, too, being a conventional system rendered irrelevant by the horrors of the times. But this changed sense of language is hopeful, and it also accords with a Sufi belief, that "the tyranny of words" reinforces "custom" and "establish[ed] patterns of thinking."[3]

Though *Landlocked* has been dismissed as "sketchy and perfunctory," "hardly a narrative at all,"[4] Lessing is doing something stunningly original here: if it seems "hardly a narrative" this is because it offers a mode more dependent on lyricism than plot, a mode that works by a richly allusive system of imagery, both pictorial and metaphorical, and that builds resonances in the course of the novel. Imagery relating to landlock, on the one hand—desert landscapes, ruined cities, nightmare houses—and to the regenerative forces of water and light, on the other, is drawn both from Martha's dreams and from her experience in a way that breaks down distinctions between objective and subjective. Dreams prefigure and influence events in ways that register dream reality as equally valid to conscious experience and render an altered sense of temporality, teaching Martha to cast imaginatively backward and forward and to speed time and slow it, in the sort of refiguration of time that becomes pronounced in *The Four-Gated City*. The imagery patterns become "what the novel is about" more than anything that actually happens. This is the mode Joanna Russ describes as "lyric" and which she contrasts to "narrative" and "dramatic" structures that depend on "chronology" and "causation"; the lyric mode is "associative" and sets "various images, events, scenes, or memories to circling around an unspoken, invisible center":

> The invisible center is what the novel or poem is about. That is, there is no action possible to the central character and no series of events which will embody in clear, unequivocal, immediately graspable terms what the artist means.[5]

The lyric mode can articulate experience made unspeakable by modes dependent on more conventional means.

On the personal level, Martha's affair with Thomas takes her into "an altogether new dimension" (153), "breaking down" (218) the boundaries of self in a way she can barely describe and teaching her new powers of intuition. On the collective level, change has been forced by the massive disruptions of the age—urbanization, industrialization, war—which require a new perspective and new kind of understanding. As Thomas tells her, "everything's changed. I'm the norm now . . . the elm tree and safety's finished . . . My family's all dead and I'm in exile" (168). Now we must "feel the stars and their times and their spaces" (193), he says, and perhaps this new understanding will make change in us: "Perhaps there'll be a mutation . . . . Perhaps that's why we are all so sick. Something new is trying to get born through our thick skins . . . everything's changed" (116).

Athen attributes the need for changed consciousness to the war: "It's not possible for us to understand . . . But suddenly human beings have to understand—in the last five years millions and millions of people have been killed . . . forty-four millions"; "You must think about it, you must think. We do not think enough about what these things mean" (130). Later, in the conversation Martha has with Jack as they speed across the African countryside, she does "think about what these things mean," when, struck by the injustice of Jack's disapproval of Maisie's several marriages, she is seized by "a new kind of knowledge" (157). So anachronistic does Jack's conventional judgment seem, in view of the many husbands Maisie lost in the war, that Martha feels disoriented: "Nothing fitted, ridiculous facts jostled with important ones, if only one knew which was which . . . and she wished she was back in the refuge of the loft, reading" (160). But the reading she longs for no longer provides a refuge, since the systems it depended on have been swept away by the cataclysms of the century, rendered as anachronistic as Jack's conventionality. Martha's derisive "who do you think I am? Madame Bovary? Well, I wish we had her problems" (58–59) expresses her sense that she inhabits "another room"—her metaphor for dislocation (220)—from that depicted by older fictions.

This is the first of Lessing's novels to show the influence of Sufism, and it is apparent in Thomas's suggestion that humanity is in the process of evolving, that something new may "get born through our thick skins."[6] The creation of the new requires the destruction of the old, in Sufi terminology, of "the web cast on humanity by the old Villain," "the bundle of . . . conditionings—fixed ideas and prejudices, automatic responses" that determine human behavior;[7] or, in Lessing's term from the preceding novel in the series, of the primeval reptile embedded in the pit. "The old Villain" must be destroyed if one is to achieve the Sufi goal of "a new way of seeing things," a way that, like Martha's "new kind of knowledge," is based on intuitive rather than logical faculties, the first step toward which is a radical disorientation.[8]

Lessing's suggestion that literary forms are complicit with the old Villain, part of the conditioning that entraps the mind in ossified patterns, reflects a further Sufi belief. In fact, Thomas's strange tale of the man who escapes his enemy only to kill himself (270–77) is a kind of Sufi teaching fable, an exercise designed to break such conditioning. Thomas's tale is one of many in the manuscript he sends out of the wilderness in his final stages of breakdown. It begins familiarly enough, so familiarly as to raise predictable expectations—"Once there was a man who travelled to a distant country. When he got there, the enemy he had fled from was waiting for him . . . he went to yet another country"—expectations which Thomas then upsets with a fiendish delight: "'No, his enemy was *not* there.' (Surprised, are you! said the red pencil.) 'So he killed himself'" (270). The pleasure in surprise, in the frustration of predictable patterns, is characteristic of the Sufi exercise designed "to free the thinking from the adhesions of rigid thinking," "to create thought in the mind and to combat the tendency to 'sleep.'"[9]

But Thomas's "last testament," a jumble of "sense" and "nonsense" (272), is testament also to the dangers of destroying the patterns of the past. Prophet, representative, and sacrificial victim of the changes he describes, Thomas Stern ends—like the speaker in Thomas Stearns Eliot's *Waste Land*—able to "connect / Nothing with nothing." This novel's closest literary analogue is not a novel but a poem, a work that similarly registers the aftershocks of a world war and the reduction of Western civilization to "a heap of broken images."[10] Lessing draws on *The Waste Land* for the same reason that Eliot draws on the grail legends and the myths on which those legends are based, to explore the possibility that this destruction may issue into rebirth and to ask "what are the roots that clutch, what branches grow/ Out of this stony rubbish?" (ll. 19–20).

The "old Villain" is dying in this novel: two old men, Johnny Lindsay and Mr. Quest, are dead by the end, as are most of the young men. Mr. Quest, who is referred to as "the old man" (197, 239), is kept alive longer than anyone could have anticipated—appropriately, by the ministrations of Mrs. Quest (246); and the scene where the slowly dying invalid claims the child Caroline's hand as his own—"the hand, bone merely . . . was gripped around the plump fresh arm of the little girl" (235)—is a striking dramatization of the dead hand upon the living. The old men die slowly, in bed; the young men—Athen, Thomas, Maisie's husbands, numerous members of the Royal Air Force—die as victims of the war or its aftermath. As in *The Waste Land* and the grail legends on which it draws, the blight of the land is expressed in the suffering of the people; but in this age of global wars it is the men who are the sacrificial victims, leaving the women to carry on as custodians of civilization. "What the father breaks, the mother makes," as Thomas's last testament suggests (271).

A "new age" has begun in this novel, though it is not the "new Jerusalem" envisioned by the young revolutionaries of the preceding novel: it is, rather, the age for which Hiroshima and Nagasaki are symbols (91) and for which the ruined city is image. The city in this novel is no longer the "realm of generous and freely exchanged emotion" (*MQ,* 79) that Martha once envisioned, but a ruin—"ruined cities . . . pulverized to ruins" (50–51), "Europe . . . in ruins" (77, 216), "the ruins of Cologne . . . a chaos of debris" (37), "the ruins that were Germany" (115). This sort of imagery is so deep in the imaginative fabric of the novel as to be invoked to describe the end of Martha's and Thomas's affair: "Soon this love . . . would have been blown apart. Like a town in Europe, dark under a sky bursting with bits of flying flame and steel" (146). Such imagery recalls the city in *The Waste Land* that

> cracks and reforms and bursts . . .
> Falling towers
> Jerusalem Athens Alexandria
> Vienna London.
>
> (ll. 373–37)

The ruined city imagery culminates in the passage where Martha tries to envision her own city as "emptied," "desiccating," "filling with drifts of dust" (190–91). What is new in the narrative mode of *Landlocked* is apparent in this surreal description of a city that, shifting shapes as images do in dreams, blends with the ruined cities of Europe then contracts, first to what seems "the shadows of leaves of grass" and then to the carcass of a grasshopper, "its big eyes staring, but empty" (191). Images are evoked to be revoked—"But it is not a leaf shadow, no"—in a ruminative process that revises and qualifies itself. This passage, set in "October again" (189)—and October is the southern hemisphere April, time of tension and transition, as well as the month of Lessing's and Martha's birth—recalls the October passage in *Martha Quest,* which accompanied Martha's succumbing to the cycles that held her "trancelike," in a "spell" of sleep and forgetting (*MQ,* 21–23); but this passage reverses that process and strips away those patterns. Like the earlier description, this both describes and effects "passage," only here, Martha strains for a "new kind of knowledge" that can include Athen's vision of destruction and Thomas's perspective of the stars (193). This desiccation is also a cleansing, as the city is purified to a shadow so thin that it allows in the light—indeed, it *is* "a kind of light." A series of unanswered questions—"but what use was it to say words like *millions,* if she couldn't imagine, really feel them?" "But what was the use of saying forty-four million . . . when one could not *feel*?" (190–91)—strains the imagination to conceive of the inconceivable; but sentences break off into ellipses as language fails with the effort. The imagery recalls Eliot's desert landscape—

> where the sun beats,
> And the dead tree gives no shelter, the cricket no relief,
> And the dry stone no sound of water.
>
> (ll.22–24)

and the nightmarish journey at the end of *The Waste Land* (ll. 331–93), a journey which is, like this "passage," initiatory.

This mode with its startling associations requires the reader to make connections and ask the significance of things. In fact, Lessing does something very like what Eliot does in *The Waste Land,* where the reader's engagement with the poem demands the same sort of imaginative comprehension required of the grail seeker if he is to lift the curse from the waste land.[11] In *Landlocked* "forty-odd million human beings had been murdered, deliberately or from carelessness, from lack of imagination" (196), and this failure is repeated on the personal level by the "failure of imagination . . . . failure of sympathy" (187) that prevents Martha from sensing the danger Thomas is in. But to read the novel sympathetically, imaginatively, is to exercise the faculty whose failure has caused the devastation. The "design" of the novel does "corroborate the process it describes" (contrary to Rubenstein's assertion, *Novelistic Vision,* 113–14), both mirroring the destruction that is its subject and suggesting a means to recreation.

Martha's condition is epitomized by two recurrent dreams, the dream of the house whose rooms she must keep separate and the nightmare of being landlocked. The dream of the house is described in language like that of the "emptied city" passage. The images are hallucinatory and shape-shifting, as the ruin Martha fears will follow from her failure to keep things separate becomes "the house on the kopje, collapsed into a mess of ant-tunneled mud, ant-consumed grass," and then turns to "the burial mound of Martha's soul," the ant tracks becoming "red veins" (14–15). The ruin looks forward to the disintegration of the Quest house, which is later described as "rotted . . . in a fierce compost"; though chronologically, it looks back to it, since this dissolution has actually already occurred (190–91). Then Martha's perspective moves "back in time, or perhaps forward—she did not know," and the house is "no longer the farm house of grass and mud; but . . . tall rather than wide, reached up, stretched down . . . built layer on layer, but shadowy above and below" (15). Whereas in the preceding *Children of Violence* novels, houses like Colonel Brodeshaw's and the house on the avenues were substantial and real, here houses shift shape and disintegrate. Past, present, and future conflate, as the dream points both forward and backward in time—back to the South London scene of Mrs. Quest's childhood and forward to Mark Coldridge's house in Bloomsbury.

The dream of the house instructs Martha to "keep things separate" because allowing them to merge would mean chaos, "disintegration" (14). But "keeping separate meant defeating, or at least, holding at bay, what was best in her . . . the need to say yes, to comply, to melt into situations" (15). She follows the instruction of the dream by saying "no" to several male characters: to Mr. Robinson when he offers her a job; to Mr. Maynard when he tries to bully her about Maisie; to her husband Anton when he suggests that they remain married. Above all she must separate herself from the pain of her parents and refuse even pity for them, lest they "get her, drag her down into this nightmare house like a maze where there could be only one end" (76), a nightmare house that is also an actual house where people "sat around, waiting for an old man to die" (197). Houses in the past and in the future, houses present and "a hundred miles away" (190), real houses and nightmare houses, blend in a mode that confounds chronology.

The other dream that expresses Martha's condition and acts as her guide is the dream of being landlocked: "On this high dry plateau where Martha was imprisoned, forever, it seemed, everything was dry and brittle, its quality was drought." Like the dream of the house, this both cautions her against a condition and suggests a way out of it: "Far away, a long way below, was water. She dreamed, night after night, of water, of the sea" (199). This dream also predicts the deaths of significant men in her life: "Across this sea, which she could not reach . . . sailed people she had known . . . Athen . . . Thomas" (128).

The images of both dreams—the house and the landlock—are combined in a waking reverie when Martha, visiting the "nightmare house" of her parents, half listens to her daughter Caroline, who both knows and does not know that she is her daughter, "playing" with Mr. Quest, taunting the old man with her youth and vitality. The situation—Caroline's teasing, Mrs. Quest's manipulating the situation so that it becomes a reproach to Martha—

pulls Martha back into "the nightmare." But dream imagery infuses her consciousness, as the sound of the sprinklers in the background—"water, water falling water"—recalls to her the possibility of rescue from the sea:

> And one day . . . Martha would . . . stand on a shore and watch a line of waves gather strength and run inwards, piling and gathering high before falling over into a burst of white foam . . . . White flowers tossing against a blue sky. White foam dying in a hissing gulf of blue. White birds spreading their wings against blue, blue depths.
>
> . . . Meanwhile, the old man lay, whimpering in his cage of decaying swelling flesh. (238–39)

The "lock," the landmass of Southern Rhodesia, becomes, in this passage, the prison of mortal life, with the light-illuminated water beyond suggesting a transcendent reality of which Martha's consciousness, instructed by her dreams, has intimation.

Besides her prophetic dreams, Martha has several mystical experiences that demonstrate her development of new faculties. Instructed by her dreams, Martha reconfigures time: on the drive across the countryside with Jack, she imagines a prewar Europe and a postwar Europe, envisions a Europe in famine and a Europe revitalized, and conjures an image of Maisie as she would have been if there had been no war and juxtaposes this to Maisie now. It is this "dislocation" that leads to "a new kind of knowledge":

> Turn her upside down, she would be floating on pale blue depths where white foam flowers hissed and died, looking up at a great bubble of pale gold, where the movements of wind showed in mile-long currents of whitening light. (157–59)

Again, striking images of light and water suggest the existence of forces beyond comprehension or description. The night she and Thomas spend dancing and drinking at the Parkland Hotel she again perceives herself as "a space of knowledge" able to leave her body. She sees that their present fleshly forms are "guises" and envisions the scene from a perspective of millennia:

> The others . . . sat around her like many-coloured ghosts of people she had known a thousand years ago, under the cool light trees over which the stars stood—but differently, they had moved across the sky. Trunks rose into remote starlight from pools of music, firelight, faces. (147)

What is new in this novel is an increasingly strong intimation of a transcendental reality and a sense of an "essential self" that is in touch with it—"what was real in [Martha] underneath these metamorphoses" (13), "what people are" (118)

It is Martha's relationship with Thomas that enables her to develop new intuitive powers. This relationship takes her into the "new dimension" (153) she has been seeking, a dimension that recalls her visionary moments as an adolescent on the veld. The description of their love in terms of light and opening doors—"as if doors were being opened one after another inside their eyes as they looked" at each other (101); "sinking deeper and deeper into light" (153)—suggests that it allows access to the ideal city she sought in the earlier novels. It provides the integration Martha associated with the city: "Adding a new room to her house has ended the division. From this centre she now lives" (98; see also 108). Their union amidst the "leaf smelling warmth" of Thomas's shed and "reflected beams of orange light . . . greenish sun-lanced light" suggests that it also allows access to the rejuvenating forces of nature.[12] Their first lovemaking occurs in a scene of light streaming through a window, with Martha "dipping her arm in and out of the greenish sun-lanced light . . . as if into water" (97) in a way that recalls Caroline's play with the sun beams. Later in this scene, when "loud splashing drops [rain] through a strong orange evening sunlight," they run to the window, their mouths open to the wet, and watch "the greenish reflections from the deep tree outside": "All around them were soaked sparkling lawns, dripping boughs, a welter of wet flowers. Everything was impossibly brilliant in the clear washed light" (103–4). But this ecstasy, like Martha's illuminations on the veld, has a terrifying side, representing a fusion that threatens dissolution, the "breaking down" (218) of the self: "No, it was too strong . . . much easier to live deprived, to be resigned, *to be self-contained*. No, she did not want to be dissolved" (90).[13]

Though it is "the most sure, the most real thing that happened to her" (159), this relationship defies definition or description. No one, not "newspapers, films, literature, the people who are supposed to express us," ever told her this sort of thing was possible "in a way that she could believe" (154). She can only express it metaphorically, evoking again a sense of vague, powerful forces beyond reason or language:

> The relationship—whatever was the right word for it—was in an altogether new dimension. They were in deep waters, both of them. And neither understood it, could not speak about it.

> Together in the loft, they spoke less . . . . To be together was like—she could not say . . . . Sometimes when they made love it was so powerful they felt afraid, as if enormous forces were waiting to invade them. But they did not know what this meant. (153)

She and Thomas eventually declare their love for each other, but Martha finally refuses the word "love" as a description for what happens between them, though she has no better term:

> She did not understand any of this . . . her experience with Thomas had been so deep, in every way, that she was changed to the point that . . . but here it was that she was unable to go further.
>
> . . . she did not know what had taken place between her and Thomas. Some force, some power . . . had made such changes in her—what, soul? (but she did not even know what words she must use) pschye? being?—that now she was changed and did not understand herself . . .
>
> But she could not use the word Love, for she did not know what it meant . . .
>
> . . . But what has been the essential quality of being with Thomas? Well, she did not know. (218)

Again, ellipses and questions express an amazement that stuns her into speechlessness—"surely she ought to be able to say" (218). And Thomas is no more able than she is to say what the experience has been about: "No one knows anything about that sort of thing . . . . We haven't any idea about it really" (219).

After he leaves for Israel, Martha continues to "talk" with Thomas, to carry on "conversations" with him wherein she tries to understand his reasons for leaving. It is this effort that prompts the "emptied city" rumination and the "passage" to "a new kind of knowledge" that comprehends the violence that has overcome Thomas. Again, a series of unanswered questions—"what does it mean, saying: I don't believe in violence?" "what does it mean to say: I don't believe that violence achieves anything?"—suggests a straining to conceive of the inconceivable. And the "answer" that concludes this passage is as illogical as it is irrefutable: "Martha did not believe in violence. Martha was the essence of violence" (195).

Thomas succumbs to violence. He is destroyed by what Lessing later terms the "self-hater," by a process of projection she will analyze more fully in *The Four-Gated City*. It is not his relationship with Martha that destroys him, as Rubenstein asserts (*Novelistic Vision,* 117–18), for while their relationship may exacerbate his instability, Thomas's fate is no more bound up with Martha's than hers is with his. Love is no longer "an end," either a personal destiny or a literary conclusion, in this world; and though his death and the deaths of other main characters occur at the end of the novel, they do not provide resolution or even closure. Thomas's fate is that of a Jew in this century, one whose family has been destroyed in the death camps of a Europe from which he is forever exiled—"my family's all dead and I'm in exile" (168); "I hate myself all the time" (176). His self-hatred, which may be understood as a kind of "survivor's guilt," is projected onto Sergeant Tressel, whom he makes into "the enemy"—an enemy who is, Martha realizes, "too strong for her" (146). Thomas knows it is impossible "to escape one's fate" (131–32); and, as is suggested by the strange story in his "last testament," having escaped the enemy Tressel in Israel, "he killed himself" (270). He is, as Anna Wulf's Michael calls himself, "the history of Europe" (*GN,* 332). He is also Europe's future.

Martha's dream of Thomas as about to be hanged—as a "hanged man"—cannot help but suggest, in the context of so many *Waste Land* allusions, the Tarot figure that "represents the sacrificial victim (the Green Man, the Winter King) who must die to ensure regeneration." Though the Tarot figure is hanged not by the neck, but by the feet, the effect of the hanging—to make the figure "see the world from upside down"—is like the disorientation both Thomas and Martha experience, a disorientation so radical as to require a "new way of seeing things."[14] The series of questions Martha asks in this dream, none of which is answered—"What was this mood, or way of thinking, or mode of being, she could not name?" "What was the look on his face?" "As if he—as if . . . *as if what?*" (203; ellipses in original)—are all versions of the question the Grail seeker must ask of the dying Fisher King if the curse is to be lifted: "Why do you suffer?"[15] Thomas is the "hanged man," the Fisher King, and there is further suggestion, in the medieval setting of the execution, that he is the Christ of Dostoevsky's Grand Inquisitor. In a way reminiscent of Eliot, Lessing evokes and conflates associations from a variety of myths, producing an effect like that of double exposure or montage. The meaning of the look on Thomas's face—which is the point of the dream, why she was dreaming it—is never explained; Martha cannot even "name" it, though she does recognize it when she sees it again, as he storms out of the political meeting enraged at the group's naïveté: "It's the look on his face—I simply *cannot* understand it. Where have I seen it before? And what is happening to Thomas?" (225). But, as in the Grail legend, it is the asking rather than the answer that matters; and it is Martha's compassion, her taking responsibility for the document Thomas sends out of the wilderness, that becomes the source, in *The Four-Gated City,* of new, saving knowledge.

Thomas's last testament, an effort to "get messages out" (272), similarly conflates associations from a variety of sources. He has retired to a village whose sufferings he describes in terms reminiscent of *The Waste Land:* "Their crops had failed through drought . . . They are dying, they say, because . . . the River God . . . is angry with them" (234).[16] The document he sends back from this village confuses time, place, action, and tone, in a violation of all literary decorums. Thomas's past in Poland intertwines crazily with his present in Africa; Jewish jokes mix with African tribal history; cries for vengeance alternate with pleas for mercy—all run together in red ink interlaced by ant tracks:

> How was Martha, or anybody, to know what Thomas had meant? . . . there were notes, comments, scribbled over and across and on the margins of the original text, in red pencil. These, hard to decipher, were in themselves a different story or, at least, made of the original a different story. . . . But what was he trying to write? (269)

"Burned . . . from the hot sun . . . sharpened" (226), Thomas has been seared by too much reality.[17] His ravings resemble Lear's in their vacillation between lucidity ("Quite sensible" stories of the people in the village, "a history of the tribe") and lunacy ("If you keep your grain on stilts, to save it from the white ants, why not walk on stilts yourself" [270]); he swings crazily from pleas for mercy ("It could be said, therefore, that gentleness saves sour milk") to vindictive rage ("Vermin. Swine. Murdered. Apes. Apes with red blistering behinds. Kill. Kill" [271]).[18] He is obsessed with death—"Death in the bottom of the river"—the river god's, his own. Thomas is the dying God, the Fisher King, the hanged man, Lear with his crown of thorns. He is also a voice from the heart of darkness which, like Kurtz's, casts "a kind of light."[19] He is a Jew, ourselves, "the norm now."

But with no way of ordering his perceptions, Thomas succumbs to the chaos Martha fears in herself, enacting that potential that the nightmare of the ruined house warns her against.[20] His document is more disjointed, more mad, than any of the other "memoirs" in the novel—than Johnny Lindsay's "memoirs of a gallant and innocent boy" (269) or Solly's "Patterns of Betrayal" (270)[21]—though it is also more "true." Johnny and Solly present partial perspectives, Johnny's "schoolboy picnic . . . socialism" (268) providing the antithesis to Solly's simple cynicism. Only Thomas strains for the whole truth, though he breaks in the attempt.

Thomas's death leaves Martha feeling "as if some part of [her had] died . . . Or it is in another room, looking on" (220). But the image of "another room," which she uses to signify dislocation, appears in the tales of Mulla Nasrudin to suggest new potential: "They were like children born in a house from which they had never been allowed to stray, doomed to walk from one room to another without knowing that there could be another house, elsewhere."[22] Whereas at the beginning of the novel, Martha was wandering benightedly from room to room, in her dreams and in actuality, her experience with Thomas has taken her into "another room" by giving her new knowledge and power.[23]

The old Villain, the patterns of the past, dies hard. Imagery of nets, webs, and cages is nearly as pronounced in this novel as it was in *A Proper Marriage*—though associated here not with Martha but with those around her. Martha's father is locked in his "cage of . . . flesh" (239); her mother is "trapped, caged" in her life (197); and "the nightmare repetition" transforms Martha's women friends into the kind of women they once despised. It is most poignant in the dream Mrs. Quest has of her mother reaching down from heaven to hand her roses that turn to medicine bottles, symbol of the maternal legacy—or the loss of such a legacy—that she bequeaths Martha. "The hound Repetition" (133) is apparent in Anton's choice of mistresses and in Thomas's choice of thin, rejecting women. In Martha's sense of the change that signals Thomas's breakdown ("He sounded—not like himself" [177])—is an echo of the sentence pronounced on her father years before: "We are afraid you will never really be yourself again, Captain" (64); and Mrs. Quest's jaunty reference to her husband and son as "my two war casualties" (106) similarly suggests that the younger generation of men is repeating the errors of the elders in a recurrent cycle of war.

Martha's life in this novel is not only without the crises, turning points, and revolutions that she had expected, but almost entirely without event. Indeed, the novel is marked by a pattern of deliberate anticlimax: the strike that comes to the fore in the final pages impedes denouement then fizzles out ("The strike came to an end, both sides claiming victory, though the strikers' main demand, namely that a law should be passed insisting on a minimum wage of three pounds a month, was not gained" [265]); and the revelation of the deaths of Martha's lover and father in the second half of the same sentence short-circuits any dramatic potential they might have had (242).

But for Martha the patterns of the past are stripped away, as one by one, the illusions that held her in preceding novels are laid to rest. The relationship with Thomas ends the fantasy that love, even as compelling as this, can provide rescue. The idea of the family as support is terminated by Mrs. Quest's legacy to her daughter just before Martha leaves for England, of "all the keys she ever had in her life," "half-a-century's keys on a key ring," "black, rusty, jutting, awkward"—keys "fit for a dungeon, opening nothing" (231–33).[24] (It is cruelly ironic that the old lady ends her days high in the mountains on a farm that is even more landlocked than the Quest family farm—high and dry.) The political meeting of the last scene represents an end to the fantasy that political action can accomplish anything. Observing the meeting with ironic distance, Martha can see that "history was repeating itself" and, knowing "the signs," can "foretell the end" (275).

But the closing of the circle is not complete, for Martha is newly opened to change and there may even be hope for the desiccated civilization. The saurian so deeply embedded in the pit may not have "centuries to live" since its excavation by violent means is under way. The power of destruction is sufficient to blast the encrusted reptile out of the bedrock, to destroy the old Villain, "the bundle of conditionings, fixed ideas, automatic responses," that are the legacy of the past. Whether this civilization will survive—whether the waste land is redeemable—is left unanswered, for Lessing, like Eliot, raises more questions than she answers. Lessing gives little indication, beyond a suggestion, when Martha, Jasmine, and Marjorie emerge onto the street after the dismal political meeting of the last scene, that somewhere it has rained, "for gusts of soft damp air came to their faces with a smell of freshly wetted leaves" (280). Like the sound of rain at the end of Eliot's *Waste Land*—"then a damp gust / Bringing rain" (ll. 394–95)—this suggests the possibility of renewal.

As Martha leaves Africa, bound for the ruined city of London, the hub of Empire and heart of darkness, the "lock" has been broken, and with it, the determinism that governed the first three novels. As Lessing's sense of cataclysmic destruction increases, her focus shifts from society to a reality that transcends the social and an essential self in touch with this reality—to "what was real in [Martha], underneath these metamorphoses" (13). "What people are" (*LL,* 118) is as mysterious as Martha's relationship with Thomas: "no one knows anything about that sort of thing, we haven't any idea about it really" (219). But if we know nothing about it, we nevertheless *know* it—we know, for example, that Johnny Lindsay is "a naturally good man" (208), "naturally," essentially, inexplicably. Unable to sustain the determinism with which she began—that "everything Martha was, was because" of the violence of the times, that individuals are bound to the "twist" and "damage" (*LL,* 195–96)—Lessing resorts to a notion of an essential self that can generate something new.

Though Lessing has been criticized for being inconsistent and reactionary,[25] the evolution of her thought resolves the paradox that informed the earlier novels: she finds a way beyond determinism, a place beyond culture, by positing an essential self in touch with a "universal consciousness." Whatever one thinks of this position, it allies her with the Modernists of the early twentieth century—not only with Eliot, but with Yeats, Pound, Lawrence, and Joyce—in what Eagleton calls "a recourse to myth" that is a "flight from contemporary history."[26] It will finally be the books of mysticism and the occult that Martha discovers in *The Four-Gated City* that provide the key Martha has been seeking, in offering a perspective that turns out to be genuinely oppositional.

*Chapter 5*

# *The Four-Gated City*: "Something Quite Different"

What was demanded of her was that she should accept something quite different.

—Doris Lessing, *Martha Quest*

What we call the beginning is often the end
And to make an end is to make a beginning.
The end is where we start from.

—T. S. Eliot, "Little Gidding," *Four Quartets*

*The Golden Notebook,* published at the beginning of the sixties, and *The Four-Gated City,* published at the end of the decade, provide two very different endings to the quest begun in *Martha Quest.*[1] Anna Wulf, "a completely new type of woman" who is "living the kind of life women never lived before,"[2] attains a measure of freedom and efficacy in the world and completes her quest in a way that forged new paths for women; and it is to this novel that Lessing turns from the impasse of *Ripple.* But when Lessing returns to the *Children of Violence* she has Martha renounce not only self-realization but self. Whereas *The Golden Notebook* focuses on a striking individual, an extraordinary woman who is "made by the kind of experience women haven't had before" (*GN,* 471), *The Four-Gated City* depicts a somewhat ordinary woman who assumes a somewhat traditional role and whose journey takes her back through the ancient experience of the race. Whereas Anna learns to "name in a different way" (*GN,* 616), Martha comes to relinquish language; whereas Anna works out her salvation in this world, *The Four-Gated City* moves elsewhere.

## Circular Returns

Yet Martha's quest is, like Anna's, for freedom, a goal that she has actually in some sense already attained at the beginning of the novel. Walking the streets of London in a state of heightened awareness, draped in Mrs. Van's old coat (47, 60)—a detail that points both back in time and forward, to the formidable matron Martha herself will become at the end of *The Four-Gated City*—Martha knows her essential self to be independent of externals, of family, society, country, and name: "There she was:[3] *she* was, nothing to do with Martha, or any other name she might have had attached to her" (36). Released from the expectations of others, she experiences herself as "an empty space without boundaries" (17), "anonymous, unnoticed . . . Never before in her life had she known this freedom" (4).

Martha will try to remember this "light" through "thinned walls" (39) and this sense of herself as "clear . . . alive and alight and aware" (35)—"remember, remember, don't let it go, remember"—but she realizes,

> No use to say: remember the lit space and its marvellous brother, the turn of the spiral above it . . . . Because, having left them behind, having sunk away, one was in a place with its own memories, its own knowledge. (39)

Like the tantalizing beginning of Eliot's *Four Quartets*—"Quick, said the bird, find them, find them, / . . . Round the corner. Through the first gate" ("Burnt Norton" [118])—these images evoke a wondrous realm glimmering just beyond our perceptions, an "elsewhere" that can be apprehended only through the imagination and expressed by "as if," all the more marvelous by contrast to the dismal rubble of postwar London. Martha begins from the place that it will take her the rest of the novel to work back to, in a movement that Lessing suggests is paradigmatic of human life.

But the freedom Martha experiences in the opening episodes is premature, even dangerous, for she will need to descend from "the lit space" (39) and reenter the world—"there's no escaping it, it's like having to go down into a pit, a terrible dark blind pit, and then you fight your way up and out" (68); she will need to reconnect with the human community before she can work her way free. Martha might well protest, as she did at the beginning of *Martha Quest,* "but if I know all this why do I have to go through it?" but she does not, for she understands her need for "responsibility":

> She had debts to pay, that was it. One could not move on before all debts were paid, the accounts made up. . . . Caroline invaded her mind, the two men she

> had married so absurdly—her mother. Debts. They had to be paid. A great descent down, down, was before her. Then a wave would lift her up again (when?) to where she was now, on a height, and from where she could glimpse other perspectives. (38)

She is careful about what connections she makes, sensing that they will determine her future, and says "no" to potentially destructive situations: to Iris and Joe, who would "shut" her in her self-deprecating persona "Matty" (5); to Henry, who would "narrow" her to the conventional "slot" of legal secretary (24); to Jack, who would leave her too free, "rootless, untied" (38), "safe and unchallenged" (47). Yet connect she must: "She, Martha, had something in her which forbade her to drift and visit and slide out" (30); "something (a sense of self-preservation?)" impels her to connect to the human community (17). Paradoxically, she will find freedom by submitting to the most confining of situations, submerging herself in the pain and confusion of the Coldridges: this is the situation that becomes her growing point.[4]

Some readers object to Martha's renunciations and wonder why she can't do something more original than raise someone else's family, having just ditched a family of her own—why can't she do something new? And some have complained that Lessing gives Mark and not Martha the role of famous author. But for one thing, Lessing has already explored the problems of the woman writer, in *The Golden Notebook.* For another thing, Martha does play an important part in Mark's writing: she is "responsible for" his most significant novel, *A City in the Desert* (177), the alleged sequel to which, "Son of the City" or "Sun City" (551), becomes actualized in the refugee camps at the end; she is also responsible for his work *Rachel and Aaron,* based on the doomed sister and brother of Thomas's manuscript.[5]

But even if Martha is only the woman behind the great man, a version of Mark's muse, this hardly matters, since the very idea of "greatness" has been so impugned in this novel as to be irrelevant—it's the last thing we would wish on her. Lessing's "new sort of understanding" (357) requires renunciation of power, position, wealth, fame, and even the autonomy and achievement which Martha once sought. "Authorship" itself has been debunked along with the rest of what the world values, as a fashion, a fad, as we watch the popularity of Mark's fiction blow with "the prevailing winds" (323)—winds that change with the political climate: thus his first novel, a dispassionate analysis of recurrent cycles of war, was coolly received in the mood of passionate self-righteousness just following the war but applauded when the "reaction" set in. (This reaction began in the United States—"in

America a period of political reaction can be foretold . . . when publishers and agents and educators, those most sensitive of barometers, talk about Art in capital letters"—and decreed that "only second-rate writers dealt with social conditions, or politics, or . . . public affairs." Lessing's analysis of Ivory Tower aestheticism as the intellectual expression of cold war politics was brilliant at a time when literary and critical standards passed as "universals": "The 'Cold War' was spreading, had already spread, from politics to the arts" [131].)

Martha is drawn to the Coldridges precisely because they are familiar, for she has not only stopped seeking something new but has renounced the search for the new: "There's a pressure on us all the time to go on to something that seems new because there are new words attached to it. But I want to take words as ordinary as bread. Or life. Or death. Clichés. I want to have my nose rubbed in clichés" (97). What she lives through with the Coldridges, however, is not exactly a repetition of what she has been through before, for the roles she assumes—Mark's mistress, his surrogate wife and surrogate mother to his children—are the same but different from those she has played in the past. The literary precedent for her situation is, extraordinarily, *Jane Eyre:* Martha enters the Coldridge house as secretary-governess and becomes involved with the master of the house—but she then also becomes involved with the mad wife in the basement, accepting her as guide through the landscape of madness:[6] "'A charming *ménage à trois,*' [Margaret, Mark's mother] murmured, not so much cattily but as it were trying to define a position" (398). The parallel draws attention to the difference between the nineteenth century and the present and the inadequacy of the conventions of the past to contemporary situations, discrepancies that Martha has long understood, though it also suggests that past situations recur within the present.

Lessing's focus on "the individual in its relation with the collective" continues in this novel, though it, too, is the same but different. Episodes concerning Martha alternate with collective scenes that provide "signs of the times"—the election night party, the garden parties at Margaret's country home, the Aldermaston March, the communal scenes that take place over meals at the Coldridges. Martha's move in with the Coldridge family is not, as some critics have suggested, a refuge from the conflicts of the political or public realm,[7] for the Coldridges are at the center of London's political and cultural life and London is still "the greatest city in the world" (33); in some sense, the Coldridges *are* England. In fact Martha's quest becomes less important as the collective becomes more important, as she becomes involved first with the family, disappearing into the "Martha/Mark/Lynda" triad, and then disappearing into the general fate of humanity. But despite the novel's social and historical specificity—though the characters who crowd these pages are typical and even stereotypical representatives of politics, arts, media, and letters in mid-century England—"the collective" is, by the end, not social or political; rather, the social and political are revealed to be increasingly bankrupt and what emerges is a kind of "universal consciousness" or cosmic oversoul, what Kaplan calls the "evolving consciousness of the world."[8] Thus not only has Martha's quest changed direction, turning to the old rather than the new, but Lessing's conception of the collective has changed.

Something new has emerged from the violence of the century, in a younger generation that has been "*stripped* . . . sharpened and sensitised" and has no "intention of behaving as . . . previous generations behaved": "None cared, or so it seemed, about rewards or successes" (428); nor do they care about romantic love, marriage, money, or power. But since narrative conventions have been developed to express the dramas of individuals with whom we "identify" and who are brought into conflict over goals that are assumed to matter, Lessing faces the problem of adapting such conventions to express the renunciation of individualism and the things of this world. Whereas in *The Golden Notebook* she breaks *through* the forms of realism, here she simply drifts away from them, leaving behind not only the goals that have obsessed Martha but Martha herself, who starts out as the focal point but whose individual destiny becomes so irrelevant by the end that her death is revealed in parenthesis (609). We are not allowed to identify with a strikingly delineated protagonist or to become involved with anyone too personally. And by the end Lessing has dispensed with yet another *sine qua non* of realism, the notion that reality can be described: language is obsolete, "history" is committed to "the memories," and the last word of the novel is "misprint."

The result is a refusal of drama, a leveling, a reporting of all things as equal, individual case histories alternating with essayistic descriptions of the collective life of the times. Lessing says she "heaved the rules out" when she wrote the novel;[9] Singleton suggests that *The Four-Gated City* "simply bypasses ordinary literary values" (215);[10] Dagmar Barnouw refers to its "narrative anarchy";[11] Walker describes it as "a travesty of the accepted critical standards of a serious novel," with its "jarring yoking of the traditional *Bildungsroman* with extraordinary futuristic prophecy" (98). And such alienating techniques have alienated even Lessing fans: Paul Schlueter describes the novel as "too diffuse, too long . . . filled with . . . undeveloped ideas and plot-strands"; Rubenstein says that "even . . . absorbing events . . . are sometimes weighed down by prolixity"—"at times the author seems to be deliberately resistant to the felicities of style"; Sprague refers to the "fallacy of imitative form" "as though length and flat texture could convey the ideological deadness and paranoia of the Fifties."[12] A reviewer describes its style as

> that of an unskilled letter writer who feels he has to report everything: this happened and then that; Lynda came home from the hospital but had to go back and we had a big party and that night Colin defected to Russia so Sally killed herself and then we spent hours and hours arguing about Communism.[13]

An aspect of the novel's refusal of drama is its refusal to acknowledge beginnings and ends. Martha's affair with Mark, for example, both ends and does not end: they stop sleeping together, temporarily, as their attention turns to other things, though they later start sleeping together again, but differently; finally they achieve a relationship something like marriage—"she supposed, that in a way she was married to Mark" (285)—though it is like marriage and not like marriage. The onset of "the bad time" is announced by an "event," yet Lessing stresses that Colin's defection only seems "different in quality" from what preceded it because Martha hadn't been paying attention:

> A bad time is announced by an event . . . [the] event is different in quality from previous events. It is surprising. But it should not have been surprising. It could have been foreseen. One's imagination had been working at half-pressure . . . . Martha had been here before . . . . Martha had been here before. (149)

Martha has been most places before and will be again (468), for patterns of recurrence keep bringing her back in a movement of circular return:

> Yes, forgetting, forgetting again and again, life brings one back to points in oneself . . . over and over again in different ways, saying . . . This is a place where you could learn if you wanted to. Are you going to learn this time or not? No? Very well, then, I'll wait for you. If you're not ready now, too bad! I'll find ways of bringing you back to it again. When you are ready, then. (472)

In one sense the narrative of *Four-Gated City* is straightforwardly, even inexorably, linear, with the momentum of a driving engine. There are few flashbacks and only one startling shift in perspective, to Mrs. Quest's, just before the midpoint of the novel. As civilization plunges "towards the edge" (580) and the once-solid Radlett Street house disintegrates, we are continually reminded that time is "running out" (513), "it's later than you think" (504, 514)—"there wasn't much time, there wasn't much time" (587). There is a sense of "feverish transience" (533), "the anguish of time eating," "the wear of time" (57), time "fighting" (54), time "riding" and "bleeding away" (49), time "conspiring" (345); and, in one of many imaginative prefigurations, Martha envisions her body sagging "down over bones in a gutter of flesh" (57). As Martha grows older, time seems to move faster, and her subjective perceptions are true to *actual* processes of acceleration: "Everything went so fast, it was as if somewhere, invisibly a time switch had been altered, for processes were speeded up that previously worked slowly through years" (443):[14]

> London heaved up and down, houses changed shapes, collapsed, whole streets were vanishing into rubble . . . it seemed as if the idea of a city or town as something slow-changing, almost permanent, belonged to the past . . . if time were slightly speeded up, then a city now must look like fountains of rubble cascading among great machines, while buildings momentarily form, change colour like vegetation, dissolve, re-form. (288)[15]

The first hundred pages focus closely in on Martha's mental states, and the first half of the novel spans eight years, 1949 to 1957; the second half covers nearly twenty years, 1957 to 1977, with the ninety-odd pages of the Appendix looking back on another twenty, as time speeds up—"and it kept speeding up. We felt as if we were in the grip of some frightful acceleration" (567).

But Martha has learned something of the power of imagination to counter temporal processes, to escape what Lessing calls "the cage of time."[16] Instructed first by her dreams, and then by her own and Lynda's breakdowns, she can travel to a region of the mind "not bound by time" (476), a region that "knows nothing about our scale of time" (589). As at the beginning of the novel when she transposed herself to "another country"—"and if she tried—but not too hard . . . a light probe into a possibility, she could move back in time, annulling time . . . and stand in another country, on another soil" (36)—so in the middle, she can "walk through this city" newly refurbished and fashionable while also retaining "that other one in her mind" (287); and on a summer afternoon at Margaret's garden party, she imagines time stopped and sees Rachel and Aaron, the doomed brother and sister so strangely resurrected from Thomas's manuscript (actually, the actors who are playing Rachel and Aaron in Mark's new play), suspended in a moment of tranquility in a setting of the English country home:

> Not doomed here, no, quite safe, for it seemed as if this scene, a summer afternoon in England, had always existed and always would, as if any time of the year and in any season, one had simply to come to this glass wall and look through and there people moved smiling on deep grass beside roses. (317)

Corroborating Martha's imaginative reconfiguration of time are patterns of prefiguration and recalling, of *déjà vu* and foreshadowing. Early in the novel Martha has a vision of prelapsarian loveliness, of "a man and a woman, walking in a high place under a blue sky holding children by the hand, and with them all kinds of wild animals . . . all as tame as housepets, walking with the man and the woman and the lovely children, and she wanted to cry out with loss," for the vision immediately becomes its opposite: "And then . . . came another picture . . . she saw a large layered house, not foreign or out of another climate, but London . . . and it was full of children . . . tortured and hurt, and she saw herself, a middle-aged woman . . . with . . . an anxious face, a face set to endure, to hold on" (59–60). Which of these visions, the ideal or the anguished, comes true? Both, actually, for though it is the pain that is most immediately realized, the ideal vision reaches further into the future, becoming actualized beyond the end of the novel in the paradise regained on the island, while it also reaches further back into the past, to the lost golden age that turns out also to be the future. Thus rounded before and after, the pain is circumscribed, revealed as a blip, an aberration—like time itself, a parenthesis in eternity. When Martha has a pre-vision of Dorothy's suicide, Dr. Lamb tries to convince her that it was *déjà vu* rather than prophecy: "You imagined it," he says; "what is imagination?" she asks; and he does not answer (309). Similarly, the doctors interpret Lynda's vision of an England frozen, immobilized by a poisoned dew, in relation to Lynda's personal past, when it is actually a prophecy of the collective future. Lessing subverts Western notions of temporality and causality in the way D. M. Thomas does in *The White Hotel,* where what seems a past-fixated individual neurosis turns out to be prophecy of collective and actual doom.

Counterpointing the novel's linearity, then, are patterns of prefiguration and *déjà vu* and circular return, as Martha returns to places to know them for the first time. Her journey through "Lynda's country" (468) in the middle of the novel takes her back to beginnings, to her condition of heightened awareness as she walks the streets of London, and earlier, to the sea journey from Africa, and even earlier:

> Oh, it had been long before the voyage to England. . . . Suddenly Martha was in a room she had forgotten, looking at enormous people, giants . . . yes, she had been a child, she had felt this as a tiny child, looking at grown-up people, as they sat around a table . . . talking and smiling to each other with put-on false smiles and looks. For they did not mean what they said. . . . She had watched . . . and . . . had seen all this, understood it, had even said to herself in an anguish of fear that she could be swallowed up: Don't let yourself be sucked in, remember, remember, *remember*—but she had not remembered . . . she had become a liar and coward like the rest. (468–69)

Walking out onto the streets of London just after this realization, she is greeted by "presences from another world whose existence just behind this one made her want to cry out with longing" (483)—an intimation that looks back to her heightened awareness at the beginning of the novel and forward to the "elsewhere" discovered at the end.

Martha's development is a movement forward and backward, which is also a movement within and a relearning of what she already knows.[17] Since learning is remembering—"We keep learning things and then forgetting them so we have to learn them again . . . . you suddenly understand something you've understood all your life, but in a new way" (97)—learning requires repetition. When life brings you back to "where you could learn from," it gives you the opportunity to transform the "nightmare repetition" to a "growing principle . . . which fed one, developed one." Martha realizes this, talking with Dr. Lamb:

> One talked . . . finally one "heard" for the first time what one's life had been saying over and over again in various ways, for years. One hadn't heard before, because one had nothing to "hear" with. Living was simply a process of developing different "ears," senses, with which one "heard," experienced, what one couldn't before. (225)

Similarly, Lynda's "I know what I know" also suggests that the way forward is the way back to what is already known, as does Mrs. Mellindip's "one could never be told what one did not already know" (353, 190), an insight that Martha recovers in her breakdown—*"Here we go again . . . 'I can't tell you something you don't know'"* (521). Lynda's attempts to break through the four walls of her room during her breakdown prefigure the movement to the Appendix after the end of the novel, where the novel breaks through the structure of four parts of four to a fifth part and a fifth dimension; and this movement also harks back to earlier literary precedent, Charlotte Perkins Gillman's *The Yellow Wallpaper*. That the furthest point of futuristic fantasy, Jimmy Wood's science fiction, reaches back to the oldest knowledge of the race, to the ancient works of mysticism and the occult that are his sources, suggests that "it was clearly not a question of discovering new plots, but of developing old ideas differently" (487).

So, too, do events that look like beginnings turn out to be returns. Rita's arrival in London at the end of the novel looks back to Martha's arrival at the beginning, as Martha's arrival in London recapitulated her arrival in Salisbury in *Martha Quest,* which similarly looked forward to Marnie's arrival at the end of that novel. Just as Martha's ideal city exists both in the past and the future, both in some lost golden age and in some undiscovered future, so too does the ruined city London exist in the past and the future.[18] References to "this doomed city" and its "doomed streets" (35, 395) point both backward and forward—back to the beginning of the novel in 1949 just after the war and forward to the end in the late seventies, when the city is devastated by some unidentified catastrophe; and they point further back to the ruined cities of *Landlocked,* and further back than this (or is it forward?) to the ruined cities "Nineveh and Tyre, and Sodom and Gomorrah, and Rome, Carthage, Balkh, and Cordova" that Mark surveys flying over the desert, when "cities have become like people, refuse to be shovelled into the nearest incinerator" (610–11)—to a future that is also the past, since these cities have fallen before. But from the ruins of these earthly cities there emerges (as before) a heavenly city, prefigured by the red, black, white, yellow flags on the walls of Mark's study (the four horsemen of the Apocalypse), Lynda's mad ramblings, *"How many miles to Babylon?"* (475) and Martha's intimation of a four-gated city—the city that "lieth foursquare, and the length is as long as the breadth," the New Jerusalem of *Revelations,* chapter 21. Lessing evokes biblical history (as she will again in *Shikasta*) to suggest that all has already happened.

The narrative structure of *The Four-Gated City*—a pronounced linearity catapulting toward The End, counterpointed by patterns of recurrence and circular return—suggests a sense of time both as arrow and as circle, those notions associated with West and East, history and myth, modern and archaic, male and female.[19] If future and past are one—if Alpha is Omega—then ends are beginnings and "all time is eternally present": "Time past and time future . . . Point to one end, which is always present" (Eliot,

"Burnt Norton," 117–18). This is the oldest of mystical truths, and it is a realization that points back to the beginning, to Martha's "illumination" on the veld, when "during that space of time (which was timeless)," "while space and time (but these are words . . . ) kneaded her flesh," she sensed that "something new was demanding conception, with her flesh as host" (*MQ,* 52–53). And it also points forward to "the new children" after the end "who include . . . history in themselves and who have transcended it" (608).

## Patient Love

Midway through the novel, Martha bids a final farewell to "the long romantic tradition of love." Realizing that if she does not marry now, in her mid-thirties, she will never marry, she lays to rest the "woman in love," "that hungry, never-to-be-fed, never-at-peace woman who needs and wants and must have." Besides, "men have ceased to be explorations into known possibilities": "the hungers, the cravings, belonged somewhere else" (286–88). In divesting herself of romantic fantasy, she grows up to resemble certain of the younger generation who "knew, before they were twenty, what their grandparents knew, perhaps, as they died" (395); Jill, for instance—who asks "what was love? . . . what she had seen of that quality people called love did not make her respect it, or them" (432).

Not all young people are so "stripped," however. Rita, who arrives in London at the end of the novel, her head filled with notions from romantic fiction, seeking "doors" and "keys" to a new future, is an image of an earlier Martha, and her fantasy finds fulfillment in Mark, who remains true, however, to his fantasy of Lynda. Lessing has provided a definition of love at the beginning of *The Four-Gated City,* a definition quite unlike the romantic— "the delicate but total acknowledgement of what is" (10); but, as with other insights that occur in the opening pages, this will take Martha the entire novel to work back to.

If Rita represents a younger potential of Martha, which she has outgrown, Mrs. Quest represents an older potential of Martha, which she must avoid. The last section of part 2, just before the midpoint of the novel, is narrated from Mrs. Quest's perspective and provides insight into the workings of a mind so enmeshed in convention that she cannot undertake the "salvage operation" that saves Martha (274). Alone in her old age, rejected by her children, Mrs. Quest is thinking about many of the same things that concern Martha. She tries to "remember," to get to the truth of her childhood, to the reality underlying the "official memory" of the young man in the photograph; she tries to understand the choices she has made, the meaning of the "love" that drove her to so unrewarding a marriage—"An old lady, who had been using the word 'love' with confidence for decades, looked at it. . . . Love, she thought, love—her mind went dark" (241). She cannot move into these areas of "congealed pain" (285) and is aided in her evasion of the dark, blank places by "licensed and appropriate thoughts" (251) and "the official language" (253):

> Mrs. Quest kept running over the official words, phrases: Empire was one . . . . Duty was another. God, another. . . . Her mind rattled with words, phrases, bits of prayer, and hymns, and remarks about life and death which all her life had fed her, supported her. (254)

Such formulations deaden pain but deaden awareness as well, leaving her with no more understanding of the last thirty years than of "a bad night" in which "she had dreamed a lot" (254).

Though Martha feels the lure of such language when she first arrives in England, her consciousness is not enmeshed in it, her relation to reality is not circumscribed by it. She experiences

> a real swell of painful feeling, all kinds of half-buried, half-childish, myth-bred emotions which were being dragged to the surface: words having such power! Piccadilly Circus, Eros, Hub, Centre, London, England . . . each tapped underground rivers. (22)

But by now she has learned to control such responses. She understands the rhetoric of the Tory Press as an opiate that dazes, stuns, muddles:

> It was unreal, afflicted her with a sense of dislocation . . . . this was a country absorbed in myth, doped and dozing and dreaming . . . as if a spirit of rhetoric . . . had infected everything, made it impossible for any fact to be seen straight. (15–16)

"You're drugged, you're hypnotized. . . . You're the victim of a lot of slogans," she tells Henry, and her terms recall Mr. Maynard's analysis years before; and to Henry's "I really don't know what it is you people want," she replies, "to have things called by their proper names" (29). But calling things "by their proper names" is not her main problem, for the territory she charts, "the lit space" and "sea of sound," is not expressible by language—which is why clichés and metaphors will do.[20]

Faced with her mother's visit, Martha becomes frantic. Realizing that her repression of the pain she has felt in relation to her mother has caused her to lose parts of her self and her past, she plunges into "excavation" (220), "the battle for her memory" (484). She turns to Dr. Lamb "to give her back pity" (222), the pity she had banished as an adolescent, and though she unlocks "doors she had not known existed" (289), transforming pain from "something which engulfed" to "a landscape she could move into and out again" (285), and though she regains feelings of pity, still she cannot find a way of *acting* on pity, or at least not to her mother, for Mrs. Quest's presence incapacitates her as it always has. Martha never does bring herself to embrace the repulsive aged body (272) and mother and daughter never communicate, except in the "look of ironic desperation" they exchange just before Mrs. Quest returns to Africa, and in their brief, unsatisfactory dialogue—"then, as she vanished from her daughter's life forever, Mrs. Quest gave a small tight smile and said: 'Well, I wonder what that was about really?' 'Yes,' said Martha, 'so do I'" (273). This relationship remains one of several "loose ends" in the novel (324, 555), a "loose end" Lessing never quite ties, a relationship she never stops writing about, returning to rewrite it in *Memoirs of a Survivor, Diary of a Good Neighbor,* and *The Good Terrorist.*

As Martha says, "you start growing on your own account when you've worked through what you're landed with. Until then, you're paying debts" (432), and it is not until Mrs. Quest disappears from her life that she can begin her own "debt-paying." That the end of this relationship makes another ending—of Martha's affair with Mark—suggests that her cathexis with the mother bound her up in dependency on a man. It also coincides with the end of the "bad time" politically, since 1956 marks the beginning "of change, breaking up, clearing away, movement" (278): individual and collective mirror each other here, for the last time, before they diverge in the latter half of the novel. As in *The Golden Notebook,* endings occur in the middle, which make the second half a writing beyond endings.

The "new movement" in Martha's life takes the form of developing the mother in herself, which she does by seeing others through what they're "landed with"—with Francis and Paul, Jill and Gwen. She finds herself playing her mother's part in relation to Phoebe's daughters and assuming a strong authoritarian role in relation to Paul, becoming the powerful figure she'd once feared and hated—the "matron": "The point was, there was no cheating, no going around, the small baby, and the rest. Oneself, or Paul, had to be, for as long as it was necessary, screaming baby, sulking adolescent, then middle-aged woman" (339–40). This process must be lived through, but it is not "nightmarish" in its "repetition," partly because Martha now understands that such roles are not "the permanent person" (340) but "a character worn for a day or two" (370) and partly because it frees her from her past: "The rejuvenation a young girl gives her mother or an older woman is a setting-free into impersonality, a setting-free, also, from her personal past" (369). When the children grow up there is "the feeling of something having been got over, done with, worked through" (427):

> Well, for the opportunity to do this, the old ones owe a debt to the young. But this, of course, will not be understood (this particular variation of wry love) until the young ones come to that point where they must turn around and face towards their own past in their children. And so it is in this remarkable traffic between parents and children that there are as it were a whole series of postdated promissory notes in the currency of a contained and patient love that come due one after another when one least expects them. (428)

"This remarkable traffic," this "currency of contained and patient love," is none other than "the generous and freely exchanged emotion" (*MQ,*79) that Martha sought in her ideal city, which suggests that the way to the city is to develop it in oneself. But this liberation is earned, unlike the premature release Martha experienced in the opening episodes and also unlike the easy freedom she envisioned when she gave her daughter Caroline away.

It is "seeing others through" that accounts for Martha's development of psychic powers and puts her "in the main line of evolution" (497). When she becomes aware of her new ability to hear what others are thinking, she turns to Lynda for guidance, joining her in the basement for "work"—"they called it work" (354, 357), though what they are doing eludes description:

> It was as if doors kept opening in their brains just far enough to admit a new sensation, or a glimmer of something—and although they closed again, something was left behind. . . . What they wanted, looked for, searched for was everywhere, all around them, like a finer air shimmering in the flat air of every day . . . It was as if the far-off sweetness experienced in a dream, that unearthly impossible sweetness, less the thing itself than the need or hunger for it, a question and answer sounding together on the same fine high note—as if that sweetness known all one's life, tantalisingly intangible, had come closer, a little

> closer, so that one continually sharply turned one's head after something just glimpsed out of the corner of an eye, or tried to sharpen one's senses to catch something just beyond them. (356–57)

Tending Lynda through a breakdown, assuming responsibility for her and entering imaginatively into her experience, Martha enters "Lynda's country" (468) and glimpses the elsewhere she has known before and will know again. On the basis of these discoveries, she embarks on a breakdown of her own that similarly takes her back to regions already traveled, to the beginning of the novel and earlier, to ancient human potentials she finds within as she discovers *"I am what the human race is"* (511).

By the end of the novel, Martha has exhausted the forms of her civilization and those forms have exhausted themselves. As the Coldridge family disperses and the house faces demolition, the house with the tree outside is at an end—as Thomas predicted (*LL,*117). The "holding operation" over, Martha finds herself "at a loose end" (555), but this does not particularly trouble her since she now knows that the keys she has been seeking are in the "process": "She had learned that one thing, that most important thing, which was that one simply had to go on, take one step after another: this process in itself held the keys" (556). Martha's final epiphany, the realization she has walking in the garden of Margaret's country home, follows from this:

> She thought, with the dove's voices of her solitude: Where? But *where*. How? Who? No, but *where,* where . . . Then silence and the birth of a repetition: *Where?* Here. Here?
>
> Here, where else, you fool, you poor fool, where else has it been, ever . . . (559; ellipses in original)

Echoes of *The Four Quartets*—the dove and the roses, the knowledge of here and now—suggest that the end of her exploration is to return to the place to know it for the first time: "Quick now, here, now, always—" ("Little Gidding," 145). "The way forward is the way back" ("Dry Salvages," 136) and it is also within, to deeper and deeper levels of self. Thus Martha finds her end—in the sense both of conclusion and goal—in her beginning, an end that is "here," "now," in the present and in the process: "In my end is my beginning"; "There is only the fight to recover what has been lost / And found and lost again and again . . . But perhaps neither gain nor loss. / For us, there is only the trying" ("East Coker," 123, 129, 128). Completing the circle,

Martha finds what Eliot calls "the still point of the turning world" ("Burnt Norton," 119, 121)—though again, this is an incomplete completion: the novel proper ends in ellipsis.

But the final pages of the novel contain another epiphany—

> "Well," said Mark, "there it is."
> "I'm afraid so," said Martha. (558)

What they are seeing is a group of "discreetly powerful looking people," harbingers of "Britain's version of a Fascist phase":

> There it was now in the wings, ready to come on, gentlemanly, bland, vicious. There it was: big business, backed by the landowning landlording Church . . . and Royalty, solidly and narrowly traditional . . . and all taking orders from America . . . through groups of international bankers and vaguely named and constituted advisers. (558)

The contrast between individual and collective epiphanies at the conclusion of the novel proper completes the divergence of personal from political toward which the series has been tending. As the institutions of social and political organization congeal into bureaucracy and hurtle down the death slopes, society is revealed as "an organism which above all is unable to think . . . like one of those sea creatures who have tentacles or arms equipped with numbing poisons" and "stun into immobility" "anything new" (430). But another definition of the collective has emerged in the course of the series, a kind of universal oversoul that is, like the essential self that is part of it, transsocial. Lessing identifies individual with oversoul, microcosm with macrocosm, in a way that makes the social irrelevant—that eliminates the middleman, as it were; and in the Appendix she finds a way of stunning the social organism into immobility, vanquishing "the beast" that is harbinger of Apocalypse.

## Future for Our Race

As in *Landlocked,* the dissolution of the old allows for the emergence of the new. But in the Appendix, the various accounts of the survivors offer contradictory versions of the new: no one quite knows what happened or "how badly the world had hurt itself" (603). The refugee camp described in Mark's report, in which a powerful administering class rules over desperate, deformed hordes and what is new are "monstrous children" with two heads and fifty fingers (611), suggests a future that is an extension of the worst possibilities of the present, of the tendencies Mark articulated in his "Memorandum to Myself": *"What will happen is a development of what is already happening and what has been accelerating, out of control, since 1914 and the green light for mass extermination"* (525). But on Martha's island, those who have journeyed within reap their rewards, as the "terrible" turns round to reveal the "marvellous":

> During that year we hit the depths of our fear. . . . But it was also during that year when we became aware of a sweet high loveliness somewhere, like a flute playing only just within hearing. We all felt it. . . . It was as if all the air was washed with a bright promise. Of what? Love? Joy? It was as if the face of the world's horror could be turned around to show the smile of an angel. . . . It was as if the veil between this world and another had worn so thin that earth people and people from the sun could walk together and be companions. When this time which was so terrible and so marvellous had gone by some of us began to wonder if we had suffered from a mass hallucination. But we knew we had not. (604)

This allusion to a flute playing just within hearing on a magical island recalls the music of Ariel, and this is the novel's third reference to *The Tempest* (264, 325), a work that, like Lessing's, concerns remembrance as redemption and which similarly envisions the sympathetic imagination as the means to a marvelous transcendent realm. On Martha's island, which is the same but different from her ideal city, children of all colors and races live in harmony with one another and with people from the sun. Though Mark's nightmarish world has the power of numbers and repressive government machinery on its side, we have been told that "the new children" have powers which render this machinery obsolete, that "government by concealment, lies, trickery, even stupidity was—dead":

> The old right of the individual human conscience which must know better than any authority, secular or religious, had been restored, but on a higher level, and in a new form which was untouchable by any legal formulas. (586)

Moreover, the new children have been promised assistance as they leave the island for the devastated portions of the earth: "It was from that time, because of what we were told, that we took heart and held on to our belief in a future for our race" (604).

It is the traditional women's virtues—nurturing, compassion, seeing others through, holding things together—that assure "a future for our race," for the powers Martha and Lynda develop in their "work" in the basement predict and prepare for the Catastrophe and save the saving remnant. Lynda's powers of insight and intuition may themselves be seen as highly evolved expressions of female empathy and ability to enter others' experiences: if Lynda "had not tested certain limits . . . they would not have been able to go on" (357); and it is significant that Lessing depicts this potential in a character who has not had to contend with a mother, for Lynda's mother died when she was a child.[21] But though these saving graces may be traditional, they are by no means conventional, for the novel has provided new definitions of *love, marriage, work, heroism,* even *ménage à trois.* Martha becomes, in an odd way, not only a "free woman" but a woman who liberates others. As Elayne Antler Rapping suggests, Martha offers "a startlingly original image of feminine heroism, which goes beyond the exceptional woman" "to include all women who have anonymously contributed to the progress and civilization of the race." In this novel, "as vast and sweeping as any of Tolstoy's or Stendhal's," "the heroes are women, common women, mad women, women doing what women have always done, and at last being named and credited for it."[22] The ending of the novel allows the female virtues to reach outside the private domestic realm and affect the public world, and Lessing has defined these virtues as what is "needed"—as fulfilling the cosmic principle of "necessity" which becomes central in the Canopus series.

Lessing has changed in the twenty-odd years she spent writing the *Children of Violence,* but in a fundamental way her values remain the same. She has not given up on the idea of change, though she has changed her view of how it is accomplished: "The revolution had gone inwards, was in the structure of life's substance" (396). In an important way, her understanding of people and problems remains political—as, for example, in the description of Phoebe's unfortunate relationship with a Freudian therapist, a Mrs. Johns, who "said politics did not come into this . . . But for Mrs. Johns politics was voting once every five years"; Phoebe, giving her the benefit of the doubt, "supposed that being so ignorant about what went on in her own country did not matter to superior insights about mother-daughter relationships" (347). Though Lessing has renounced the world, she has not ceased believing in our responsibility to the human community—what drives Martha to connect is a “sense of self-preservation” that saves not only herself but others; and Lessing, too, is still trying to take others with her, using the novel as an instrument of change.

In order to save the world, however, Lessing must destroy it, for she cannot conceive of a way of breaking the chain of determinism and destruction within this world or the laws of probability and causality that govern it. The shading into the fantastic obscures a contradiction: whereas the novel proper suggests that change is accomplished by working it through—that by enduring the process one moves beyond it, and such virtues as patience and endurance are what is “needed”—the Appendix breaks the circle in a fairly dramatic way and allows a heroic resolution. And without this move to an elsewhere, where would we be? Would Lessing seriously propose that, as fascism consolidates its power, as we descend into a new ice age of tyranny and terror, of bureaucracy and barbarism—that work on the inner life is what is most needed?

But perhaps it is ungenerous to confine *The Four-Gated City* to prescriptions so literal when it has so liberally encouraged and enabled us “to be receptive, to be alert” (357). Lessing has taught us “a new sort of understanding” (357), a way of imagining alternatives to “the current orthodoxy” (548), to the empiricist mold of time and space into which western epistemology pours experience. Her narrative “annuls time,” then reconfigures it, expanding our imaginations “to apprehend / the intersection of the timeless with time” (“Dry Salvages,” 136). The “loose ends” of the Appendix allow us, the novel’s readers, to construct the shape of the future and “the End”—now, within time, now while there is still time. The structure of *The Four-Gated City* makes a “wordless statement”—like the form of *The Golden Notebook*—and forces us to exercise that faculty whose atrophy has laid the world waste. To Martha’s question “What is imagination?” *The Four-Gated City* provides an eloquent though elliptical answer.

*Chapter 6*

# *The Golden Notebook:* "Naming in a Different Way"

> That they were both "insecure" and "unrooted," . . . they both freely acknowledged. But Anna had recently been learning to use these words in a different way, not as something to be apologised for, but as flags or banners for an attitude that amounted to a different philosophy.
>
> I had to "name" the frightening things, over and over, in a terrible litany, like a sort of disinfecting . . . . But now . . . it was not making past events harmless, by naming them, but *making sure they were still there.* Yet I know that having made sure they were still there, I would have to "name" them in a different way.
>
> —Doris Lessing, *The Golden Notebook*

In the introduction to *The Golden Notebook,*[1] published nearly a decade after the novel appeared, Lessing expressed disappointment that no one had noticed its complex structure and that critics had reduced it to a "tract about the sex war," a "trumpet for Women's Liberation."[2] Though she had grounds for complaint, in fact the novel received very different kinds of readings from men and women. Male critics condemned it for deviating from the party line—not Soviet, but New Critical party line—reacting exactly in the way Lessing describes critics as reacting: "What they do very well, is to tell the writer how the book or play accords with current patterns of feeling and thinking, the climate of opinion. They are like litmus paper" (xvi). But women, untroubled by the novel's violation of New Critical canons or its status as "art," were thrilled to find themselves named: "And not censored: love, politics, children, dreams, close talk. The first Tampax in world literature."[3] Women read asking Martha Quest's question "What does this say about my life?"[4] and "what we discovered, when we read *The Golden Note-*

*book* or the Martha Quest novels, was a writer who, it seemed, knew us better than we knew ourselves . . . *this,* we felt, was what was lacking in our study and teaching of literature."[5]

## Men and Women on *The Golden Notebook*

To be sure, some men recognized its importance,[6] but most male reviewers and critics—even those who deplored the general timidity of postwar British fiction—found ways of discounting it. Anthony Burgess laments that novelists today "do not feel sufficiently strongly about anything to be urged into attempting some large-scale work of individual vision which . . . [will] radically change our view of life";[7] and, entirely missing what is visionary and transformative about *The Golden Notebook,* he dismisses it as "a crusader's novel," "unacceptable" as a "work of art." His grounds for dismissal are actually somewhat embarrassing:

> [Anna] say[s] some hard things about male arrogance, crassness, sexual impotence and incompetence, and her own sexual frustrations (which are, of course, to be blamed on men) . . . She is intelligent, honest, burning with conviction, but she ends up as a bit of a bore. So, for that matter, does Mrs. Lessing's own experiment . . . There has been too much diversion of aim, too little digestion of deeply held beliefs into something acceptable as a work of art. The crusader's best medium is the manifesto, which is not quite the same thing as a novel. (100)

Offended by Anna's attack on "male arrogance" and "impotence," Burgess counterattacks by calling her "a bore" (in a move very like Richard's in a scene in *The Golden Notebook,* when he responds to Anna's sexual rebuff by insulting her [45]). Burgess cannot let it go, either, for he returns to say in another context:

> We have seen how in Doris Lessing's *Golden Notebook* there is a powerful expression of resentment of the male—not purely social (in the old suffragette manner) but sexual as well. Woman has a sexual need of man, but she objects to having this need; she wants to reject man, but she cannot, and so she seeks to dominate him . . . and the literary expression of the female dilemma is often harsh, sensational, explosive. (122)

P. W. Frederick McDowell similarly criticizes the novel, suggesting that Anna's "intellectual difficulties . . . arise from her sexual frustrations" and that the novel is "disorganized," "subjective," "a cross between a standard novel . . . and a confession."[8]

Other critics concede that it has interest for what it reveals about women's lives but deny that it is "art." Walter Allen admits that *The Golden Notebook* is "impressive in its honesty and integrity, and unique . . . as an exposition of the emotional problems that face an intelligent woman who wishes to live in the kind of freedom a man may take for granted," but he concludes that it "fail[s]" "as a work of art": "the structure is clumsy, complicated rather than complex. . . . Its main interest [is] . . . sociological."[9] Patrick Parrinder describes it as "an almost legendary weapon in the armory of 'consciousness raising' about politics, psychoanalysis, feminism. . . . There is no lack of witnesses to the 'importance' of this novel, but I do find a strange absence of agreement or even serious debate, about its artistic success."[10] Frederick Karl calls it "the most considerable single work by an English author in the 1960s," but he too dismisses it on "purely literary" grounds:

> It is a carefully organized but verbose, almost clumsily written novel. . . . The book's strength lies . . . certainly not in the purely literary quality of the writing, but in the wide range of Mrs. Lessing's interest, and, more specifically in her attempt to write honestly about women.[11]

James Gindin criticizes "Miss Lessing's addiction to historical categories" and "the historically conditioned character" as "an aesthetic shortcoming":[12]

> Doris Lessing's intense feeling of political and social responsibility is carefully worked into specific historical situations. But the positive convictions can become heavy-handed, and the specific situations journalistic, while the strict allegiance to time and place can limit the range of perception about human beings. Miss Lessing . . . produces an enormously lucid sociological journalism, honest and committed, but . . . she lacks a multiple awareness, . . . a perception that parts of human experience cannot be categorized or precisely located, a human and intellectual depth. Intense commitment can cut off a whole dimension of human experience. (86)

The assertion that *The Golden Notebook* lacks "multiple awareness" is astonishing: but this was 1962, and Gindin's assumptions that "intense commitment" and "historical specificity" are at odds with "intellectual depth" reflect, "like litmus paper," the New Critical dicta of the day.

Notice how consistently these critics draw attention to Lessing's marital status even when they do not know what it is: whatever else they know or do not know, they do know that she is a woman, and their insistence on nailing her into this category is an insistence on categorizing *The Golden Notebook* as a "women's novel." In the context of such judgments one appreciates Bernard Bergonzi's admission that *The Golden Notebook* is "not at all easy to place or evaluate": he calls it a "disturbing achievement" that breaks down "the traditional distinction . . . between literary and sociological ways of looking at the world," "a work of great, if cold brilliance."[13] One suspects that if this novel had been written by a man, critics might have shown more humility in approaching it; of course, if it had been written by a man it would not be *The Golden Notebook*.

What one senses in these responses is an irritation, the real grounds of which are unacknowledged. New Critical criteria—"complexity," "multiple awareness," "pure literary quality"—are then enlisted to dismiss the novel as "inartistic," "unaesthetic," "clumsy," "unacceptable as a work of art." Because it violates some New Critical standards, it is faulted for violating all of them—for "lack of multiple awareness"! Lessing knew that "to say, in 1957, that one believes artists should be committed, is to arouse hostility and distrust"[14]—and sure enough, *The Golden Notebook* gets dismissed as "sociological," "journalistic," a "manifesto." But even today, when the prevalent critical approach is better suited to appreciating the novel than it was in the fifties, few men are much better at reading *The Golden Notebook;* few (in my experience) *have* actually read it, let alone read it carefully. Of the fifty-six writers, critics, and reviewers surveyed in the 1978 *New Review,* a few mention Lessing as among the major novelists of the day, though only one gives her her due, as "the outstanding novelist of our time" (47).[15] As recently as 1983, John Holloway and Gilbert Phelps omit *The Golden Notebook* from their surveys of contemporary literature.[16] A 1987 collection of essays on *British Novelists Since 1900* contains nothing on Lessing.[17] In his learned and provocative study of the novel, *Resisting Novels* (1987), Lennard Davis says, "There has never been a novel, to my knowledge, that actually seriously addresses" or "reveal[s] the ideology of the novel through the novel"[18]—as though *The Golden Notebook* had never been written.

*The Golden Notebook* presented problems for some women readers as well. Alice Bradley Markos sees Lessing's women as the most badly mangled victims of the contemporary world, "almost humans manqué";[19] Elaine Showalter and Ellen Morgan argue that it is alienated "from the authentic female perspective";[20] Catharine Stimpson sees Lessing as apart "from the 'feminine' and from feminism";[21] Jenny Taylor claims that "the novel certainly isn't an explicitly feminist text."[22] But I think such assessments derive from the assumptions of early feminist criticism, that literature should provide strong "role models," "explicit feminism," and "authenticity." If one reads the novel according to such prescriptions, it is sure to disappoint, but one approaches it this way at risk, for Lessing's parody of the Soviet "literature of health and progress"—"where are the working masses in this book? Where the class conscious fighters?" ask Soviet reviews of Anna's *Frontiers of War* (443–45)—make it unlikely that she will be much interested in providing models of heroic behavior.

That Anna is no model of feminist rectitude and independence she would be the first to admit. Catapulted out of a long, draining relationship with a man who has denigrated her as a writer and mother and who ditches her for the security of a dead marriage, Anna is "in pieces," a state of "awful moral exhaustion" (44). "'Free women,' said Anna, wryly" (4), and the reiteration of *Free Women* in the chapter headings drives home the irony—that "women's emotions are still fitted for a kind of society that no longer exists. My deep emotions, my real ones, are to do with my relationship with a man. One man" (314). But from this unpromising beginning Anna writes beyond "the end of the affair," forges "a new way of looking at life" and "new imaginative comprehension" (61), and makes something new (472–73). *The Golden Notebook* is about breaking "a habit of nerves from the past," "shedding a skin"—"what is happening is something new in my life . . . a sense of shape, of unfolding" (479)—and its narrative takes its protagonist (and many of its readers) through an evolution of consciousness.

Joanne Frye claims that the novel "does not argue a feminist position or even center exclusively in female experiences; instead it examines broadly the crises of twentieth-century society and the problems of characterizing those crises in novelistic form."[23] But Frye's divisions are not Lessing's: the novel *does* center in "female experience" *and* it relates that experience both to novelistic form and to the crises of twentieth-century society. It not only centers in female experience but charts that experience compellingly, powerfully, originally: Anna is delineated in relation to her body ("the first Tampax in world literature"), to her child, to men, women, work, and politics. It depicts female friendship in a way that is unprecedented in fiction: Irving Howe rightly praises the "precise and nuanced dialogue" of the "remarkable conversations between Anna and Molly as some of the strongest writing in the novel" (178). It renders the "role conflict" that riddles women's lives today: Anna is torn between roles of single parent, political worker, writer, lover, friend, "living the kind of life women never lived before" (472).

Anna herself does not separate her personal experience from problems of narrative form or from the crises of the twentieth century; as she says of her "writer's block," "If I saw it in terms of an artistic problem, then it'd be easy, wouldn't it? We could have ever such intelligent chats about the modern novel" (41). The first novel of the century to name "the disease of women in our time" (333) as a political "disease," this work is fundamentally concerned with relationship—with (in Lessing's words) "the personal [as] general," "look[ing] at things as a whole and in relation to each other" (xiii–xiv). *The Golden Notebook* depicts "form" as a literary *and* a personal *and* a political problem, for it is only when Anna can cast off conventional forms in her life that she can risk something new in her fiction; and the freedom she aspires to—"I want to walk off, by myself, Anna Freeman" (471)—requires a world in which all can be free.

I will argue that *The Golden Notebook* is a feminist novel, both in terms of content and textual strategies.

## Men and Women in *The Golden Notebook*

*The Golden Notebook* concerns change on individual, collective, and narrative levels. It is about people who "try to be something else" (466) and try to change the world—"world-changers" (624). In a conversation that takes place in "The Shadow of the Third," the novel Anna writes in the yellow notebook, Ella's father claims "a man is what he is. He can't be anything else. You can't change that"; to which Ella replies: "That's the real difference between us. Because I believe you can change it" (466). When Ella imagines "writ[ing] about that—people who deliberately try to be something else, try to break their own form as it were" (466), she realizes that something else requires new forms because it cannot be expressed within the familiar "patterns of defeat, death, irony" or "patterns of happiness or simple life." What she envisions—"a man and a woman—yes. Both at the end of their tether. Both cracking up because of a deliberate attempt to transcend their own limits. And out of the chaos, a new kind of strength" (467)—prefigures what happens later, when, in the blue notebook, Anna and Saul break down into each other.

On the collective level, the novel concerns humanity's slow, painful progress toward (in Anna's phrase) "the end of being animals" (276). On the historical level, this is not an easy time to believe in progress—"not an easy time to be a socialist" (21)—as leftists, "determined to be honest, yet fighting every inch of the way even now not to have to admit the truth about the

Soviet Union" (481), "are reeling off from the C.P. in dozens, broken-hearted" (448). But to Tommy's "What do you live by now?" Anna replies,

> Every so often, perhaps once in a century, there's a sort of—act of faith. A well of faith fills up, and there's an enormous heave forward in one country or another, and that's a forward movement for the whole world. Because it's an act of imagination—of what is possible for the whole world. In our century it was 1917 in Russia. And in China. Then the well runs dry, because . . . the cruelty and the ugliness are too strong. Then the well slowly fills again. And then there's another painful lurch forward.

Meanwhile it is our "acts of imagination" that "keep the dream alive": "Yes—because every time the dream gets stronger. If people can imagine something, there'll come a time when they'll achieve it" (275–76). (A version of this hope gets stated by Anna's fictional character, Paul, in his description of the "boulder pushers" [210]).

Lessing refers to *The Golden Notebook* as expressing her "dissatisfaction" with "the conventional novel" (intro, xiv), and she expresses this dissatisfaction by making her protagonist a novelist who is similarly dissatisfied: as Anna says, "I keep trying to write the truth and realizing it's not true" (274). Though Lessing describes "the artist" as the "theme of our time"—"every major writer has used it, and most minor ones" (xi–xii)—*The Golden Notebook* is one of only two novels where Lessing "uses" it (*The Diaries of Jane Somers* is the other) and the only one where she endows the novelist-protagonist with her own considerable talents. It is actually surprising that Lessing addresses this "theme" at all, in view of her contempt for "the cult of the artist" and her skepticism about why most people wish to write—their desire to attain fame and to escape the tedium of their lives (*MQ,* 211–12). But as she explains in the introduction, she is not interested in "that isolated, creative sensitive figure" that is the usual subject of the *Kunstlerroman;* she finds "intolerable" "this monstrously isolated, monstrously narcissistic, pedestaled paragon":

> I decided [the theme] would have to be developed by giving the creature a block and discussing the reasons for the block. This would have to be linked with the disparity between the overwhelming problems of war, famine, poverty, and the tiny individual who was trying to mirror them. (xii)

The "theme of the artist" is thus for Lessing a political theme and "the reasons for the block" are political as much as personal, for, as Anna says, the "moment I sit down to write, someone comes into the room, looks over my shoulders, and stops me . . . It could be a Chinese peasant. Or one of Castro's guerrilla fighters. Or an Algerian fighting in the F.L.N . . . . They stand here in the room and they say, why aren't you doing something about us, instead of wasting your time scribbling?" (639)

In order to write "the only kind of novel which interests" her, a work "powered with an intellectual or moral passion strong enough to create order, to create a new way of looking at life" (360), Anna must "enter those areas of life [her] way of living, education, sex, politics, class bar [her] from" (61). In order to do this, she must remain vulnerable to "the overwhelming problems" of others: rather than closing and dividing herself off, as most of the male characters do, she must keep herself "open for something"; this becomes the means to new creation, the "gap" through which "the future . . . pour[s] in a different shape" (473). In the final episodes, when Anna and Saul " 'break down' into each other, into other people, break through the false patterns they have made of their pasts" (as Lessing describes them [vii–viii], Anna "break[s] . . . [her] own form"; and "changed by the experience of being other people" (602), she "expand[s] [her] limits beyond what has been possible" (619).

It is her ability to risk the dissolution of the self that enables her to expand the boundaries of the self, and Anna is able to take this risk because she is a woman: "because we aren't the same. That is the point" (44). Lessing articulates differences between men and women to women's advantage, portraying women as "tougher . . . kinder" (663). Whereas Anna's boundary fluidity, empathy, relatedness, enable her to change,[24] the men in the novel remain fixed within bounded egos; as Chodorow says, the male "has engaged, and been required to engage, in a more emphatic individuation and a more defensive firming of experienced ego boundaries."[25] This contrast is established in the first scene, in the conflict between Richard and Molly/Anna for the loyalty of Tommy, Molly and Richard's son. Whereas Richard prides himself on "preserv[ing] the forms," Anna and Molly pride themselves on not "giving in" ("to what?" Richard asks; "if you don't know we can't tell you," they reply [25–26]); and Tommy understands that "the forms" by which Richard defines himself (money, status, power) fix him and freeze him, whereas the "formlessness" of the women's lives allows them to "change and be something different" (36). Yet Tommy, in Anna's "Free Women" version, is so terrified of formlessness that he kills off a part of himself rather than risk it; and this measure, though extreme, symbolizes what most of the men do, who "stay sane" "by block[ing] off at this stage or that . . . by limiting themselves" (469); their "locking of feeling" is a "refusal to fit conflicting things together . . . [which] means one can neither change nor destroy" (65). Most have performed "leucotomies" on themselves that leave them diminished but unaware of their limitations—a principle that is caricatured in the American brain surgeon, Cy Maitland, who boasts of "cut[ting] literally hundreds of brains in half" (328).

Divided in themselves, they are divided from others; incapable of wholeness, they are incapable of seeing others whole and so reduce women to stereotypes that deprive them of humanity: "Even the best of them have the old idea of good and bad women" (485). Unwilling to risk freedom in any basic sense, every one of them (except Saul) clings to the security of marriage. Richard remains faithful to Marion "just as long as most men are, that is, until . . . her first baby" (27), then embarks on a series of affairs with increasingly younger but otherwise interchangeable "nut-brown maids"; he then defends his infidelities on the grounds of "a problem you [women] haven't got—it's a purely physical one. How to get an erection with a woman you've been married to for fifteen years"; to which Anna retorts, "At least we've got more sense than to use words like physical and emotional as if they didn't connect" (31). Whereas men's sexual pleasure depends on a division of the physical from the emotional, women are unable to "have an orgasm unless [they] love" (458).

The men Anna becomes involved with after the end of the affair with Michael (Paul in the yellow notebook) are "sexual cripples" (484) who are afflicted with "mother trouble" (581) and frozen in postures of "cool, cool, cool" (545).[26] Even Saul, the one man in the novel who is "free" in the most elementary sense (of being unmarried), who risks breakdown and survives able to write—even he remains locked into an "I" that rattles through his speech like a machine gun (556), and leaves at the end, unable to love, "not mature yet" (642).

## Working It Through: Textual Feminism

Lessing demonstrates that both male and female behavior represent crippling adjustments to a destructive society, but that men are more crippled because they are locked into postures that prohibit change. In "the sex war" (572) Saul and Anna engage in as they break down into each other, they assume typical, stereotypical, male-female roles, which they play out in extreme form. Enacting the various potentials of women and men, they "play against each other every man-woman role imaginable" (604): he becomes "the position of man," "a classic . . . story of our time" (560), as she assumes "the position of women in our time" (579). Anna begins "stuck fast in an emotion common to women of our time" (480), "self-pitying," "Anna betrayed" (596), to which Saul responds with "his need to betray" (597). He admits that he resents her success as a writer and that he "enjoys a society where women are second-class citizens" (604–5), that he's "competitive about everything" "because I'm an American. It's a competitive country" (578). They enter into a "cycle of bullying and tenderness" (581), he railing against women as "the jailers, the consciences, the voice of society," she responding with "the weak soft sodden emotion, the woman betrayed" (630), "the white female bosom shot full of cruel male arrows" (636). He is "repeating a pattern over and over again: courting a woman with his intelligence and sympathy, claiming her emotionally; then, when she began to claim in return, running away. And the better a woman was, the sooner he would . . . run" (587–88).[27]

But out of these unpromising materials they forge a new kind of relationship, noncompetitive and supportive—"You're going to write that book, you're going to write it, you're going to finish it . . . because if you can do it, then I can," he tells her (639)—and they part as a "team": "we're a team, we're the ones who haven't given in, who'll go on fighting" (642); "I felt towards him as if he were my brother, as if, like a brother, it wouldn't matter how we strayed from each other, how far apart we were, we would always be flesh of one flesh, and think each other's thoughts" (641).

In this relationship, as in the novel as a whole, "something . . . [is] played out . . . some pattern . . . worked through" (583). As in the *Children of Violence,* working through requires repetition; as in *The Four-Gated City,* where Martha's circular returns allow her to learn on deeper levels, here the organization of material into several notebooks allows Anna to rework the material of her life until she can get it right. In the course of her breakdown, she circles closer in on cathected material, and, as her self dissolves, so too do the basic categories of experience: she loses all "sense of time" (593–94), and "words . . . become . . . not the form into which experience is shaped, but a series of meaningless sounds," "the secretions of a caterpillar" (476). This is why she would like to communicate through nonverbal shapes, a circle or square (633)—and in a sense the "wordless statement" made by the form does just this, for (as Rubenstein notes) "the major divisions of the novel into four groups of four are abstractions of the square" ("Novelistic

Vision," 107), as opposed to which are "the cyclic repetitions, layerings, and recombinations of the same essential emotional events from a variety of perspectives" (75): *The Golden Notebook* "moves forward in time and in the narrative unfolding of the novel, while turning back on itself both in the repetition of images and themes in the circularity of the organization" (90).[28] Reworking the material in four notebooks and two novels, Anna can circle back over experience and "the end of the affair," repeating the loss of Michael in the loss of Paul and repeating the loss of Michael/Paul in the loss of Saul/Milt in a way that puts an end to repetition. The form of *The Golden Notebook* allows repetition that is a release from repetition and allows Anna to revise, reevaluate, redescribe—to know "on deeper and deeper levels" (239) and "'name' . . . in a different way" (616). And as in *The Four-Gated City,* where four parts of four yield to a fifth, to the new dimension of the "Appendix," so, too, in *The Golden Notebook* do four sections of four notebooks yield to a fifth, the golden notebook, which similarly renders breakthrough to a fifth dimension.

In the introduction Lessing stressed the importance of the form: "My major aim was to shape a book which would make its own comment, a wordless statement: to talk through the way it was shaped . . . this was not noticed" (xiv). It was "not noticed" because *The Golden Notebook* was ahead of its time, and, like other innovative works, it had to teach us how to read it. After Lessing published the introduction the form was noticed, and the next decade of criticism focused on it, though most readings emphasized Anna's attempts to find wholeness through Jungian psychology and Marxism, which, as Lessing says, "looks at things as a whole and in relation to each other—or tries to" (xiv).[29] A more recent stage of criticism has been less focused on the text's unities than its disunities, its uses of splitting and fragmentation, and less concerned to resolve Anna into a homogeneous, unified self than to celebrate her complex, heterogeneous identity.[30] This shift illustrates (like litmus paper) the shift from the New Critical focus on unity to contemporary theory's interest in discontinuity and illustrates, as well, reassessments of the subject as the site of competing systems.[31]

But the political implications of Lessing critiques of "the forms" have still not been much noticed, which is why the novel's feminism continues to be misunderstood. Lessing drew on Marxist critiques that were coming out of the Left in the fifties and sixties for her analysis of the ideological complicity of the forms, conventions, and institutions of literary production. The novel combines Marxist exposure of the ways ideology is inscribed within literary forms with deconstructive critiques of an epistemology based on hierarchical oppositions, with a feminist analysis of personal as political and of female identity as processive, in a radically deconstructive feminist text that is also a "writerly" text (in Barthes's term), a "polyphonic" text (in Kristeva's term), an "interrogative" text (in Belsey's term).[32]

## Ideology and Form

Like feminist theorists Adrienne Rich and Mary Daly, Lessing sees naming as crucial to remaking the world: "It would be a help at least to describe things properly, to call things by their right names" (xvi).[33] But how to call things by their proper names when names are themselves "contaminated, full of traditional associations," as Lessing says?[34] Anna seeks truth in words, only to find "untruths" everywhere, encoded in slogans, jargon, "parrot-phrases" (21, 401, 590–91): "How many of the things we say are just echoes" (52).

Lessing was drawn to Marxist aesthetics because it was concerned with the questions that concerned her—about the ideological complicity of linguistic and narrative convention, the relationship of politics to art, the possibility of revolutionary form. Though she left the Communist party in 1956, her break precipitated, like that of many other British leftists, by Stalin and the invasion of Hungary, she was on the first board of the *New Left Review* in 1960, on the editorial board of the *New Reasoner,* and took an active part in the emerging New Left that focused on analyses of literature, media, communications, and the possibility of "cultural intervention."[35] She knew Brecht's drama and probably also knew Walter Benjamin's work on Brecht;[36] she had read Lukács and was aware of his analysis of the novel as counteracting the alienation and fragmentation of capitalism and re-creating the totality or relatedness of life;[37] Antonio Gramsci's *Prison Notebooks,* written between 1927 and 1935, was translated into English in the fifties (or at least portions were, in *The New Prince*) and was being discussed in leftist circles.[38] Louis Althusser's refinements of the "vulgar Marxist" definition of ideology in "Marxism and Humanism" (in *For Marx*) and "Ideology and Ideological State Apparatuses" (in *Lenin and Philosophy*)[39] were published a few years after *The Golden Notebook,* but his ideas were in the air.

Anna uses the word *myth* as Gramsci and Althusser use *ideology,* to mean that system of beliefs and assumptions—unconscious, unexamined, invisible—by which we imagine and represent the world. "It all comes out of the myth," Anna says, referring to the "flat, tame, optimistic . . . curiously jolly" (349) Soviet fiction she and her friend Jack read, "the literature of health and progress" (445):

> The writing is bad, the story lifeless, but what is frightening . . . is that it is totally inside the current myth . . . This novel touches reality at no point at all . . . It is, however, a very accurate re-creation of the self-deceptive myths of the Communist Party at this particular time; and I have read it in about fifty different shapes or guises during the last year. (346)

Though, as Althusser says, "the accusation of being in ideology only applies to others, never to oneself" ("Ideology," 175), the numerous parallels Lessing suggests between Communist and "capitalist publishing racket[s]" (346) make the point that Western literary and critical practices are every bit as enmeshed in ideology as Soviet propaganda is. As Lessing says, everyone is "a prisoner of the assumptions and dogmas of his time, which he does not question, because he has never been told they exist" (xvi); as Anna says, "well, surely the thought follows—what stereotype am I?" (49).

Though originating in particular social and political conditions, ideology authorizes those conditions as "natural" or "universal."[40] Gramsci analyzes ideology as working through "1. language itself, which is a totality of determined notions and concepts . . . 2. 'common sense' . . . 3. the entire system of beliefs, superstitions, opinions, ways of seeing things and of acting, which are collectively bundled together under the name of 'folklore.' "[41] Althusser describes two types of "State Apparatuses" that "ensure *subjection to the ruling ideology*" ("Ideology," 133): the Repressive State Apparatuses such as the army and police and the Ideological State Apparatuses, mainly "the educational" but also including "the communications apparatus" (press, radio, and television) and "the cultural" (literature, the arts) (143, 145, 154). His analysis of "the School" as "the dominant Ideological State Apparatus" (153, 156–57) resembles Lessing's critique of formal education as inculcating "received opinion" and a respect for authority; and his analysis of coercion as both psychological and materialistic (like Gramsci's) represents a "union of Marx and Freud"[42]—"Grandfathers Freud and Marx," as Anna calls them (643). Ideology masks contradictions, offers partial truths and a false coherence, thereby obscuring actual conditions and prohibiting change; as Coward and Ellis say, "It defines the limits for, and works to fix the individual within, a certain mental horizon" and masks the very "contradictions, ambiguities, and inconsistencies" that might function as "a source of possible change."[43]

Literature transmits ideology not merely or most significantly in content; rather, as Eagleton suggests (drawing on Lukacs), "the true bearers of ideology . . . are the very forms" (24): "In selecting a form . . . the writer finds his choice already ideologically circumscribed"; "The languages and devices a writer finds to hand are already saturated with certain ideological modes of perception, certain codified ways of interpreting reality" (26–27). Jameson says "formal processes" "carry ideological messages of their own, distinct from the ostensible or manifest content of the works";[44] Barthes says that "every Form is also a Value": "It is under the pressure of History and Tradition that the possible modes of writing for a given writer are established . . . writing . . . remains full of the recollection of previous usage, for language is never innocent."[45] Raymond Williams describes conventions as "involving . . . social assumptions of causation and consequence";[46] DuPlessis applies this specifically to romance, which she analyzes as a "trope for the sex-gender system."[47] Forms, conventions, and language are bearers of ideology; and so, too, are genres, which emerge in response to specific historical situations, as the novel did to meet the needs of the bourgeoisie in the eighteenth century. In fact, Jameson extends *"the ideology of form"* to apply to "the aesthetic act" itself: "The production of aesthetic or narrative form is . . . an ideological act in its own right, with the function of inventing imaginary or formal 'solutions' to unresolvable social contradictions" (*Political Unconscious,* 79).

## Representation and Its Discontents: The Four Notebooks

The central question of *The Golden Notebook*—how to oppose a system by means of linguistic and literary conventions that have been forged by that system—was raised though not worked through in the *Children of Violence*. Anna's four notebooks contain commentary, explicit and implicit, on the ideological complicity of literary and critical forms—novels, short stories, journalism, parody, "propaganda," literary criticism, reviews. They discuss—and demonstrate—the complicity of forms with the systems, capitalist and Communist, that produce them, exploring a kind of "worst possible case," the possibility that all discourse is inextricably and inevitably and always bound to "reproduction," bound to a circular process of reproducing the ideology that produces it, determined and determining.

In the yellow notebook Anna explores the conventions of the "women's novel" by writing "The Shadow of the Third," which "comes out of" the myth of romantic love—"the property of the women's magazines" (204), as

Ella calls it. The red notebook, a record of Anna's political activities, consists of Soviet short stories and speculations about Soviet art. The black notebook is a record of transactions relating to Anna's first novel, *The Frontiers of War,* which includes attempts of the capitalist literary marketplace to commodify it and Soviet reviews that condemn it for deviating from the Party line. The blue notebook, a journal, contains "facts," attempts at parodies and discussions of parody, of film, "High Art," and pastiche, including Anna's last-ditch effort to "cage the truth" by means of the newspaper clippings she pastes around her walls.

The form that is easiest to critique as ideological—because it expresses someone else's ideology—is the Soviet fiction Anna reads for the Communist publishing house she works for. Though the cheerful, bland Soviet writing is superficially the antithesis of the "unhealthy," "immoral" fiction she repudiates in *Frontiers of War,* Anna realizes that this "dead stuff," "this bad, dead, banal writing is the other side of my coin . . . of the psychological impulse that created *Frontiers of War*": "And so this is the paradox: I, Anna, reject my own 'unhealthy' art: but reject 'healthy' art when I see it" (349). The parallels between these forms imply similarities in the societies that produce them. The lonelyhearts letters Ella answers for the women's magazine she works for, *Women at Home,* have their counterparts in the comrades' letters Anna answers for the Communist party publishing house, and when this publisher advertises its interest in fiction it is inundated by manuscripts. As Molly exclaims,

> Everyone was going to be a great writer, but everyone! . . . every one of the old party war horses . . . everyone has that old manuscript or wad of poems tucked away . . . Isn't it terrifying? Isn't it pathetic? Every one of them, failed artists. I'm sure it's significant of something, if only one knew *what.* (16)

"What" it signifies is stated in *Martha Quest*—no one can "face the prospect of a lifetime behind a desk" (211–12). Such manuscripts may "come out of" different "myths," but they express the same despair (38–39, 167–68, 175, 236, 284, 353, 653).

Overt forms of coercion in the Soviet Union are paralleled by blacklisting in the United States. As Nelson, a blacklisted American writer, says, *"they've beaten me* . . . they don't need prison and firing squads to beat people" (490). On both sides, the political situation makes it impossible to know the truth: "the communist language" and "the language of democracy" are both "safe unreal jargon," "a means of disguising the truth" (294–95). "This is a time when it is impossible to know the truth about anything" (302); "anything might be true anywhere . . . Anything is possible" (163).

But that "anything is possible" makes parody impossible, since truth is so fantastic that it outdoes attempts at caricature, as Anna keeps discovering—"something had happened which made parody impossible" (440). The "journals" of a young American traveler and a "lady author" "afflicted with sensibility," which Anna and her friend write as parody, are accepted as authentic and published (434–40). Anna's "Blood on the Banana Leaves" expresses the melodrama and sensationalism implicit in her first novel, *Frontiers of War,* as "the Romantic Tough School of Writing" (539–41) expresses a potential of Saul's writing. When Anna assumes the voice of June Boothby, a lovesick adolescent girl, she realizes how close this style is to her own: "I wrote in the style of the most insipid coy woman's magazine; but what was frightening was that the insipidity was due to a very slight alteration of my own style, a word here and there only" (620). Conversely, Anna finds parody where there is none: Comrade Ted's story of his meeting with a Stalin eager to follow his advice is so fantastic that Anna "thought it was an exercise in irony. Then a very skillful parody of a certain attitude. Then I realised it was serious. . . . But what seemed to me important was that it could be read as parody, irony, or seriously"; and this gives her a sense of "the thinning of language against the density of our experience" (302).

The Western literary world co-opts by the power of money, on the one hand, and by the power of "culture," on the other hand, the former reducing art to a commodity, the latter enshrining it as High Art; "the literary world is so prissy . . . so classbound; or if it's the commercial side, so blatant, that any contact with it sets [Anna] thinking of joining the Party" (154). Anna's encounters with Reggie Tarbrucke of Amalgamated Vision and Mrs. Edwina Wright of Bluebird Screenplays illustrate "the commercial side." Reggie tries to convince Anna that her novel is "really a simple moving love story" (285), and in an effort to outrage him Anna suggests making a comedy of it, but, again, this attempt at parody is defeated when Edwina, representative of American television, assures her that "it would make a marvellous musical" (292).

The belief in "Art" and "the artist" is represented by Anna's Jungian therapist, Mrs. Marks. "A pillar of reaction" (237) who insists that the artist is "sacred" (235), "a European soaked in art," her room is "like a shrine to art" (253)—"all that damned art all over the place" (5); "the walls are covered with reproductions of masterpieces and there are statues. It is almost like an art gallery" (236). Anna can see that this view of the artist is part of the same myth that sanctions the term *real woman* and that this myth is "reactionary"—Mrs. Marks "uses this word, a woman, a real woman, exactly as she does artist, a true artist. An absolute" (237): "I no longer believe in art," Anna tells her (232). The name Anna and Molly give her, "Mother Sugar," refers to "a whole way of looking at life—traditional, rooted, conservative" (5). Besides, Anna can see that Mother Sugar's "complacent smile" "when the word Art cropped up" is another expression of the attitude of the marketplace, of "the money-changers, the little jackals of the press, the enemy": "When a film mogul wants to buy an artist—and the real reason he seeks out the original talent and the spark of creativity is because he wants to destroy it, unconsciously that's what he wants, to justify himself by destroying the real thing—he calls the victim an artist" (62–63). Anna rejects both preciousness and popularization, "culture" and commerce, and realizes that they are opposite sides of the same coin.

Criticism, like literature, "comes out of the myth," and while purporting to offer new perspectives, only recycles received ideas. Reviews of *Frontiers of War* demonstrate the way criticism monitors what can be thought and said. Soviet journals condemn the novel: "A true artistic work must have a revolutionary life . . . this author must learn from our literature, the literature of health and progress, that no one is benefited by despair. This is a negative novel . . . unhealthy, even ambiguous" (445). In the West academic taste shifts with political winds, so that an article on China that is refused publication one month becomes lucrative the next month (157–58); critics and reviewers "adapt themselves to authority figures, to 'received opinion,'" and are incapable of "imaginative and original judgment" (this commentary occurs extratextually, in Lessing's remarks on the critical reception of *The Golden Notebook* [xvi]). Anna imagines herself writing a review of *Frontiers of War* that asks "the only question worth asking":

> The most interesting question raised by this new report from the racial frontiers is: why, when the oppressions and tensions of white-settled Africa have existed more or less in their present form for decades, it is only in the late forties and fifties that they exploded into artistic form. If we knew the answer we would understand more of the relations between society and the talent it creates, between art and the tensions that feed it. (60)

In both novels she is writing, *Free Women* and "The Shadow of the Third," Anna shapes the rough, raw material of the blue notebook into more conventional, marketable form. In *Free Women* there are clearer crises and denouements, scenes that are more dramatic and definitive, than anything in the blue notebook: Tommy attempts suicide and blinds himself; Anna offers advice that improves the situation between Tommy and Molly and earns Richard's thanks (521–22); and the novel ends with Anna "'integrated with British life'" (666), taking a job as a marriage counselor and giving up writing. In "The Shadow of the Third" Ella has a more conventional job than Anna does, at the women's magazine *Women at Home,* and she and her friend Julia "considered themselves very normal, not to say conventional women" (171); though Ella has qualms about how her magazine "pushes taste on" its readers (179, 220), she is generally untroubled by questions of the truth or morality of art—she publishes a novel about suicide and has "no politics." Anna names the "coy little-womanish, snobbish" atmosphere (178) of Ella's magazine and adjusts her language to it ("it was Patricia Brent, editress, who suggested Ella should spend a week in Paris" [306]). Romantic love is associated with conventional form: "Broken hearts belong to old-fashioned novels. . . . They don't go with the time we live in" (103), as Paul Blackenhurst says[48]—though this novel concludes more interestingly than *Free Women* does, breaking off into fragments that lead to new beginnings.

Though Anna is critical of the forms, she also makes various nostalgic efforts to cling to them. The form she clings to longest is that provided by romantic love—"my strongest need—being with one man, love, all that" (625). Though she can criticize the system of beliefs that sanctions Mrs. Marks's terms *true artist* and *real woman,* she has more difficulty with the term *real man,* which she uses without irony (391–93, 404, 455, 484, 561): she strives for liberation from the romantic myth, yet she is also enmeshed in it, and the emotional thralldom she is exploring in "The Shadow of the Third" is her own.

The "end of the affair" coincides with the end of therapy with Mrs. Marks and the end of her involvement with the Communist party: "Michael is leaving me, that's finished"; "And I'm leaving the Party. It's a stage of my life finished. And what next? I'm going out, willing it, into something new . . . I'm shedding a skin, or being born again" (353). Endings occur in the middle, with the second half of the novel "writing beyond" them: the "skin" Anna "sheds" is no less than her conditioning, "a habit of . . . nerves from the past" (365), and her change puts her on a "kind of frontier" (482).

*The Golden Notebook* registers the loss of the master narratives—social, moral, philosophical, political—that once gave life meaning: "My God, what we've lost, what we've lost, what we've lost, how can we ever get back to it, how can we get back to it again?" Saul exclaims (629). Anna's efforts "to get back to it" are thwarted by her own honesty, on the one hand, and by history, on the other, which preclude the possibility of romantic or political innocence. Against Mrs. Marks's attempts to fit her experience into an "old pattern," to get her to "put the pain away where it can't hurt, turn it into a story or into history" (471), Anna insists on remaining true to what is new in her, to "areas of me made by the kind of experience women haven't had before" (471)—to what is "raw" and "unfinished" in her life (236–37). Anna's interrogation of literary-critical forms is thus one with her efforts to move beyond conventional forms in her life. To be true to what is new in her requires that she invent a new kind of story.

## New Moves

To remain stuck in the role of victim is to validate the "helpless lists of opposing words" (71) Anna named at the beginning—"Men. Women. Bound. Free. Good. Bad. Yes. No. Capitalism. Socialism. Sex. Love" (44)—and so to reaffirm the dualisms that are the basis of Western thought, confirming not only male power but the whole epistemological and linguistic structure that sanctions it. But in the course of the novel, nearly every important event, issue, question, quality, attitude, and action comes up for renaming: in the visionary and re-visionary final episodes, words, phrases, events recur, the same but different, as the value of "boulder pushing," of "taking a stand," of the forms, of "making patterns," of irony, and of naming itself—all are renamed as Anna wrests strength from chaos. Most crucial is the principle of destruction represented by her dream of the dwarf, which she names "joy in malice, joy in a destructive impulse" (477). Anna first dreams it negatively and then, realizing "it was up to [her] to force this thing to be good as well as bad" (478), dreams it positively, releasing a "third friendly" creature—male and female, "the third" or "the shadow of the third," the figure onto whom she had projected those powers she relinquished in her relationship with Michael/Paul.

But the way to this power is by giving up power, just as the way to new form is through formlessness. This is why Anna's route in the latter half of the novel seems so bizarre. Rather than finding redemption through the love of a good man, Anna becomes involved with men who are worse and worse, even more divided and destructive than Michael/Paul—Nelson, de Silva, Saul Green—and submerges herself in their destructiveness. They take her through an "emotional no-man's land" (457) to a realm where "it didn't matter" (de Silva's phrase), but they also jolt her out of the passive, unthinking stance she assumed with Michael into more active, creative roles that do not fall within the rubric of romantic love or, indeed, within any rubric. Those critics who have blamed Lessing for depicting woman's sexuality as "contained" or "created" by the man's (445, 215)[49] have confused the author with the protagonist, for Lessing shows Anna as needing to outgrow this idea: the cost of being Michael's "creation" has been her own creative self.

Anna's sense of agency begins as she learns, with Cy Maitland, that she can "do the directing" (323); with the Canadian script writer she also "gives pleasure," though she resents this new role, criticizing him on the grounds that "the man's desire creates a woman's desire, or should, so I'm right to be critical" (546). Blaming de Silva on similar grounds—"Of course it's him, not me. For men create these things, they create us"—she has a new insight: "Remembering how I clung, how I always cling on to this, I felt foolish. Because why should it be true?" (501). Anna does not easily relinquish the claims of the passive self, but against her clinging to old patterns there emerges a new sense of her powers of creation—as suggested by the short story sketches concerning the creation of selves in response to relationships (460–61) and by the insight that a man with an "ambiguous uncreated quality" (532) is more attractive than one who is formed. By immersing herself in the destructiveness of these men, she comes to acknowledge the destructive principle within her, a process symbolized by the dream of the dwarf, which evolves through various male incarnations and then comes to rest finally in her.

As she comes to see herself as participant rather than victim and as her role in relationships becomes more "creative," she can relinquish the illusion that "the truth" is outside, in some external form, and accept that it is, rather, in the patterning, structuring power of her mind. In her search for the truth, Anna has assumed that there is a reality independent of the mind, but all her attempts to record "simply, the truth," "the straight, simple formless account" (63), throw her back on her "own ordering, commenting memory" (585). On the day she attempts to record "everything," September 17, 1954, "the idea that I will have to write it down is changing the balance, destroying the truth" (341): "No, it didn't come off. A failure as usual" (368). She realizes that knowing the end has altered the shape: "As soon as one has lived through something, it falls into a pattern. And the pattern of an affair . . . is seen in terms of what ends it"; "literature is analysis after the event" (227–28). She realizes that memory distorts: "How do I know that what I 'remember' was what was important? What I remember was chosen by Anna, of twenty years ago. I don't know what this Anna of now would choose" (137).

She imagines that visual images might provide greater certainty—"the absolute assurance of a smile, a look, a gesture, in a painting or a film" (110): "Probably better as a film. Yes, the physical quality of life . . . not the analysis afterwards" (228). But in the dream she has of herself filming her life, she realizes that visual images are also shaped by memory: "What makes you think that the emphasis you have put on it is the correct emphasis?" (619), asks the "projectionist." All attempts to "cage the truth" (660) by means of visual images or facts are as dependent as fiction is upon the ordering, selecting faculty of the mind.

When Anna can accept that there is no reality apart from the mind that perceives it and the words that shape it, she can accept that none of her versions is true—or all are true, or truth itself is a fiction, invented rather than discovered. It is this that gives her the power of renaming. New possibilities incur ontological instability, and as Anna's role becomes more creative, we cannot always tell what is real and what is created. Toward the end of the novel Anna's notebook divisions break down: the political meeting where Anna meets Nelson is recorded in the blue notebook rather than the red notebook, and observations occur in the yellow notebook that prompt her to say: "This sort of comment belongs to the blue notebook. I must keep them separate" (537). Both red and black notebooks break off into newspaper clippings; the yellow notebook breaks off into Ella's short story sketches (531–34), sketches that prefigure Anna's breakdown with Saul and raise questions: if Ella is "writing" Anna, is she "authoring" her author? if Ella writes Saul, is he real—a "real man"? The blue notebook becomes a record of breakdown, which becomes, in the golden notebook, a record of breakthrough; and in both, dreams figure prominently, prefiguring "actual" incidents (or recalling them? it is not always possible to tell). Impugning the blue notebook as the truth on which the other notebooks draw, Lessing blurs the boundaries between truth and fiction and calls into question not only "the true story" but the real man.[50] It may be that Anna "invents" Saul, fabricates him from all the men she has known, a kind of composite male who expresses her own "masculine" potential (in Jungian terms, her animus) and guides her through breakdown: she does dream of him as her "projectionist," "a person concerned to prevent the disintegration of Anna" (614).

Though Lessing enlists Marxist critiques of linguistic form as determined and determining, she also critiques this critique and, allowing Anna the power of "naming in a different way," she gives her a way of tapping into the subversive and liberatory potentials of language. Coward and Ellis critique Marxist thought about language as being "capable [only] of negative formulations about language," reducing it "to ideology" or "to a passive medium of communication with no effective determinacy of its own"; but language is not "reducible to ideology," for "language and thought . . . engender [each] other: language makes thought possible, thought makes language possible" (78–79).[51] *The Golden Notebook* qualifies its Marxist critiques with a poststructuralist sense of the truth of interpretations, that (in Molly Hite's term) "there is no truth apart from the telling, no real story, no authorized version" (90).[52] Not that there is no reality, as in extreme poststructuralist positions, but that, as Raymond Williams suggests, "all human experience is an interpretation": "We create our human world as we have thought of art being created." This view of interpretation as agency, as creative and culture-building, is different from relativistic deconstructive positions. It makes the imagination integral to "everything we see and do, the whole structure of our relationships and institutions," and it provides the way through Anna's writer's block by justifying art, making it crucial to culture building and linking it with life: "To see art as a particular process in the general human process of creative discovery and communication is at once a redefinition of the status of art and the finding of means to link it with our ordinary social life." This is the answer both to High Art and commodification, as Williams explains, for it eliminates "the distinction of art from ordinary living, and the dismissal of art as unpractical or secondary (a 'leisure-time activity')," which "are alternative formulations of the same error."[53] When Anna can accept her own fictions, she can allow her various versions to "come together" into the novel we have just read, a form that admits to its own uncertainties and contradictions, to its own processes of production, and that celebrates the "crude, unfinished, raw, tentative" in her life as "precisely what was valuable in it" (236–37).

## Naming in a Different Way

Before she can know, with a knowledge that is "part of how [she sees] the world" (589), that truth is in the patterning, structuring power of the mind, Anna must first experience the dissolution of language, know that "words mean nothing" (476–77). This possibility is suggested in several places in the novel and is finally worked through in the golden notebook:

> I think, bitterly, that a row of asterisks, like an old-fashioned novel, might be better. Or a symbol of some kind, a circle perhaps, or a square. Anything at

> all, but not words. The people who have been there, in the place in themselves where words, patterns, order, dissolve, will know what I mean and the others won't.

This realization prompts Anna's encounter with the "terrible irony," a nihilism that represents the defeat of all human effort, but this low point is also the turning point, for

> Once having been there, there's a terrible irony, a terrible shrug of the shoulders, and it's not a question of fighting it, or disowning it, or of right or wrong, but simply knowing it is there, always. It's a question of bowing to it, so to speak, with a kind of courtesy, as to an ancient enemy: All right, I know you are there, but we have to preserve the forms, don't we? And perhaps the condition of your existing at all is precisely that we preserve the forms, create the patterns. (633–34)

That the terrible irony calls forth "a kind of courtesy" recalls the association of *irony* with *courtesy* in relation to Tom Mathlong, "a courteous, ironical figure" "who performed actions, played roles, that he believed to be necessary for the good of others, even while he preserved an ironic doubt about the results of his actions": Anna describes this stance as "something we needed very badly in this time" (597). "We have to preserve the forms," the phrase Richard used to justify his idiot complacency, is renamed positively as "creating the patterns" and transformed from a self-limiting self-justification to a saving grace; and though Tommy has dismissed "just making patterns" as cowardice—"I don't think there's a pattern anywhere—you are just making patterns, out of cowardice" (275)—Anna re-envisions "making patterns" as an act of creative imagination. Similarly, "it doesn't matter," the phrase that expressed the nihilism of de Silva and the "total sterility" of Anna's dream of her life as a film—"it doesn't matter what we film, provided we film something" (525)—is associated now with commitment: "It doesn't matter" which stand we take as long as we take a stand; "We've got to make stands all the time . . . the point is to make a stand at all" (552). The value of boulder-pushing, about which Paul felt hopeless—"We are the failures," he says, because "all our lives . . . we'll put all our energies, all our talents, into pushing a great boulder up a mountain. The boulder is the truth that the great men know by instinct, and the mountain is the stupidity of mankind" (210)—gets restated by a character Anna dreams in the golden notebook, a composite of Paul and Michael:

> But my dear Anna, we are not the failures we think we are. We spend our lives fighting to get people very slightly less stupid than we are to accept truths that the great men have always known . . . It is our job to tell them. Because the great men can't be bothered. Their imaginations are already occupied with . . . visions of a society full of free and noble human beings . . . [but] they know we are here, the boulder-pushers. . . . And they rely on us and they are right; and that is why we are not useless after all. (618)

In this crucial instance of "naming in a different way," "boulder-pushers" are renamed as "not failures," "not useless," and the second version goes on to envision "a society full of free and noble human beings."

Naming itself is transformed from a defensive "fixing," "a 'naming' to save . . . from pain" (489), to the imaginative re-creation Anna practices in "the Game" and in the novel as a whole. Naming is reenvisioned as "rescue-work . . . rescuing the formless into form" (470), and "something new and terrible" (481) becomes something "terrible . . . or marvellous" (473). "Everything has two faces," as Anna tells Mrs. Marks (251), which is also what Martha discovers in her breakdown: *"Every attitude, emotion, thought, has its opposite held in balance out of sight but there all the time. Push any one of these to an extreme, and boomps-a-daisy, over you go into its opposite"* (*FGC*, 521).[54] This involvement of each quality with its opposite, this dialectical interchange of each with other, dissolves the binding force of binaries.

This release of new potentials enables Anna to dream, again, of her life as a film, but unlike the "glossy," "conventionally, well-made films" of the first golden notebook dream sequence, "all false" (614–21), this film has a "realistic," "rough, crude, rather jerky quality" (634), and it not only transcends her experience but brings "together" images previously separate:

> The film was now beyond my experience, beyond Ella's, beyond the notebooks, because there was a fusion; and instead of seeing separate scenes, people, faces, movements, glances, they were all together . . . it became a series of moments where a peasant's hand bent to drop seed into earth . . . or a man stood on a dry hillside in the moonlight . . . his rifle ready on his arm. (635)

The golden notebook dream sequences show Anna transcending her own form and attaining a "new imaginative comprehension" (61) of the Algerian soldier and Chinese peasant, figures that recur to symbolize the collective life she feared her art was debarred from (596, 600, 635, 639). Having confronted the worst possibility, "the terrible irony"—"all right, I know you are there" (634)—Anna can get on with her life.

After the four notebooks merge in the golden notebook and after Anna's selves merge with Saul's, Anna steps back into the forms and frames the experience with the short, conventional novel *Free Women,* which—unlike the notebooks, whose endings fragment to become new beginnings—is a closed form that contains or "buttons up" (625). Having dissolved the forms, she can remake them on her own terms and "preserve the forms" that enable her to endure, forging a new relation to the forms that is not a capitulation but enables her to take stands, in full recognition of the arbitrariness of these stands, in a spirit of courteous irony.

Lessing makes terms with the forms similar to those that she makes with language, terms that acknowledge what Fuoroli calls "the paradoxical nature of referential language—that it is always inadequate and always necessary."[55] *The Golden Notebook* has been criticized for discussing the inadequacy of language in adequate language, for "talk[ing] about disorder in a very orderly way—in an accessible style, and a determinedly everyday vocabulary, one usually nonallusive, even pedestrian."[56] It is true that Lessing assumes the efficacy of language for practical purposes; as the protagonist of *Briefing for a Descent into Hell* says, quoting T. S. Eliot, *"I gotta use words when I talk to you."*[57]

The "wordless statement" made by the form of *The Golden Notebook* affirms the value of forms while also acknowledging their partiality and incompleteness. But these forms are different from those by which Richard defined himself: it is irony, with its acknowledgment of other perspectives and the incompleteness of each, that makes the difference—irony, not "terrible" but "courteous."[58] By juxtaposing the forms, Lessing creates a whole which includes and goes beyond them, a whole that is complex, heterogeneous, and processive.

## Breaking the Circle

Though Anna began with the passivity of earlier Lessing protagonists—Mary Turner of *The Grass Is Singing* or Martha Quest of the first four *Children of Violence* novels—drifting into destructive relationships and staying in them too long, she becomes, by the end, "intelligent enough to let [men] go": "You could do worse," Milt quips; "you could keep them" (568).[59] Anna does not get it "all," and her failure is in some sense a failure to resolve the traditional female conflict between love and writing. But her breakdown into Saul has transformed male-female relationships from a power struggle to a cooperative venture, and her response to the end of the Saul/Milt affair is measure of how far she has come since the end of the affair with Michael/Paul: the skin she sheds is no less than her sexual and emotional conditioning, the female dependence that is the legacy of the past. In a sense this is a personal resolution—only in the fantasy structures of the science fiction are Lessing's characters allowed powerful public roles that enable them to save their worlds; yet in another sense, Anna's triumphs and affirmations—culture-building, boulder-pushing, keeping the dream alive—are more than personal.

The main affirmation of the novel is the novel itself. I am assuming that Anna writes *The Golden Notebook,* though I realize that there is some debate about this. The most persuasive argument that she does not is made by Molly Hite, who claims that since Lessing disallows "a hierarchy of ontological levels," it is impossible to decide whether the blue notebook or *Free Women* (in which Anna says she will no longer write) provides the real ending (98). Hite argues that if we see Anna as the author of *The Golden Notebook,* we need to posit "a controlling consciousness to preside over *The Golden Notebook,*" "an 'invisible Anna'" who is "the 'editor' of the entire work." But where is this Anna, author of *The Golden Notebook*? "If the authorial 'Anna' is not in the story, she is completely unknowable. There is no basis for calling her 'Anna' or for supposing that the experiences she recounts are in any sense her own" (98).

Perhaps it is just that I cannot tolerate this much ontological insecurity,[60] but it seems obvious that Anna writes *The Golden Notebook* because she has been writing it all along: these are *her* notebooks. (As a student of mine commented, "She wasn't suffering from writer's block—she was writing the whole time; she had an attitude problem.") It is true that Anna nowhere says she intends to bring the notebooks together into a single novel, but she does say that she intends to put all of herself into one notebook, a golden notebook.

If *Free Women* is all Anna writes as a result of her breakthrough, it hardly seems worth the effort. In *Free Women* Anna tells Molly that she will no longer write but intends to be a marriage counselor and to work for the Labour party and Molly tells Anna that she is getting married; both women are resigned to the forms, "integrated with British life at its roots" (666). A tone of what Hite calls "debilitating irony" (99) informs the ironically titled *Free Women,* a "tone" that has been defined by Anna as "a locking of feeling, an inability or a refusal to fit conflicting things together to make a whole . . . [a] refusal [that] means one can neither change nor destroy" (65)—an irony not courteous. But as Lessing explains in the introduction, to use "Free Women" as a frame for the notebooks was to make a "comment about the conventional novel," to show "how little I have managed to say of the truth, how little I have caught of all that complexity: how can this small neat thing be true when what I experienced was so rough and apparently formless and unshaped" (xiii–xiv). What is missing from *Free Women* is what is most essential about *The Golden Notebook:* the wresting of strength from chaos, the transformation of terror to courtesy, the process of working through, of renaming and reclaiming.

This situation of an Anna who writes a novel about an Anna who gives up writing is a closed, self-canceling circle: like the novel Anna writes about an Ella who writes a novel about suicide or like the "sadistic-masochistic cycle" (606) in which Saul and Anna are caught, "a cycle [in which they] go around and around" (621), or Anna's dream of the firing squad, a nightmare in which two men cynically exchange glances as they change places before a firing squad before being shot—a dream that shows history as "simply a process, a wheel turning," and that "cancels all creative emotion" (345). But Anna and Saul break their cycle, and the novel Saul writes, to which Anna gives him the first line, reverses the nightmare of the firing squad, for in Saul's novel the two men talk to each other, though they are shot for it. So, too, does the novel Anna writes, to which Saul gives her the first line—"the two women were alone in the London flat" (639)—transform the closed circle to an open, liberatory form, for the opening line sends us back to the beginning not only of *Free Women* but of *The Golden Notebook:* end circles back in a "self-begetting novel" that concludes with the protagonist ready to begin—or, in this case, realizing that she has already completed a task she had thought was impossible. Though the linearity of narrative means that there is no escaping what John Fowles calls "the tyranny of the last chapter,"[61] and *Free Women* is the last chapter, it is not the last word.

That each ending sends us back through the other, searching for a resting place that cannot finally be found (Hite likens this effect to that of a Möbius strip), enlists the reader's imagination in an exercise of perceiving relationships that strengthens the sympathetic imagination envisioned as a saving grace in the novel. For there is another "consciousness" in *The Golden Notebook:* besides Anna's, besides Lessing's, there is the reader's imagination—that essential component of any literary enterprise—that brings the notebooks together and completes them. It is the reader who "imaginatively fuses" *The Golden Notebook,* who provides the creative moral response, the "act of imagination" that Anna likens to an "act of faith" (275) and that she defines as necessary to the realization of better selves and better worlds: "I was thinking that quite possibly these marvellous, generous things we walk side by side with in our imaginations could come in existence, simply because we need them, because we imagine them" (637).

As dismayed as Lessing was by readers' failure to understand the novel, she has also admitted to being instructed by her readers: "This novel continues to be, for its author, a most instructive experience." She describes how "ten years after I wrote it, I can get, in one week, three letters about it," one "entirely about the sex war," "the second . . . about politics," the third, about "mental illness": "But it is the same book." What she has learned from such letters is (what one suspects she already knew)—about the role of the reader in the production of meaning. She concludes, characteristically, that

> the book is alive and potent and fructifying and able to promote thought and discussion *only* when its plan and shape and intention are not understood, because that moment of seeing the shape and plan and intention is also the moment when there isn't anything more to be got out of it.
>
> And when a book's pattern and the shape of its inner life is as plain to the reader as it is to the author—then perhaps it is time to throw the book aside, as having had its day, and start again on *something new*. (xxii; emphasis mine)

Naturally, I would like to believe that Lessing's "plan and intention" are plain to me. Nevertheless *The Golden Notebook* remains "alive and potent and fructifying" to me, since each time I read it, it yields something new. It provides "a new way of looking at life" (61) and "expand[s] one's limits beyond what has been possible" (619), and its structural and formal innovations affirm the possibility of psychic and political transformation. Lessing writes not only beyond romantic endings but also beyond the idea of the ending, with its inevitable nostalgia, and beyond those fictions by women who refuse their protagonists powers equivalent to their own. "A woman if she is to write must have a room of her own," said Virginia Woolf, and Lessing gives Anna "Wulf" not only a room of her own but the literary and critical gifts neither Woolf nor Austen nor the Brontës nor Eliot ever lavished on their protagonists and then demonstrates that this is not enough, for the room in which Anna and Saul break down becomes a place where new possibilities are forged, terrible and marvelous: "The floor . . . bulging and heaving. The walls seemed to bulge inwards, then float out and away into space . . . I stood in space, the walls gone" (599). *The Golden Notebook* represents more than an "act of imagination" that "keeps the dream alive." It has been for many of us a "lurch forward" into new possibilities (275); it is what Margaret Drabble calls "territory gained forever."[62]

*Chapter 7*

# *The Summer Before the Dark*: Closed Circles

> It is always a question, when in a cul-de-sac, of seeing what there is for you, one has to be listening.
>
> —Doris Lessing, *The Summer Before the Dark*

"Like the start of an epic, simple and direct," this novel begins—"a woman stood on her back step, . . . waiting"—and it unfolds with similar starkness: "What was she going to experience? Nothing much more than, simply, she grew old."[1] As elsewhere in her fiction, Lessing is concerned with the individual in its relations with the collective, only here the individual is so representative as to be a type or "Everywoman," a woman who is not even named until several pages into the novel, when we learn, on page 8, that her name is Kate—"that well-documented and much-studied phenomenon, the woman with grown-up children and not enough to do" (19). "Everything does seem pared down, stripped of essentials, the diction and syntax reminiscent of those in parables, fables, archetypal myths," as Sydney Janet Kaplan says;[2] Betsy Draine, responding to its "emotional flatness," calls the novel an "apologue," "a simple narrative vehicle for conveying an idea," "a fiction generated and closely controlled by a theme" or "didactic function."[3] But if *Summer Before the Dark* is a novel pared down to convey a theme, its message is by no means clear, for despite its apparent simplicity there is critical disagreement about the most basic questions it raises—such as the meaning of its central symbol, Kate's dream of the seal, and its ending.[4]

In this novel, even more than in *The Golden Notebook,* "the personal is general" and Lessing's sense of the general is cataclysmic: Kate's "twilight condition" (67), the "dark" that awaits her, is also the world's. "The atmosphere of the summer coast" in Spain where she and her young lover Jeffrey travel is the "more poignant because of the general feeling that . . . [it] was doomed, soon to be ended, and for good" (76); as Kate's son Tim asserts, "The end of civilization was close, and . . . we should shortly be looking back from a worldwide barbarism formalised into a world bureaucracy to the present, which would, from that nasty place in time seem like a vanished golden age" (79). The "chill wind from the future" that threatens to "strip" Kate "of color, texture, form," threatens civilization as well: "The public, or communal, events—wars, strikes, floods, earthquakes, once high and rare . . . were moving into the first place of everyone's experience, as if an air that had once been the climate of a distant and cataclysmic star had chosen to engulf our poor planet" (3). This backdrop of cataclysm, of natural and social disaster, dwarfs and diminishes Kate's story, making it impossible even for Kate to take herself seriously: "The fact was that the things happening in the world, the collapse of everything, was tugging at the shape of events . . . and making them farcical. A joke. Like her own life. Farcical" (155).

Lessing describes the experience Kate is about to undergo as apparently "so personal," when "in fact it would be pressures from the other, the public, sphere pressing on her small life that would give what she experienced its urgency?" (this is one of many sentences in the novel that appears to be headed toward a simple declaration but takes a surprising turn, with the punctuation, to become a question): "However that might be, the summer's events were not going to be shaped through any virtues or capacities of her own" (6). But apart from the power failure in the opening episode that occasions the family cookout and the strikes that inconvenience Kate on her journey to Istanbul (48), pressures from the public sphere do not significantly impinge on Kate's story. How, then, does the catastrophic public realm, "the collapse of everything," shape "the summer's events," as it is claimed to?

For one thing the summer's events are less a matter of event, what happens to Kate, than they are about her inner discoveries. The plot consists of little more than Kate's efforts to avoid doing what she needs to do, which is to confront herself—first, taking a job at Global Foods, then letting herself get sent to Istanbul, and finally going to Spain with a young man, Jeffrey. It is only when Jeffrey becomes ill and Kate says "no" to staying in Spain and nursing him that she begins to recognize her own needs. Speculating on her situation at this point, Kate realizes, "It is always a question, when in a cul-de-sac, of seeing what there is for you, one has to be listening": it finally becomes clear to her that she could become "a person operating from her own choices" if she could learn to "see" and "listen" (96). Finally, she chooses to be alone, taking "a room of her own" in a hotel in Bloomsbury, where she recovers from an illness of her own; and then, at a flat she takes with a young woman, Maureen, she makes the inner discoveries she's been avoiding, finishing the dream of the seal which has expressed her "voyage of self-discovery" and learning to see and to listen and to some extent operate from her own choices—though the notion of choice has been severely qualified by this time in her story. The real "events" of the summer are internal: in a continuation of the process articulated in *Four-Gated City,* "the revolution had gone inwards."

Lessing shows public impinging on personal, then, not by means of plot or event—not by having Kate get caught up, say, in a dramatic political situation in Istanbul like the Caribbean revolution that Rennie of Margaret Atwood's *Bodily Harm* gets embroiled in—but by exploring the ways consciousness is enmeshed in "convention." The word *convention* recurs in the novel (2, 75, 90–91, 96), and it refers most obviously to the social and sexual conditioning that has shaped Kate's life, her socialization as woman-in-love, wife, mother, sex object. But more interesting is Lessing's interrogation of convention as a system, or, rather, as a set of interlocking systems, circular and self-referential, that includes not only romantic love and political ideology but forms of representation such as high art and language itself. That there is value in art, love, political action—these our most cherished beliefs, ideals that we assume most express us, Lessing exposes as self-enclosed, stifling systems that admit nothing new. The problem Kate faces, of separating "what she really feels" from the socially fabricated, is no less than breaking the circle of convention that defines and determines us. No wonder she fails, that her victory is so qualified—that she has no choice but to return home and resign herself to the domestic situation which is the source of her problem.

But contrary to this ending is another movement, symbolized by the dream of the seal, that allows her a kind of triumph. As at the end of the novel proper in *Four-Gated City* internal events take a separate course from external event, here too internal progress diverges from plot—though without the facilitating move to fantasy allowed by an Appendix, the disjunction is stark and disturbing.

### Dresses off a Rack

Kate seeks the truth, what she really felt, beyond the conventional phrases that fix and determine her:

> A woman stood on her back step . . . waiting.
>
> Thinking? She would not have said so. She was trying to catch hold of something, or to lay it bare so that she could look and define; for some time now she had been "trying on" ideas like so many dresses off a rack. She was letting words and phrases as worn as nursery rhymes slide around her tongue: for towards the crucial experiences custom allots certain attitudes, and they are pretty stereotyped. *Ah yes, first love!* . . .
>
> The truth was, she was becoming more and more uncomfortably conscious not only that the things she said, and a good many of the things she thought, had been taken down off a rack and put on, but that what she really felt was something else again. (1–2)

The problem with which the novel begins, Kate's sense of a slippage between the stereotypical attitudes allotted by convention and her "real" feelings, is linguistic and epistemological.[5] Kate has a sense of the gap between language and reality, and her search is, like Anna Wulf's, for a truth beyond the "myths" of her society, beyond "custom" (1) and "popular wisdom" (65)—beyond the prefabricated attitudes that present themselves "like so many dresses off a rack." These attitudes that Kate "tries on" are like the conventions Anna experiments with, and though Kate is not a writer and does not work this through by experimenting with literary forms, Lessing does: like *The Golden Notebook, Summer* evokes and repudiates various literary conventions as it works through to a form of its own. Though apparently realist, *Summer* has elements of metafiction that work against the realist assumption that language provides an unproblematic reflection of reality.

The situation from which Kate begins sets up certain conventional expectations: her family grown, her husband unfaithful, she takes a glamorous well-paid job that takes her to Istanbul then sets off with a younger man for a romantic trip through Spain. But "the convention 'older woman, younger man'" (80) no more defines Kate than the "doll's house" ending could define Martha at the end of *A Proper Marriage,* and the repudiation of this "convention in love" (75) is also the refusal of a literary form, the poignant romance of an older woman and a younger man. But neither can *Summer* be described as a woman leaving a stifling domesticity for a rewarding career, the formula of much "mad housewife" fiction of the late sixties and early seventies and a convention that Lessing herself helped conventionalize in the early Martha Quest novels. Lessing has Kate reject this version of her life early on: "But good God, she would have been mad not to marry, mad to choose Romance languages and literature" (15)—to the dismay of some critics.[6] Kate views her marriage as "successful and satisfactory" (62)—or at least mainly so; and Lessing's exposure of Global Foods as an organization that does nothing but talk eliminates "career" as a source of significant action. So, then, is the novel a *Bildungsroman,* concerned with the process of learning, growing, developing? Well, yes and no. It concerns a woman coming of age—but really of age, old age; and Kate does learn something. But such learning as she accomplishes is attenuated, for, as she realizes early on, "a lot of time, a lot of pain, went into learning very little" (4).

Like all Lessing's works, this novel confronts the question of change, the possibility of making something new. But Kate's quest is mainly retrospective, for she is trying to understand processes that have already occurred: "It was all nonsense to see things in terms of peaks and crises: the personal events, like the public ones, were long-term affairs, after all . . . It is after—at least months, but it is usually years—that a person will say, *My God, my whole life has changed*" (3). Her own change has not been a process she has caused or controlled any more than the events she is about to live through will be:—"Choose? When do I ever choose? Have I ever chosen?" (6). People do not change by deciding in advance on a course of action that they then make happen: "That was not how people changed; they didn't change themselves: you got changed by being made to live through something, and then you found yourself changed" (95). Kate faces the problem of understanding changes that have already taken place, and she also faces further change, but again, not the sort she chooses or controls: "By the time it was all over with, she would certainly not have chosen to have it differently: yet she could not have chosen it for herself in advance, for she did not have the experience to choose, or the imagination" (6).

At the outset Kate has become aware that her image of herself and her marriage is out of date and she has been tending the image rather than herself—that the truth is, she is no longer the warm, nurturing center of her family, but that she has been long starved:

> The fact was, the picture or image of herself as the warm centre of the family, the source of invisible emanations like a queen termite, was two or three years out of date. (Was there something wrong with her memory perhaps? . . . ) The truth was she'd been starved for two years, three, more. . . . The fact that this had taken some time, that it had been a process . . . was it because of this her memories were turning out to be liars? . . . But she had *not* allowed herself to feel it. . . . She had instead carefully tended the image of the marriage. (51–52)

These changes have created a "gap between formula and what happened" and she is coming to see her memory as "false memory" that must be revised (62). She becomes aware of another slippage between formula and feeling when she catches sight of the ironical grimace that contorts her face at the thought of Michael's infidelities—the visual image here, as elsewhere in the novel, providing access to a truth deeper than language—and it is this truth that she must now try to confront: "I'm telling myself the most dreadful lies! . . . *Now,* look at it, try and get hold of it, don't go on making up all these attitudes, these stories—stop taking down the same old dresses off the rack" (12). (This is the second time convention is associated with dress, and the association is appropriate considering what Kate, who is Everywoman, learns about the importance of appearance.) "But perhaps this is where she should begin . . . her feeling, childish, irrational, but absolutely undeniable, that because of Michael she felt like a doll whose sawdust was slowly trickling away" (65).

But beyond this there lurks the larger question whether it matters that Kate change or that she understand her changes: "But why should anyone care that he, she, has changed, learned, matured, grown?"

> For there is no doubt at all that there does persist the feeling, and it is probably the deepest one we have, that what matters most is that we learn through living. This feeling should be attributed to habit, a hangover from earlier, more primitive times? . . .
>
> We are what we learn.
>
> It often takes a long and painful time.
>
> Unfortunately, there was no doubt, too, that a lot of time, a lot of pain, went into learning very little . . .
>
> She was really feeling that? Yes, she was. (4; ellipsis in original)

What Kate learns is "very little" indeed compared to what Anna and Martha do: she will not forge new forms for life or her writing, nor will she get to save the world. She will attain a glimmer of understanding, a slight change in her way of seeing and knowing, and the courage to endure—though this will be the "small painful courage" that Anna Wulf comes to see as "larger than anything."

## A Lot of Rubbish

Kate's progress consists mainly of repudiations of the conventions that have defined her. The most crucial of these involve her socialization as sex object, mother, wife, and woman in love—conditioning that she now sees as "nonsense," "rubbish," a "con trick." The most disastrous of these has been her training as a sex object, not only because it left her so "bamboozled" (de Beauvoir's term for women's consciousness)[7] but because it left her so grotesquely unprepared for the strengths she would need as a mother: "Looking back now at the beautiful girl, indulged by her mother, indulged and flattered by her grandfather . . . she was tempted to cry out that it had been a gigantic con trick, the most monstrous cynicism. . . . Nothing had prepared her for what she was going to have to know, and soon" (91–92)—

> With three small children, and then four, she had to fight for qualities that had not been even in her vocabulary. Patience. Self-discipline. Self-control. Self-abnegation. Chastity. Adaptability to others—this above all. This always. . . . She had acquired the qualities before she had thought of giving names to them. She could remember very clearly the day when, reading certain words that seemed old-fashioned, in an old novel, she had thought, well, that's what *this* is. . . . And as for being a sponge for small wants year after year . . . what was the word for that? She had been amused by big words for what every mother is expected to become. But virtues? Really? Really virtues? . . . If so, they had turned on her, had become enemies . . . it seemed to her that she had acquired not virtues but a form of dementia. (92)

Again, the sense of change as a process incurred not by deciding upon and naming a direction, but by being made to live through events and then finding words for them. Kate finds the words for this adjustment to motherhood, surprisingly, in "an old novel," though for some of the skills she needs—"being a sponge for small wants year after year"—no words exist; and she now even questions whether these skills are virtues or dementia. What seems to her "almost a definition of motherhood in this enlightened time" is "feeling guilty": "It was a lot of nonsense, it was all a lot of rubbish, all of it—somewhere along the line they have gone wrong—Who? Herself? . . . Society?" (98).

Kate is in the grip of a revulsion from qualities she has had to develop as a mother—her "adaptability to others" (18), "not being able to say no" (65): "Dislike of her need to love and give made her call herself dog, or slave" (42). She protests "the long, grinding process of always, always being at other people's beck and call, always having to give out attention to detail, minuscule wants, demands, needs," which has turned "an unafraid young creature" into "an obsessed maniac" who is "always available, always criticized, always being bled to feed these—monsters" (94, 89). She is outraged at being cast off "like an old nurse" (94) or "like a wounded bird, being pecked to death by the healthy birds" (98). No wonder that her symbol for herself in the serial dream that expresses her self-discovery is a scarred, wounded creature. Moreover, the talk with which the family has always dealt with problems leaves her unable to say the most important thing: "If all those years of 'love talk' had been any use at all, she now could have used it, could have said: And now, enough, I'm like a cripple or an invalid after years of being your servant, your doormat. Now help me. I need your help. But she could not say this"; "They would see it as a claim on their attention, their compassion." Now the "discussion and the talk and the blueprinting" seem to her to have been "all nonsense" (95), "not the healthy and therapeutic frankness she had imagined, they had all imagined, but a form of self-deception" (87).

Also dismissed as "talk"—*"nonsense, it was all nonsense, . . . eternal talk, talk, talk, . . . a great con trick"*—is Global Foods. Supposedly an organization that is solving the problems of world starvation, Global Foods is actually *"a mechanism to earn a few hundred men and women incredible sums of money"* (38); rather than doing necessary or useful work, "they talked" (32). On neither the personal nor the collective level is talk sustaining: rather than solving familial or global problems, talk leaves people starved. Besides, Kate finds herself doing the same kind of work here that she does in her family: "This is what women did in families—it was Kate's role in life," to be a "provider of invisible manna, consolation, warmth, sympathy," "the supplier of some kind of invisible fluid or emanation": "She was beginning to see that she could accept a job in this organization or another like it, for no other reason than she was unable to switch herself out of [this] role" (45–46). So much for the idea that a glamorous, well-paid job provides a viable alternative to domesticity. The most Kate can expect from Global Foods is to stave off her "chill wind" for a time.

Kate's affair with Jeffrey is another attempt to avoid the chill wind that succeeds in eliminating another conventional solution—"the convention 'older woman, younger man'" (80). Kate finds herself, with this lost young man, back in the role of mother and listener; and, having embarked on an affair of the flesh, she finds herself grotesquely embroiled in the flesh, as he falls ill and in need of a nurse. Even before he gets sick, however, the affair is a parody of "those unwritten but tyrannical values of the emotional code" that dictate that this type of affair "should be desperate and romantic" (75). Anyhow, Kate has already lived through this convention, in an earlier affair with a younger man, and ought to know better: though "popular wisdom claims that this particular class of love affair is the most poignant, tender, poetic, exquisite one there is, altogether the choicest on the menu" (65), the truth was, it had been "humiliating"—"It had been false memory again, she had dolled it up in her mind, making something presentable of it to fit the convention 'older woman, younger man.' But really it had been humiliating" (80). Again, Kate has tended the image rather than the actuality and has rewritten the experience to conform to the convention; again, the term *dolled up* associates the convention with dress; and again, what promises nourishment—the choicest item on the menu—leads to starvation. This convention can no more provide Kate's life definition or sustenance than a career at Global Foods could.

Turgenev's *A Month in the Country,* the play Kate attends once she is back in London, is one expression of this "convention in love." It also illuminates certain assumptions about High Art (159) that Kate dismisses as a "con." Though Kate once turned to the theater for "confirmation" ("confirmation of what?"), this play now strikes her as "rubbish," "a farce, and not at all a high-class and sensitive comedy filled with truths about human nature." Natalie Petrovna, whom Kate had once imagined that anyone, anywhere would "recognise . . . at once," who had once seemed "the mirror of every woman in the audience who has been the centre of attention and now sees her power slip away from her," now strikes her as "Mad. Nuts. Loony . . . She should be locked up." Kate no longer finds herself "mirrored" in this nineteenth-century woman, nor does she imagine that the women in the Spanish village would either, though their lives are considerably closer to the nineteenth century than is her own. While supposedly expressing universal "truths about human nature," High Art is actually timebound, culturebound, and classbound, mirroring only the values of a small elite: while passing as universal, it is profoundly provincial. Though such plays once gave Kate "the feeling of having eaten well . . . of having been filled, sustained, supported," this now leaves her starved: and by this time she actually is starved, for she is ill and losing weight (153–55).

In fact High Art is only designated "high" because it confirms what we already know. Like the applause of the audience, described as "a ritual confirmation of self-approval on the part of the audience and the actors . . . a fantastic ritual" (159), this sort of play "where one observed people like oneself" (53) is merely self-affirmation and self-aggrandizement—a closed, circular process that admits nothing new. It is a kind of culturally approved narcissism, self-involved and self-serving as the mirror-gazing that has consumed so much of Kate's life. No wonder that she reaches for a mirror when she gets back to the hotel room and that her thoughts turn to another narcissistic process, falling in love. Kate now sees woman's choice of a man as a matter of letting herself be chosen by him because he admired that face that he saw as she saw:

> Oh it was all so wearying, so humiliating . . . had she really spent so many years of her life—it would almost certainly add up to years!—in front of a looking glass? Just like all women. Years spent asleep, or tranced. Did a woman chose *him,* or allow herself to be chosen by *him,* because he admired that face she had so much attended to. . . . For the whole of her life . . . she had looked into mirrors and seen what other people would judge her by. (161)

The process of loving and being loved now seems to her "a confirmation of self-approval," a circular process as self-enclosing and stifling as admiring one's reflection in a glass: "And now the image had rolled itself up and thrown itself into a corner, leaving behind the face of a sick monkey" (161).

Kate thus repudiates the sexual codes and signals to which she's been "twitching" all her life (186). She demystifies these conventions utterly by walking back and forth in front of a group of construction workers, first dressed invisibly, in a sack dress, with her hair covered frumpily, and then dressed sexily, "set to receive notice" (179), and concludes that "men's attention is stimulated by signals no more complicated than what leads the gosling; and for all her adult life, . . . she had been conforming, twitching like a puppet to those strings" (186), to sexual codes so crudely simple that they ought to have insulted her: "What a lot of rubbish, what a con it all was, *what a bloody waste of time*" (199); "This is what you have been doing for years and years and years"—"That's what it is all worth. That's all. Years and years and years of it" (219–20).[8]

Finally, she dismisses love itself as "a load of shit," responding to the word *love,* which she finds scrawled at the bottom of a note from Maureen, with *"Shit to that!* . . . What a load of shit" (200). Using the word *shit* "was like entering forbidden territory"—"so much for a word"; and saying "shit" to *love,* Kate appropriates some of her neighbor and friend Mary Finchley, who has functioned as a corrosive commentary on Kate's illusions, a kind of double who vents an energy and anger of which Kate is incapable. Indeed, Kate has been carrying Mary around with her, recalling the hilarity of their "cow sessions," where words like *home, Mother, father, family,* and *husband* would send them off into gales of "ribald laughter at the whole damned business" (34), and one of the questions she needs to confront is what this means: "She was going to have to understand what Mary meant to her, what she was standing for" (94).

Also dismissed as "useless" are Kate's revolutionary feelings about the theater audience, her speculations that what was spent on the hair of certain of these heads "would keep a dozen families alive for months" (158, 156). These thoughts strike her as useless because "that lot," the Russians, "had been swept off the boards by a revolution, and what of it . . . nothing had changed, and the same thoughts went revolving and revolving in their grooves in peoples' heads . . . like a lot of old scratched gramophone records" (158). This line of thought is developed later, when Kate meets Maureen's boyfriend, Philip, who "sees himself as new, fresh-minted by history" (194) while he is actually only repeating the clichés of an earlier generation of fascists and demonstrating that "things had come round again, they always did" (197). Talking to Philip makes Kate reflect again upon the futility of political attitudes and slogans:

> More and more the political attitudes seemed like the behaviour of marionettes, or little clockwork figures wound up and continuing to display their little gestures while they were being knocked about . . . in all directions in a typhoon.
>
> Yet the Browns were political, like all the people like them. . . . All their adult lives, ever since the war that had formed them, they had been setting their course, holding themselves steady in self-respect, with words like liberty, freedom, democracy. . . . Yet the truth was she was thinking . . . more and more, that it was all nonsense. (196)

The wonderfully tautological comparison of the Browns to "all the people like them" suggests the self-reinforcing and self-aggrandizing nature of political attitudes: people surround themselves with people with political views like their own, thereby affirming their sense of their own rightness and importance but accomplishing nothing new.

But the most disturbing of Kate's insights is that none of the above insights matters, that the very process of understanding and describing is itself futile: "What she thought about it was probably not important at all . . . now *that* was the truth, it was the truth . . . we spend our lives assessing, balancing, weighing what we think, we feel . . . It's all nonsense" (232). The final "nonsense" is to imagine that we learn from experience—a realization that impugns the value of Kate's experience, of the novel itself, and indeed, of all human effort.

## Working it Through

What goes on at Maureen's flat enables Kate to come to terms with these rejections, to qualify them and incorporate them into positions she can live with.

Being with strangers, placing herself in a situation where nobody knows her, releases her from the expectations of others: Kate doesn't need to oblige anyone's conception of her now since no one here has a conception of her. Liberated from the mirror of other peoples' gazes, she realizes that she needn't return to her former self; for the first time it strikes her that she might actually "stay as she was . . . What an interesting idea!" (167)—"a thin monkey of a woman . . . her hair tied into a lump behind her head" (166), gaunt, unkempt, with a "bush of multi-hued hair" (153). This realization is liberating, but it is also frightening, for "outside a cocoon of comfort and protection, the support of other people's recognition" (172), she finds her sense of self slipping away. But from this insight that "all her life she had been held upright by an invisible fluid, the notice of other people" (180) comes the understanding that she has derived support from others as well as supported them—that she has been fed by the process of feeding others—which makes her feel less a victim, less "devoured" by monsters. (Margaret Drabble's Kate Armstrong works through her midlife crisis to a similar realization—"if so many people weren't leaning on me . . . I might fall over.")[9]

Entering into a surrogate mother-daughter relationship with Maureen, Kate is able to work through some of her problems about motherhood. Maureen comes to her with questions of the sort a daughter would ask, about whether to marry, what to be, and Kate is able to say, "I can't answer that" (185): refusing the burden of responsibility for another person's life, she is able to divest herself of the guilt she has seen as "a definition of motherhood" (98). When Maureen calls her mother "a failure," "a sad sack," "who'd want to be like that?" and when she weeps "because of [Kate's] power to darken her future" ("I'd do anything . . . rather than turn into *that*" [203]); "All day long, busy busy busy—at what?" Kate can reply, "At bringing you up . . . and making not a bad job of it" (205). To Maureen's protest, "No, it's not good enough," Kate replies, "The best of luck to you. And what are you going to be instead?" (206). Though Maureen voices Kate's own previous criticisms, that being a mother is an education in fussing and a form of dementia, Kate is now able to counter such accusations and to see some dignity in what she has done with her life: "Where I think you may be wrong is that you seem to be thinking that if you decide not to become one thing, the other thing you become has to be better" (205).

Kate and Maureen enter into a relationship of the sort that Anna forms with Saul, playing roles off one another in a way that enables them to extend the boundaries of their experience. Kate learns, both by observing Maureen and by interacting with her, something about herself. In Maureen she encounters a young woman facing the choices she herself faced—whether to marry and have children—and by understanding the constraints upon Maureen, she comes to understand those circumscribing herself and all women. Maureen knows how to say "no" and is free in ways Kate never was: her ability to change costumes, to move from role to role, represents "some kind of freedom" (212)—but still she is not free. She seems perversely drawn to the hyperfeminine, constrained styles of the past, and it never occurs to her to contemplate a future without a man (though each of the men she considers, the neofascist, the hippie, and the aristocrat, has obvious limitations). She is doomed to live through each stage of the life process, to endure it, as Kate herself has, as women in Lessing's fiction do;[10] and Kate dreams of her as a bird in a cage (208).

Playing off Maureen, responding to her needs, Kate is able to reenact the stages of her own life, but to a different end—to live through a kind of repetition with revision. In response to Maureen's "Tell me a story," Kate searches her memory for happiness ("It almost seemed as if the things she remembered were because of Maureen's interest—Maureen's need? It was Maureen who was doing the choosing?") and in the course of remembering things that had not "struck her before as important or even as interesting" (222), she remembers the good times in her marriage. She turns out to be remembering not only for Maureen but for herself, for these memories enable her to revise her view of her marriage as "black" and "ugly," "a web of nasty self-deceptions," and to arrive at other possible views: "For Michael had his difficulties too, she had not been remembering that"; "What it all amounted to was that because family life was difficult at times . . . because Kate played the role she had to, a mother who had to be resisted, fought, reacted against, because she wasn't always loved and appreciated, then she had to damn it all, see it all as black, as ugly. . . . Was that all it was?" (231–32)[11]

Kate puts an end to these happy memories, however, by telling Maureen about Mary Finchley and, in the course of this, understands some of "what Mary meant to her, what she was standing for" (94), "why . . . she [was] thinking so much about Mary" (35). Kate tells Maureen,

> It took me a very long time to understand that Mary was really quite different from me. From every woman I've known. . . . Something's been left right out of her. . . . Nothing has taken on Mary. She hasn't any sense of guilt—*that's* the point. We are all in invisible chains, guilt, we should do this, we must do that . . . Mary's isn't, it's been left right out of her.
>
> Love—all of it, romantic love, the whole bloody business of it—you know, centuries of our civilisation—it's been left out of her. She thinks we are all crazy. (225–26)

When Maureen asks angrily, "what do you want me to conclude from that?"—"what use is Mary to me or to you? She's no help at all" (230)—Kate at first replies, "I've never been able to conclude anything from it—except that she's quite different from me"; though she then goes on to describe how this view of Mary has changed: "At one time thinking of Mary was a kind of comfort and support—I'd think I'm much better and finer-feelinged and sensitive. . . . But now I wonder." From thinking of her as "quite different," firmly "other," she has begun to take her more seriously, to incorporate her perspective into her own:

> If you are with someone who really does think it is a joke, but really . . . then it's odd, it changes your perspective. There are times you know when there's a sort of switch in the way I look at things—everything, my whole life since I was a girl—and I seem to myself like a raving lunatic. (228–29)

Mary is what people might be without social conditioning, and Kate's education is a deconditioning that draws her closer to Mary. Like other doubles in contemporary women's fiction—Gerda in Gail Godwin's *The Odd Woman,* Jocasta in Margaret Atwood's *Bodily Harm,* Doreen and Joan in Sylvia Plath's *Bell Jar*—Mary represents a subversive potential, outspoken and cynical; but whereas most doubles remain "other" and protect the protagonist from the taint of the unconventional, Mary represents qualities Kate will incorporate: she changes her.

Kate, however, insists that it doesn't matter what she concludes, since it will all look different later—in a year the summer "will not seem anything like it did now. So why bother to assess and weigh?" (232). But this is not her last word, for when she is confronted with this same attitude from Maureen—"It doesn't matter a damn what you do. Or what I do" (242)—she bounces back, "I don't believe it." To Maureen's despair, Kate responds carefully, thoughtfully:

> Various arrangements of words suggested themselves, probably from newspaper leaders, then there was what she was thinking herself: Millions of people are dying, will die, perhaps you and me among them, but there's got to be some with cool heads to carry on. . . . What you are really looking for is a man who knows all the answers and can say, Do this Do that. There's no such animal. (243)

When confronted with the indifference and meaninglessness at the heart of the universe, the "terrible shrug of the shoulders" Anna meets in the depths of her breakdown, Kate's response is, like Anna's, to acknowledge "all right, I know you are there," but we still have to carry on. There may be no truth, no certainty, and any version of events may be qualified and disqualified by later versions, but we cannot abandon our efforts to know and to act. "Kate could not do anything for Maureen. But she had children: it would be nice to take them home presents" (243)—a gesture like Clarissa Dalloway's to decorate the dungeon with flowers. Besides, "this is what she was thinking herself"—this is her thought, her feeling, not an attitude taken down from a rack.

## Circular Returns

Though Kate does learn to see and to listen and to operate from her own choices, it is not clear that this provides a way out of her "cul-de-sac." Though she says "no" to a number of things, she is left at the end with no alternative but to return to the situation that has left her so wounded.

I find the ending hard to take, but I understand it and I respect it—precisely because it is hard and refuses the consolation of facile resolutions: no Nora slamming the dollhouse door, Kate does something more difficult, heroic precisely because it is so unheroic. The muted, understated quality of the ending—and of the novel itself—suggests that small, painful courage which Anna found so difficult.

Kate has arrived at a clearer sense of what she feels, given up on the idea of a man who knows all the answers or a convention that will provide her life shape and significance. As she is shopping for her children, she catches sight of her reflection in the shop window and sees that "her face had aged. Noticeably. . . . The light that is the desire to please had gone out. And about time too" (243). She has penetrated the veil of commonplace wisdom, seen through her dolled-up memories, and—hardest of all—she has recognized the triviality of her own story.

Kate's most important statement is made in her hair:

> Her discoveries, her self-definition . . . were concentrated here—that she would walk into her home with her hair undressed . . . like a statement of intent. . . . All her adult life . . . she had been in an atmosphere where everything was said. . . . She had lived among words. . . . But now that it was important to her, a matter of self-preservation, that she should be able to make a statement, that she should be understood . . . she was saying *no:* no, no, no, NO: a statement which would be concentrated into her hair. (244)

"No" is an assertion of boundaries and separation from others, important to one who was so close to her children that she felt "devoured" and so close to her husband that his infidelities made her feel like a doll losing its insides. Given the association of appearance with convention, the change in hairstyle is a serious statement (contrary to some readings of it).[12] It is also a nonverbal statement: whereas Anna gave up on the idea that visual image provided greater certainty, Kate finds significance in the nonverbal.

Also nonverbal is Kate's working through of her problems by means of the dream of the seal, "a dream that developed like a fable or myth" (128) and is "as much her business for this time in her life" as anything that happens to her: "What she was engaged in was the dream, which worked itself out in her" (129) and which provides a movement counter to the somewhat dismal return to her marriage. This dream begins when Kate takes the job at Global Foods, when she finds "a seal lying, stranded and helpless among dry rocks high on a cold hillside," and "she knew that she had to get it to water" (30). She loses the dream as she becomes embroiled with Jeffrey, dreaming instead of a turtle that loses its sense of direction—"she was in the wrong dream" (68). She retrieves the seal, but under ominous circumstances—in a northern landscape with "a low and sullen sun," "a small sun, it had no heat at all, everything was getting very dark" (119), and the dream warns her to leave Jeffrey: "The seal's life was very weak, she knew that" (130). She fights for the seal's life as she fights for her own, battling her illness as she tries to get it to the sea, to get it to water, as she tries to get herself back on course. The dream disappears when she arrives at Maureen's flat, when Kate takes over some of its unconscious work by her conscious interactions with Maureen, but it starts up again after she tells Maureen about Mary Finchley—and this time it appears alongside a "cherry tree in full bloom" (229): this is the "use" of Mary, the dark double whose subversiveness Kate incorporates.

Kate finishes the dream by returning the seal to the sea, where it swims off and joins its kind:

> The sea was full of seals swimming beside each other, turning over to swim on their backs, swerving and diving, playing. A seal swam past that had scars on its flanks and its back, and Kate thought that this must be her seal, whom she had carried through so many perils. But it did not look at her now.
>
> Her journey was over. (241)[13]

Having done this, however, she sees that "the sun was in front of her, not behind, not far behind, under the curve of the earth, which was where it had been for so long. She looked at it, a large, light, brilliant, buoyant, tumultuous sun that seemed to sing" (241). What is striking about this is that the end of the dream works counter to the coming of the dark that is the prognosis for Kate and for us all. Whereas Kate in her life has drawn boundaries and resigned herself to "the dark," Kate in her dream as the seal merges with the whole and is left staring at the sun: whereas on the external level Kate draws firmer ego boundaries, on the internal level she merges with the cosmic oversoul. This contradiction is understandable in view of Lessing's changed sense of the collective: Kate needs to defend herself against the sorts of conventions that represent the collective in its social manifestation, but she can risk merging with the collective as Lessing is reconceptualizing it—as a collective unconscious or universal oversoul. But the contradiction between internal and external developments, which was obscured by the fantasy of *Four-Gated City,* becomes glaring in the absence of fantasy: Kate is left practicing work on the inner life, while the world sinks into barbarism and bureaucracy.[14]

It is clear why Lessing's next move has to be to "another order of world altogether."[15]

*Chapter 8*

# *The Memoirs of a Survivor:* The Breaking of the Circle

> . . . a scene, perhaps of people in a quiet room bending to lay matching pieces of patterned materials on a carpet that had no life in it until that moment when vitality was fed into it by these exactly answering patches . . .
>
> —Doris Lessing, *The Memoirs of a Survivor*

To ask what is real in this novel—the realm behind the wall or what goes on in the flat—is to miss the point. To be troubled by these questions—what is the relationship of the realms, spatially, temporally, logically? whose childhood is the narrator remembering, or is she imagining what goes on behind the wall, or dreaming it, or is she mad?—is to remain stuck within a paradigm of knowledge the failure of which is Lessing's subject. Yet we cannot help asking such questions: the novel makes them irresistible. By engaging us with them and thwarting our efforts to answer them, by frustrating our usual modes of explanation, Lessing leads us to question not only the evidence of our senses but the paradigm of Western rationalism we've inherited to deal with experience.

Such questions are unanswerable because what is happening is "impossible" according to Western notions of time, space, and possibility. The rooms beyond the wall "occupy the same space" as the corridor beyond the wall,[1] yet Western science tells us that two objects cannot occupy the same space. The "personal" scenes beyond the wall are from Emily's past, "of course" (*Memoirs,* 45), yet they are chronologically too far back in the past to be from Emily's childhood. Such impossibilities have led some readers to reject the novel[2]—of all Lessing's works I think this has been the most unimaginatively read[3]—but if we can suspend disbelief, they may teach us to question our perceptual equipment and the spatial-temporal mold of Western empiricism and lead us to something new. To insist on realistic explanations is to be bound to an outmoded epistemology, to notions of possibility and probability that derive from the "scientific method"—which, as Francis describes it, "evolved centuries before, [and is] useful for some things, but useless for others,"[4] and which Lessing shows here to have run its course: "As for our thoughts, our intellectual apparatus, our rationalisms and our logics and our deductions . . . as we sit in the ruins of this variety of intelligence, it is hard to give it much value." Our kind of intelligence has proved bankrupt and dangerous—in fact, "the perceptions and understandings" of animals are "far in advance of" it (82).

Both the setting and the subject of this novel are the End. Set in "the protracted period of unease and tension before the end" (3), when "everything, all forms of social organization, broke up" (18), it is written from a time after the end, looking back on the end. Lessing takes us through the end, not only of our world, but of the "intellectual apparatus" that explains it and the conventions that express it—including the epistemological assumptions and narrative conventions of realism. *Memoirs of a Survivor* has the feel of "a letter to the past" (a term Lessing uses in the introduction to *The Golden Notebook*): "I write all these remarks with exactly the same feeling as if I were writing a letter to post into the distant past: I am so sure that everything we now take for granted is going to be utterly swept away in the next decade." Faced with this sense of final things, how does one write a novel, or indeed, why? (a question Lessing poses in the introduction to *The Golden Notebook:* "So why write novels? Indeed, why! I suppose we have to go on living *as* if . . .").[5] One response would be to stop writing novels—the response of the late Tolstoy; but Lessing's is to devise new fictional forms to express a new vision. Though *Memoirs of a Survivor* is unreadable within the conventions of realism, it teaches "a new imaginative comprehension" (as it is termed in *The Golden Notebook* [61]), "a new kind of knowledge" (as it is termed in *Landlocked* [157]), which is beyond language and logic and the forms into which Western rationalism pours experience. Like the Sufi teaching fable (as described by Nancy Shields Hardin), it " 'teach[es]' a shift in perspective from a more logical linear mode of thought processes, which we of the Western world have been taught to hold in the highest esteem, to a more intuitive perception."[6] As elsewhere in Lessing's fiction, this entails not only a shift from linear to circular modes but also a breaking of the closed, vicious circle of determinism for an open form that accommodates change.

## Last Days

The novel begins plausibly enough, in the final days of our civilization amidst "the general break-up of things" (29), depicting events become even more plausible in the three decades since its publication—events that seem an all too probable "development of what is already happening and what has been accelerating, out of control" (in the terms of Mark's "Memorandum to Myself" [*FGC,* 525]). The title "memoirs" anchors the novel in realism, as does the term *history*—"This is a history, after all, and I hope a truthful one" (110). Lessing, on the dustjacket of the original edition, referred to this novel as "autobiography," and though this seems an odd term, since it does not resemble autobiography in any obvious sense, it is an accurate term, as will become clear. *History* is also an odd term, considering that the work is set in the future, and *hope,* an even odder term for this spectacle of the destruction, the collapse, of all systems—social, economic, political, ecological. Nothing works, services have ground to a halt, gangs and marauders roam the streets, food has become scarce and illness is everywhere, the environment having become toxic and the air unbreathable. A government still exists, but it does nothing but interfere, intermittently and ineffectually, in the new social arrangements that spring up in spite of it; and administrative agencies exist, yet they do nothing but "talk."

Anchoring her narrative in "history," Lessing gains our assent. But the narrator tells us that the quality of life at this time combines the "extraordinary" with the "ordinary" (18), "the bizarre, the hectic, the frightening, the threatening . . . with what was customary, ordinary" (19)—terms that apply not only to the quality of life but to the novel itself, with its mingling of the familiar and the fantastic: "Yes, it was extraordinary. Yes, it was all impossible. But, after all, I had accepted the 'impossible.' I lived with it" (18). Thus does the narrator explain the sudden and inexplicable arrival of Emily in her life: "In such an atmosphere, in a time of such happenings, that an unknown man should arrive in my home with a child, saying she was my responsibility, and then leave without further remark, was not as strange as all that" (21).

This intermingling of the extraordinary and the ordinary makes the point that the world we think of as real is actually quite fabulous:

> For instance, on the newscasts and in the papers they would pursue for days and days the story of a single kidnapped child. . . . But the next news flash would be about the mass deaths of hundreds, thousands, or even millions of people.

> We still believed, wanted to believe, that the first—the concern about the single child, the need to punish the individual criminal . . . was what really represented us. (19)

"Or what can one say about the innumerable citizens' groups that came into existence right up to the end, for any ethical or social purpose you could think of," organizing meetings "about the 'decay of family life,' about 'immorality,' about 'sexual indulgence.' This was comic, of course. Unless it was sad. Unless . . . it was admirable" (20–21). This is typical of the way statements in this novel qualify and revise themselves, allowing us several possible attitudes—is it comic, sad, or admirable, this belief that individual actions matter, that old values still apply, this belief that persists against all evidence to the contrary: "Spitting into a hurricane; standing in front of a mirror to touch up one's face or straighten a tide as the house crashes round one" (21).

"This is the sort of thing we accepted as normal. Yet for all of us there were moments when *the game we were all agreeing to play* simply could not stand up to events: we would be gripped by feelings of unreality, like nausea," the "feeling, that the ground was dissolving under our feet" (19). Lessing posits, again, contradictory possibilities: is it reality that is "the enemy" or is it the sense of unreality that is the enemy and the adherence to decorum that is the necessary and saving grace, even if it is only a game[7]—like the forms Anna comes to understand as essential to survival? Whichever is true, the sense of unreality becomes overwhelming and produces a widening gap between personal and public versions: "It was not from official sources that we were getting the facts which were building up into a very different picture from the publicized one"; "we apprehended what was going on in ways that were not official" (4–5). The situation is like Kate's at the beginning of *Summer,* when she is faced with a sense of a widening rift between the conventional attitudes allotted her and "what she was really feeling"—and here, as in that novel, the space provides the opening for a new kind of understanding. If we can acknowledge the unreality of the so-called real, if we can accept this bizarre and fantastic world we live in, what is to prevent our assent to "another order of world altogether"?

The structure of *Memoirs of a Survivor* involves complex and unsettling play with space and time. The novel takes place in three spaces: a "comfortable, if shabby flat" (11) where the personal lives of the characters are played out; outside, on the street, where the narrator observes "the public, outer life" (18), the life of the collective; and behind the wall, which represents the inner life, an inner reality in touch with a "collective" of a different sort from the social—the collective consciousness of the race, or universal oversoul. Most of the novel takes place in the flat, whose window offers a view of the life outside, through which the narrator observes the formation of new social units, the tribes that migrate off to unknown destinations, and from which she occasionally ventures forth herself, on excursions through devastated neighborhoods or a visit to Gerald's commune. What goes on in these realms is generally explicable within conventional notions of time and space—except perhaps for the mysterious appearance of Emily in the narrator's life, along with the impossible Hugo, half-dog and half-cat; and except for the way time is speeded up, so that Emily moves with impossible rapidity through "chrysalis after chrysalis" (60), hurtling from first love to middle-aged jadedness—an acceleration matched by the rapid formation and dissolution of social arrangements, processes of creation and destruction that occur with similarly impossible speed. Though again, this accelerated change is merely an extension of "what is already happening," of the processes dramatized in *The Four-Gated City,* fantastic but actual.

It is when the narrator moves to the realm beyond the wall that our customary notions of reality are strained. Here she encounters first the spacious possibilities of the "impersonal" realm and then is made to live through the "prison" of the personal—to relive scenes in the coming of age of a girl. The narrator's means for moving beyond the wall are primarily "watching and waiting" (81)—"simply waiting. I watched to see what would happen next. I observed. I looked at every new event quietly, to see if I could understand it" (102)—and listening: "I sat listening" (148). (This becomes especially apparent in the film version, where the viewer is aware of how much we simply watch the protagonist, played by Julie Christie, who is herself "watching and waiting," and we realize how little she actually does; this inactivity is something else that has troubled readers.[8]) Yet this passivity becomes potent, since it is her ability to wait out events while being compassionately involved with them, her wise receptivity and attentiveness, that enable her to develop the strengths to lead the characters of her world "into another order of world altogether." Like Martha, she develops extrasensory powers by opening herself to the experiences of others; and in the same way that Martha's moving between Lynda's basement and Mark's study represents her negotiation of personal and public, individual and collective, and becomes her means of holding the Radlett Street house together, so too does the narrator's movement among the various spatial and temporal realms of *Memoirs* perform a "holding operation" for her world.

Betsy Draine sees the novel as a "failure" because Lessing has mismanaged its "shifting frames": "Throughout the novel, the narrator negotiates frequent shifts between these two radically incompatible universes"; no sooner has the reader settled into a "realistic" frame "than an alternative frame presents itself—a mystic or mythic dimension in which the laws of time and space are suspended." Draine finds these shifts impossible to follow because she feels that the mythic dimension is insufficiently vivified; she is unconvinced by what she calls "a most unpersuasive prose style," "toneless and unaffecting," filled with "inarticulate gropings and repetitions."[9] But I find them enormously effective, partly because I find the style persuasive and partly because I find the process of disorientation and readjustment interesting and instructive: to ask the relationship of things, to ascertain the connections, is to exercise the imaginative faculty that can rebuild the world. When the narrator becomes aware of "the growth of that other life or form of being behind that wall," of "that other life, developing there so close to me" (7)—"I even found I was putting my ear to the wall, as one would to a fertile egg, listening, waiting" (12)—she wonders about the "link" (25), the "connection" (40) between this life and her own[10]—and the novel teases the reader also to wonder about this connection. Images of gestation—the egg, "a weight redistribut[ing] itself, as when a child shifts position in the womb" (12)—connote new life; and we, like the narrator, like Martha, must submit to a process of gestation that will germinate a wise receptivity in us, that will teach us to see and listen and imagine a way out.

At first when the narrator finds herself behind the wall, she wanders blissfully, aimlessly, in a realm of lightness and freedom, where all she had ever yearned for seemed capable of fulfillment—"it held what I needed, . . . had been waiting for, all my life" (13). She names it the "impersonal." This realm consists of spacious, high-ceilinged rooms, in disarray and often in ruins, which she must repair and then repair again, for she returns to the rooms to discover that they've been trashed in her absence.[11] Yet

> the impersonal scenes might bring discouragement or problems that had to be solved—like the rehabilitation of walls or furniture, cleaning, putting order into chaos—but in that realm there was a lightness, a freedom, a feeling of possibility. Yes, that was it, the space and the knowledge of the possibility of alternative action. (42)

The narrator is struck by "how much work needed to be done," yet always there is "a sweetness . . . a welcome, a reassurance. Perhaps I did see a face, or the shadow of one"—and increasingly, the "promise" is imagined as a mysterious presence, an "exiled inhabitant": "The face I saw clearly later was familiar to me. . . . This was the rightful inhabitant of the rooms behind the wall" (14). Later, the walls of these rooms dissolve, to reveal the abundance of nature, the boundless gardens of the old world: "Straying through room after room all open to the leaves and the sky, floored with the unpoisoned grasses and flowers of the world, I saw how extensive was this place, with no boundaries or end that I could find" (100–101). Its boundlessness is suggested by the "gardens beneath gardens, gardens above gardens; the food-giving surfaces of the earth doubled, trebled, endless—the plenty of it, the richness, the generosity" (161).

After Emily appears in her life, however, the narrator is made to enter a personal realm that intrudes on her joyous experience of the impersonal, and is forced to relive the oppressive scenes of a childhood. In this personal realm, which is governed by "child time" and by strict, unalterable laws of necessity, the narrator follows scenes in a life from early childhood through age fourteen, the age Emily is when she is presented to the narrator. Though these scenes take place in a time too remote to be from Emily's childhood, the narrator insists that they are from Emily's childhood: "The small child was of course [Emily]"; "I had been watching a scene from her childhood (but that was impossible, of course, since no such childhood existed these days; it was obsolete): a scene, then, from her memory, or her history, which had formed her . . ." (45–46; ellipsis in original), from "a hinterland which had formed her." The idea of inevitability is stressed by the reiteration of the word *formed,* and the narrator adds, "from that shadowy region behind her came the dictate: *You are this, and this and this—this is what you have to be, and not that*" (94). Though in terms of conventional chronology, "that was impossible, of course"—we are given the pieces of an "impossible puzzle" and are left trying to piece together the relationship between Emily's past, the narrator's, and Lessing's.

However impossible the chronology, the scenes depicted in the personal realm are entirely possible, familiar to the point of tedium, conventional to the point of cliché—the ambiguously sexual, absent-present father; the child made to feel guilt for her very existence, blamed by a mother who does not begin to understand her own misery because she imagines she has chosen her life:

> She was trapped, but did not know why she felt this, for her marriage and her children were what she personally had wanted and had aimed for—what society

> had chosen for her. Nothing in her education or experience had prepared her for what she did in fact feel, and she was isolated in her distress and her bafflement, sometimes even believing that she might perhaps be ill in some way. (70)

The personal is a prison in that it admits no possibility of alternative action: "To enter the 'personal' was to enter a prison, where nothing could happen but what one saw happening, where the air was tight and limited and above all where time was a strict unalterable law and long" (42); "this was . . . claustrophobia, airlessness, a suffocation of the mind, of aspiration. And all endless" (43). This is endlessness of a quite different sort from the boundlessness of the impersonal realm; this is the endlessness of repetition, where all that can happen is what is already happening. The personal is also a prison in that it locks the individual into the defenses Emily has had to develop against guilt at being born. Observing Emily on the street, the narrator is struck by how isolated she seems (71), and observing her responses to others, she realizes "what a prison we were all in" (31).

In the scene the narrator labels "Guilt," the pronoun shifts from *she* to *I,* from Emily to the narrator, in a way that suggests that what is being recalled is from the narrator's own past:

> The hard accusing voice went on and on, would always go on, had always gone on; nothing could stop it, could end these emotions, this pain, this guilt at ever having been born at all, born to cause such pain and annoyance and difficulty. The voice would nag on there forever, could never be turned off, and even when the sound was turned low in memory, there must be a permanent pressure of dislike, resentment. Often in my ordinary life I would hear the sound of a voice, a bitter and low complaining just the other side of sense . . . still there, always there. . . . (71)

Yet when the narrator finds the child she hears wailing behind the wall—wailing for being beaten because it has eaten its own excrement—the child turns out to be not Emily, but Emily's mother:

> I never found Emily. But I did find . . . the thing is, what I did find was inevitable. I could have foreseen it. The finding had about it . . . the banality, the tedium, the smallness, the restriction of that "personal" dimension. . . . Who else could it possibly be but Emily's mother? . . . Up went the little arms, desperate for comfort, but they would be one day those great arms that had never been taught tenderness. (151)

That the sobbing child turns out to be not the child but the mother epitomizes the endless tedium of this process—unloved daughters make unloving mothers who produce unloving daughters who become unloving mothers, and so on; and the child eating its excrement is an apt image for this self-enclosed, stifling circularity. This is the "nightmare repetition," the "nightmare of fated and recurring evil" that Martha dreads. Nor is it anyone's fault—behind one inadequate mother is another, and so on and so on, and "none of them could help themselves" (45). Finally, it does not matter whose past we are reliving: it is our past, it is everyone's, and without some break in the circle, it will be our future as well, and the future of our children.

That Lessing's mother and grandmother were both named Emily suggests why *autobiography* is a relevant term. Indeed, Lessing has already written much of this story in *Children of Violence*. Emily is—like Martha, like Lessing—born old; she begins life with a sense of weariness that she has to go through it: "Her face was old and weary. She seemed to understand it all, to have foreseen it, to be living through it because she had to. . . . Time, through which she must push herself till she could be free of it" (45). The relationship between mother and daughter replays that between Martha and Mrs. Quest, which is also that between Lessing and her mother—which Lessing describes vividly, poignantly, in the essays in *Granta*.[12] Emily's pert, chattering little style, her hard, bright, vivacious shell, is the persona "Matty" that Martha develops as a defense against her mother. Lessing thus condenses her autobiography and speeds it up—we observe it as though through the wrong end of a telescope and move through it as though on fast-forward; but she contextualizes it so as to suggest a way out, by making it only one element, one piece of the puzzle. Our attempts to make temporal connections, to make sense of the chronology, are thwarted, though also weirdly satisfied, when we realize that all are one: Emily, the narrator, Lessing, ourselves; that we are reliving a personal past that is also a generalized past, the experience of "a woman of our time."

Our efforts to figure out the spatial and logical relationships are similarly baffled, and satisfied, when the narrator realizes that, as dissimilar as the personal realm behind the wall and the anarchy on the street seem to be—as apparently disconnected as the stifling order imposed by the family and the disarray of society—the one follows inexorably from the other. This becomes clear in the discussion the narrator has with Emily about Gerald's commune. When Emily complains that the children have made her and Gerald into authority figures, contrary to what they had intended in building the commune—"We had everything so that we could make a new start" (133)—

the narrator tries to explain the connection between peoples' personal conditioning, the conditioning that takes place in the family (particularly vivid to her because she has been reliving the scenes behind the wall), and the children's insistence on a "pecking order." "It starts when you are born. . . . She's a good girl. She's a bad girl . . . *Don't you remember?*"—

> On the one hand, "you're a good little girl a bad little girl," and institutions and hierarchies and a place in the pecking order; and on the other, passing resolutions about democracy, or saying how democratic we are . . . all that has happened is what always happens. (132–33)

As in the family, where nothing can happen but what is already happening (42), so too in the social order, for the conditioning that occurs in the personal realm assures that in the public realm "all that has happened is what always happens"—the tautology turning back on itself in a closed circle. Human beings produced by the prison of the family are incapable of making a free society, and the ruined garden of Gerald's commune represents the impossibility of making anything new from existing social conditions: you can't get there from here.

The impossibility of getting there from here is further suggested by the Ryan family, which represents the sort of extended, communal arrangements becoming frequent amidst the general breakdown. The Ryans are unassimilable in terms of conventional paradigms of family or society, but they might conceivably hold out the possibility of a sort of compromise between the prison of the family and total anarchy: their loose family structure provides some support for its members while also allowing more flexibility than allowed by the nuclear family; and the Ryans represent, in their communal sharing, their poverty, their ability to live in the present time, what the narrator terms the values of the saints. Yet when June Ryan leaves, suddenly and inexplicably taking off on a migration without even saying good-bye to Emily or the narrator, her behavior shows only a chilling "inconsequence," different in degree but not in kind from the principle of inconsequence that characterizes the behavior of the new gangs of children. The new gangs of children, who have grown up entirely outside the family, are also beyond all appeal, to reason, punishment, kindness, even self-interest; they are driven by pure, uninhibited aggression. It would seem, then, that though life within the family is crippling, life outside it is worse—as is of course corroborated by studies of children raised in institutions. The destruction of the family brings not "freedom" but anarchy: the release from "necessity" produces not liberation but "inconsequence."

"Stale social patterns" persist even in the midst of the destruction of everything, absurdly anachronistic, obsolete, dysfunctional, yet intransigent:

> Old thoughts, about stale social patterns. Yet one had them, they did not die. Just as the old patterns kept repeating themselves, re-forming themselves even when events seemed to license any experiment or deviation or mutation, so did the old thoughts, which matched the patterns. (136)

Emily assumes her woman's place and prefers to be Gerald's woman rather than a leader in her own right—which is what prompts the narrator to say "this is a history" (110). She lives through "'the first love' of tradition" (84), "feeling as girls traditionally did," and then through the stages of a "woman in love"—"what she wanted was inappropriate. . . . She was an anachronism" (86), "her emotions had not accommodated change" (99).

This is why the move forward is actually a move backward: though hurtling ahead with precipitous speed, this world is also returning "to an earlier time of man's condition" (99), "reverting to the primitive" (105). Both personal and collective speed into a future that is also the past, time circling back on itself. Nor is this a redemptive return to the past, but a circle of repetition become even more nightmarish and frenetic the faster it moves. Against this, the timeless space behind the wall, the realm of myth, archetype, and the impersonal, emerges the more attractively, compellingly.

The narrator realizes that she wants something new for Emily: "What I was really waiting for . . . was the moment she would step off this merry-go-round, this escalator carrying her from the dark into the dark. Step off it entirely. . . . And then?" (94; ellipsis in original). Both "merry-go-round" and "escalator," both circular and linear processes, are inexorable, destructive, and lead only to the "dark." Nothing new can come from the life of society or the personal realm that shapes it.

## New Beginnings

"And then?" How to step off this merry-go-round and get from this dark place to the light? from this prison to freedom? How to break the circle, or, rather, to transform the closed, nightmarish circle to an open liberatory form that admits something new? How to transform a dead end to boundlessness—to remake the ruined garden of Gerald's commune into the paradisical gardens beyond the wall?

In part it is nature that provides example of the generosity and abundance, the rejuvenating processes that are occurring even in the midst of destruction. Even when things are at their worst, "where we were was alive," and the narrator is reluctant to leave because the new growth springing up through the cracks in the pavement is a promise of new life:

> The old city, near-empty as it was, held people, animals, and plants which grew and grew, taking over streets, pavements . . . forcing cracks in tarmac, racing up walls . . . life. When the spring came, what a burst of green life there would be, and the animals breeding and eating and flourishing. (211)

This time of "watching and waiting" is also a time of ferment, "when everything is in change, movement, destruction—or reconstruction" (81). But nature alone cannot yield what is needed—new social arrangements require culture, cultivation, and the imagination of alternative possibilities.

It is the impersonal realm that presents "the possibility of alternative action," but this realm is difficult to describe. It is rendered imagistically, by metaphors and allusions replete with ancient and powerful associations—the walled garden with the stream running through it, the "gardens beneath gardens, gardens above gardens," the mysterious presence the narrator keeps sensing, which she can only glimpse out of the corner of her eye. Visual images are the language of dreams and the unconscious, as Freud tells us, and Lessing uses them here to evoke a rich underworld of the unconscious. The ineffability of this realm is suggested by frequent ellipses and qualifications—"it was as if"; "but no, I did not see that." Draine dismisses these as "inarticulate gropings" but they seem to me perfectly understandable attempts to express the inexpressible, to reach beyond language, necessary because language is another convention bound to the epistemological paradigm that the novel repudiates.

But how to get there from here? How to translate symbol to action and actuality? When the narrator protests, outraged at the unfairness that the man who left Emily left no instructions, that she must carry on without knowing the rules—"I didn't know if I was doing the right thing"—in response to her confusion, the wall opens up to reveal a six-sided room containing figures at work on a carpet, engaged in efforts that bring the pattern in the carpet to life. The carpet is initially "without . . . life"; though "it had a design, an intricate one," its "colours had an imminent existence, a potential, no more" (79).

The "work" consists of finding pieces of material that match with a part of the pattern, and this matching of the part with the whole brings the carpet to life, fulfills its potential: "It was like a child's game, giant-sized; only it was not a game; it was serious, important not only to the people actually engaged in this work, but to everyone"—important also because "there was no competition here, only the soberest and most loving co-operation." This mysterious scene offers an image of loving and cooperative effort that will go on, independent of anyone's individual will: "I left that tall room whose ceiling vanished upwards into dark where I thought I saw the shine of a star, a room whose lower part was in a bright light that enclosed the silent concentrated figures like stage-lighting," "but I knew it was there waiting; I knew it had not disappeared, and the work in it continued, must continue, would go on always" (80–81). The figures, silent and concentrating, the intricately patterned carpet, the shine of the star, recall scenes associated with the magi, the revelation of divinity—and this marvelously resonant scene does offer an epiphany, though not of an individual messiah but of a communal effort that will save us all.

But how to get there from here? Is there something we can do, some effort within our reach, some "small, painful courage" that will transport us to this visionary realm?

Lessing suggests that there is. The narrator guards Emily, who is given to her by a "guardian, protector, or whatever he was" (99), and Emily guards Hugo, and Hugo in turn guards Emily; and Gerald, "guardian of the young," remains stubbornly faithful to his savage children. The narrator believes that it matters that Emily care for Hugo, though he is only a dog: Emily couldn't abandon him without doing harm to herself (79), any more than Gerald could abandon the children without abandoning "the best part of himself" (213). It is this band of survivors—Emily, Hugo, Gerald, Gerald's children—who get through the wall, and they do so because they fulfill their responsibilities toward one another; and the children get through because of the strength of Gerald's caring. This is the loving, cooperative effort symbolized by work on the carpet, the forms it is necessary to observe—not a game, though perhaps like a game in the apparent arbitrariness of its moves, but serious, and important to everyone.

As in *The Four-Gated City,* the way to the city is a journey within, and as in that novel, the protagonist does not travel alone. The narrator's work on the inner life is symbolized by her efforts to make order in the rooms behind the wall and by her reliving of scenes from her past. When she first starts on this work she longs "simply to walk through the wall and never come back," but she realizes that "this would be irresponsible. It would mean turning my back on my responsibilities" (24). Like Martha, whose glimpse of the lit space and the spiral above at the beginning of *The Four-Gated City* is premature, who can't simply step off the cycle but must return and take others with her—the narrator must return because Emily has been entrusted to her. She can only escape time and history by living through time and history. This is the way off the merry-go-round into a realm of "alternative possibilities."

The focus of this novel is the life of the group, the "we" announced in the opening line—"we all remember that time." "We all" suggests that others have survived, and one of the mysteries of the novel is who these others are. One possibility is that they are those who disappear on the migrations, whom the narrator imagines as freed from "responsibility" (35): "Free. Free, at least from what was left of 'civilisation' and its burdens. Infinitely enviable, infinitely desirable, and how I longed simply to close my home up and go" (167). But freedom for Lessing is never attained by abjuring responsibility; it is only gained by adhering to responsibility—"But how could I? There was Emily. As long as she stayed, I would" (167). Going off with the tribes offers the kind of freedom Martha imagines she's found each time she joins up with a group—the Sports Club, the life in the town, the Communist party—which each time turns out to be only a release into pack mentality. But the narrator tells us that she sees all around her instances of "self-restraint, even a caring for others" (83), so presumably others have performed the kind of "mutual aid and self-sacrifice" (96) enacted by her, Emily, Hugo, and Gerald. This is perhaps the reason for her assurance, when she loses the room with the carpet in it, that the work would go on, must go on, always.

## "Our Future Like a Fable"

Draine criticizes the ending of the novel on the grounds that Lessing fails to make the realm behind the wall sufficiently vivid or emotionally interesting, that it never becomes compelling enough to make us relinquish our hold on the real and follow the characters there: "The reader, unwilling to accept the new frame as primary and unable to retreat into the old one (which has just disappeared) is forced to step outside both frames and disengage from the act of participation in the novel as world. This is experienced as a repudiation of the text as a whole."[13] What Draine finds "disengaging," however, I find engaging; and it's difficult to say why it works for me, but it does. It may be, as Draine says, that a reader finds it convincing if s/he's already convinced, but I am neither a mystic nor a Sufi nor a Christian, and I am convinced. (It worked for my students also, who were intrigued by the impossible Hugo, by the process of piecing things together—though it may have worked for them because it worked for me.) I find the language persuasive—the inarticulate gropings pointing beyond this reality to another, the imagery shimmering with new possibilities and resonant with old allusions, biblical and medieval, the generosity of the gardens recalling the Medieval doctrine of *"kynde."* Maybe since I approach this work from Medieval and Renaissance literature, these images have more resonance for me. I do not find the mysticism so bizarre: after all, it was only relatively recently that this world view fell into disrepute. I find pleasurable the process that the reading puts us through, and I like to think that what is pleasurable is also instructive—that by testing one reality off against the other and puzzling out the relationships between them, we develop the imaginative flexibility that enables us to follow the characters through the wall.[14]

The ending has the quality of fable, myth, fairy tale, folktale, romance. As in *The Four-Gated City,* the way forward is the way back, not only through one's personal past but through the collective past—back to the oldest knowledge of the race. (It is significant that when Emily arrived in the narrator's life, she had in her possession the Bible, some science fiction, and a book of photographs of animals [23].) This novel is fabulous in the sense that Shakespeare's late romances are: it presents a vision of life that is apparently unreal though ultimately more real than the world we inhabit, truer to our sense of rightness and fairness than the nightmare we are accustomed to imagine is the whole of reality. What Lessing asks us to do is release the universe from our limited and reductive conceptions of it, and I, for one, am willing. The ending asks us to accept "another order" of reality, to assent to "our future . . . like a fable where we would walk hand in hand, together. And then 'life' would begin, life as it ought to be, as it had been promised—by whom? When? Where?—to everybody on this earth" (34).

"Our future like a fable"? If the past is history, locked into the inexorable laws of cause and effect that fix and determine us, the future is "a fable," and the means to it is the means by which we respond to fable—wonder, awe, imagination. The novel asserts that the realm beyond the wall is finally more real than our so-called reality, the realm of causality and probability that is revealed to our senses and apprehended by our reason. It holds out a "blueprint for the future" like that which Anna imagines: "I was thinking that quite possibly these marvellous, generous things we walk side by side with in our imaginations could come in existence, simply because we need them, because we imagine them" (*GN,* 637). It offers a realm attainable by sober, collective effort—by those who have the imagination to work it through, to work it out, to work together. We are, reading this novel, like the figures working on the carpet: matching the piece with the pattern brings life to the whole, intricate design and is part of the serious, important work that will go on, that must go on, forever.

When the wall opens up, "and now it is hard to say exactly what happened," there appears "a giant black egg" around which "stood Emily, Hugo, Gerald, her officer father, her large laughing gallant mother, and little Denis, the four-year-old criminal, clinging to Gerald's hand": "There they stood, looking at this iron egg until, broken by the force of their being there, it fell apart." Out of its disintegration comes "a scene, perhaps of people in a quiet room bending to lay matching pieces of patterned materials on a carpet that had no life in it until that moment when vitality was fed into it by these exactly answering patches." As this world "folds up," "was vanishing, dwindling and going—all of it . . . the one person I had been looking for all this time was there: there she was":

> No, I am not able to say clearly what she was like. She was beautiful: it is a word that will do. I only saw her for a moment, in a time like the fading of a spark on dark air—a glimpse. She turned her face just once to me, and all I can say is . . . nothing at all. (216)

The broken phrases, ellipses, questions, qualifications, and retractions suggest that what happens is finally ineffable.[15] At the end of history we see face to face, but of the mysterious presence who is finally revealed, the narrator can say—"nothing at all." That the animating presence is "she" suggests, perhaps, the "good mother," the animating, nurturing principle of *kynde.* It revokes and reverses the nightmare repetition through which one bad mother produces another and so on indefinitely—this she restores those losses. As in Shakespeare's *Winter's Tale,* the restoration of the lost mother inspires a wonder that strikes dumb.

The novel leaves us with many unanswered questions: Who are the other survivors? How did they survive? What happens to those who migrated? And how exactly does the narrator get through the wall, since she seems to be, as usual, observing—it's not clear where she is positioned in relation to the scene she describes "while the world folded itself up" and Gerald, Emily, and Hugo "walked quickly behind that One who went ahead showing them the way out of this collapsed little world into another world altogether" (217). And that One, the mysterious she, "the *exiled* inhabitant" of the rooms (14)—is it the narrator's work on the rooms that has brought her home? And in bringing her home, does the narrator become her? If the narrator, like Emily, Hugo, and the others, is "transmuted into another key" (216), is she transmuted into her—the Good Mother, mother to us all, nurturing, hatching out the world of her creatures, as Martha did hers, as Lessing does hers?[16] And if so, what does this imply about the woman writer? There are finally no answers to these questions, there is only the asking.[17]

Like *The Four-Gated City,* this novel ends with the end of the world and a breakthrough to another world and way of knowing. But breakthrough does not require the breakdown of the individual, as in *Four-Gated City* and *Golden Notebook: Memoirs* suggests that we can get there from here by means less dire than madness. It suggests that something recognizably human, within our capacities, is of value—love, fidelity, responsibility. Like Shakespeare's romances, it acknowledges the worst in the world but transmutes it to "something rich and strange." It asks the same sorts of ultimate questions as *The Winter's Tale* and *Tempest*—what can endure the wreck of a lifetime, of a civilization?—and, acknowledging the worst, shores up something of value against the ruin. Part history, part autobiography, part fable and fantasy, and a curious blend of dystopia and utopia—it offers an elsewhere accessible to human capacities. It holds out the possibility that if we can read this novel imaginatively, sympathetically, we may follow Lessing's characters "out of this collapsed little world into another order of world altogether."

## Chapter 9

# Re: Colonised Planet 5, Shikasta: "After Long Circling and Cycling"

Things change. That is all we may be sure of.

—Doris Lessing, *Shikasta*

Everything changes in *Shikasta,*[1] and frequently—time and place, speakers, settings, cities, continents, planets, galaxies, eons. Like the planet Rohanda, like the universe itself, this novel is "sizzling with change" (14)—"this is a catastrophic universe, always; and subject to sudden reversals, upheavals, changes, cataclysms" (3). Lessing herself seems to have changed, for neither the form nor the content of this novel is like anything else she has written. She speaks of the "exhilaration" she felt turning to science fiction, at "being set free into a larger scope": "It was as if I had made—or found—a new world for myself" (xi).

Mona Knapp claims that Lessing is no longer using "literature as a consciousness-raising tool," but as an "escape from an altogether imperfect reality."[2] But in fact Lessing *is* still using fiction for purposes of consciousness-raising: what is different is that she has found in biblical history a way of mythologizing and also of defamiliarizing some familiar concerns—our defects of imagination and failure to know ourselves as part of one another and the universe, our "fall . . . into forgetfulness" (9). *Shikasta* is a creation myth of Miltonic scale and splendor, an epic that addresses—like *Paradise Lost* and *Paradise Regained*—the origin of evil and "all our woe":[3] only it combines Christian myth with a history of contemporary times and with future history. It takes dizzying leaps backward and forward in time, offering a perspective of ages and eons, then zeroing in on a few years in the life of one adolescent girl, Rachel Sherban—tunneling in and telescoping out, taking both "the long view" and "the near, the partial views" (170). It offers a mélange of genres and voices, from the impersonal, "objective" records of Canopus to the chatty diary of Rachel, and a range of tones from the detached to the denunciatory, soaring at times into powerfully moving laments for the human condition that resemble Old Testament exhortation. There is no literary precedent for it. There is nothing like it.

Its moves were too disorienting for most reviewers, and Lessing lost many readers over it,[4] but she is in some sense her own harshest critic—she calls it "a mess, but at any rate it is a new mess."[5] But I think it's magnificent—eloquent, inventive, passionate, compelling. Parts of it bring tears to my eyes, sorrow for my ruined planet and race, "creatures infinitely damaged, reduced and dwindled from their origins, degenerate, almost lost" (203). I find its roughness a pleasure and a challenge: the pleasure comes from piecing things together, recognizing the familiar in the strange, the strange in the familiar, as characters and events from biblical history turn up side by side with characters and events from our present time, together with beings from other planets and galaxies. Figuring out the relation of the parts is a "process of imaginative effort" (130), which is what is "needed" if we are to survive these "dreadful last days" (347): the novel puts us through a reading process that works, like the Canopean agents, to "heal [our] woeful defects of imaginative understanding" (349) and make us *"see things differently"* (254).

The "now" of the novel is time present, the "last days" just before the end—the time of *The Four-Gated City* and *Memoirs.* That Lessing feels compelled to return to this dreadful time of ours suggests, again, the need to re-cover this ground until it is recovered, the impulse to repeat in order to revise, to get it to come right. As an epic, *Shikasta* begins *in medias res* and moves back through events that have already occurred; and this epic convention suits Lessing well, for, as in *The Four-Gated City* and the *Children of Violence,* ends work back to beginnings in a circular pattern in which all has already happened. Here, too, the end is foretold in the beginning: the ten-page history of the "Century of Destruction," which recounts how each war brings a new "descent into barbarism" and how the rampant consumption of the planet is "built into the economic structure of every society" (89), points the way to the end of our world that occurs at the end of the novel, in famine, disease, and nuclear holocaust. But it also points the way to a time after the end, when Shikastans are "restored to themselves" and "wondered *why* they had been mad" (93), when, "after long circling and cycling" (202) we reach the end which is also the beginning in a circular return that is Alpha and

Omega: the cities are rebuilt, the lion lies down with the lamb—"And here we are all together, here we are."

## The Uses of Dismay

*Shikasta* is not an easy novel to read and not an easy novel to take. It teaches some hard lessons about "necessity"—about what is needed in these terrible times—and it's right that it be hard: "Dismay has its degrees and qualities. I suggest that not all are without uses" (3), as Johor tells us early on; later, he says that "the hidden power, or force" that drives Shikastans "nearer to self-knowledge, understanding" is never "'happiness' or 'comfort'" (175). This is a novel that dramatizes what Shakespeare, in *As You Like It,* termed "the uses of adversity," what King Lear terms "true need."[6] Since comfort and security are not what is needed—here, as in Shakespeare's tragedies, "security / Is mortal's chiefest enemy" (*Macbeth,* 3.5.32–33; p.1124)—it is right that this novel discomfort and unsettle, that it frustrate our attempts to settle in, that, by breaking narrative sequence and requiring us to engage and disengage and readjust our relation to events and the fictional frame, it make us work to construct meaning. Also, since consumption is at the heart of the rot of our civilization, it is right that this novel not be easily consumed but that it require thoughtful and energetic reconstruction.

*Shikasta* is also difficult to grasp in terms of its central doctrine, the coexistence of "freedom" with "necessity" and obedience to the whole. In the state of prelapsarian harmony Johor describes,

> everybody accepted that their whole existence depended on voluntary submission to the great Whole, and that this submission, this obedience, was not serfdom or slavery— . . . but the source of their health and their future and their progress. (26)

Some critics see such "submission" as "slavery": several object that it makes human beings into "mere pawns of Good and Evil, so thoroughly manipulated by these great abstract powers that human actions have no moral import at all."[7] Some compare Lessing's views unfavorably with Christian doctrine, seeing Lessing's vision as "morally inferior . . . to that of the Old Testament"—in that "every good development on earth is due to these heavenly visitants," her "philosophy . . . dwarfs the individual."[8] But in fact Christianity also makes good emanate solely from God and salvation depend solely on grace, even while it holds human beings accountable for their actions, and these positions involve it in some contradiction. When Milton wrote *Paradise Lost* "to justify the ways of God to man" (1.26, p.212), it was this paradox—the coexistence of man's free will with God's providential plan—that he was justifying: that God foreknew yet man is free, "sufficient to have stood, though free to fall." "If I foreknew," God says, "Foreknowledge had no influence on [human] faults / Which had no less prov'd certain unforeknown" (3.99 and 117–19, pp. 260–61). The Canopean doctrine of necessity no more precludes the idea of free will than Christian doctrine does.

But while Milton writes to justify the ways of God to man, Lessing writes to justify the ways of man to God: Johor's purpose is to demonstrate that Shikasta "*is* worth so much of our time and trouble" (3). Critics who object that the Canopean perspective "dwarfs the individual" overlook this. It is true that *Shikasta* punctures our inflated "ideas" of ourselves—"This planet knows nothing of the little scum of life on its surface," "this film of liquid that the profusion of life depends [on]"; it "has other ideas of itself" (5);[9] and true also that it posits a geography so radically redescribed as to reduce England to the status of "the northwest fringe." Nevertheless, this spectacle of Shikastans as "scuffl[ing] and scrambl[ing] and scurry[ing] among [our] crumbling and squalid artifacts" also shows us "reaching out" "to heights of courage and . . . *faith*" (203). Such heights are exemplified by Lynda Coldridge and others of the meek and downtrodden who provide instruction to Dr. Hebert and inspire his "testament of faith"—

> All these people can take weight, responsibility, burdens, difficulties, delays, the loss of hope. As we know, this is essential equipment for these hard times. . . . I want to say something to you that I regard as a testament, an act of faith! It is that if human beings can stand a lifetime of the sort . . . that it has been Mrs. Coldridge's lot to undergo . . . if we, the human race, have in us such strengths of patience and endurance, then what can we not achieve? (353)

Lynda demonstrates not only "what . . . is possible in a human being," but what is "essential"—patience, endurance, responsibility. Thus Lessing faces a challenge similar to Milton's in *Paradise Lost,* a version of his problem of making Christianity heroic, of adapting the conventions of classical epic to dramatize inherently undramatic Christian virtues of humility, obedience, and meekness: Lessing similarly needs to make glorious the inglorious qualities of patience, endurance, and compassion.

The difficulties are apparent from the outset. We enter the world with Johor, a Canopean agent who is, as Draine says, less a character than a "presiding presence" (151). Jeannette King points out the echo of "Yahweh" in Johor and describes the effects of this beginning:

> Instead of beginning with an individual human experience, taking place in a world recognizably our own, this novel confronts us with an alien universe, and a disconcertingly remote narrator. . . . The reader's perspective is . . . wrenched into an unfamiliar alignment with another, by which our own world and its assumptions are made to appear not only lacking but incomprehensible.[10]

We not only enter the world with an alien; we are confronted with a chronology that defies human comprehension: "And so, returning again after an interval—but is it really so many thousands of years?" (4). As in *Paradise Lost,* we first glimpse our world through the eyes of an alien—and Johor's cosmic journeys recall Satan's trips through hallucinatory landscapes[11]—only here the alien is not the enemy of our race but a friend. We are plunged into "a hard place, full of dangers" (5), a limbo or purgatory full of "chimeras, ghosts, phantoms, the half-created and the unfulfilled" (6) pressing against Shikasta to be reborn.

Starting *in medias res,* then, we begin with Johor's third "mission" (6)—the third for him, that is, though the first for us; immediately after which, Johor recalls his first trip, "in the First Time, when this race was a glory," and recounts the evolution of life, hastened by a "blast of radiation" and a Canopean "booster" (14–15), the establishment of the Lock between Canopus and the people of Rohanda, the building of the cities according to "the closeness, the match, between individual and surroundings" (32), the paradise where humans lived in "the strong quiet purpose which I have always found to be evidence, anywhere— . . . of the Necessity" (33). Johor then proceeds to describe the disturbance of the Lock by the malalignment of the stars and the invasion of Shammat, the destruction of harmony and the desolation of paradise—"This paradise . . . is where now lie deserts and rock, sands and shales. . . . Ruins are everywhere" (30)—and the ruin of our intelligence, our falling off into the degenerative disease, against which the codification of Canopean knowledge in the form of the Ten Commandments (62) shores up such understanding as remains. After which, we leap forward thirty thousand years ("I now return to my visit in the Last Days" [74]), a leap forward that is also a return to the beginning of the novel and to "now," "these terrible end days" (197). Again the return—again and again—to "now."

We have heard that "Taufiq had been captured" (6), and we now turn to Taufiq, who is, in his Shikastan incarnation, John Brent-Oxford, a lawyer led astray from his Canopean mission by the temptation to prideful involvement in "political" causes; we then move to the ten-page history of the Century of Destruction. Then, in one of the most dizzying leaps in this novel, we return to "penultimate Time" and reports by Taufiq on postlapsarian events—the earth shifting on its axis, the Flood, the Covenant, Babel, the choice of the chosen people—all of which prompts Taufiq's request, "I again apply for transfer from Shikastan service" (101), eloquent in its understatement. We then proceed to Johor's second trip, at the time of Abraham and the destruction of the cities (104–8), including a five-page official history of the "period of public cautioners" or prophets—and again, a spectacle of devastation, the laying waste of the cities: "Deserts lie where those cities thrived" (108). We then leap forward in time, to now, to an account of "individuals who, if Taufiq had not been captured, would have been in very different situations" (113) and a continuation of contemporary records, with "illustrations: the Shikastan Situation," which include a portrait of the artist (114) and a portrait of the father of the artist (the one-legged farmer in southern Africa [160–62]), of Patty Hearst and the Baader-Meinhof gang. Spliced into this is another hallucinatory journey through Zone Six, which turns out to be not another journey but the same journey with which the novel began, a harrowing traversing of "shivering and swirling sands" (147) that coalesce into treacherous whirlpools—"a vast whirlpool, all the plain had become one swirling centrifuge, spinning, spinning . . . some appalling necessity was dragging and sucking at this place" (149).

From the suck and swirl of these forces—the most sinister circles in Lessing's fiction—Johor is rescued by an eagle (an eagle also guides Dante out of hell), in whose care he leaves Ben and Rilla. These scenes are interspersed with "Additional Explanatory Information" on the Generation Gap and the most amazing passage in the book, which asks us to bore into the molecular structure of a leaf and contemplate a universe like a "roaring engine" of change in which Shikastans nevertheless rise to heights of dignity and courage—another testimony to faith, this time Johor's. Thence follows another journey through Zone Six, which is again the same journey with which we began, during which Johor picks up Ben and Rilla to take them back to Shikasta. This journey ends as they enter flesh, about to be reincarnated as George, Rachel, and Ben:

> In a thundering dark we saw lying side by side two clots of fermenting substance, and I slid into one half, giving up my identity for the time, and Ben slid

> into the other, and lay, two souls throbbing quietly inside rapidly burgeoning flesh. . . . The terrible miasmas of Shikasta close around me. (210)

So by the middle of the novel, we have returned, after long circling and cycling, to the beginning.

But with the double line on page 210, we lose the presiding consciousness of the novel: Johor is reborn as George, though we reemerge not into George's consciousness, but into that of his sister, Rachel, whose journal recounts their growing up. This part of the novel proceeds more chronologically and comprehensibly, but since Rachel's perspective is partial and limited, it presents us with other problems of interpretation: we see things from her perspective, while also bringing to bear on her story the point of view we have learned from the first part of the novel, which means that we have a sort of double vision of her: her dashing off to save George looks different to us than it looks to her, and we are left to find our own meaning in her melodramatic suicide. We also have to piece together Chen Lieu's account of the Trial of the White Races and speculate why the mock trial dispelled the rumor of the extermination of the European populations. Finally, at the end, George disappears, Rachel dies, and we're in the consciousness of Kassim, one of the children rescued by George, from whose point of view we witness the rebuilding of the cities: what has happened is that the Canopean perspective has yielded to the human, as the human perspective—the survivors' and ours—has expanded to encompass the Canopean.

Draine describes *Shikasta* as "a movement without end, an action without climax" and refers to the text's "refusal . . . to resolve into unity":

> As the book drifts to an end, with an instruction to consult other volumes of the archive, the reader is implicitly asked not to conclude, not to settle on a single perspective, but to sustain tentatively and simultaneously the appreciation of both the science fiction saga still in progress and the spiritual fable that has only begun to be developed. (160)

But actually the ending is unusually unambiguous for Lessing: though the evolution is on-going and uncompleted, since "the object and aim of the galaxy . . . [is] ever-evolving" (35), there is little doubt about what has happened. The old cities are rebuilt in a way that suggests that the Lock is back in place, that Shikastan minds are back in harmony with the purpose. This is the clarity of "divine comedy," where we emerge from a past that was "a thick ugly hot darkness" (364), into the light and new beginnings: "It is Paradise nowe" (354).

## Saving Graces

But if the overall plan and purpose are clear, what is less clear is our part in this scheme—what is to be done, how we should behave in these terrible last days, in order not only to survive but to salvage something of value. This is a message that needs some teasing out, for it is not so simple as that propounded by *Paradise Lost,* "the sum of wisdom" stated by Milton's Adam:

> Henceforth I learn that to obey is best,
> And love with fear the only God, to walk
> As in his presence, ever to observe
> His providence, and on him sole depend.
>
> (12. 561–64, p. 467)

While Milton and Lessing would agree that blessed are the meek, their reasons for believing this are quite different.

Lessing has set herself the hardest of tasks, to write a novel that engages without recourse to the usual means of engagement—identification with striking individuals who are brought into dramatic conflict over the things of this world—yet which nevertheless inspires us to feel for the human plight. Her task is to get us to feel deeply, for she knows that human beings do not learn where they do not feel, and to feel differently, to engage us emotionally about "voluntary submission to the great Whole" (26). So far is she from allowing us to "identify" with an individual that she hardly even allows us a human protagonist, for to identify with a striking individual would be to incriminate ourselves, to share the degenerative disease: "To identify with ourselves as individuals—this is the very essence of the Degenerative Disease, and every one of us in the Canopean Empire is taught to value ourselves only insofar as we are in harmony with the plan, the phases of our evolution" (38). Even what looks like a dramatic situation turns out not to be. "Taufiq's capture," for example, turns out to refer to his descent into mortal oblivion and his lapse from purpose, and lest we derive any suspense from Johor's "search for Taufiq," Johor tells us its outcome:

> I could foresee . . . that later in the frightful time in front of us, I, a young man, would confront [Taufiq] and say to him some exact and functioning words. An

> enemy—for he would be that for a time—would become a friend again, would come to himself. (82–83)

Whatever suspense this situation might hold is further dispensed with when their confrontation takes place off-stage, as it were; though we hear that Johor and Taufiq (George and John Brent-Oxford) meet at the Trial of the White Races and are much seen together (326), we never observe their meeting. Even death does not provide drama, since there is no death, only a movement to another state. Rather than drama and rhetoric, what Lessing offers is—"exact and functioning words": exact and exacting, functioning and functional.

The closest we come to identifying with an individual is with Rachel, and what her brief, unsatisfactory tale illustrates is how disastrous it is to identify with the individual and with the old conventions of heroism and histrionics: these are no longer what is needed. When we meet Rachel after the double line on p. 210, we welcome a human consciousness; as Draine says, "By this point in the narrative, we are starved for characters to follow consistently"[12]—though our hunger is hardly assuaged by the thin gruel of her story. Rachel is keeping her journal at the suggestion of Hassim, one of George's "friends," and that such friends all turn out to be Canopean representatives suggests that the journal will be "functional." And the record she keeps does turn out to be instructive, though more instructive for us than for her, for we have a perspective on it that she lacks, which we've gleaned from the first part of the novel; we read knowing who George is, what his mission is; we read knowing Rachel's history in Zone Six, scrutinizing her story for signs that she is passing or failing her test. We have become informed readers, have learned to see and hear in new ways—to hear double meanings, to see a variety of possible perspectives on an event.

In her efforts to record the truth, the facts, Rachel confronts many of the obstacles encountered by Anna Wulf. Like Anna, she writes to discover "what to think" (254). Like Anna she is dismayed by the unreliability of her thoughts: "If what we think now is different from what we thought then, we can take it for granted that what we think in a year will be different again" (224). Her awareness of the way emotions distort her perceptions, her sense of herself as "a sort of sack full of emotions" (255), recalls Martha's (*RS*,226). Her development recapitulates that of earlier Lessing protagonists, only like Emily in *Memoirs,* she moves through the stages more rapidly and efficiently. She can reject the conventional female roles, partly because she feels them as "a terrible snare or trap" (243) and partly because she realizes that biological motherhood is no longer what is needed: "I don't want it. How could I want to be grown-up and marry and have six kids and know they are going to die of hunger or never have enough to eat?" (244). She is right, what is needed now is a generalized kindness and caring for the children who already exist—which George gives her an opportunity to exercise when he brings home two children for her to "look after" (276), Kassim and Leila, whom he has rescued from the childrens' camps. Like the protagonist of *Memoirs,* Rachel feels inadequate to the task, but when she draws back from it George warns her to toughen up (267): "If you can't face all this, then you'll have to come back and do it all over again. Think about it" (270).

After George leaves Rachel begins to drift toward death, and it is Suzannah who takes over responsibility for the house. Finally, Rachel rushes off after George to save him, against his command that she stay and care for the children, and is arrested and commits suicide—"theatrical events" (294) that are not only not needed, but disastrous. Comment on suicide has been provided by Olga: "There is evidence to suggest that there is hell to pay. Literally. But in any case, *we do not commit suicide*" (256–57). "Hell to pay" is one of those clichés that turn out to have an exact and functional meaning. George's words when he hears of Rachel's death, "Well, better luck next time" (300), are also exact and functional—Rachel will have to return to Zone Six and endure another round of Shikasta because she hasn't managed to "toughen up" and work herself free; she has shirked the hard way for the easy way of martyrdom and heroics and has succumbed, again, to the miasma of Shikasta. It is Suzannah who, though more stolid and less intelligent, "more like a servant" (291), is what is needed; Suzannah, who is both "tougher" and "kinder" (and these terms recur in relation to her and recall Milt's description of Anna in *The Golden Notebook*) and is a "householder," literally, in that she stays behind and holds the house together. The only way to "freedom" is, as in the *Children of Violence,* "the hard way": "by enduring it, to be free of it forever" (*Shikasta,* 207, 9).

To identify with Rachel's heroics would be to incriminate ourselves of the degenerative disease, though actually, there is not much chance that we will do this: Lessing has not lavished the dramatic and rhetorical appeal on this character that Milton lavishes on Satan. But Milton enlists our identification with Satan, not because he is "of the devil's party," as some readers have claimed, but rather—as Stanley Fish demonstrates—as a rhetorical device calculated to teach us that we are fallen: insofar as we respond to Satan's histrionics, we demonstrate how ruined our hearts and minds are, how defective our wills and intelligence, how much we need grace.[13] Like

Milton, Lessing puts the reader through a series of responses that demonstrate the ruination of our faculties and emphasizes the need to renounce ego, but she deploys her rhetoric on the side she endorses—in Johor's laments for the human condition and exhortations to endurance and faith. Like *Paradise Lost, Shikasta* teaches us to feel differently and to strengthen the faculty that is the means to our restoration. But for Milton it is obedience that is the saving grace, our one hope of resisting the devil's snares, whereas for Lessing it is the creative imagination whereby we may repair our defective understanding—and to strengthen this, she appeals to poetry rather than renounces it. It seems to me that her vision confers greater dignity on human beings—it is less humbling, more enabling.

## The Uses of Irony

King claims that Johor shows no "subjective bias, and seems to have little interest in the usual concerns of the individual"—that he is "too disembodied, too removed from the world and assumptions of the reader" to provide "a focal point for his or her concerns."[14] But in fact Johor does become involved with what he describes, and his involvement is a source of considerable interest. The novel instructs us in the doctrine of "necessity," the governing principle of the Canopean universe (25–26; 33); but Johor devises "additional material"—since "*facts* are easily written down: atmospheres and the emanations of certain mental sets are not," he provides "sketches and notes made in excess of his mandate" (153–54), "setting down thoughts that perhaps fall outside the scope of the strictly necessary" to justify that Shikasta "*is* worth so much of our time and trouble" (3). This "additional material" is the most compelling writing in the novel, and its effects derive from Johor's engagement with his material, from a compassionate involvement with Shikastans that wells up in spite of himself, which is the more moving for his determined restraint and subordination of purpose to the whole. In this sense Johor does become a focal point for our concerns, and as he comes to share our perspective, we align ours with his, stretching our imaginations to attain the vision of Canopus.[15]

Johor's involvement emerges the more powerfully by virtue of its understatement:

> But the ability to cut losses demands a different type of determination from the stubborn patience needed to withstand attrition, the leaking away of substance through centuries, then millennia . . .

> Dismay has its degrees and qualities. I suggest that not all are without uses. The set of mind of a servant should be recorded. (3)

No headlong rush to judgment, this, but rather, the caution, the restraint: "Not all the degrees and qualities of dismay are without uses." The ambiguity of "a servant" makes it unclear who Johor is referring to, himself or us: *whose* losses need cutting, *whose* patience is required? And the ambiguity is purposeful and evidence of his identification with Shikastans, for both Johor and we are servants. The need to cut losses is Canopus's but "the stubborn patience needed to withstand attrition" is Shikasta's.

Johor's "Additional Explanatory Information" consists of two powerful, lyrical laments for the human condition which are the emotional center of the novel and are rhetorically in "excess" of what is "needed." Though rhetoric is debunked in this novel—in Ben's account of the political rhetoric deployed at the Trial of the White Races—as it is elsewhere in Lessing, particularly in *The Sentimental Agents* (the fifth of the Canopus novels), Johor's "additions" do not stint on rhetorical appeal.

The first of these passages describes the generation gap, the dislocation in human life due to our drastically shortened life spans (171–74). The sense in this passage is of time speeded up, hurtling toward the end, of a frenzy that makes for a desperate grab and snatch on the part of the young:

> They do not know what their own history is . . . they know nothing, understand nothing, but are convinced because of the arrogance of their education that they are the intellectual heirs to all understanding and knowledge. Yet the culture has broken down, and is loathed by the young. They reject it while they grab it, demand it, wring everything they can from it. And because of this loathing, even what is good and wholesome and useful left in traditional values is rejected. So each young person finds himself facing life as if alone. (172–73)

The disruption of natural temporal processes interrupts processes of germination and growth and, above all, of learning: the older generation is left, having "learned so much, so painfully, at such a cost to themselves and to others," unable to teach the young anything (174). George's dream of "a civilization once" that lasted the ages, in which there is time for sane and loving relations between parents and children and men and women, a civilization based on "close links with the stars and their forces" and with "necessity" (285–89), offers an image antithetical to this, the ideal against the actuality.

The second additional explanatory note describes Shikastans' attempts to find "some good or substance that will not give way as they reach out for it" (201), their frantic and failed efforts to find in ideologies (religion, nationalism, politics, science) some purpose larger than themselves, something solid to which the heart can cling, all of which turn out to be transient. Even what was once certain—pleasure in the young, in the nourishment of food and in nature—is now poisoned. Looking for some lasting good or substance in nature, a Shikastan woman and a man look at a tree, then a leaf; and I quote most of this full-page sentence because it is so amazing:

> And this is what an eye tuned slightly, only slightly, differently would see looking out of the window at that tree . . . no, not a tree, but a fighting seething mass of matter in the extremes of tension, growth, destruction, a myriad of species of smaller and smaller creatures feeding on each other, each feeding on the other, always—this is what the tree is in reality, and this man, this woman, crouched tense over the leaf, feels nature as a roaring creative fire in whose crucible species are born and die and are reborn in every breath . . . every life . . . every culture . . . every world . . . the mind, wrenched away from its resting place in the close visible cycles of growth and renewal and decay, the simplicities of birth and death, is forced back and into itself, coming to rest—tentatively and without expectation—where there can be no rest, in the thought that always, at every time, there have been species, creatures, new shapes of being, making harmonious wholes of interacting parts, but these over and over again crash! are swept away! crash go the empires and civilisations and the explosions that are to come will lay waste seas and oceans and islands and cities, and make poisoned deserts where the teeming detailed inventive life was, and where the mind and heart used to rest, but may no longer, but must go forth like the dove sent by Noah, and at last after long circling and cycling see a distant mountaintop emerging from wastes of soiled water, and must settle there, looking around at nothing, nothing, but the wastes of death and destruction, but cannot rest there either, knowing that tomorrow or next week or in a thousand years, this mountaintop too will topple under the force of a comet's passing, or the arrival of a meteorite. (201–2)

This is a vision of catastrophic change that goes beyond the merely social and political upheavals of the century of destruction—this is change built into the substance of life, pushing life itself into new substances. Yet it is not depressing, partly because it is so compelling—"The woman may . . . think that the laws that made this shape must be, must be, stronger in the end than the slow distorters and perverters of the substance of life"—and partly because it is only "one truth":

> The man . . . forcing himself to see the tree in its other truth, that of the fierce and furious way of eating and being eaten, may see suddenly, for an instant, so that it has gone even as he turns to call to his wife: Look, look, quick! behind the seethe and scramble and eating that is one truth, and behind the ordinary tree-in-autumn that is the other—a third, a tree of a fine, high, shimmering light, like shaped sunlight. A world, a world, another world, another truth. (202–3)

As in *The Four-Gated City,* the other world is glimpsed fleetingly and fitfully, shimmering just beyond the reach of our senses, just out of sight beyond this one—"Quick, said the bird" (Eliot, "Burnt Norton," 118):

> This, then, is the condition of Shikastans now . . .
>
> Nothing they handle or see has substance and so they repose in their imaginations on chaos, making strength from the possibilities of a creative destruction. They are weaned from everything but the knowledge that the universe is a roaring engine of creativity, and they are only temporary manifestations of it.
>
> Creatures infinitely damaged, reduced and dwindled from their origins, degenerate, almost lost— . . . they are being driven back and away from everything they had and held and now can take a stand nowhere but in the most outrageous extremities of—patience. It is an ironic and humble patience, which learns to look at a leaf, perfect for a day, and see it as an explosion of galaxies, and the battleground of a species. Shikastans are, in their awful and ignoble end, while they scuffle and scramble and scurry among their crumbling and squalid artifacts, reaching out with their minds to heights of courage and . . . I am putting the word *faith* here. After thought. With caution. With an exact and hopeful respect. (203)

Again the restraint, as Johor ventures "the word *faith,*" after thought, with caution, and with an "exact and hopeful respect." Again the ambiguity: the "faith" is Shikastans', but it is also Johor's, on behalf of Shikastans.

Thus Johor is drawn into a compassionate involvement with Shikastans that goes beyond necessity, into identification with the race that, though so nearly lost, is capable of heights of courage and faith. Johor may be an alien but he is also familiar, an extension of qualities toward which Lessing's protagonists have been tending—the compassionately observing protagonists of *Memoirs* and *The Four-Gated City,* who shed their personalities to blend in with the lives of those they care for. This is now what is necessary—this identification with the collective, "I" become "we," the "we" that emerges triumphant at the last: "And here we are all together, here we are." The protagonist is finally the human race, about whom we learn to think and feel differently. Lessing is teaching another kind of "identification with ourselves" that is regenerative rather than degenerative, collective rather than individual; she is teaching "kindness"—and the etymological coincidence that *kindness* derives from *kynde, nature* in Middle English, implies that it is human nature to be gentle. As always it is the life of society that Lessing cares about,[16] and she makes this identification as emotionally charged and compelling as the romantic love and flashy heroism that have long been the mainstays of narrative and that have served us so poorly in building a better world.

Though the way forward is the way back, to old truths and values, the novel also moves us ahead to new levels of awareness, to the next step of evolution implied in *The Four-Gated City* and *Memoirs*. This is what the Trial of the White Races suggests, in which the white races are put on trial by the dark races. From one point of view the entire episode, narrated in a letter from Chen Liu to Ku Yuang, is anticlimactic and unsettling. The issues seem to evaporate, as it becomes apparent that the dark races have behaved every bit as badly as the white races; Knapp sees this as "a laconic outcome typical of these novels' shoulder-shrugging indifference to political issues" (138). But looked at another way, the trial accomplishes something important: it makes it impossible for the white races or the dark races to project enmity onto an "other" and demonstrates (what Martha discovered in her breakdown) that there is no "enemy," that the enemy is always us—the trial makes everyone accountable. Moreover, as we see the participants beginning to understand what is happening, all at the same time and without words, as we see that the young are developing telepathic powers, we realize that the catastrophic events of the century of destruction have pushed life into new forms.

Besides, the traditional values to which the novel refers us—faith, endurance, patience—may be old, but they are also new, re-envisioned in a way that makes them the same but different from the traditional Christian virtues, reimagined in a way that answers the question Lessing's works always ask, how to get there from here? In *Shikasta* the meek inherit because they can tolerate uncertainty, can suspend judgment—which is quite different from the solidly certain "sum of wisdom" that Milton espouses: what is new in Lessing's conception of meekness is this linking of humility with irony.

As Dr. Hebert describes Lynda and others who have endured lifetimes of being treated as lunatics:

> These are all people . . . who, because of their experience are inured to hardship, misunderstanding, uncertainty, and a capacity for suspending judgement that is the inevitable reward of having to undergo years of suspending judgement on the workings of their own minds. These are most useful qualities! (352)

So too is the reader encouraged to cultivate these "useful" qualities, for the experience of reading forces us to suspend judgment and tolerate multiple viewpoints and develop a capacity for irony like Lynda's, like Johor's: the capacity Johor evidences in his double attitude toward his subject, an ability to hold opposite, even logically contradictory perspectives in tension. The "use of dismay," then, is not only the "stubborn patience needed to withstand," the small painful courage that is larger than anything, but the "courteous irony" that emerges as a saving grace from *The Golden Notebook.*[17]

Irony is "needed" because of what Shikasta is—"This planet is above all one of contrasts and contradictions. . . . Tension is its essential nature. This is its strength. This is its weakness" (5). These "contradictions" require ability to entertain a multiplicity of perspectives. But irony also has immediately tangible benefits as regards survival, because without it one is vulnerable—because "it takes one to know one" (343). "It takes one to know one" is one of those gnomic utterances, reiterated in *The Four-Gated City,* that is both utterly obvious and utterly opaque. In *Shikasta* its meaning becomes clearer because it explains why Canopus is continually misjudging Shammat ("that revolting empire") and also why Shammat cannot finally understand Canopus: because "benign and nurturing minds" are unable "to credit the reality of types of minds keyed to theft and destruction" (22) and evil minds are similarly incapable of comprehending good. Yet the principle "it takes one to know one" locks one into one's own perspective and makes one defenseless: so the question becomes, how "to know one" without being one—how to develop understanding of what one is not so that one can defend oneself? How to resist Shammat without being Shammat? This is the question at the heart of Shakespearean tragedy, which asks why the good are so vulnerable to evil, and which also shows evil being obtuse about goodness. Irony, the ability to suspend judgment and tolerate multiple perspectives, is what enables one to know one without becoming one, to defend oneself without succumbing, and so it turns out to be of enormous value in survival.

Like *Paradise Lost, Shikasta* puts us through a reading experience that repairs the ravages of the fall, teaching us to see and hear new meanings and reconstruct the world. To read this novel attentively is to learn to hear and see as Canopeans, for when at the last Johor's perspective gives way to Kassim's, our perspective becomes Johor's. Yet Lessing does not teach a simple Miltonic doctrine of obedience. She teaches us, rather, how to realize our full human intelligence and imagination—to reach out amidst the mad scramble for profit to a creative, redemptive irony.

Chapter 10

# *The Marriages Between Zones Three, Four, and Five:* "An Enquiry and a Remaking and an Inspiration"

There was a lightness, a freshness, and an enquiry and a remaking and an inspiration where there had been only stagnation. And closed frontiers.

—Doris Lessing,
*The Marriages Between Zones Three, Four, and Five*

Approaching this novel from *The Four-Gated City, The Summer Before the Dark, Memoirs of a Survivor,* and *Shikasta*—as we do reading Lessing's works chronologically—*The Marriages Between Zones Three, Four, and Five* comes as an enormous relief.[1] After the rush to destruction of the "last days," after the anguish and exhortation, we are given some space to pause and remember what we loved about life—a scene of humans living in harmony with one another in an unspoiled natural landscape, an ambience more of "olden times" than of "space fiction."[2] We are allowed to rest awhile and breathe easily, in a place like the prelapsarian paradise glimpsed briefly in *Shikasta.* Lessing refers to *Marriages* as one of her favorite novels. She describes it as being easily written—"There's never been a book that I enjoyed as much as that one. . . . When I finished, I was sad that it was ended"[3]—though also as coming "out of years of the closest possible work of the imagination."[4] And indeed its narrative flows effortlessly, gracefully. Undivided into sections or parts, it has the effect of a seamless whole, the polish and play of an intricately faceted gem. It has an elegance both simple and artful, a stylization like that of Medieval tapestries—though this simplicity is (as usual in Lessing) only apparent, for the narrator's frequent references to previous artistic renderings create a layered intertextuality that raises complex questions.

Lessing refers to *Marriages* as "a sort of legend," yet "also, oddly enough, [as] . . . realistic."[5] And notwithstanding its elegant stylization, this is a tale about the breaking of forms and transgressing of boundaries. Though in one sense strikingly different from anything Lessing has written, it is still centrally focused on the same questions that have always concerned her—on the individual in its relations with the collective, the relation of representation to reality, and the possibility of change.

Lessing depicts an ideal society then sets about demonstrating that it is not ideal if it has stopped growing and developing. Zone Three is a utopia, a society living in accord with egalitarian principles and with "Necessity" (121), a world whose individuals are so closely attuned to their environment that they communicate telepathically with their animals and so much in harmony with one another that "everything was entwined and mixed and mingled, all was one" (58). As the narrator, Lusik, one of Al.Ith's "mind fathers" says, "There is no 'I' here, can only be the 'we' of equals and colleagues. . . . We are all the visible and evident aspects of a whole we all share" (197)—which explains why "Al.Ith am I, and I Al.Ith" (199). This is a society functioning so well that its people are "free"—free to realize their potentials as individuals, free to create in accord with their best potentials—while also remaining subservient to the whole. The creations of Zone Three—the elegant yet functional towns, buildings, artifacts, ornaments, clothings—demonstrate the heights a culture could attain if its resources were not drained into war:

> If the fat and the fullness of a land were not continually poured away into war, then everything, but everything, would start to fill, and flower, and grow lovely and lavish with detail. In hands and in minds lived skills and cleverness that had only to be fed and given room. (224–25)

Al·Ith is its ruler, insofar as Zone Three can be said to have a ruler, for since there is no hierarchy or rank, she is not so much its ruler as its representative—"She *was* this land, this realm. It was she who embodied and contained it" (118); she represents "the best part of . . . [her] people" (59). That utopia is governed by a female, a female who is also a mother (to more than fifty!) suggests the centrality of the female principle to the ideal society: only a woman can be its "best part," since this is a system whose customs—of child rearing, animal husbandry, government—are informed by compassion, nurturing, openness to all creatures, human and animal, and in which "the Mothers" play a strong though unspecified part. But more importantly, a woman is what is "needed" in that it is Al·Ith's boundary fluidity that allows her to accomplish what this society needs to do, to take it through its next step in evolution.

For when the mysterious order comes commanding the marriage between Zones Three and Four, it is revealed that there is trouble in paradise, that there has been for some time: Zone Three is suffering from smugness, complacency—provinciality. "We were not even sure where the frontier was . . . [we were] afflicted with repugnance, or at least by an antipathy to foreign airs and atmospheres that showed itself in a cold lethargy, like boredom" (4); "And we saw how long it had been since we had thought at all of what lay beyond our borders. . . . We had perhaps grown insular? Self-sufficing?" (6); later the words *malaise* and *stagnation* would be used (141). The order prompts the realization, first in Al·Ith and then in others, that the birthrate has fallen, the crops are failing, and there is a sadness in the animals. As queen, Al·Ith feels remiss for having been inattentive to the changes in her realm: "She had not been listening" (56). Though guilt is an inappropriate emotion because it is contrary to "the knowledge, which was the base of all knowledges, that everything was entwined and mixed and mingled, . . . If there was a wrong, then this must be the property of everyone" (58); and though she is not responsible in the sense of having caused the problem, yet, as representative of her people, she is responsible for setting it right. This means that she must discover what is beyond the borders, must cross boundaries, both internal and external—that she must descend into a lower realm and, like Christ, take on flesh and submit to a kind of martyrdom: "When Al·Ith made her forced descent into that dreary land it was for us all" (142). Since Al·Ith is already human, and female, taking on flesh means bringing forth flesh, having a child who will unite the Zones.

The descent into Zone Four jostles Al·Ith out of former certainties and makes her see things differently. After the first trip (of several trips) to Zone Four and the first return (of several) to Zone Three, after she has been submerged in Zone Four and estranged from her own realm, she gains a new perspective on it, sees new potentials of it: her realm "had been finite, bounded, known . . . self-enclosed . . . but now it lapped and rippled out and upwards beyond there into hinterlands that were like unknown possibilities in her own mind" (61). Zone Three appears suddenly to be rippling with new possibilities, and it is this sense of promise that draws Al·Ith's attention to Zone Two and reminds her of her former fascination with it:

> What lay there? She had no idea! She had not thought! She had not wondered! Or had she, a long time ago? She could not remember ever standing as she did now, gazing, wondering, allowing her eyes to be drawn into those long, blue, deceiving distances . . . her eyes seemed to be drawn and follow, and become dissolved in blue, blue, blue . . . a mingling, changing, rippling blue. (59)

She imagines Zone Two as a dissolution of self and a merging with the ineffable, but she "came to herself . . . with a knowledge born that she knew would hatch out. Not yet, but soon" (59). Gazing at Zone Two jostles her memory:

> Yes, as a child she had come here. Now she remembered. She had been a very young girl. . . . She had . . . looked up and out and it had been as if her whole self had filled with a need to leave her and let herself be absorbed by that endless blue! . . . And . . . then what? She could not remember! (81)

As in *Children of Violence* and *Shikasta,* the problem the protagonist faces is one of remembering; and, as in those novels, the beginning provides a glimpse of the end, but it is an end for which the protagonist is not yet prepared. Like Martha, Al·Ith will have to endure a long descent—literally, into Zone Four, and figuratively, into potentials of herself—before she can work her way back up and out of Zone Three and into Zone Two. Also, like earlier Lessing protagonists, she must return and take others with her, so that her personal progress can allow evolution for the whole.

One of the striking things about this novel is the contrast between its elegant form and the anguish it depicts,[6] for Al·Ith's is a hard road that she must travel alone: "I do not know myself. I do not trust myself. I must go alone" (57); "she was a fallen creature, poor Al·Ith, and she knew it" (60). The descent into Zone Four is "a descent into possibilities of herself she had not believed open to her" (58). Her story is pitiable, wrenching, and, like other of Lessing's works, it demonstrates that freedom can only be earned the hard way. On several occasions Al·Ith imagines that freedom will come easily: "When [the child] is delivered, then I shall be delivered, too?" (112); "one day, . . . she would be free," restored "to her own country and be her own real self" (181–82). Freedom does not come easily or in any of the ways she can imagine, but it does eventually come, for Al·Ith will not only be freed, "translated into something other than anything she had known or imagined" (116)—she will also become the liberator of her people. As Lusik says, "Al·Ith freed us" (198).

Al·Ith's descent into Zone Four takes her to a realm more oppressive than anything she has ever known, a "realm of low and seething mists" (168) where "love" is a swamp, a bondage, a "desperation, questioning, an unfulfillment" (166). Zone Four is a society in thralldom to war, its "economy entirely geared to war" (87) and to notions of male and female behavior that follow from a commitment to war. In fact there has been no war and no cause for war within living memory—"that was a displacement of something else, some other aim, or function, something enjoined that they had forgotten" (140)—but it hardly matters, for this society's militarism affects everything, diminishing human potential by a rigid polarization of masculine and feminine that turns male-female relationships into power struggles.

When young children are left to the exclusive care of women, "when [boys] have known nothing but women," as Al·Ith explains to Ben Ata in an analysis very like Chodorow's, "boys have to turn against women . . . in order to become men at all"; this is why "to be brought up by women is to bring up a nation of soldiers. Men without softness for women, only contempt for them, and hardness" (203–4). Denied and repressed, women are forced underground, and Al·Ith discovers Zone Four's underground women's movement through Dabeeb, the wife of Ben Ata's general Jarnti, exemplar of this society's rigid militarism (104–5). Secret, subversive, they come to seem sinister: "It seemed to [Ben Ata] that half his realm, the female half, was a dark dangerous marsh, from which monsters might suddenly appear" (179). This fear and suspicion gives men further incentive for oppressing women, and women retaliate as they can, "treat[ing] . . . men as if they were enemies, or idiots . . . or small boys" (177) and devoting themselves excessively, aggressively, to motherhood.

Lessing demonstrates how the conventions of each Zone determine the way love, sex, friendship, and parenting are conceived of and carried out: in no other novel does she dramatize the social construction of gender so clearly and convincingly as here.[7] The word *love* means different things in the two realms, as Al·Ith painfully discovers. In Zone Three "it means . . . being with someone. Taking responsibility for everything that happens between you" (92); and, recently arrived from Zone Three, she succeeds in teaching Ben Ata this kind of love and teaching him a sexual play filled with "lightness, . . . impulsiveness . . . grace" (185). But in Zone Four love is a weight, a bond, a "possession," as Ben Ata teaches her, and sex is a "having" or being "had" (110, 114, 144), "all grab and grind" (109), "being ground and pounded into . . . ecstasies of submission" (96). Whereas in Zone Three Al·Ith is freed to do many things, "so much, so variedly," in

Zone Four her attentions are contracted to her physical person, concentrated on her wardrobe in a way that intensifies narcissism and obsessive eroticism: "If one devoted one's energies to self display, to the exact disposition of parts of one's body, and always with one idea, that one should be seen, and attract—then presumably that was enough to call forth this raging desire?" (180).

Childbearing also has different meanings. In Zone Three men are involved from the start "in sustaining and feeding and reassuring" (155), brought in as both mind fathers and gene fathers, whereas in Zone Four the child is "born into [a] clutch of women" (112), "sustained . . . by women, by the talk of women, the love of women." Women identify "fiercely" "with the birth of a child as if it was some sort of a self-fulfillment. More: as if a birth was a triumphing over a threat or even a wrong"—or as if maternity were a compensation for all the powers denied them. Motherhood is, like love, a "passionate need to have and to hold and to exult" (155), a drive to possession that obliterates all else: "This *mine, mine, mine* about a child paid reverence to the flesh, but where was the acknowledgement of the high and fine influence that fed every child?" (156).

Though Zone Three is superior to Zone Four and Al·Ith is more in touch with what is going on than Ben Ata is (she realizes that "we are here for a purpose—to heal our two countries and to discover where it is we have gone wrong, and what it is that we should be doing, really doing" [76])—it is not simply a matter of her teaching and his learning, but of each submerging themselves in and learning from the other. As in a Laingian breakdown, as with Saul and Anna, both hazard boundaries and identities and both grow in the process. Though it is harder to see what Zone Three learns from Zone Four than what Zone Four learns from Zone Three, Al·Ith needs to be jostled out of her comfort and complacency in order to grow—she needs to be dispossessed from both realms and endure a painful exile while she "wandered in the in between place, unknown, ignorant of what was needed from her or what her future was to be" (119). Ben Ata also must risk "boundaries" (175) and be "laid open" "to emotions he had no desire at all to feel" in order to be "introduced to his potentialities beyond anything he had believed possible" (68): "He was out of his depth, faced with a problem beyond his powers, and unsure of himself and his purposes" (154); "He was no longer himself, not a warrior, a great soldier. He had become . . . a man whose purposes had gone" (158), facing the possibility "that this new Ben Ata who had been given birth to by Al·Ith had destroyed in him all joy for ever" (171). But bit by bit, both begin to understand: he comes to see his country as a place horribly impoverished, "in every way poorer and more brutal than he had ever suspected, and his people more dissatisfied" (165), and Al·Ith comes to see her society as stagnant and as purposeless as Zone Four and to realize that "something else, some other aim, or function," "had [been] forgotten" (140)—*"We must find out what we are for"* (119).

Though Ben Ata is more impatient than she is—"Why don't they tell us what is wrong, quite simply, and be done with it. And then we could put it right"—Al·Ith soon suspects, "I think we are supposed to think it out for ourselves" (42). As elsewhere in Lessing's fiction, it is the process of thinking it out, of piecing it together—theirs and ours—that is instructive: and what the characters do in the novel mirrors what the reader does in relation to the novel. Also—as elsewhere in Lessing's fiction—the characters need to live through a process before they can understand it: as the narrator says, "My experience is that discussion is fruitless. What sets forth and demonstrates is the sight of events in action, is living through these events, and understanding them" (141). As Ben Ata comes to realize, "these messages from the Providers . . . it was not that they were ambiguous, but that you had to wait for events to interpret them" (207).

Just as the couple has achieved understanding of their relationship—just as "everything comes into balance between them, all based on the love-making that was a marvel of lightness, gaiety, wit, and fire" (201)—then a new order comes that Al·Ith must return to Zone Three and Ben Ata must marry Vashi, queen of Zone Five. Ben Ata must now endure the kind of process A.Ith had with him, being "savaged" by "a dirty primitive queen" (207) and submerged in a baser element, a process that wrenches him once more from all he knows and puts him through a torment like Al·Ith's: "He could no longer be as he had been, the Ben Ata who had never doubted what he should do; nor could he yet react from any higher or better centre or state. He was in between, and horribly uncertain." But from this dislocation comes understanding: "He believed he was beginning to see the outline of [the Providers'] plans for Zone Five" (212), which is to educate Vashi, as Al·Ith has educated him, and also to submit to the process of learning from her, as Al·Ith has with him. Their marriage represents another clash of cultures that produces another painful lurch forward—and so the process of change ripples from one character to the next and from one Zone to the next. Soon after their marriage Vashi also is changed:

> There was nothing in this marriage that she had wanted, or expected—she certainly could not say she had enjoyed it, for there had been too much uncom-

> fortable newness in it for that. And yet everything in her was changed, and she felt set apart from the life of her people, and responsible in a way she did not understand. (217)

After the order comes to part Ben Ata and Al·Ith, what follows is Al·Ith's most painful time, a period of exile from both Zones in which she feels "doomed always and from henceforward to be a stranger everywhere she went" (189). Returning to her sister Murti, she realizes how far she has traveled from her people and that she is forgotten, "a stranger" (116, 190): "I do not belong here, I do not belong anywhere, where do I belong" (191); "a fugitive, unwanted anywhere," she wonders "if perhaps she was mistaken about her path and direction" (120). Even Murti sees her as a "contagion" (118) and puts her under a kind of arrest. But Murti sees her this way because she has forgotten the bad times and rewritten the past; as Al·Ith tells her, "you have forgotten, Murti! Things were very bad before I was sent down to Ben Ata. . . . And now, instead of lethargy, and listlessness, and sorrow . . . we have the opposite" (241). Murti is unable to move with the times—and in this she is like Jarnti, Ben Ata's general, who is incapable of change.[8]

Al·Ith takes up residence on the pass near Zone Two, where she lives quietly, humbly, though still under surveillance, and where she becomes a focal point for the new restlessness in the land, as others join her on pilgrimages of their own. She makes various attempts to get to Zone Two, but she can only visit it in dreams and visions—visions that give her intimations of presences hovering just beyond her perception: "*Almost* she could see them. Almost, in the thin blue of this high air it was as if flames trembled into being" (194). As in *Memoirs,* the reality intimated here is ineffable, and Lessing can only suggest it by means of analogies, "as if's" and ellipses: "There are beings like flames, like fire, like light . . . it is as if wind had become fire, or flames . . . the blue is only the matrix of the real light" (230). Al·Ith's problem—and ours—is that we are approaching Zone Two still accouterd in "the senses of Zone Three and . . . Zone Four": "Probably, with different eyes, the eyes of someone set much finer than Al·Ith's, this world she was walking through would show itself as one of springing flames" (192); "Who could tell her what in fact she could have seen there, if differently tuned, if more finely set?" (196). But as her earthly senses are purged away, she is being refined into that realm she is drawn to, and when Dabeeb visits, she finds her much changed, "could see from her eyes how far she had been gone from them" (229): "a worn thin woman who seemed as if she was being burnt through and through by invisible flames" (228). One day she simply disappears up the pass: "One day when Al·Ith climbed the road to visit the other Zone, she did not come back. Others of her friends disappeared in the same way" (244). This passage allows the opening of boundaries and inspires new life and creation:

> There was a continuous movement now, from Zone Five to Zone Four. And from Zone Four to Zone Three—and from us, up the pass. There was a lightness, a freshness, and an enquiry and a remaking and an inspiration where there had been only stagnation. And closed frontiers. (244–45)

Despite its apparent simplicity, then, *Marriages* is a novel that asks us to stretch our imaginations and conceive of "another world" and another order of world. It depicts a utopia where people live in harmony and freedom, and then it asks us to reconceive of utopia as a process of movement and change. A society is not ideal if it rests in the smug assurance that it is the best there is and, indeed, all there is. Being at harmony within one's own isolated borders isn't sufficient, for "what goes on in one Zone affects the others" (142). Nor is a society ideal when it has stopped growing, when being rich and comfortable makes it "forget [its] proper purposes" (76), which is to evolve.

The novel asks us, further, to accept a view of art as part of the process of growth, as a delving and probing that opens the artist to risks like those hazarded by Al·Ith and Ben Ata. Lusik understands that he is taking a risk by submerging himself in the subject of Al·Ith. He is writing in order to combat the view of Al·Ith taken by Murti—"Al·Ith was being connected in the general mind with that time"; she is being forgotten or thought of with "distaste," thought of as "those who represent places in ourselves we find it dangerous to approach." He is hoping to evoke "another idea" of her, to get his society to re-remember her, to set the record right: "One of the motives for this chronicle is an attempt to revive in the hearts and memories of our people another idea of Al·Ith, to re-state her in her proper place in our history." Lusik understands why people have distanced themselves from her, why they withdraw from "the damaged, the hurt": "Fear is the root of it: that they might be brought low themselves" (142–43). She has been scapegoated—the bad time has been projected onto her. Yet since (as we know from *Four-Gated City*), when we meet the enemy it is always us, trying to get people to accept a different picture of Al·Ith is asking them to make terms with themselves.

It is precisely this risk that the narrator—any narrator—incurs, for "describing, we become. We even—and I've seen it and have shuddered—summon. The most innocent of poets can write of ugliness and forces he has done no more than speculate about—and bring them into his life."[9] Lusik "speculates" on this dangerous submersion—

> Yet there is a mystery here and it is not one that I understand: without this sting of otherness, of—even—the vicious, without the terrible energies of the underside of health, sanity, sense, then nothing works or *can* work. I tell you that goodness—what we in our ordinary daylight selves call goodness: the ordinary, the decent—these are nothing without the hidden powers that pour forth continually from their shadow sides. Their hidden aspects contained and tempered. (198)

Thus Lusik is writing to get his world to accept not only Al·Ith but the principles her story illustrates—that growth requires "the sting of otherness," the interaction of "the underside" or shadow side with our "ordinary daylight" realities; that change requires discomfort, disorientation, and this is the only way anything can "work" or grow.[10]

In the course of telling this story, the narrator repeatedly interrupts himself to describe and comment on scenes as they have been represented pictorially, and usually his remarks draw attention to the inadequacy of those representations. We are continually asked to readjust our perspective, to move from engagement to disengagement; as Whittaker suggests, "the reader is involved in what happens, and then asked to stand back, as it were, and look at the scenes as rendered into art: formal, distorted from reality, and imbued with symbolism merely by the fact of their selection for a permanent record."[11] Yet Lusik's calling attention to the unreliability of earlier renditions inevitably raises the question of the veracity of his own version. Why should we take Lusik's word any more than the others'? What makes him a reliable narrator, if he is one?

Well, mainly because Lusik cares about the same questions Lessing does—the relation of ideology to form, the relation of representation to the society that produces it, the inscription of ideology within aesthetic conventions. What interests Lusik is what interests Lessing: "I have always been a student of the different emphasis given by the two realms. Scenes popular with us are indifferently received by them, . . . and of course, the other way around as well" (146). He notes the difference between the two Zones' depictions of Yori, the riderless horse, for example, on Al·Ith's first entrance to Zone Three: "In their Zone the riderless horse gave birth to songs of death and sorrow; in ours to songs about loving friendship," for "a certain type of ballad is impossible with us: the kind that has as its ground or base lamentation, the celebration of loss." He describes what happens when tales from Zone Four pass into Zone Three: "Zone Four ballads . . . found themselves transformed as they crossed the frontier . . . there was no need of the inversions, the ambiguities, that are always bred by fear of an arbitrary authority" (27)—implying that a hierarchical social order will dictate rhetorical device whereas egalitarianism allows clarity.

Its militarism determines Zone Four's obsession with scenes depicting martial valor. The scene of Al·Ith "parading herself before the armies has always been the favourite one in Zone Four. In fact it would be easy to believe this was the only event of importance in the marriage, judging from the number and size of the pictures: the ballads, the songs, the tales" (146). Whereas "with us this scene has never been popular. This was not only because it was felt to be painful and demeaning. . . . There was an ambiguity in it that all of us could feel, . . . [concerning] what it meant to Al·Ith to descend to that Zone in the way she did" (147–48). Only later do the artists of Zone Three even begin to undertake this scene, and when they do, Lusik says, "I do not believe that any of our artists, or our ballad-makers or songsters, have got anywhere near the truth of that scene" (149), for "all these representations failed to come to terms with Al·Ith's real feelings" (148).

Lusik's judgments reveal both what is valuable and what is limited about Zone Three's conception of art. It is more cheerful than that of Zone Four, and it is more rhetorically straightforward, but it has also so missed the truth of Al·Ith that Lusik feels called upon to set the record right. In fact it sounds somewhat like the healthy Soviet art that makes Anna uncomfortable. Though unlike Soviet realism, it eschews scenes of vulgar heroism, its cheerful complacency, its confidence in surfaces, makes it ultimately inadequate. How, then, can art, which serves as a repository of the wisdom of the race, be kept from rigidifying into symbol, into formula: How can it be kept a living, fluid form capable of change and depicting change? Lessing's elegant, apparently simple fable urges, and exemplifies, a difficult view of art, as challenge and risk and growth.

Lusik's taking on the tale of Al·Ith reveals his commitment to a socially responsible art, to an ideal of art that not merely reflects the values of a society but also creates those values, an art that participates in the work of the world—so that rather than freezing the subject into symbolism and making meaning static, the artist frees it into fluidity and makes it open to interpretation and reinterpretation, makes it part of the process of delving and questioning and risking that is necessary to growth.[12] Art is not separate and different from life, but is, as Raymond Williams says, part of the impulse that builds culture.[13] *Remaking* is the word for what happens when the Zones are opened, and it is significant that this word can apply to both life and art, to conventions both social and aesthetic. The artist thus participates in, is implicated in, re-forming society—in movement and change, in extending the boundaries—a process that requires delving into parts of ourselves we might rather forget. Of course in performing these functions, the artist runs risks, for his/her compassionate receptivity incurs the danger of summoning the shadow areas and being, like Al·Ith, contaminated by them: in describing we become. Yet such risks are necessary to keep a society alive and changing. This gives the artist the function of a healer who diagnoses and prescribes and who, by plumbing the past and the self, can help make us free—as Lessing's fiction has. It also puts her or him at risk of contagion.

Lessing describes Al·Ith as a character who came out of long and serious "work of the imagination," work that was Lessing's attempt to "fantasize" herself strong:

> It was written out of this experience. When I was in my late thirties and early forties my love life was in a state of chaos and disarray and generally no good to me or anybody else and I was, in fact, and I knew it, in a pretty bad way. Unconsciously I used a certain therapeutic technique which just emerged from my unconscious. What I did was I had a kind of imaginary landscape . . . in which I had a male and a female figure in various relationships . . . I made the man a man who was very strong as a man, responsible for what he had to do and autonomous in himself and I made the woman the same because I was very broken down in various ways at that time, and this went on for some years in fact. And then I read about it; it is a Jungian technique. They tell you that if you have some area in yourself which you can't cope with, to do this; you take some part of you which is weak and deliberately fantasize it strong . . . So this book has come out of years of the closest possible work of the imagination.[14]

A projection of Lessing's stronger self, one might also see Al·Ith as a projection of Lessing's pain, of her own sense of being twice exiled and at home nowhere: Al·Ith's anguish has the force of Lessing's behind it. I suspect, also, that something else is going on. I wonder if Lusik's attempt to exonerate Al·Ith may not be Lessing's attempt to exonerate herself, to clear her name of the "contagion" she above all—as Cassandra—must know inevitably accrues to the bearer of bad news.

*Chapter 11*

# *The Diaries of Jane Somers:* Filial Atonements and New Romances

With her revelation, in the *New York Times,* on September 23, 1984, that she had published two novels under the name Jane Somers, Doris Lessing blew the cover off one of the most fascinating literary hoaxes of recent years. The main reason she gave for this "little experiment" was her desire to make a point about the literary marketplace; she wished, as she said, "to highlight that whole dreadful process in book publishing that 'nothing succeeds like success.'"[1] In the preface to the novels (published together as *The Diaries of Jane Somers* shortly after Lessing came out as their author) she said that she wished to be "reviewed on merit, as a new writer, without the benefit of a 'name,'" suggesting that this would "cheer up young writers, who often have such a hard time of it."[2] In this preface she gave reasons related to her own writing: she hoped that the pseudonym might set her "free of that cage of associations and labels that every established writer has to learn to live inside," "free to write in ways [she] had not used before." What interests me most is Lessing's association of Jane Somers with her mother, her suggestion that "reflections about what my mother would be like if she lived now" went into the creation of this protagonist—"practical, efficient, energetic . . . conservative . . . a little sentimental . . . though always kind" (viii).[3]

Lessing's mother must have been much on her mind, for besides influencing her characterization of the protagonist, Jane, she seems also to have been behind the ninety-two-year-old woman Jane befriends, Maudie. Not only is Maudie old enough to be Jane's (and Lessing's) mother: her name is the diminutive of the name Lessing's mother went by, Maud. Lessing's mother was named Emily Maud, but, as Lessing tells us, she preferred Maud to Emily[4]—perhaps because Emily was the name of her own mother, a redundance that must have reinforced Lessing's horror of "the direct line of matriarchy" (in Martha Quest's term when she gives birth to a girl).[5] If thoughts of her mother influenced her characterization of both Jane Somers and of Maudie, what *The Diary of a Good Neighbor* depicts, in a veiled way, is the situation of the daughter becoming mother to the mother and "delivering" her from life.

Lessing has only recently begun to speak and write about her mother. Though she has had much to say about her father,[6] her first published personal statements about her mother appear in two essays in *Granta,* in 1984 and 1985. She is frank about their antagonism—"she paralysed me as a child by the anger and pity I felt. Now only pity is left, but it still makes it hard to write about her"—yet she is generous in her praise: "She was such a brave woman, so resourceful, and all of that of course was wasted in a much too small arena for all this talent she had";[7] "what an awful life she had, my poor mother" (*Granta* 1: 68). "Now I am appalled at how I treated them both," she laments, while acknowledging, "I could not have done differently" (*Granta* 2: 237–38). I think that one function of the Jane Somers pseudonym was to allow Lessing to deal with matters she could not confront as Doris Lessing, still cathected matters related to the mother.

From the beginning the mother has loomed large in Lessing's fiction. There is much of Emily Maud Tayler in Martha Quest's mother, though Mrs. Quest is more than a personal failure: she is "the nightmare repetition" (*PM,* 77, 95), both victim and representative of the recurring cycles of behavior—biological, psychological, social, historical—that threaten Martha, of the pain and guilt passed from one generation to the next. In *The Four-Gated City* Martha turns to an analyst "to give her back pity," the pity she had banished as an adolescent, but though she regains feelings of pity, she never finds a way of acting on pity, for Mrs. Quest reduces her to rage, as she always has, and Martha never does bring herself to embrace her aged body.[8] Lessing returns to the mother-daughter relationship in *The Memoirs of a Survivor*—which she calls "an attempt at autobiography"[9]—where a young girl, named Emily, who has been damaged by her relationship with a bad mother (who has in turn been damaged by *her* bad mother), is given to the care of the narrator; the narrator, by assuming responsibility for her and by coming to understand the historical processes that have shaped them all, "delivers" them from the nightmare of history into the transcendent realm of myth—though this liberation requires a framework of fantasy.

In the Jane Somers novels, a decade after *Memoirs,* Lessing again confronts the mother-daughter relationship, replaying it, again, in the guise of a surrogate relationship, though this time without the fantasy—and complicated by the pseudonym. In *The Diary of a Good Neighbor* Lessing constructs a fictional situation that enables the protagonist to enter the perspective of a mother figure, to love her and tend her and *act* on pity in the way Martha could not. As Jane learns to enter into Maudie's experience—and, by extension, to participate imaginatively in the lives of other old people, to understand "the interest of their lives, their gaiety" (148)—she is released from her bounded self and becomes capable of intimacy, the intimacy she risks in the sequel, *If the Old Could,* with her nieces Jill and Kate, and with Richard.

## Repetitions and Reversals

Though at first glance the Jane Somers novels are, as Ellen Cronan Rose calls them, "a good read, densely realistic," with nothing of "the epistemological gymnastics of *The Golden Notebook,*"[10] they are actually more complicated than they first appear. They include the stories of several women: Jane and Maudie, Jane's sister Georgie, her nieces Jill and Kate, her friend and coworker Joyce, and her younger coworker Phyllis. We learn about the past histories of these women and about their present lives, their families, husbands, children, and work. Their stories are interwoven so that they comment on one another and comment on such subjects as youth and age, living with others and living alone, responsibility, commitment, work; and they raise such questions as the value of families, motherhood, marriage, male-female relationships and female friendships, and the value of a life—"how do we value ourselves," what *use* are we? (25). *The Diary of a Good Neighbor* also investigates, in an unobtrusive way, some questions similar to those addressed by *The Golden Notebook,* as Jane considers how to express Maudie's story, what literary modes best suit it, and problems of memory, language, and style.

The Jane Somers novels concern the processes by which youth turns to middle age and middle age to old age. They include young people (Jill, Phyllis, Kate, Richard's children) and very old people (Maudie Fowler, Annie Reeves, Eliza Bates), with Jane in the middle, aware of the processes by which each stage becomes the next, able to remember herself at an earlier age and to imagine herself at a later. Jane watches younger women watching older women "for signs of processes that would lead to their being replaced" (46); she is able to imagine the steps by which Maudie let herself go (55), and when her own back gives out, she is incapacitated in a way that makes her understand Maudie's helplessness. But whereas in the *Children of Violence* Lessing's sense of life as process reduced everything to a meaningless repetition, in the Jane Somers novels it makes life more meaningful, enhancing the value of what passes so quickly. Jane understands that merely "a bone the size of a chicken's rib" separates her from the helplessness of Maudie, and this sense of fragility makes her appreciate life as "a miracle": "I love—all of it. And the more so because I know how very precarious it is" (166). Lessing describes Jane Somers as freeing her from "a kind of dryness, like a conscience, that monitors Doris Lessing whatever she writes" (preface, viii), and these novels do show more geniality than one is accustomed to in her fiction. They also show a mellowness about other matters that were stringently critiqued in her earlier fiction—such as romance, romantic novels, even glamor magazines.

These novels are celebrations of life and of London. London is rendered in loving detail, its parks, streets, pubs, food, seasons, weather, registered with "wonder" and "admiration" (237), a "feast of possibilities" (165): "Oh, the good humour of this city, the pleasantness, the friendliness!" (198). "If the young knew," the unstated other half of the proverb from which the title *If the Old Could* is taken, is as important as the stated half of the proverb, for both novels concern what the young do *not* know: "I was thinking of them all [the young] as possessors of some treasure, but they disregarded it; a marvelous inheritance, but they did not know it; though warnings enough reach them of the vast deserts" (*IOC,* 491–92). Richard's caution, "You [English] don't know what you have," expresses an attitude toward life generally. What the young do not know is what the old *do* know, or ought to know: to love that well which must be left ere long. What neither the old nor the young know, however, is how to enter imaginatively into the experience of the other, and Lessing is centrally concerned here with this failure of sympathy that fixes people within the limits of their experience.

Most remarkably, the Jane Somers novels are celebrations of old people. *The Diary of a Good Neighbor* breaks what de Beauvoir calls "the conspiracy of silence" surrounding old age[11] and celebrates age in a way that is unprecedented in fiction: "Once I was so afraid of old age, of death, that I refused to let myself see old people in the streets—they did not exist for me. Now, I sit for hours . . . and watch and marvel and wonder and admire" (237). Jane comes to know the value of life from the aged: "I could learn real slow full enjoyment from the very old, who sit on a bench and watch people passing, watch a leaf balancing on the kerb's edge. . . . I love sitting on a bench by some old person, for now I no longer fear the old, but wait for when they trust me enough to tell me their tales, so full of history" (166). In fact, the same sense of life as process that in Lessing's earlier fiction reduced people to clichéd expressions of what has "been done and said before" (*PM*,34), in these novels humanizes people: "One day we will be old" may be (as Jane suggests) "a cliche so obvious, so boring" (21, 24), but it is our denial of this commonplace that reduces old people to "other" and so excuses our indifference and cruelty (as Simone de Beauvoir argues), whereas it is the recognition that "one day we will be old" that allows us to understand the aged as ourselves at a later stage. To understand the processes by which "we" become "they" is to break down the boundaries between young and old and to learn how not to "other."

This new interest in and empathy for the aged has to do with the fact that Lessing herself is aging, but it also has to do with her reevaluation of her mother—a reevaluation that is reflected in the protagonist's reassessment of her mother. Jane comes to admire her mother and even at one point wishes to be like her: "The doctors could not talk to me about what was happening to my husband, but they could talk straight to my mother about what was happening to her. *Because of what she was*. It was the first time in my life I wanted to be like her. Before that I had always found her embarrassing" (7). Jane's befriending of Maudie is an atonement for her withdrawal from her mother and grandmother—as Jill says, Maudie is "a substitute for Granny, you weren't nice to her, so you are making it up with Maudie Fowler" (231)—and also for her withdrawal from her husband's death by cancer ("I had not taken in these events, had armoured myself" [67]). When her mother became ill, she tried to "take it in," but she still "couldn't do it"; "I hate physical awfulness"; "I couldn't touch her, not really. . . . I could hardly make myself meet her eyes"; "I couldn't think of anything to say" (7–8). Her sister Georgie was capable of the physical and emotional intimacy of which she was not: their mother "held Georgie's hand. The point was, Georgie's was the right kind of hand"; and their talk "was interesting. Because they were so involved in it" (9).

Jane's withdrawal from her mother leaves her feeling unreal, without "substance": "It must have seemed to her that there was nothing much there—I mean, as if *I* was nothing much" (8). Though she attributes her failures to who she is—"I had let Freddie down and had let my mother down *and that was what I was like*"—and though she says "it is not a question of will, but of what you are," she *wills* herself to become something different: "That is why I decided to learn something else" (11). Jane has always been "real" at work, at the magazine *Lilith,* where her life centers; there she is "the one" person she knows how to look for in any organization, the one who takes responsibility and makes things happen (45, 56). Entering into a relationship with Maudie, she sets about becoming that "one" in a friendship—learning to be present, substantial, and to have, like sister Georgie, "the right kind of hand" for holding.

Though Jane panics at committing herself to a relationship with someone whose need is so boundless, she commits herself nevertheless, accepting the responsibility and adhering to the "promise" it entails (70). She learns to be capable of physical contact by washing Maudie and "lifting" her in response to her desire to be held, and she learns to listen to Maudie's stories, to participate imaginatively in her life, to *see* old people who were formerly invisible to her, to understand "the interest of their lives, the gaiety" (148). She learns to be "the one" in a relationship (104)—"someone has got to do it" (145)—and to assume the kind of responsibility she has always accepted at work. From caring for Maudie, she learns, as she says, "the cost": "now I know what it costs, looking after the very old, the helpless." She now realizes what her sister went through looking after their mother and what their mother went through looking after her mother (58)[12] and she understands that "everything has to be paid for" (157). But she also comes to realize the benefits, as caring for Maudie enables her to enter perspectives formerly closed to her: their relationship is not a matter of one taking, the other giving, but is mutually beneficial, for Maudie may be old and infirm, but she becomes a growing point for Jane.[13]

After Maudie's funeral, when confronted with Maudie's dreadful family, Jane tells a story of how once, when Maudie was starving, she found a coin in the street that appeared as though in answer to a prayer; after using it to buy food, she returned the change to the church box, saying, "You've helped me, and now I'll help you" (252). Jane tells this to contradict Maudie's family's anecdote of a Maudie who returned one cherry for one strawberry, a tale that confirms their image of her as calculating and mean-spirited. But Maudie's line "You've helped me and now I'll help you" resonates beyond the immediate context to suggest a right relationship between youth and age, an exchange based on reciprocity, which Jane has understood and fulfilled. So, too, does the friendship between Jane and Maudie, with its exchange of kindness for kindness, resonate with more than a personal meaning, transforming the vicious cycle of pain for pain, the nightmare repetition, into a loving interchange that signifies a right relationship between the generations.

Of course theirs is not a real mother-daughter relationship, but a surrogate relationship of the sort that Lessing's characters often enter into with strangers in order to repair the ravages inflicted by the biological family. In *The Four-Gated City* Martha Quest "pays debts" to Mark's family that she has incurred by her failures to her own, and in *The Summer Before the Dark* Kate Brown works out her relationship to motherhood by becoming surrogate mother to Maureen. By means of such relationships Lessing deals with a central ambivalence: her attraction to and fear of intimacy. On the one hand, she has a deep aversion to the nuclear family; on the other hand, she feels the need for connections and has the sense, as she puts it, that "the only thing that really matters in life is not wealth or poverty, pleasure or hardship, but the nature of the human beings with whom one is thrown into contact, and one's relation with them."[14] This tension leads her to explore, in her fiction, relationships that are chosen rather than inherited. Surrogate relationships are safer than kin, since they are entered into voluntarily and have built-in limits. (It seems significant in this respect that nearly all the great loves of Lessing's protagonists—Richard in *If the Old Could,* Thomas Stern in *Landlocked,* Michael/Paul in *The Golden Notebook*—are safely married to someone else.) But surrogate relationships may also offer radical alternatives to the nuclear family.[15]

In the first Jane Somers novel the protagonist enters into a surrogate mother-daughter relationship in order to atone for failures with her biological mother—though Jane learns to say yes where Kate Brown learned to say no, as the intimacy that once threatened her substance now becomes the source of her substantiality. Jane has always been capable of autonomy—"I love being by myself" (124): what she needs to learn is connectedness. In the second Jane Somers novel, as in the first, the protagonist similarly atones for an earlier guardedness—though in *The Diary of a Good Neighbor* Jane atones for a failure of compassion and in *If the Old Could* she atones for a failure of passion, expiating her failures with Freddie by enduring tormenting and unfulfilled desires for Richard. Jane regrets "the girl I was once," "that cold girl, negotiating allowances of emotion, of sex—did I ever use the word love?" (277) and recognizes her former self in the guarded young women around her, especially in her niece Jill—"myself, at her age" (195), "my younger self" (263–64)—but also in Phyllis, who can no more be asked for help than Jane could at her age. She wants to warn Jill against "locking up" such "treasures"—"I . . . want to say, Jill, Jill, *don't*" (292, 434)—and weeps that she herself was so foolish—"I know one thing . . . I look back and think I was the greatest bloody fool" (323). But the romantic relationship between Jane and Richard is less convincing than the Jane-Maudie relationship, which has the full force of Lessing's filial atonements behind it. Though Lessing seems to have intended the sequel to show the effects of Jane's "rebirth," I am not persuaded by this recuperation of the romantic fantasy she has so thoroughly repudiated elsewhere.

## Real and Apparent Structures

In *Changing the Story,* I categorized *The Diary of a Good Neighbor* as "postfeminist" for its depoliticization of issues and severing of personal from political.[16] I should have known that Lessing was up to something more interesting than this—but Jane Somers is so unlikely a feminist heroine that it's easy to miss. Jane spends an inordinate time fussing with her appearance; she is conservative, apolitical—"revolutions are hardly my line," she says (159)—and critical of feminism. Whereas Martha Quest and Anna Wulf condemned romance and nostalgia in their pursuit of the truth, Jane not only works on a glamor magazine, *Lilith,* but writes romance novels in her spare time, which she defends on the grounds that "the truth is intolerable" (151) and people need "escape" (140).

But what is feminist and revolutionary about this novel is its portrayal of women in relation to work and to one another through work. As is usual in Lessing's fiction, the family is stifling, but what is less usual is the way Lessing shows women finding alternatives to the family in their work: this pleasurable, even passionate relation of a woman to her work is a rare subject in fiction. Jane derives identity, self-esteem, and sustenance from her work—and so too do Maudie, Joyce, and Jill, though Jane is the only one who has the sense to realize that she does, that work is where her life centers. It is work on *Lilith* that enables Jane to grow, that gives her a sense of competence and value—"I wasn't good enough for university! It just didn't present itself as a possibility" (74):

> At school no one had ever even suggested I might have capacities, and certainly my parents never did. But in the office, I was able to turn my hand to anything. I was soon just the one person who was able to take over from anyone sick or incapable. I cannot remember any pleasure in my life to match that: the relief of it, the buoyancy, tackling a new job and knowing that I did it well. I was in love with cleverness, with myself. (75)

Jane blossoms in work, loves her own efficiency, her sense of *"being in control"* (45), and acknowledges this as the greatest "pleasure" in her life.

Nor is this merely career feminism: it is work with women, for women, on a women's magazine, in situations where women mentor one another—Jane learns from Joyce, Phyllis learns from Jane, Jill from Jane. It is true that women's magazines function ambiguously in women's lives: they offer up happiness for the price of the advertisers' products, but they also take women's issues seriously, as few other types of publications do, and are important sources of information;[17] *Lilith* represents this ambiguous mix: "Two thirds of *Lilith* is useful, informative, performs a service" (140).

Maudie similarly comes from a wretched family and she, too, blossoms in a work situation that enables her to discover her talents. Maudie's family has always ground her down to their conception of her, insisting that she is an opportunist at the same time that they mercilessly exploit her; and when Maudie takes Jane to meet them, they try to deprive her of her one real accomplishment, a friend of her own, by insisting that Jane is a "good neighbor," paid to be her companion. Maudie finds her "value" in her work as a milliner, where she realizes that she has "a gift": "I loved that work so, I loved it all . . . and then the other girls, we had worked together so long . . . and we knew each other and all our troubles"; "they were the best [times] in my life" (92)—though, unlike Jane, she never really incorporates this experience into her sense of her life. Jill, too, "emerging from loving family life, which grinds people down so," finds "confidence at her abilities, which are bubbling in her," contrary to her family's image of her (195).

These are novels in which "Chloe likes Olivia," a world whose "emotional center of gravity," as Rose aptly puts it, is women. In fact the only real love in *Diary of a Good Neighbor* exists between women—between Jane and Maudie and between Jane and Joyce. As in Woolf's *Room of One's Own,* where the friendship of Chloe and Olivia grows out of their work together—they share a laboratory—so also here, female friendship develops from shared work. Jane's friendship with Joyce begins in their work on *Lilith* and is based on a kind of wordless communication: "Joyce is the only person I have talked to in my life. And yet for the most part we talk in smiles, silences, signals, music without words" (64). It is also based on laughter: "those sudden fits of laughing, music without words, that are among the best things in this friendship of ours" (67). Jane also communicates wordlessly with Vera in a "shorthand" that similarly grows out of shared work (105), and Maudie's happiest memories are of working with women, at the hotel in Brighton (32–33) and at the milliner's workshop, "singing and larking and telling stories," all the while she is being exploited by a lecherous boss and roughed about by her "man" (90–93).

This depiction of women and work implicitly answers the question, How do we value ourselves? by what "yardsticks and measurements"? (25) Yet what is tragic is that none of the women, except Jane, really understands this "yardstick," really gets it: none realizes how central a joy and sustenance work is to their lives. Maudie never values her gift as a milliner, ambitious young Phyllis gives up her work to marry her lazy boss Charlie, and most disastrously, Joyce follows her husband to America. Underrating their real skills and strengths and their ties to other women, women disempower themselves.

I think this is the significance of the sociological treatise that Jane writes, "Real and Apparent Structures." Jane's interest in the way things work—"what is developing inside a structure, what to look for, *how things work*" (75)—leads her to observe, again and again, that it is women who do the work of the world while men are given the credit and authority. Women run *Lilith* while pretending that their incompetent male bosses do—first Jane and Joyce defer to Boris, then Phyllis to Charlie. In the caring professions "female" qualities of giving and empathy provide the "real structure" on which everything depends. The "home help" hold together their own homes as well as the homes they are paid to help, and in the hospital "it is the nurses who monitor the changes of need, of mood, of the patients, and the doctors who appear from time to time, issuing commands" (241–43). What Jane calls a "freemasonry of women" "keep[s] things together . . . underpin[s] our important engagements . . . by multifarious activities so humble" (199). Women working, "doing the same kind of thing at home as . . . at work" (249)—this forms the fabric of caring that knits society together.

Women do the work while men have the power, and "the power men have" is not gently wielded but a "stick they beat you with" (110), as Maudie asserts, who nevertheless clings throughout her life to a pitiful notion of "her man": "such is the power of—?—that Maudie refers to that awful husband of hers, even now, as My man" (110). But both novels suggest that *men have this power because women give it to them,* acting against their own best interests by overrating "romance" and underrating their real ties to other women and to work. Following her man, Maudie gave up the chance to work in Paris as a milliner, at a job she would have loved (92), just as following her husband to America, Joyce leaves behind work, friends, and home—choices that both women live to regret. Similarly, Phyllis's marriage to Charlie takes her away from work she loves to raise a family she does not particularly want. And though "Maudie is the one real thing that has happened to me" (135), Jane can't discuss her with Joyce or Jill because this attachment is viewed with suspicion by everyone; it is so unconventional that it falls beyond the bounds of expression—and certainly beyond the bounds of literary expression, for I know of no other novel that centers on a relationship such as this.

The boundaries of what is imaginable and expressible are delineated by an article in *Lilith,* on "images of women":

> The Images. (a) A girl of twelve of thirteen, . . . a frank healthy sensuality . . . Miss Promise. (b) A girl about seventeen . . . Still at home but you are ready to leave the nest. (c) Leading your own life. Mid-twenties . . . pretty and vulnerable. Needing Mr. Right but able to do without. (d) Young married woman, with a child. Emphasizing the child. (e) Married woman with part-time job, two children, running home and husband.
>
> And that was that. (21)

"And that was that": the tautology of a closed circle. A similar phrase is used with regard to Joyce's "choice" to follow her husband to the States—"and that's the end of that" (54)—and in fact Joyce's decision enacts what is scripted in *Lilith*'s "images," the old plot that makes woman's value and identity derive from marriage and family, a plot which buttons things up, closes things off. Against these errors we may see Jane's decision at the end of the second novel, to stay and work at *Lilith* rather than follow Richard to Canada, as heroic.

### "That Was That"

Joyce is a double to Jane, a negative potential who enacts the wrong plot. *The Diary of a Good Neighbor* begins (like *Summer*) with the protagonist thinking about the process of thinking and realizing "there are things I need to *think* out which I haven't got around to yet. Joyce for one" (10)—Joyce, who, when faced with a decision whether to stay in London and continue her work at *Lilith* or follow her husband to the States, feels that she has no choice but to go:

> Joyce *is* going to America. She will give up a wonderful job. Very few women ever get a job like this one. She will give up family, friends, home. Her children are nearly grown up. She will be in a country that she will have to learn to like, alone with a man who would have been happy to go with another, younger girl. *She has no choice.* (69)

Jane realizes, "I had made a long journey away from Joyce, and in a short time . . . something had changed in me, quite profoundly. And there was Maudie Fowler, too. It seemed to me . . . that Joyce was a child" (67). Knowing Maudie has confirmed her in the rightness of her choices—"I like being alone. Period" (62)—and made her see that it is the fear of being alone that gives a woman "no choice."

Joyce is also uncompassionate about Maudie, and her failures of imagination are of a piece: her inability to extend her imagination to Maudie is one with her inability to conceive of other options for herself. Her attitude toward Maudie is a characteristic denial: since old people are other, they are not us and we don't have to treat them humanely. Though she and Jane spend hours on the phone discussing "her marriage, my marriage, my mother, our work," "we do not talk about Maudie"—Joyce's attitude is "'Look, I don't want to know, do you understand?' I said to her, 'You don't want to talk about the one real thing that has happened to me?'" to which Joyce replies, "it didn't *happen* to you . . . for some reason or other you made it happen" (135). Joyce is pleased to be putting thousands of miles between herself and her father: "He's an old pet, but enough's enough." Jane tries to get her see that the way we talk about old people implies that they "are something to be *outwitted,* like an enemy, or a trap. Not that we owe them anything";[18] Joyce swears that she won't expect her children to look after her, that when she gets to be helpless she's going to bow out, though as Jane notes, that's what everyone says: "'And so I'm going to end up, some crabby old witch, an incontinent old witch—is that what you are saying?' 'Yes.'" (136). Joyce's denial that she'll ever get old or that she'll want to go on living if she does is a failure to imagine herself otherwise or to imagine that old people are herself at a later age. Yet her inability to imagine herself otherwise is actually no different from Maudie's or Phyllis's inability to conceive of a different "yardstick," to incorporate their work into a sense of themselves. The pleasure of work, of working with other women, isn't a yardstick by which we are taught to measure ourselves: "A crisis in the family, a choice, you wonder if perhaps you might actually have to live alone at some time, along with x billion other women—and all you are in your work counts for nothing, falls to pieces" (82).

Why? Because the ideology of marriage and family has so strong a hold on our imaginations that it prevents us from experiencing the pleasure and sustenance we actually derive from female friendships and work: because ideology obliterates experience. But part of the reason ideology has such a hold is the pernicious influence of romance novels and glamor magazines, and even Jane has to admit that magazines like *Lilith* may actually help *produce* the situation that necessitates the escape that they then provide: "at this very moment a million girls tapping away at their typewriters . . . are dreaming . . . not of women's lib and emancipation—but of *I love you* and a wedding dress . . . . Why? For one thing, because of the efforts of *Lilith* and her sisters" (454).

In the next novel, *If the Old Could,* Joyce admits, "I made a mistake. . . . Now I know it. You were right" (341). I think this is why Lessing needed the second novel—to show processes working themselves out, in Joyce and in Jane, to show Jane refusing Richard and choosing to be alone. "Clever Janna," says Joyce, "not to have children" (343). But Jane does have a child: she adopts Maudie. Jane and Joyce each describe the other as having "something missing": "There's something missing in you, I've always said so," says Joyce; "or perhaps there is in you," Jane responds (108). Jane figures out what is missing, however, and sets about fixing it—"that is why I decided to learn something else" (11). She gets "it all," in an odd way, both autonomy and intimacy, whereas Joyce's conventionality and failure of imagination leave her with neither.

Though Jane disavows feminism, she nevertheless works with women and identifies with women and understands "the freemasonry of women that glues society"; and one of her most important accomplishments is to write a day in the life of Maudie and a day in the life of the "home help." Despite its "apparent structure," then, the "real" structure or substance of this novel is deeply feminist: in Jane's attachment to Maudie and to her work, in her pleasure working with other women and living alone, Lessing demonstrates alternatives to the closed, dead-end system wherein "that was that." The novel challenges "whatever the power is that makes Joyce feel she has no choice" by locating value and intensity in other relationships and activities and giving women another yardstick by which to measure the value of their lives. (As Jane says to Joyce, "Those years we sat working together, never a cross word, understanding each other, that was love, as far as I am concerned" [165].) The reader, like Jane, has to develop a vision that allows us to look inside a structure and see how things work: "I hadn't learned *how* to see what was going on: what is developing inside a structure, what to look for, *how things work*" (75). I hadn't either, when I first wrote on this novel.

But I still have trouble with Jane's denigration of "women's lib." To Joyce's feeling that she has "no choice" but to sacrifice her life to a husband who does not particularly want her, to leave everything and follow him to America, Jane thinks,

> Well, women's lib, . . . what do you have to say to that?
>
> What, in your little manifestoes, your slamming of doors in men's faces, your rhetoric, have you *ever* said that touches this? As far as I am concerned, nothing . . .
>
> The reason why girls these days get themselves together in flocks and herds and shoals and shut out men altogether, or as much as they can, is because they are afraid of—whatever the power men have that makes Joyce say, I have no choice. (69)

"Women's lib thoughts" "aren't the point; they never were the point, not for me, not for Joyce" (66). This seems perversely obtuse, for, as Lessing doubtless knows, "women's lib" "manifestoes" are centrally concerned with "the power men have" that makes Joyce feel she has no choice. And she has herself analyzed this "power" in terms that could be right out of those manifestoes.

Jane may be missing the wider social and political implications of her identification with other women, and so too may Lessing—she did say that in becoming Jane Somers she found herself becoming "very narrow."[19] Though the pseudonym releases her from "a kind of dryness, like a conscience, that monitors Doris Lessing whatever she writes and in whatever style" (*JS,* viii), it also seems to dissipate the moral indignation I've always found bracing in her work.

## Aesthetic Qualifications

A similar contrast between "real" and "apparent" structures is evident in the contrast between Jane's defense of romance writing and her practice of graphic realism: for Jane may defend romance writing, but she offers, in her diaries, the starkest of realism, and the qualification makes for an interesting complexity. As elsewhere in Lessing's fiction, the reading of the novel requires a piecing together, an exercise of the sympathetic imagination analogous to what the protagonist goes through.

Just after she meets Maudie and sees the squalor she lives in, Jane feels ashamed of working on *Lilith,* but she soon realizes that Maudie loves this sort of magazine, just as she loves her beautiful clothes. Jane defends her romantic novel, *The Milliners of Marylebone,* on the grounds that "Maudie would love her life, as reconstructed by me." In this "reconstruction" the powerful males in Maudie's life "value" and "cherish" her (244): the fantasy of this novel, as of romances generally, is that men behave gallantly and respectfully toward women, rather than exploiting and discarding them, as has been the case in Maudie's life. Similarly, Jane's delight in the stories by which Maudie reconstructs her past implies an acceptance of the "lying nostalgia" repudiated in the *Children of Violence* and *The Golden Notebook*. The "coy, simpering" *persona* constructed by Annie Reeves (172–73) recalls the "humorous and gay" facade of Mrs. Quest (*PM,* 97) that so infuriated Martha, but this sort of fabrication is tolerated here, just as Annie's clichés are (168, 171). The conventional formulations that were condemned as "lies, evasions, compromises" in *Martha Quest* (7, 168, 171) are here accepted as the way a mind deals with experience and approved of as softening intolerable truths: "I know very well what I heard from Eliza about her life is not at all the truth, probably nothing like it; and I commend her as I would the writer of a tale well-told" (153). "Lovely things . . . to think about" are all old people have (112).

But though these novels contain an *apologia* for romantic novels, they are not themselves romantic novels. Of the two kinds of writing that Jane tries out as ways of representing Maudie's life, she may approve of the romantic—"I know only too well why we need our history prettied up. It would be intolerable to have the long heavy *weight* of the truth there, all grim and painful"—but she uses a realistic record of facts and events to render that grim and painful truth, to render even the "unprettied," unadorned "freezing smelly lavatory" that Jane claims will *not* be on Maudie's mind as she lies dying (141). In the process she contemplates questions like Anna Wulf's: "I wrote Maudie's day because I want to understand. I *do* understand a lot more about her, but is it true?" (126). She wonders whether even her straightforward account may be a way of "presenting" for an "observing eye" (64), and she is bewildered by the shifts of liking, anger, and irritation, "the grit and grind of a meeting" (31), that make it so difficult to capture the quality of her time with Maudie. Jane may approve of romantic rewritings of reality, but it is the "grit and grind," the hard task of understanding, that she undertakes in her diaries.

In fact, to write about another person is to take on that person's perspective, to feel what they feel. Jane's writing is a means of entering experiences other than her own—Maudie's day, the home help's day, Eliza Bates's day. As Lessing in *Diary of a Good Neighbor* uses writing to reconstruct Jane's and Maudie's life, so Jane uses her diary to reconstruct Maudie's life, and as she does so she confronts the limits of understanding, for she cannot imagine what Maudie feels as she lies dying: "Sometimes it is not possible to put oneself into the place of another" (233).

In a fascinating passage Jane ruminates about writing as "presentation": "Writing is my trade," she says; "to *present* ideas . . . I postulate the outside eye . . . I see that as I write this diary, I have in mind that observing eye . . . It's a funny thing, this need to write things down, as if they have no existence until they are recorded. Presented." From this she moves to thoughts about her "style" of dress and "the trouble we take" which suggest an association between dressing and writing (64–66). But whereas dress is mainly presentation, writing is only partly presentation, for writing is also a matter of penetration, of getting beneath the surfaces. In the course of the novel Jane shifts her attention from her dress to her diary, from a focus on self-presentation ("I did not ask myself what I was really like, but thought only about how other people judged me" [5]) to a focus on writing—as she says, "It has been a choice between proper baths and the diary" (86). And the truth she seeks in her writing—that vexed question for Anna Wulf—becomes truth to the feelings of others: like Shakespeare in *King Lear,* Lessing defines seeing as feeling, knowledge as compassion, and writing as a delving beneath surfaces to feel what others feel.

In a quiet, unobtrusive way, *The Diary of a Good Neighbor* challenges conventions, psychological, social, and generic. Like other Lessing protagonists, Jane transgresses boundaries, internal and external. In taking on Maudie, she ventures into areas of feeling that expand her bounded, defended self; and since "one did not have *friends* with the working classes" (38), their friendship crosses class lines as well. The novel pushes against genre in that its protagonist's apologia for romance is contextualized by the most graphic realism and a further complexity is introduced by the use of a pseudonym. And finally, Lessing takes the novel beyond its customary purviews by making women's relations to work and to other women through work the locus of emotional intensity. As I find myself repeating in relation to Lessing's novels, there is nothing quite like it.

## *Chapter 12*

# *The Good Terrorist:* Lessing's "New Upsetting Phase"

> But it was possible that she was tired, and perhaps sickened by a life-time's battle with stupidity.
>
> —Doris Lessing, *Landlocked*

*The Good Terrorist* is Lessing's most disturbing novel. What I find horrific about it is the way Lessing seems to turn on her own former beliefs in a mood of savage caricature. Lessing's fiction has always urged us to "make the effort of imagination necessary to become what we are capable of becoming," an effort that requires remembering and connecting. But what Martha learned in the long course of the *Children of Violence* series—to excavate her past and hold the Radlett Street house together in a way that assures a future—is not even a possibility for Alice. Alice, Lessing's "good terrorist," is a figure so furiously at odds with herself that though she directs her considerable energies to salvaging, repairing, bringing together, her efforts are at best futile and at worst, lethal: for Alice is incapable of understanding what is going on around her, let alone doing anyone any good.

Another ideal central to Lessing's earlier work that appears here like a mockery of its former self is the notion that we are being watched over and guided by superior beings. Though Lessing posited this quite seriously in the Canopus series and in *Briefing for a Descent into Hell,*[1] here it appears as one of Alice's infantile delusions, an instance of what one character calls her "arrested development."[2] Alice surmises—a fantasy fabricated from her attraction to Comrade Andrew next door and bolstered by stale leftist rhetoric—the existence of benign and helpful networks of revolutionaries who are guiding us to useful ends:

> All over the country were these people—networks, to use Comrade Andrew's word. Kindly, skilled people watched, and waited, judging when people (like herself . . . ) were ripe, could be really useful. Unsuspected by the petits bourgeois who were in the thrall of the mental superstructure of fascist-imperialist Britain, the poor slaves of propaganda, were these watchers, the observers, the people who held all the strings in their hands . . . everywhere, in fact, was this network . . . It gave her a safe, comfortable feeling. (251)

Alice turns out to be right that there are "watchers," though far from being kindly, they are sinister, and what they protect is their self-interest. These are the "layer of people" at the top, who, invisible and unsuspected, "run everything," "pull the strings"; these are the people Alice's mother warns her of: "This world is run by people who know how to do things. They know how things work. They are *equipped*. . . . But we—we're just peasants. We don't understand what's going on, and we can't do anything" (334). These are "the professionals" "poor baby" Alice goes off to meet at the end.

## England in the Eighties: The Dispossessed

As in *The Four-Gated City,* Lessing focuses on a household as microcosm of English society, but the difference is measure of change—of how much further down the death slopes England has slipped in the sixteen years between these two novels. Mark Coldridge's house on Radlett Street in Bloomsbury begins by being rooted firmly in the power structure of Britain—rooted, like the tree outside Martha's bedroom window, in solid soil. The Coldridge family is connected, by family relations and Oxbridge alliances, to the aristocracy, parliament, the world of arts, letters, publishing, and the media—to the people who "run everything." When Mark's brother Colin defects to the Soviet Union it is an act sufficiently momentous to attract the attention of media and government and provoke a national outcry. In the course of *The Four-Gated City* the house comes apart, its physical materials get shoddier, and the family takes in more marginals and misfits until it finally transmutes to new shapes, moves to the country and thence to an island, where what's left after "the catastrophe" evolves to a higher stage of consciousness—and what happens to the Coldridge family happens to the human race, for *The Four-Gated City* is epic in scope and significance, celebrating no less than the founding of a new order.

43 Old Mill Road—the name is grotesquely anachronistic—is also "a large house. Solid" (3). But it has been abandoned, condemned by the Lon-

don Council, slated for demolition, its wiring torn out to discourage squatters, its toilets filled with concrete (its sole occupant, Jim, a black man, has to resort to buckets which he stashes in the rooms on the top floors). When Alice arrives, with Jasper, her homosexual boyfriend of fifteen years, they are joined by a lesbian couple, Roberta and Faye, by a heterosexual couple, Pat and Bert, and by Philip, an unemployed repairman who is brought in to fix the toilets and wiring. Later Mary, a sympathetic woman from the London Council who helps Alice get legal squat status for the house, moves in, along with her boyfriend, Reggie. Jim invites them in as unsuspectingly as indigenous populations characteristically welcome their white despoilers. The group that converges at 43 Old Mill Road is made up of transients from here, there, and everywhere—displaced persons so cut off from their social origins that all (except Jim) speak in "made up voices" (125), as Alice, with her keen ear for accents, realizes.[3] In focusing on this group, Lessing shows a society further along in the process of uprootedness that Thomas Stern prophesied: "It was once like this: a child was born in a house that had a tree outside it . . . the child grew up while the tree shed its leaves and grew them again . . . and felt at peace"; but "everything's changed" now; "I'm the norm now . . . the elm tree and safety's finished . . . that's what normal is now. My family all dead and I'm in exile" (117, 168). In focusing on this ragtag collection who have been spit out by the system, Lessing suggests that the dispossessed are "the norm now."

Alice sets about setting this house in order, making the squat a stronghold for the Communist Centre Union—"Centre," Alice explains, "because we wanted to show we were not left deviants or revisionists"; "union" to indicate "a union of viewpoints, you see" (98). And indeed she accomplishes amazing feats of reconstruction: within a week after they move in she has managed to get the London Council to rescind the order for demolition, to unplug the toilets, get the buckets of shit emptied into a pit in the yard, get vast amounts of rubbish packed up in plastic bags and hauled away, and get the gas and electricity turned on—though she can do nothing about the rot in the upper beams of the roof (186, 212, 282) or about the squat next door, Number 45, whose yard is also filled with trash and whose occupants bear a mysterious relation to those of Number 43.

Alice sweeps up and washes up and washes down and clears away, patching, painting, repairing, and trying to make not just a house but a home—"It is like a family, it *is*" (234). But Alice can't really bring this group together into a whole, and her illusion that she can wars with her better sense that she cannot (103, 178). Philip, who tries hardest to help, is the frailest;

Bert and Jasper, the leaders, are useless; and the couples—Roberta and Faye, Mary and Reggie—break off into separate units with separate interests. Alice is seized by "a vision of impermanence" when Philip tells her that his former place of business, the address on his letterhead, has been "pulled down, demolished. It isn't even there." She and Philip share this vision, "star[ing] at each other with identical appalled expressions, as if the floorboards were giving way"—"houses, buildings streets, whole areas of streets, blown away, going, gone, an illusion" (124). And indeed, in this world, households, "families," living arrangements, businesses mushroom into existence and disappear overnight: in the process begun in *Four-Gated City* and accelerated in *Memoirs* and *Shikasta,* time is moving faster. All Alice's efforts succeed only in bringing the group together long enough for them to take part in a few demonstrations, blow up a concrete pilon, and explode a bomb in a crowded downtown street, killing five people and injuring twenty-three.

In its satire of a group of revolutionaries *The Good Terrorist* has similarities with *A Ripple from the Storm* (1958), though the satire is more biting and Alice is more complicitous with her cohorts than Martha was, who was just passing through, using the group as a growing point. Though *Ripple* concerned the Communist party in southern Africa in the forties and *The Good Terrorist* concerns what's left of the Left in Thatcher's England, both political groups are completely out of touch with the workers and the political realities of the countries. In *Ripple* the Communists are cut off from the real proletariat of Africa, the black workers, and in *The Good Terrorist* the revolutionaries are cut off from the working class of England, which they purport to represent but in fact know nothing about (though they imitate working-class accents, they do not, except for Philip, work themselves; nor do the workers welcome them at their strikes).

Both groups are in it for the excitement, but in *The Good Terrorist* Lessing's exposure of the personal pathology of political extremism is more ruthless. The politicos in *The Good Terrorist* need danger as a turn-on, a sexual aphrodisiac—"the intoxication of it, the elation: *Pleasure.* There was nothing like it!" (13, 126, 147, 157)—and Alice is one with them in this sense as in others: "She yearned for it, longed for the moment when she would feel the rough violence of the policemen's hands on her shoulders, would let herself go limp" (239). When their explosion of the concrete pilons gets them only a paragraph in the local *Advertiser,*

> They felt it was a snub of them, another in a long series of belittlings of what they really were, of their real capacities, that had begun—like Faye's vio-

lences—so long ago they could not remember. They were murderous with the need to impose themselves, prove their power. (318)

United only in their determination to destroy "this shitty fucking filthy lying hypocritical system," what they share is a sense of dispossession, of personal damage which they project outward in murderous rage on the world: in all, "the political serves personal ends" (as Jeannette King says),[4] and political rhetoric and obscenities (shitty, fucking) substitute for analysis. Only Mary seems to be honestly concerned with finding a responsible way of protesting the abuses of the system: she is drawn to Militant because she is appalled at the corruption of the London Council, some contractor making "a packet" out of tearing down houses, "jobs for pals." And though she leaves Militant, repelled by its tactics, to join the harmless Greenpeace, "that Mary had gone anywhere near Militant, that was the impossibility!" (93).

In both groups the men are the leaders, while the women do the real work. Jasper's "familiar phrases of the Socialist lexicon" (222) recall Anton's cliché-choked rhetoric, and in both men political incompetence is associated with sexual inadequacy. Jasper is cold to Alice and shameless in his exploitation of her, though it's also true that she uses him and is in this sense, as in others, complicitous with what happens to her. Alice is as entranced by Jasper's high-flown words as Martha is by Anton's, and the sexual politics of both groups are the same: the women not only accept, but welcome, their subordinate positions. (Andrew, the charismatic revolutionary next door, whom Alice admires as "the real thing," succeeds in recruiting female spies for the KGB on the basis of his sex appeal.) Though both protagonists value and trust other women—Martha respects Maisie and Marjorie as Alice trusts and likes Pat and Caroline—neither Martha nor Alice incorporates this into a view of the world that might challenge male authority: Alice is incapable of generalizing her affection and trust for women to feminism, of which she has no understanding.

But a major difference between *Ripple* and *The Good Terrorist* is that the women here are angrier, crazier, scarier. Whereas the women in *Ripple,* not only Martha but Maisie, Marie, and Marjorie, provided a bedrock of sanity and common sense, a counter to the delusions of the men, Alice is more caught up in the group's lunacies than Martha was, more complicitous. And though she is not much of a terrorist, let alone a "good terrorist," the character who is the good terrorist, the bomb maker, is a woman—Jocelyn; and the person who mis-sets the deadly timer and explodes herself along with others, in her second and finally successful suicide attempt, is Faye. So much for the hope that women are the center and salvation of civilization. Contrary to Alice's description of the group as the Centre Union, there is no center and no union.

## Alice the Wonder, the Wondrous Alice

Alice directs her considerable energies to cleaning, salvaging, restoring, building, bringing together—making "well and whole" (370). People call her a marvel, a wonder (40, 73)—"Alice the wonder, the Wondrous Alice" (81)—and though they do so in tones verging on mockery, Alice does have some fine qualities: she is the only one of the group who has a feeling for the value of individual life and compassion for the world's victims, whom she instinctively knows. She instantly senses Philip's vulnerability and when he helps with the house, she is determined to pay him, if she has to turn thief to do so (which she does); when he asks her to help him with the painting job he will otherwise lose, she does this too (though it costs her, delivering her back to Jasper, whom she has at this point decided to leave [270–72]). When he dies and no one else gives him a thought, Alice sees it through, assuming responsibility for the details of his death and mourning him like a brother—"and her heart ached for poor little Philip, who had tried so hard, been so gallant. *It wasn't fair*" (284). Philip, "her saviour, the restorer of the house" (36), had been inadequate to the task—too frail to save himself let alone tackle the rot in the beams upstairs. She sees his accident as a self-destruction: "Of course he had got himself run over, or whatever had happened, because he needed to . . . make himself helpless: Make his helplessness visible" (279). She sees him as "a brave little orphan" (36), a frail leaf swept away by the wind or the current; "she was thinking that this is what happened to marginal people, people clinging on but only just" (280); or rather, "It was not a question of Philip's having 'lost hold.' He had never grasped hold" (279).

Alice shows a similar concern for Jim, who can't find a place in the system because he is black. She gets him a job with her father and watches him come alive and alert with his good luck (193). She even curbs her tongue about her "shitty father" in order not to spoil his happiness, though she also shows a fatal carelessness in not imagining the connection that will be made between her theft of her father's money and Jim's presence in his office, a carelessness that crushes him and drives him away. And this cruelty resonates with more than a personal meaning: as the British Empire has drained the Third World, for its supposed good, these supposed champions of the underdog only succeed in dispossessing the dispossessed further—as Jim moans, "I was here before any of you, this was my house" (73).

Alice's compassion for the victims of this world is epitomized by her distress over the bird's nest that she and Pat knock down as they are fixing the roof of the house: "'Oh *no,*' said Alice, 'Oh, how awful!' She sounded suddenly hysterical, . . . and began to cry"; "Then something crashed onto the tiles of the roof: an egg. The tiny embryo of a bird sprawled there. Moving. Alice went on crying, little gusts of breathless sobs" (85). The crushed embryo represents the waste of life, the thwarted potential, that outrages Alice everywhere[5]—"Life simply oughtn't to be like this" (245). She understands—and here her perception shades into Lessing's—"Something had not happened that should have happened: a teacher, or someone, should have said: This one, Philip Fowler, he must be a craftsman, do something small, and delicate and intricate" (281). But her assurance that "one day, it would be impossible that fine people like Philip would be misused, kept down, insulted by circumstances; one day—and because of her, Alice, and her comrades—things would be different" (156), is wacky, given what she and her comrades are up to. Still, she has a keen sense of the value of life: "poor old thing" (317), she responds upon hearing that an old woman was injured by the explosion of the pilon—though it was *their* bomb that injured her. The term *a good person* still means something to her—she assures Gordon O'Leary that Comrade Andrew is "a fine person. A really good human being" (307)—though this judgment is so wildly irrelevant that it convinces him she is mad. Alice's humanitarianism is ludicrous in her world: as her upset over the broken eggs shows, she has no understanding of the first law of revolutionary politics, that you can't make an omelette without breaking eggs.

Yet some of her instincts about people are shrewd to the point of telepathy. Her intuitions tell her who is good and who is bad, who can be counted on and who cannot, and her knowledge does not depend on words. Many of her political judgments are similarly astute. She is outraged at the waste and corruption of a profit-driven system, appalled that the council is closing down the market that provided people with "proper food" "to build another of their shitty enormous buildings, their *dead* bloody white elephants that wouldn't be wanted by anyone but the people who made a profit out of building them. Corruption. Corruption everywhere" (17). She is scandalized by the fact that it is human beings who make these decisions, who destroy a house, build atrocities like the concrete pilings the group decides to blow up: "These hideous and pointless and obstructive objects. . . . People did this"

(297). Of desperate, displaced people like Monica Winters and her husband and baby, living in a squalid room of a converted hotel, Alice feels that these "young couples with their spotty, frustrated infants had been presented to her by Fate, as her responsibility" (137), and as Mary says "There are hundreds, thousands of them" (138), and the council can do nothing for them.

Alice has capacities that would make her a heroine in an earlier Lessing novel, qualities that make civilized life civilized.[6] In a sense she is justified in identifying with "the English tradition" (304), "the democratic tradition" (306), for the concern she expresses for the dignity of the individual represents what's finest about Western humanism and liberalism, and her outrage on behalf of the marginal, the homeless, the aged, and her sense of responsibility, are Lessing's. But in Alice these qualities are screwed in wrong, so that however she may patch and repair and nurture and care, her efforts are as doomed as she is. Partly, the materials she works with are doomed—both the human materials and the physical materials, rotted not only in the "superstructure" but in the base. But mainly what defeats her are her own mental and emotional deficiencies, some rot in her own structures. Her problems bringing the group together are minor compared with the problems she has getting herself together, for Alice's right hand knows so little of her left hand that each undoes the efforts of the other.

Alice is a case study in dissociation. She is dissociated from her body, whose "messages" occasionally "puzzle" her (200) but which she avoids by staying with a man who can't bear to touch her (167, 210). She is disconnected from her own deepest feelings and from her past, which is why she has drastic memory lapses: she can't remember that her mother planned to sell her house, even though she helped make the phone calls to arrange for the sale; she still thinks of herself as her mother's daughter, though she has destroyed their relationship—as is clear from their interaction early on, a telephone call that ends with Alice reviling her as a "doomed" "bourgeoisie" (16). Only gradually does she take in, and then only on one level, that the home is no longer there for her to return to, and even then she never understands her own part in its loss.

Alice has no understanding of politics—of revolution, communism, the IRA, the KGB, or of terrorism. Ideology is simply not her line, as Jasper says at one point when Alice tries to expand the notion of Trotskyite to include all of them (95); it is one of his few astute remarks. Her political convictions go contrary to her deepest intuitions, which is why they ring so hollow. She is committed to the idea that "it was capitalism that was so hard and hurtful"

(110)—"When we have abolished fascist imperialism there won't be people like that" (53)—though her instincts tell her that people are what they are, regardless of social or political systems: "'It's human nature,' said Alice, feebly, using a phrase that of course was simply beyond the pale" (94).

In Alice the personal and political are most drastically at odds in that her personal energies go to creating while her political efforts go to destroying. Creative and nurturing, on the one hand, and destructive and murderous, on the other hand, she is at cross-purposes with herself—hence the oxymoron "good terrorist." But Alice isn't really a good terrorist: she's more like a "good Samaritan" (which she twice calls on) or a good daughter (which she thinks of herself as [45]); "good girl Alice, her mother's daughter," as Lessing describes her as she throws a stone through her father's window (131), "every granny's dream" (213–14). Alice is a good terrorist only in the self-contradictory sense that she is anything: a good person who is nevertheless a terrorist, a good Samaritan who throws bombs, a good daughter who is no longer a daughter and no longer good—each term canceling out the other, as all her efforts do.

A major part of her problem is that Alice is a case of arrested development. She looks prepubescent, or middle-aged, but never her own age, which is thirty-six (10), and she persists in believing that her parents are omnipotent, that her mother could resume possession of her former house if she weren't so perversely stubborn. Her temper tantrums are like an infant's (123, 140, 158, 211), as is her inability to imagine consequences: after the stone goes through her father's window she doesn't give a thought to what happens. She doesn't imagine the consequences of accepting the five hundred pounds from Comrade Andrew and is surprised when Gordon O'Leary turns up expecting her to render services in exchange for it. Her mother mentions "contracts" as a feature of the real world about which Alice knows nothing (331), and it is true that her failures of understanding and memory make her incapable of following through on anything long term, though she does honor immediate human responsibilities, as to Philip. Her infantilism is further evident in her attitude toward the system—it owes them a living, though they are committed to destroying it—and in her belief in omnipotent beings who care for them unconditionally. Her desire for a protector makes her turn blindly, trustingly, to Peter Cecil, because he is "English," and deliver herself over to a system she does not begin to understand.

Alice's contradictions are most apparent in her teary-eyed musings about the good intentions of terrorists like herself:

> Ordinary people simply didn't understand, and it was no good expecting them to. Here the tenderness that had been washing around the place, inside and outside her, not knowing where it belonged, fastened itself on these ordinary people, and Alice sat with tears in her eyes, thinking, "Poor things, poor things, they simply don't understand!"—as if she had her arms around all the poor silly ordinary people in the world. (371)

This is one of those moments when we see the full force of her lunacy, and that it occurs so near the end, as she is about to go off to meet Peter Cecil, suggests that she has learned nothing—though this particular delusion, that you can save people by killing them, is hardly unique to her.

## Narrative Dislocations: "Rapid and Total Readjustments"

Not only is Alice disturbing in herself; our relation to her is disorienting. For much of the novel we are in her consciousness, sharing her perceptions of people and situations: narrative perspective hovers somewhere between Alice's and Lessing's, with Alice's perspective at times indistinguishable from Lessing's. Take Alice's reflections on the hideous pilon they decide to blow up: "People did this. First, in some office, they thought it up, and then they made a plan, and then they instructed workmen to do this, and then workmen did it. It was all incomprehensible. It was frightening, like some kind of invincible stupidity made evident and visible" (297). The series of short staccato statements, Alice's, gradually builds to an abstract summation that becomes Lessing's. It is enormously effective, not only for the way it builds, but for its imperceptible shading from a limited perspective to an informed one.

But we are also continually having to distance ourselves from Alice and make "readjustments." This becomes especially apparent at the end, when Alice's nattering on about their being "English revolutionaries" who "act according to the English tradition" (304) and Comrade Andrew's being "a really good human being" makes Gordon O'Leary draw back and reassess her:

> What was happening with him now was that he was thinking—as, after all, happens not so rarely in conversations—But this person is mad! Bonkers! Round the twist! Daft! Demented! Loco! Completely insane, poor thing. How was it I didn't see it before?
>
> At such moments, rapid and total readjustments have to take place. For

> instance, the whole of a previous conversation must be reviewed in this new, unhappy light, and assessments must be made. (306)[7]

Readjusting our view of Alice means readjusting our view of her views, and identifying with a protagonist who is "bonkers" makes it difficult to know what is "true."[8] If we can't accept her judgment of Jasper, what do we make of her contempt for Mary and Reggie, who may have redeeming qualities she is not in a position to appreciate? Or of her insistence that O'Leary is Russian rather than American, as he insists? And what about her certainty that Peter Cecil is "the essence of an Englishman, to match his name," when, as he himself suggests, and as Alice herself knows, "accents are not always what they seem" (354)? What do we make of Peter Cecil's "authentic" accent or of Jocelyn's, for that matter? Are they the ultimate disguise or is Alice simply wrong about them? Since even Alice's authentic tones are constructed—Alice had not "reclaimed her father's Northern tones" because she considered this "dishonest," "yet her own voice dated from the days of her girls' school in North London, basic BBC correct, flavourless" (26)—when she hears Jocelyn's flawless "Irish accent, perfect," she wonders if Jocelyn is in fact Irish: "And if so, what does it mean? Does it matter? Here is another of us with a false voice!" (342). The search for authenticity leads to further constructions.

Besides, the closer we move in on an explanation of Alice, the more information we get about her, the further we are from understanding her—understanding recedes, like the home Alice seeks. Behind Alice's efforts to make a family at 43 Mill Road is her dispossession from the home of her parents, "a comfortable house in Hampstead" where she grew up in "the golden age" of the sixties (202). When she finally understands that her mother has sold the house, she is "dissolved in grief because of the loss of her real, her own home" (219)—"she had no real home now. There was no place that knew her, could recognize her and take her in" (214)—and this sense of bereavement unlocks childhood memories. But what she remembers is that her parents made her give up her room during their parties: "How could they have done that to me? They took my room away from me, just like that, as if it wasn't my room at all" (219). Then, as if that weren't enough, they went to sleep. Some reviewers point to this as an explanation for the feeling of dispossession at the heart of her—"for it had been with her since she could remember: being excluded, left out" (101)—but it is a wildly inadequate explanation, as even Alice realizes:[9] "But this is all *silly,* Alice was thinking. . . . Most of the people in the world don't have half of what I had, and as for their own rooms" (219). The point is that Alice's past experiences do *not* account for her: the more information we get about her, the less we understand. Though Lessing teases us with the possibility of an explanation, at the heart of what makes Alice tick is an absence, a blank, just as at the heart of the home Alice is trying to get back to is an originary dispossession.[10]

It would seem, then, that Lessing shares Alice's impatience with "unhappy childhoods": "I've had all the bloody unhappy childhoods I am going to listen to. People go on and on. . . . As far as I am concerned, unhappy childhoods are the great con, the great alibi" (121). Alice excuses Jasper on the grounds of his past but doesn't want to go into it: "His mother—well, Alice wasn't going to get involved even with the thought of all that dreary psychology, but no wonder he had problems with women" (152). It goes without saying that unhappy childhoods make unhappy grownups, though sometimes it is true that happy childhoods do too: Lessing draws a curtain over this aspect of her characters' lives, in a spirit of impatient dismissal.

## Quest for Origins

The novel builds to Alice's confrontation with her mother, Dorothy Mellings, working back to this relationship as though to a point of origin or explanation. Her mother has been on Alice's mind throughout. Alice carries her around like an aching conscience, a gnawing awareness of something she needs to remember but would rather forget: in some sense this story is a quest for the mother, a quest that turns up yet another displaced person.[11]

When Alice finally tracks her to her new address, she still cannot get it through her head that her mother has to live here; indignant at this "paltry and ugly" little room, she demands "What do you think you are doing, in this place?" (325) and can barely recognize her mother in this stern, frowning old lady. Dorothy tries to explain that she and Jasper have literally eaten her out of house and home, for instead of using the money that her father gave her to convert an apartment so that she could afford to keep her home, she took in Alice and Jasper: "The point is, I would be there now, at home, if it weren't for you and Jasper" (330). But she claims to be glad to be "free of all that. Who said I had to spend my life buying food and cooking it? Years, years of my life I've spent, staggering around with loads of food and cooking it and serving it to a lot of greedy-guts who eat too much anyway" (331). Sounding like Kate Brown, she dismisses years of her life spent *"fussing"*

(332): Dorothy Mellings represents Kate Brown with a different ending (which may make one rethink one's dissatisfaction with Kate Brown's return). When the mother speaks she turns a searing beam on everything she once believed in—"Nothing was safe from her sarcastic hostility: not her children, her friends, her former husband, or anything in her past" (333).

Alice wants to protest, "Stop, please stop, before you destroy everything, even the memories of our lovely house. But this dangerous, destructive force that was now her mother did not hear her" (331). Nor does Alice hear her mother's lament for her own lost potential—"I had no proper education, as you know . . . I just kept house and looked after you and your brother and cooked and cooked and cooked. I am unemployable"—or for Alice's lost potential: "Oh, I did so want something decent for you, Alice" (333):

> I haven't done anything with my life. . . . Well, at least I'll make sure that Alice gets educated, she'll be equipped. I won't have Alice stuck in my position. . . . But it turned out that you spend your life exactly as I did. Cooking and nannying for other people. An all-purpose female drudge.

So much for the idea that female nurturing is the basis of civilization. Their exchange degenerates into mutual recriminations, as mother accuses daughter of "playing at revolutions" and daughter calls mother a "shitty old fascist" (334–35). Their final confrontation reiterates their first as the circle closes in a pattern of nightmarish repetition.

More illusions are blasted and more relations are unraveled as Alice remembers, after leaving her mother, the argument Dorothy Mellings had with her closest friend, Zoe. Dorothy and Zoe met on the first Aldermaston March, but while Dorothy is rethinking earlier positions—"I am doing a stock-taking. . . . I am *thinking* . . . about my life. That means I am examining a lot of things"—Zoe remains locked into old leftist clichés. Dorothy has come to see that "All you people, marching up and down and waving banners and singing pathetic little songs—'All You Need Is Love'—you are just a joke. To the people who really run this world, you are a joke. They watch you at it and think: Good, that's keeping them busy" (339–40). Dorothy's arguments represent Lessing's repudiation of her own former beliefs.

There is a lot of Lessing in Alice, in her strong intuitive responses, her belief in human nature over the ideological[12]—and in Alice's failed attempts to save the world is perhaps Lessing's comment on the futility of her own lifelong efforts. But it is Alice's mother, in what Alice thinks of as this "new, upsetting phase" (257), who most directly speaks for the author. And Alice's sense of her mother's "new mode," as "bitter and brief and flat" (53), describes Lessing's style here—stark, unlovely, flat.[13]

The futility that informs Lessing's vision in this novel is epitomized by the image of shit. Alice wages war on shit, rot, and rubbish, in the house and in the political system—"We are going to pull everything *down.* All of it. This shitty rubbish we live in" (334). But shit and rubbish are everywhere—"Everything is *rotten*" (335)—pervading a system "doomed to be swept into the dustbins of history" (203). *Shitty, rotten,* and *rubbish* are Alice's all-purpose terms (180, 184, 200, 203, 281, 296, 305, 336)—"the state of Britain. Rotten as a bad apple and ready for the bulldozers of history" (169). At the end her mother turns these adjectives on Alice, calling her "spoiled rotten" and accusing her of speaking "rubbish" (328).

This shit is simply shit, not a resource capable of being transmuted to gold (as it is in Drabble's *Middle Ground*),[14] but a revelation, as Kate Brown says, of what it's all worth. Moreover, it is "systemic," produced both by the physiological system, the body, and by the socioeconomic system, the body politic. After Alice, Jim, and Pat spend the day emptying the buckets Jim has filled, Jim is shaken to realize how much shit he alone has produced: "How much shit we make in our lives," "suppose the sewers just packed up?" (66–67). Dorothy laments a life wasted in fixing food for "a lot of greedy-guts" (331) and Alice hates the "greedy-guts" middle class (180). Such images suggest a vision of humanity as a shit-producing mechanism whose consumption produces only shit and make the point that the system is shitty because human beings are. The personal turns out to be political, after all.

This is realism with a vengeance, but realism with a difference, that disallows the consolation of explanations or origins, of "sequence" and "consequence" (to use Drabble's terms in *The Radiant Way*).[15] *The Good Terrorist* offers none of the usual consolations of narrative: that what has happened in the past accounts for the present, that what we do in the present affects the future, that we can learn through experience, that the next generation will do better than the last. Gone is Lessing's belief that the next generation might make a better life than the generation before, and with it, the hope of progress.[16] Gone is any vision of a reality that transcends this one: we are in the dark pit, with no glimmer of an elsewhere. Lessing's vision is Swiftian not only in its excremental quality but in its rage, the rage of someone who has spent her life trying to educate, warn, re-form, and has watched the world slide from bad to worse to rotten.

In the end Alice is, for all her creative energy, as parasitical as the classes she opposes, a greedy guts who eats her mother out of house and home. All Dorothy's efforts to nurture have produced only Alice, and all Alice's efforts produce only senseless killing. Notwithstanding their hatred of the system, the revolutionaries in fact take on its worst traits and are incapable of anything but futile repetition—they exploit the working class, oppress the black man, and take for granted the traditions of England in a way that is destroying what is finest about those traditions. In Alice and her cohorts Lessing depicts an England unable to learn from past errors or move with the times or imagine itself as part of a global situation—they have the audacity to insist, after they've succeeded in establishing alliances with the IRA, that they are English and not to be bossed around by "foreigners" (288). And this incomprehension makes them futile: the only revolution they take part in is "revolution" in the sense of circular return, each generation repeating what's worst about the generation before.

At the end Alice sits alone in the empty house, contemplating the meaning of events:

> She sat on quietly there by herself in the silent house. In the *betrayed* house . . . She allowed her mind to move from room to room in it, praising her achievements . . . The house might have been a wounded animal whose many hurts she had one by one cleaned and bandaged, and now it was well, and whole, and she was stroking it, pleased with it and herself . . . Not quite whole, however. (370; ellipses in original)

No, "not quite whole." Still, the structure is left standing, "a lot of people had found shelter for a time" (46), and, despite the rot in the superstructure, it won't be torn down, it will be converted. So too does England still stand, its welfare services provide shelter to "a lot of people," the sewage system still works.

Though for how long? "The future of Britain," point number two on the agenda of the Communist Centre Union Congress, is never got to (225).

*Chapter 13*

# Conclusion

Empathetic exploration demands of the investigator the creative capacity to suspend closure. The founders of phenomenology and psychoanalysis developed methods to facilitate a process of not-concluding, ways of keeping the mind open to new possibilities.

—Alfred Margulies, "Toward Empathy: The Uses of Wonder"

It feels presumptuous to conclude a study of a living writer, and especially presumptuous with regard to a writer who is herself so resistant to conclusions as Doris Lessing, for no writer I know of is so reluctant to make endings as Lessing is. It is this that draws her to write series, where the spillover from one novel to the next allows for investigation of processes usually cut off by literary closure. Yet even when she comes to the end of a series she leaves a "loose end," as situations and characters from the *Children of Violence* get picked up and developed in the *Canopus in Argos* series; and when she interrupts *Canopus* after the penultimate novel—as she interrupted the *Children of Violence* after its penultimate novel—even the novel with which she interrupts the series, *The Diary of a Good Neighbor,* sprouts a sequel. This straining against endings is consistent with her restlessness, her claustrophobia, her search for a position beyond systems. It is also indicative of the cast of mind she values in her characters, an empathetic receptiveness, an openness to experience, a reluctance to shut down or shut off.

The circular structures I've traced throughout the *Children of Violence, The Golden Notebook, The Memoirs of a Survivor,* and *Shikasta* thwart endings and allow new beginnings. If, as Frank Kermode suggests, the ending is a figure for death,[1] then the refusal of endings is, crudely put, an affirmation of life. Lorna Irvine suggests this with regard to the "continuous fictions" of Margaret Drabble: she sees Drabble's "insistence on the continuance of the fictional universe"—her open endings and the way her characters wander in and out from other novels—as affirmation of "the human capacity to survive," of a "generative view of human life."[2]

The same may be said of Lessing, but this is somewhat more surprising with her, since her works suggest so strong a sense of the End. And this is another paradox about her: few writers are so reluctant to make ends, yet few writers are so fixated on the End. The dark that awaits Kate in *The Summer Before the Dark* is not only hers but her civilization's, and *Memoirs of a Survivor* takes us through Apocalypse, as do *The Four-Gated City* and *Shikasta*. Yet in these works ends issue into new beginnings: even Anna Wulf's nightmarish fixation on nuclear holocaust allows for the possibility of a blade of grass pushing its way up through the ruins.

However, in her most recent novel, *The Fifth Child,* ends are absolute, final. In *The Fifth Child* the belief in evolution central to Lessing's fiction since the *Children of Violence* turns to a vision of devolution, of humanity regressing to an earlier, savage stage—and this is a vicious circle of nightmarish return rather than a movement issuing into new beginnings. Ben, the mutant throwback fifth child, is an invader not from outer space or from the lower classes (as some reviewers have suggested), but from the womb. And he is not abnormal, a freak, for it turns out that there are many like him, the entire "sediment of the uneducable, the unassimilable, the hopeless"[3]—armies of young people who are violent, destructive, amoral, incomprehensible (and addicted to television) and who may represent, contrary to what Lessing had suggested in *Four-Gated City,* "the main line of evolution." Whereas in *The Four-Gated City, Memoirs,* and *Shikasta* fantasy was a means of exploring better possibilities, here the fantastic, too, has become nightmare.

But *The Fifth Child* is not Lessing's last word.[4] In her latest collection of short stories and sketches, *London Observed* (*The Real Thing* in the United States),[5] that geniality that she needed the Jane Somers pseudonym to express gets expressed in the name of Doris Lessing. Here Lessing's love of London—its parks and café life and even the underground—comes through strong: here is a mellowness and peace far from the biting anger of *The Good Terrorist.* "It's far from the apocalyptic visions of the city which appear in her earlier writing, indeed, it's a defense, even a celebration of much that others might find simply squalid," as Lorna Sage says:

> She is always interested in seeing around the corner of what is the current orthodoxy, and if London is now seen to be, as I think it is by very many

> people, very much the horrible city that she described twenty years ago, she will now discover in it the other city that they're not seeing.[6]

At present Lessing is working on her autobiography; she wishes to do this, she told me, "because there is so much I do not understand."

What none of the photos show and what I saw only at close range are the laugh lines at the corners of her eyes—not only at the far corners but at the inside corners—which give her face a marvelously mischievous look. What struck me most meeting Doris Lessing was her openness, her curiosity, her willingness to listen. When I commented to Margaret Drabble, "She's not even remotely arrogant," Drabble replied, "oh no, she's anything but arrogant. She's whatever's the opposite of arrogant."

So I think I'll conclude with a few snippets from that May 1992 radio profile of Lessing. Brian Aldiss describes her as a "tremendously good-humored and a witty lady"; of her new audiences at science fiction conferences he says, "People just love her, they love her." Drabble describes her surprise at finding "that somebody who was quite often dealing with the ends of the universe also had strong views on cats and kitchen shelves and houseplants." And she describes visiting her home,

> The first time I went to Doris's, no, it must have been the second time. . . . I noticed that her house was full of strange little plants growing in yogurt pots, and I inquired about these and she told me that they were grown from grapefruit pits or avocado stones, and that I ought to try this too, and I think she gave me some yogurt and said that this would be excellent, this mother of yogurt plant and this would go on and on forever, and I think she has this nurturing instinct, if she sees a seed or a pit, she really wants to make it grow, . . . it's just that she doesn't like the waste of all these things and that seemed to me very Doris—if you see something that might grow, plant it.

# Notes

## Chapter 1

1. Iris Rozencwajg, "Interview with Margaret Drabble," *Women's Studies* 9 (1979): 341.

2. Bookshelf, "Profile of Doris Lessing," produced by Abigail Appleton, BBC Radio, May 1, 1992 (hereafter Bookshelf).

3. "My Father," in *A Small Personal Voice: Doris Lessing, Essays, Reviews, Interviews,* ed. Paul Schlueter (New York: Vintage, 1972), 86 (hereafter "My Father").

4. "My Mother's Life," part 1, *Granta* 14 (Winter 1984): 55 (hereafter *G,* 1).

5. "I think the title explains what I essentially want to say. I want to explain what it is like to be a human being in a century where you open your eyes on war and on human beings disliking other human beings" (inter. by Roy Newquist, in Schlueter, *Small Personal Voice,* 57 [hereafter Newquist]).

6. "He could not face being a bank clerk in England, he said, not after the trenches. . . . Besides, the civilians did not know what the soldiers had suffered, they didn't want to know, and now it wasn't done even to remember 'the Great Unmentionable'" ("My Father," 89).

7. "My Mother's Life," part 2, *Granta* 17 (1985): 229 (hereafter *G,* 2).

8. Lessing points out this same sort of contrast in the family of Olive Schreiner, suggesting that this is one of the "psychological ingredients" that goes in "to the creation of a woman novelist . . . at least, often enough to make it interesting":

> A balance between father and mother where the practicality, the ordinary sense, cleverness, and worldly ambition is on the side of the mother; and the father's life is so weighted with dreams and ideas and imaginings that their joint life gets lost in what looks like a hopeless muddle and failure, but which holds a potentiality for something that must be recognized as better, on a different level, than what ordinary sense or cleverness can begin to conceive. (Afterword to *The Story of an African Farm,* by Olive Schreiner, in Schlueter, *Small Personal Voice,* 108)

9. Television interview.

10. A horror that is expressed particularly in *Briefing for a Descent into Hell* and in the introduction to *The Golden Notebook,* where she describes education as indoctrination of the individual to the will of society (New York: Bantam, 1973), xv–xviii (hereafter *GN*).

11. "Testimony to Mysticism: Interview with Doris Lessing," by Nissa Torrents, *Doris Lessing Newsletter* 4, no. 2 (Winter 1980): 12.

12. Henry Kellermann and Hans-Peter Rodenberg, *"The Fifth Child:* An Interview with Doris Lessing," *Doris Lessing Newsletter* 13, no. 1 (Summer 1989): 4.

13. The term is Sandra M. Gilbert and Susan Gubar's (*The Norton Anthology of Literature by Women: The Tradition in English* [New York: Norton, 1985]), 1678. Lessing describes the experience of being doubly exiled in *The Marriages Between Zones Three, Four, and Five* and *The Sirian Experiments.*

14. Minda Bikman, "A Talk with Doris Lessing," *New York Times Book Review* 85, Mar., 30, 1980, 1ff (hereafter Bikman).

15. Doris Lessing, *Martha Quest* (New York: New American Library, 1964), 57–58 (hereafter *MQ*).

16. Doris Lessing, *A Ripple From the Storm* (New York: New American Library, 1966), 7.

17. Lorna Sage describes Lessing as a "demystifier" or "critical observer of social processes and systems" (*Contemporary Writers: Doris Lessing* [London: Methuen, 1983], 11, 24). Susan Lardner describes her as "an exile, a philosophical hobo, temperamentally restless"; she paces at the confines of the world, her demon is claustrophobia ("Angle on the Ordinary," *New Yorker,* Sept. 19, 1983, 140).

18. Doris Lessing, *The Summer Before the Dark* (New York: Bantam, 1974), 62.

19. I've said more about this indebtedness in "Looking at History," in *Changing Subjects: The Making of Feminist Literary Criticism,* ed. Gayle Greene and Coppélia Kahn (London: Routledge, 1993), 4–27.

20. *MQ,* 53, 141, 216; *GN,* 61, 353, 472–73, 479.

21. "A Small Personal Voice," in Schlueter, *Small Personal Voice* (hereafter "SPV"), 6. And as Kate Fullbrook suggests, there is no contemporary novelist who has "accepted this ethical role more conscientiously or over a longer period of time than Lessing" (*Free Women: Ethics and Aesthetics in Twentieth-Century Women's Fiction* [Philadelphia: Temple University Press, 1990], 141).

22. *A Proper Marriage* (New York: New American Library, 1970), 61–62 (hereafter *PM*).

23. *The Four-Gated City* (New York: New American Library, 1976), 131 (hereafter *FGC*).

**Chapter 2**

1. *GN* xi.

2. *Doris Lessing Newsletter* 8, no. 2 (1984), 3 (hereafter *DLN*).

3. *FGC,* 558.

4. "Sage, seer, prophetess—the epithets frequently invoked in response to Doris Lessing's work acknowledge her significance, for many readers, as a visionary teacher

and guide" (Kate Fullbrook, *Free Women: Ethics and Aesthetics in Twentieth-Century Women's Fiction* [Philadelphia: Temple University Press, 1990], 141).

5. "I believe she is one of the twentieth-century writers by whom literary critics of the future will know us," as Erica Jong says; "and perhaps this is because she is intelligent enough to be unfashionable" (Review of *Summer, Partisan Review* 40 [1973], 501).

6. The term *something new* occurs in *MQ,* 53, 141, 216; *Landlocked* (New York: New American Library, 1964), 117 (hereafter *LL*); and *GN,* 61, 353, 472–73, 479. "The nightmare repetition" is from *PM,* 77, 95.

7. As she herself says, "Critics tend to compartmentalize, to establish periods, to fragmentize, a tendency that university training reinforces and that seems very harmful to me. . . . This tendency to fragmentize, so typical of our society, drives people to crisis, to despair" ("Testimony to Mysticism: Interview with Doris Lessing," by Nissa Torrents, *Doris Lessing Newsletter* [Winter 1980], 4, no. 2, p. 360).

8. Mona Knapp, *Doris Lessing* (New York: Fredrick Ungar, 1984), 21.

9. Preface, *The Diaries of Jane Somers* (New York: Vintage, 1984), xi. See also the preface to *Shikasta* (New York: Vintage, 1981), where she expresses a sense of exhilaration that science fiction has "set her free" (ix).

10. See Randall Stevenson, *The British Novel since the Thirties: An Introduction* (Athens: University of Georgia Press, 1986), chap. 3 for nostalgia in postwar British fiction.

11. Bernard Bergonzi calls Snow "the most deeply backward-looking and nostalgic of living English novelists" and criticizes Powell for his complacency about English society (*The Situation of the Novel* [Pittsburgh: University of Pittsburgh Press, 1970], 137, 122). See also John Holloway, "The Literary Scene," in ed. Boris Ford, *The New Pelican Guide to English Literature: The Present,* 417–49 (Penguin, Harmondsworth: 1983).

12. *The Grass Is Singing* (New York: New American Library, 1976), 33.

13. Patricia Hill Collins, "Learning from the Outsider Within: The Sociological Significance of Black Feminist Thought," in *(En)Gendering Knowledge: Feminists in Academe,* ed. Joan E. Hartman and Ellen Messer-Davidow (Knoxville: University of Tennessee Press, 1991), 46. The "simultaneity of oppression" is discussed in the Combahee River Collective, "A Black Feminist Statement," in *But Some of Us Are Brave: Black Women's Studies,* ed. Gloria T. Hull, Patricia Bell Scott, and Barbara Smith (Old Westbury, N.Y.: The Feminist Press, 1982), 16. See also Barbara Smith, intro., *Home Girls—A Black Feminist Anthology,* ed. Barbara Smith (New York: Kitchen Table / Women of Color Press, 1983), xxxii.

14. Susan Lydon, review of Lessing's *Four-Gated City, Ramparts,* Jan. 1970, 48 (hereafter *Ramparts*).

15. Intro., *Doris Lessing: Critical Studies,* ed. Annis Pratt and L. S. Dembo (Madison: University of Wisconsin Press, 1974) (hereafter *DL*).

16. Marilyn Webb, "Feminism and Doris Lessing: Becoming the Men We Wanted to Marry," *Village Voice,* Jan. 4, 1973, 14.

17. Bookshelf, "Profile of Doris Lessing," interview produced by Abigail Appleton, BBC Radio, May 1, 1992.

18. Laurie Stone, *Ms.*, July–Aug. 1987, 29.

19. Jean McCrindle, "Reading *The Golden Notebook* in 1962," in *Notebooks, Memoirs, Archives: Reading and Rereading Doris Lessing,* ed. Jenny Taylor (Boston: Routledge, 1982), 50.

20. Kate Millett, *Flying* (New York: Simon and Schuster, 1990), 357.

21. Rachel Blau DuPlessis and Members of Workshop 9, "For the Etruscans: Sexual Difference and Artistic Production—The Debate over a Female Aesthetic," in *The Future of Difference,* ed. Hester Eisenstein and Alice Jardine (New Brunswick, N.J: Rutgers University Press, 1980), 128–56, rpt., *The New Feminist Criticism: Women, Literature, and Theory,* ed. Elaine Showalter (New York: Pantheon, 1985), 279–80.

22. Margaret Drabble, "Doris Lessing: Cassandra in a World under Siege," *Ramparts,* Feb. 1972, 52 (hereafter "Cassandra").

23. Lisa Alther, "The Writer and Her Critics," *Women's Review of Books* 6, no. 1 (Oct. 1988): 11 (hereafter *WRB*).

24. Jane Marcus, "Invisible Mending," in *Between Women: Biographers, Novelists, Critics, Teachers and Artists Write about Their Work on Women,* ed. Carol Ascher, Louise De Salvo, and Sara Ruddick (Boston: Beacon Press, 1984), 391.

25. Doris Lessing, *World Press Review,* July 1981, 61; see also x; and Lessing's talk in Marin, Apr. 1984.

26. Susan Lardner, "Angle on the Ordinary," *New Yorker,* Sept. 19, 1983, 144 (hereafter "Angle").

27. Margaret Drabble, quoted in Elaine Showalter, *A Literature of Their Own: British Women Novelists from Brontë to Lessing* (London: Virago, 1978), 311.

28. Interview with Peter Firchow, *The Writer's Place: Interviews on the Literary Situation in Contemporary Britain* (Minneapolis: University of Minnesota Press, 1974), 107.

29. Elizabeth Wilson, "Yesterday's Heroines: On Rereading Lessing and de Beauvoir," in Taylor, *Notebooks,* 57–74. See also Anna Davin and Anna Paczuska, in *Once a Feminist: Stories of a Generation,* ed. Michelene Wandor (London: Virago, 1990), 56, 151; and Mary King, *Freedom Song: A Personal Story of the 1960s Civil Rights Movement* (New York: William Morrow, 1987).

30. Ellen W. Brooks, "The Image of Women in Lessing's *Golden Notebook,*" *Critique: Studies in Modern Fiction* 11 (1973), 101.

31. Elayne Antler Rapping, "'Unfree Women': Feminism in Doris Lessing's Novels," *Women's Studies* 3 (1975), 30.

32. Showalter refers to the novel's "aversion to the feminine sensibility" (*Literature,* 309); Ellen Morgan calls it "alienated from the authentic perspective ("Alienation of the Woman Writer in *The Golden Notebook,*" in Pratt and Dembo, *Doris Lessing,* 63). See also Catharine R. Stimpson, "Doris Lessing and the Parables of Growth," *The Voyage In: Fictions of Female Development,* ed. Elizabeth Abel, Marianne Hirsch, and Elizabeth Langland (Hanover: University Press of New England, 1983), 193–94.

33. "I learned from her, to my enormous surprise, that a novel could be serious and philosophical even if the protagonist were an ordinary woman, neither a whore nor a goddess, and even if the content were nothing more ambitious than the stuff of daily life. Lessing's books were a revelation" (in conversation with Carey Kaplan and

Ellen Cronan Rose, eds. *Doris Lessing: The Alchemy of Survival* [Athens, Ohio: Ohio University Press, 1988], 6).

34. Dee Preussner, "Talking with Margaret Drabble," *Modern Fiction Studies* 25, no. 4 (1989–90): 568; review of Lessing's *Stories* in the *Saturday Review,* May 27, 1978, cited in Ellen Cronan Rose, "Twenty Questions," *Doris Lessing Newsletter* 4, no. 2 (Winter 1980), 5.

35. I discuss *The Waterfall* in relation to *The Golden Notebook,* in *Changing the Story,* chap. 6; and *The Middle Ground* in relation to *The Summer before the Dark,* in "Feminist Fiction and the Uses of Memory," *Signs,* 16, no. 2 (Winter 1991): 310–14; and I discuss *The Radiant Way* and *The Four-Gated City,* in "Bleak Houses: Doris Lessing, Margaret Drabble, and the Condition of England," *Forum for Modern Language Studies* 28, no. 4 (1992), 304–19.

36. Lois Gould's, *Final Analysis* (New York: Avon, 1974), 41; Valerie Miner's, *Movement* (New York: Methuen, 1982), 116; Anne Oakley, *The Men's Room* (New York: Ballantine, 1988). For Lessing's influence on Jong's *Fear of Flying,* see *Changing the Story,* chap. 4.

37. Dorothy Bryant, *Ella Price's Journal* (Berkeley: Ata, 1972), 88.

38. Jenny Taylor, "Introduction: Situating Reading," in Taylor, *Notebooks,* 5.

39. For histories of the women's movement in the United States, see Barbara Sinclair Deckard, *The Women's Movement: Political, Socioeconomic and Psychological Issues* (New York: Harper and Row, 1983); Rochelle Gatlin, *American Women since 1945* (Jackson: University Press of Mississippi, 1987); Myra Marx Ferree and Beth B. Hess, *Controversy and Coalition: The New Feminist Movement* (Boston: Twayne, 1985). For the women's movement in England, see Elizabeth Wilson, *Only Halfway to Paradise: Women in Postwar Britain, 1945–1968* (New York: Tavistock, 1980); Olive M. Banks, *Faces of Feminism: A Study of Feminism as a Social Movement* (Oxford: Basil Blackwell, 1986); Sheila Rowbotham, *The Past Is before Us: Feminism in Action since the 1960s* (London: Pandora, 1989); Harold L. Smith, ed., *British Feminism in the Twentieth Century* (Amherst: University of Massachusetts Press, 1990).

40. Such as Margaret Laurence's *The Fire-Dwellers* (Toronto: McClelland and Stewart, 1984); Alix Kates Shulman's *Memoirs of an Ex-Prom Queen* (New York: Knopf, 1972); Sheila Ballantyne's *Norma Jean the Termite Queen* (Harmondsworth: Penguin, 1986); Marge Piercy's *Small Changes* (New York: Fawcett Crest, 1973); Sue Kaufman's *Diary of a Mad Housewife* (New York: Bantam, 1970); Fay Weldon's *The Fat Woman's Joke* (Chicago: Academy, 1967). I discuss this in some detail in *Changing the Story,* chap. 3.

41. "Afterword to *The Story of an African Farm,* by Olive Schreiner," in "SPV," 99.

42. *Prisons We Choose to Live Inside* (New York: Harper and Row, 1987), 7.

43. "Doris Lessing at Stony Brook," interview by Jonah Raskin, "SPV," 66. Doris Lessing, *The Sirian Experiments: The Report by Ambien II, of the Five* (New York: Knopf, 1980), vii (hereafter *SE*).

44. Susan Kress says, "No novelist convinces us more forcefully of the need to change ourselves, actively, morally, and responsibly" ("Lessing's Responsibility," *Salmagundi* [Winter–Spring 1980]: 131). Kaplan and Rose describe her as "an al-

chemical writer" who "challenges her readers and changes them; alters their consciousness" (5). Betsy Draine notes that "Lessing's unchanging subject is itself change" and that she, "perhaps more than any other living writer, has succeeded in moving her readers from one order of perception to another" (*Substance under Pressure: Artistic Coherence and Evolving Form in the Novels of Doris Lessing* [Madison: University of Wisconsin Press, 1983], xiii, 141–42. Katherine Fishburn reads her as "trying . . . to modify the way we experience everyday reality," to "force us to reconsider what reality itself might be" (*The Unexpected Universe of Doris Lessing* [Westport, Conn.: Greenwood Press, 1985], 11).

45. *Memoirs of a Survivor* (New York: Bantam, 1976), 217.

46. Sometime in the late sixties Lessing became a Sufi, attracted by the works of Idries Shah. Sufism is a form of Islamic mysticism. Its literature, a compilation of fourteen hundred years and several strains—European, Near Eastern, African—and including the scientific as well as the philosophical, is not codified, and there is no church. Coming at this literature from the Renaissance, as I do, I find many of its metaphors familiar: its belief that the world we inhabit is not the whole of reality, that nature is immanent with the divine and reflects a cosmic harmony in which microcosm reflects macrocosm, is recognizable from sixteenth-century Christianity. Even the belief in cosmic evolution, in the quest to achieve harmony with the One, recalls the Renaissance "great chain of being."

47. See Jerome A. Miller, "Wonder as Hinge," *International Philosophical Quarterly* 29, no. 1 (March 1989): 53–66.

48. This is why I omit *Retreat to Innocence* and *The Sirian Experiments* from this study. I've omitted *Briefing for a Descent into Hell* and *The Making of the Representative for Planet 8* because they have male protagonists, and I'm primarily interested in the question of change in relation to female consciousness.

49. Freedom is not, as Fullbrook notes, "an absence of relatedness and duties, not a Nietzschean matter of the triumph of superior, individual will, but a wise arrangement of the instances of interrelationship that are necessarily part of the human condition". "How 'free' one can be is seen by Lessing to be less a matter of exercising personal choice (though it certainly is that), than an entire culture's cultivation of qualities of good faith, mutual tolerance, and honesty. One simply cannot be free alone" (*Free Women,* 157).

50. See reviews of *Memoirs* and *Shikasta,* cited in chap. 8 n.20, and chap. 9 nn. 2 and 7.

51. Roland Barthes, *S/Z* (New York: Hill and Wang, 1974), 135.

52. George Lukács, "The Ideology of Modernism," *The Meaning of Contemporary Realism* (1963), trans. John and Necke Mander (London: Merlin Press, 1969), 19; *Studies in European Realism* (New York: Universal Library, 1964), "1946 Preface," 1–9.

53. See Catherine Belsey's explanation of Barthes's views of realism as "the accomplice of ideology," as a closed, fixed system that appears realistic "precisely because it reproduces what we already seem to know" (*Critical Practice* [London: Methuen, 1985], 73, 46–47, 52).

54. Nancy Chodorow, *The Reproduction of Mothering: Psychoanalysis and the Sociology of Gender* (Berkeley: University of California Press, 1978).

55. This capacity may be seen in relation to Keats's "negative capability," an ability to tolerate "uncertainties, Mysteries, doubts." Alfred Margulies analyzes negative capability as akin to empathy as described by Freud, which "plays the largest part in our understanding of what is inherently foreign to our ego" and is the means by which "we are enabled to take up any attitude at all towards another mental life." Margulies also links this to the ability to tolerate uncertainty and to the refusal of closure ("Toward Empathy: The Uses of Wonder," *American Journal of Psychiatry* 141, no. 9 [1984]: 1025).

56. Lyn Sukenick, "Feeling and Reason in Doris Lessing's Fiction," in Pratt and Dembo, *Doris Lessing,* 102.

57. Patricia Waugh notes that "the solubility of . . . ego boundaries" becomes "a source of utopian strength" in Martha and Anna: "Lessing suggests that the continued existence of the human race will depend upon the displacement of the primacy of the 'masculine' values of war and competition by those such as care and nurturance, at present associated with women and thus regarded as secondary" (*Feminine Fictions: Revisiting the Postmodern* [London: Routledge, 1989], 204, 208).

58. *The Summer before the Dark* (New York: Bantam, 1974), 244.

59. Most recently, in "Women's Quests," *Partisan Review* (May 1992): 189–96:

> I want at this point to quote a piece some time ago in *Ms.* magazine about me, and the entire piece was about the view of one of my characters about the female orgasm. Now, I've done quite a lot of things in my life which the women's movement, I should have thought, would approve of; but to be reduced to one of my character's views on the female orgasm made me extremely annoyed and I began to wonder if this movement was for me at all. This was when I began to think it was not. (191)

Marilyn Webb describes Lessing's visit to the United States in 1970: "New York feminists gathered by the hundreds, sure of hearing what they wanted a heroine to say, only she disappointed them enough to be denounced. They said she wasn't a feminist and wasn't interested in the women's movement." In 1973 "none of the vocal feminists came to Lessing's talks":

> On this visit she was nervous and defensive. "Wherever I went before people asked me about feminism," she said. . . . "I was tired of the same question. Of course I'm a feminist but I also have other interests. I was appalled by it all. In America I'm a 'hot item.' That is not the case in England." (14)

Ruth Whittaker describes subsequent events: "During a tour of North America in 1984 Mrs. Lessing was taken to task for her 'betrayal' of the feminist cause. She was unrepentant, and said that 'women's politics are exactly like men's politics,' and regretted that women have not co-operated with men to solve problems common to them both: 'a great opportunity has been missed'" (*Modern Novelists*). See also Roberta Rubenstein, "An Evening at 92nd Street Y," "Reports: Lessing in North America, March–April, 1984," *DLN* 8, no. 2 (Fall 1984): 6.

60. Adrienne Rich, "Disloyal to Civilization: Feminism, Racism, Gynephobia," *On Lies, Secrets, and Silence: Selected Prose, 1966–1978* (New York: Norton, 1979), 279.

61. Teresa de Lauretis, "The Technology of Gender," in *Technologies of Gender* (Bloomington: Indiana University Press, 1987), 25.

62. See Julia Kristeva, "Women's Time," *Signs* 7, no. 1 (1981): 32; and Wendy Kaminer, *A Fearful Freedom: Women's Flight from Equality* (Reading, Mass.: Addison-Wesley, 1980), who is quite critical of this tendency.

63. Carolyn Heilbrun, for example, suggested that women should emulate "male" qualities in our search for autonomy and independence, that we "reinvent womanhood" on the male model (*Toward a Recognition of Androgyny* [New York: Knopf, 1973]; *Reinventing Womanhood* [New York: Norton, 1979]).

64. Dorothy Dinnerstein, *The Mermaid and the Minotaur* (New York: Harper and Row, 1976); Jane Flax, "The Conflict between Nurturance and Autonomy in Mother-Daughter Relationships and within Feminism," *Feminist Studies* 4 (1978): 171–89; Jean Baker Miller, *Toward a New Psychology of Women* (Boston: Beacon Press, 1976); Carol Gilligan, *In a Different Voice: Psychological Theory and Women's Development* (Cambridge: Harvard University Press, 1982).

65. In "Reading Doris Lessing" Judith Stitzel says, "I read Lessing not as a stimulus to *think this or that* but as a stimulus to *thinking about thinking*" (*College English* 40, no. 5 [Jan. 1979]: 502).

66. In *Prisons* Lessing articulates the hopeful possibility that "the whole push and thrust and development of the world is towards the more complex, the flexible, the open-minded, the ability to entertain many ideas, sometimes contradictory ones, in one's mind at the same time" (71–72).

67. John Leonard refers to "page 353 of *Four-Gated City,* when Martha went through the 'door' into mystical razzmatazz" ("The Spacing Out of Doris Lessing," *New York Times Book Review,* Feb. 7, 1982, rpt., *Critical Essays on Doris Lessing,* Sprague and Virginia Tiger [Boston: G. K. Hall, 1986], 205). Mona Knapp comments that "more than one reader has expressed the sense of having lost a friend with Lessing's abandonment of earthlings" (130). But see Ann Snitow's "A Vindication of Doris Lessing," *Voice Literary Supplement* 39 (Oct. 1985): 6ff.: "In her galactic fantasies, she is never talking about any world but ours." To the extent that she uses science fiction to get outside, she also uses it to look back in.

68. Walter Allen, *The Modern Novel in Britain and the United States* (New York: Duton, 1964); and Richard Kostelanetz, *On Contemporary Literature* (New York: Avon, 1964). Kaplan and Rose also cite reviews of *Martha Quest* and *A Proper Marriage* (*New York Times Book Review* [1964]; *The Canon and the Common Reader* [Knoxville: University of Tennessee Press, 1991]). David Lodge describes her "as faithful to Eliot's lofty conception of responsibility to instruct, heal, unify" ("Beyond the Catastrophe," review of *Shikasta New Statesman* 98 [Nov. 30, 1979]: 860).

69. Gore Vidal, "Paradise Regained," *New York Review of Books* 26 (Dec. 20, 1979): 3.

70. William Pritchard, "Fictional Fixes," *Hudson Review* 33 (Summer 1980): 263. Pritchard adds, "With *Shikasta* she has succeeded in squeezing out all possibilities for

tone from her writing . . . and it is too bad to have people, mainly academic ones, still try to her hold her up as a noble contemporary novelist" (236).

71. Richard Jones, *Listener* 112 (Dec. 6, 1984): 34.

72. Rosemary Dinnage, "In the Disintegrating City," review of *Memoirs* and *The Grass Is Singing, New York Review of Books* 22 (July 17, 1975): 38. Dinnage adds, "Leaden dialogue, faceless characters, and the grinding of worthy ideological axes have all occasionally marred" her novels (38). According to Rene Kyhn Bryant, "Complex character creation, spell-binding plot-spinning, delicate character interplay, bright dialogue—none of these has been regarded as Mrs. Lessing's forte in earlier novels, and *Memoirs,* alas, is no exception" ("Mrs. Lessing's Vanishing Point," review of *Memoirs, National Review* 28, Apr. 30, 1976, 462). Denis Donoghue describes her as "not a stylist": "Mostly, her style is a prose without qualities. . . . The words on the page are there to be seen through, not regarded. They seem to want to be rid of themselves" ("Alice, the Radical Homemaker," *New York Times Book Review,* Sept. 22, 1985, 3). Ronald Bryden claims that "Doris Lessing's intelligence is swifter and finer than the prose style she commands" ("On the Move," review of *Memoirs, New Statesman* 88, Dec. 6, 1974, 827). Kingsley Amis says, in a review of *The Four-Gated City,* that "anyone with so little to narrate should . . . make more concessions to her readers than Mrs. Lessing does with . . . her thousand-word paragraphs, and her tissues of abstract commentary doing duty for characterization" (*Spectator,* Oct. 8, 1954, 450; rpt., Sprague and Tiger, *Critical Essays,* 174).

73. Even sympathetic readers miss the qualities of her style. Here is Kaplan and Rose: "Lessing . . . rarely indulges in word play, *double entendre,* trope, motif, symbol, mythology, in all the playfulness that characterizes much of the most highly regarded literature of the past fifty years"; "Lessing is all passionate engagement; she repudiates again and again the distancing implicit in the chilly cerebral detachment of highly wrought style. . . . Her novels are often presented as diaries, memoirs, personal archival records, letters, notebooks, and rough drafts. Her material is notoriously autobiographical . . . her tone is passionate, deeply personal, emotional, and even physical" (*The Alchemy of Survival,* 7). While much of her material is certainly autobiographical and her tone is of passionate engagement, this description does Lessing a disservice: her style is also highly wrought and characterized by a complexity of play and allusion worthy of the highest of Modernists.

74. Jerome Miller describes "the poetic image as it emerges out of marveling" as giving "us the first inkling of that which we cannot know except through wonder and the inquiry it provokes. . . . [It] leaps ahead toward something which becomes accessible to us for the first time in the poetic evocation of it." ("Wonder as Hinge," *International Philosophical Quarterly* 29, no. 1 [Mar. 1989]: 61).

**Chapter 3**

1. All references to the *Children of Violence* are to the New American Library editions and are referred to as *MQ* (*Martha Quest*), *PM* (*A Proper Marriage*), *RS* (*Ripple From the Storm*), *LL* (*Landlocked*), and *FGC* (*The Four-Gated City*).

2. Catharine R. Stimpson describes "Lessing's primary lesson" as "the necessity of growth, particularly of consciousness," and the narrative as "a detailed, subtle

account of the methodology of growth" ("Doris Lessing and the Parables of Growth," *The Voyage In: Fictions of Female Development,* ed. Elizabeth Abel, Marianne Hirsch, and Elizabeth Langland [Hanover: University Press of New England, 1983], 190, 193). Betsy Draine discusses "images of . . . growth, conversion, and evolution" throughout the series (*Substance under Pressure: Artistic Coherence and Evolving Form in the Novels of Doris Lessing* [Madison: University of Wisconsin Press, 1983], 46). See also Mary Ann Singleton, *The City and the Veld: The Fiction of Doris Lessing* (Lewisburg: Bucknell University Press, 1977), 166.

3. As Roberta Rubenstein says, Lessing's focus evolves away from "psychological realism" to "the symbolic, mythopoeic, and mystical dimensions of experience that go beyond language" (*The Novelistic Vision of Doris Lessing: Breaking the Forms of Consciousness* [Urbana: University of Illinois Press, 1979], 109). See also note 20.

4. "The Small Personal Voice," in *A Small Personal Voice: Doris Lessing, Essay, Reviews, Interviews,* ed. Paul Schlueter (New York: Vintage, 1975), 14 (hereafter "SPV"). Georg Lukács, "The Ideology of Modernism," *The Meaning of Contemporary Realism* (London: Merlin Press, 1963), trans. John and Necke Mander; rpt., *Twentieth-Century Literary Criticism,* ed. David Lodge (London: Longman, 1972), 476, 486.

5. Sydney Janet Kaplan, *Feminine Consciousness in the Modern British Novel* (Chicago: University of Illinois Press, 1975), 140.

6. "Doris Lessing at Stony Brook: An Interview by Jonah Raskin," in Schlueter, *Small Personal Voice,* 65; *Doris Lessing Newsletter* 8, no. 2 (Fall 1984): 3.

7. Rubenstein, *Novelistic Vision,* 35, 45. According to Michael Thorpe, the "narrative owes nothing to structural experimentation and supplies little debatable symbolism" (*Doris Lessing,* London: Longman, 1973), 19; Mary Ellmann finds "the effect of tedium . . . so predominant . . . [that the] whole intention seems to have driven the writer toward the dulling of her own talent" (*Thinking about Women* [New York: Harcourt, 1968], 198); Kingsley Amis refers to Lessing's "thousand-word paragraphs, and her tissues of abstract commentary doing duty for characterisation" (*Spectator,* Oct. 8, 1954, 450; rpt., Sprague and Tiger, *Critical Essays,* 174).

8. Patricia Spacks writes: "If Martha Quest . . . figures as a heroine, she must be a heroine of a very peculiar sort. She stands for nothing, defies nothing successfully, cannot endure her condition without self-defeating gestures of escape. She is passive when she should be active, obtuse when she should be perceptive. Her heroism consists merely in her suffering and her rage, not in any hope or promise of effect" (*The Female Imagination* [New York: Knopf, 1975]). Sydney Janet Kaplan criticizes her for a passivity that "approaches tropism": "Things just seem to happen to Martha," "who finds herself married twice to men she does not love, who bears a child after she decided she would not, who winds up in the Coldridge household permanently as caretaker and helpmeet, sailing along from one situation to the next with plans for change, plans for decisive action, but nonetheless carried along on a tide of contingency" (*Feminine Consciousness in the Modern British Novel* [University of Illinois Press, 1975], 53). Jean Bethke Elshtain ("The Post–*Golden Notebook* Fiction of Doris Lessing," *Salmagundi* [Winter–Spring 1980]: 95–114), criticizes Lessing's women for "a passive or re-active stance towards the world: they are beings to whom, or

through whom, things happen" (99). Betsy Draine's distinction "between fatalistic resignation and a fruitful receptivity" (65) speaks to this criticism.

9. From "Little Gidding," *The Complete Poems and Plays* (New York: Harcourt, 1958):

> We shall not cease from exploration
> And the end of all of our exploring
> Will be to arrive where we started
> And know the place for the first time.

10. Peter Brooks describes repetition with a view to revision as the primary impetus of narrative (*Reading for the Plot: Design and Intention in Narrative* [New York: Vintage, 1984], 98, 235, 285). Roy Schafer describes narrative as like psychotherapy, aspiring to "a narrative re-description of reality," to a "new story" ("Narration in the Psychoanalytic Dialogue," *On Narrative,* ed. W. J. T. Mitchell [Chicago: University of Chicago Press, 1981], 46, 44).

11. The term *no man's land* recurs in Mr. Quest's obsessive ramblings about the war, and it is Sandra Gilbert and Susan Gubar's metaphor for the early twentieth-century literary landscape, with its many dying and wounded male figures (*No Man's Land: The Place of the Woman Writer in the Twentieth Century* [New Haven, Conn.: Yale University Press, 1988]).

12. Rachel Blau DuPlessis notes that Martha "adheres to literary and attitudinal scripts of womanhood" and that "literature offers structures and resolutions that bear no resemblance to her life as a woman" (*Writing Beyond the Ending* [Bloomington: Indiana University Press, 1985], 188).

13. Roland Barthes refers to "the constraints of the discourse" (*S/Z* [New York: Hill and Wang, 1974], 135). In her discussion of the post-Saussurean position represented by Barthes, Catherine Belsey describes realism as "the accomplice of ideology" (*Critical Practice* [London: Methuen, 1980], 73): "It is intelligible as 'realist' precisely because it reproduces what we already seem to know" (47); "to this extent it is a predominantly conservative form" (51; see also 46, 52). Stephen Heath describes realist narrative as "aimed at containment." "The point of the action, the goal of its advance, is the recovery of homogeneity" (*Touch of Evil, Screen* 16, no. 1 [1995]: 49; and 16, no. 2 [1975]: 91); in *Language and Materialism: Developments in Semiology and the Theory of the Subject,* ed. Rosalind Coward and John Ellis [London: Routledge, 1977], 49. Fredric Jameson refers to "containment strategies which seek to endow their objects of representation with formal unity" (*The Political Unconscious: Narrative as a Socially Symbolic Act* [Ithaca, N.Y.: Cornell University Press, 1981], 54).

14. Audre Lorde, "The Master's Tools Will Never Dismantle the Master's House," in *This Bridge Called My Back: Writings of Radical Women of Color,* ed. Cherríe Moraga and Gloria Anzaldúa (New York: Women of Color Press, 1981), 98–101.

15. Rubenstein, *Novelistic Visions,* 38. Cf. "down the slopes of disintegration" (*Women in Love* [New York: Viking, 1960], 196 and 36). At the end of the novel, as Birkin wonders if Gerald might have escaped his doom by finding "the old Imperial Road," he reflects: "Was it a way out? It was only a way back in again" (469).

16. Simone de Beauvoir," *The Second Sex* (New York: Vintage, 1952), 71. For a discussion of the archetypal resonances of this theme, see Katherine Fishburn's "The Nightmare Repetition: The Mother-Daughter Conflict in Doris Lessing's *Children of Violence,*" in *The Lost Tradition: Mothers and Daughters in Literature,* ed. Cathy N. Davidson and E. M. Broner (New York: Ungar, 1980). Fishburn discusses Mrs. Quest in relation to Erich Neumann's idea of "The Dark and Terrible Mother," "the devouring womb of the grave and of death" (*The Great Mother: An Analysis of the Archetype,* trans. Ralph Manehim [Princeton University Press, 1972]).

17. Indeed, she dispenses with endings wherever possible. Even when she comes to the end of the *Children of Violence* series, she leaves a "loose end" (*FGC,* 324, 555), which is picked up in the next series, *Canopus in Argos,* when Lynda Coldridge makes a startling reappearance in *Shikasta;* and rather than finishing this series, she interrupts it with Jane Somers's *Diary of a Good Neighbor,* which itself sprouts a sequel, *If the Old Could.*

18. There are numerous images relating to light screened or filtered, as though it were too overwhelming to be apprehended directly: sunlight filters through the window (*PM,* 171), "slants through the slats of the blind" (12), through the doorway of the military bungalow (212), "through the cream-shaded windows" of Stella's mother's house (207), through the "gauze window" of the pantry, which is the coolest room in Martha's house (248). Imagery relating to light mediated by human contrivances becomes even more pronounced in *A Ripple from the Storm,* which also opens on a scene of two women talking, only here they are inside a room looking out on an urban scene—"from the dusty windows of a small room over Black Ally's Cafe." The world of this novel is even further from the light, more cut off from rejuvenating forces of nature: the veld is "soiled, factory-littered, smudged" (28); the midday sun strikes painfully into Martha's skull (87). The only benevolent brightness that occurs in these novels is in the scene where Martha's daughter Caroline wakes at dawn and tries to catch the mote-filled sunlight—"a shaft of yellow light . . . swam with golden dust," the room "filled with sunlight, like a glass bowl full of quivering bright water" (*PM,* 200–202): the child is still near the light.

19. For a provocative discussion of the liberating effect of the Great War on women, see Sandra M. Gilbert, "Soldier's Heart: Literary Men, Literary Women, and the Great War," *Signs* 8, no. 3 (1983): 422–50; and *No Man's Land*

20. Brooks, *Reading,* 22. See also Walter Benjamin, "The Storyteller," in *Illuminations,* trans. Harry Zohn (New York: Shocken Books, 1969): "Death is the sanction of everything that the storyteller can tell. He has borrowed his authority from death" (94); and Frank Kermode, who suggests that since people are born and die in medias res, "to make sense of their span they need fictive concords with origins and ends, such as give meaning to lives . . . the End is a figure for their own deaths. So, perhaps, are all ends in fiction" (*The Sense of An Ending: Studies in the Theory of Fiction* [London: Oxford University Press, 1975]).

21. In "My Mother's Life" Lessing describes her mother's "real love, the man she ought to have married," as "dead": "He had been a young doctor. . . . His little picture, torn out of a newspaper that recorded his death by drowning in a ship sunk by the Germans, stood forever on her dressing table" (*Granta* 14 [Winter 1984]: 56). As Simone de Beauvoir suggests, "There are women who devote themselves to dead or

otherwise inaccessible heroes, . . . for beings of flesh and blood would be fatally contrary to their dreams" (*Second Sex,* 727). de Beauvoir discusses the function of the dead hero in preserving women's illusions (391–92).

22. Women's subjection to the reproductive cycle makes her what de Beauvoir terms "the victim of the species" (*Second Sex,* 23; and chap. 1, "The Data of Biology").

23. Stokley Carmichael's remark was one of those notorious provocations that caused women to realize that the interests of women and men, even those who were working for radical change, were not necessarily allied. See Judith Hole and Ellen Levine, *Rebirth of Feminism* (New York: Quadrangle Books, 1971), 110–11; and Sara Evans, *Personal Politics: The Roots of Women's Liberation in the Civil Rights Movement and the New Left* (New York: Vintage, 1980), 87–88.

24. Claire Sprague notes the discrepancy between men's "professions of dedication to equality" and "their private patriarchal behavior patterns" (*Rereading Doris Lessing: Narrative Patterns of Doubling and Repetition* [Chapel Hill: University of North Carolina Press, 1987], 132).

25. "All of these violent hostilities are unreal. They've got very little to do with human beings" (interview by Roy Newquist, Oct. 1963, *Counterpoint* [Chicago: Rand McNally, 1964]; rpt., Schlueter, *Small Personal Voice,* 45–60).

## Chapter 4

1. Parts of this chapter reiterate "Doris Lessing's *Landlocked:* 'A New Kind of Knowledge,'" *Contemporary Literature* 28, no. 1 (Spring 1987): 82–103. I am breaking with the chronology of Lessing's works in discussing *Landlocked* and *The Four-Gated City* before *The Golden Notebook* because I want to trace the evolution of ideas and structural patterns throughout the series.

2. Doris Lessing, *Landlocked* (New York: New American Library, 1966), 175. All references to the *Children of Violence* are to the New American editions and are referred to as *MQ* (*Martha Quest*), *PM* (*A Proper Marriage*), *RS* (*Ripple from the Storm*), *LL* (*Landlocked*), and *FGC* (*The Four-Gated City*).

3. "The Teacher, the Teaching, the Taught," Idries Shah, *The Sufis* (New York: Doubleday, 1971), 392.

4. Lorna Sage, *Contemporary Writers: Doris Lessing* (London: Methuen, 1983), 58.

5. Joanna Russ, "What Can a Heroine Do? or Why Women Can't Write," in *Images of Women in Fiction,* ed. Susan Koppelman Cornillon (Bowling Green, Ohio: Bowling Green University Popular Press, 1972), 3–20; rpt., *Woman as Writer,* ed. Jeanette L. Webber and Joan Grumman (Boston: Houghton Mifflin, 1978), 158–63.

6. For the idea of evolution in Sufism, see "The Travelers and the Grapes," 33; and "The Elephant in the Dark," 38, 61, in Shah, *Sufis.*

7. For "the old villain," see "Our Master Jalaluddin Rumi," Shah, *Sufis,* 134.

8. "Our Master," 141; "Travelers and Grapes," 17; and "Elephant," 45. Mary Ann Singleton notes that in this novel "Martha begins to show a more profound knowledge that reaches below the level of rational thought. . . . evident partly in her

increased powers of intuitions" (*The City and the Veld* [Lewisburg: Bucknell University Press, 1977], 196).

9. "Elephant," 52–53.

10. *The Waste Land,* T. S. Eliot, *The Complete Poems and Plays, 1909–1950* (New York: Harcourt, 1952), ll. 22, 301–2. Further references are to this edition. Bluett voices the Communist party line on Eliot, in his sarcastic response to Jasmine's attempts to educate Tommy with *War and Peace*—"'Well, well,' he said, 'why not T. S. Eliot? Why not T. S. Eliot, while you're about it?' He began reciting: 'April is the cruellest month, breeding lilacs out of the dead land'" (*RS,* 74). Lessing does not share his contempt.

11. I argue this more fully in "Shakespeare's *Tempest* and Eliot's *The Waste Land:* 'What the Thunder Said,'" *Orbis Litterarum* 34 (1979): 187–300.

12. The opening scene of *Landlocked,* like that of each preceding novel, evokes a play of light—except that here Martha does not shun it: the sun burns through her office window at Robinson's, irradiating everything within (4–6); then, through the open windows, comes the smell of cut grass—"the grass fell in jade-green swathes, frothy with white flowers . . . and the smell of cut grass wafted in" (9)—anticipation of the fresh foliage that becomes the setting for her love with Thomas.

13. The failure of this relationship recalls that in *The Waste Land* when the speaker withdraws from "the hyacinth girl," similarly described in terms of fresh foliage and light:

> —Yet when we came back, late, from the Hyacinth garden
> Your arms full, and your hair wet, I could not
> Speak, and my eyes failed, I was neither
> Living nor dead, and I knew nothing,
> Looking into the heart of light, the silence.
>
> (ll. 36–41)

14. *A Feminist Tarot,* ed. Sally Gearhart and Susan Rennie (Watertown, Mass.: Persephone Press, 1977), 14. Their reading of the hanged man as "the male principle" that must be sacrificed to assure "the regeneration of the female principle" is interesting in view of the deaths of so many male characters in this novel.

15. See Jesse L. Weston, *From Ritual to Romance* (Garden City, N.Y.: Doubleday Anchor, 1957), chap. 2, "The Task of the Hero."

16. According to Weston, "the feat by which the Grail heroes, Gawain and Perceval, rejoiced the hearts of a suffering folk [was] the restoration of the rivers to their channels, the 'Freeing of the Waters'" (*From Ritual,* 26).

17. "Human kind / Cannot bear very much reality" (T. S. Eliot, "Burnt Norton," *The Four Quartets, Complete Poems,* 118).

18. Lear's madness encompasses a comparable range, from "Thou must be patient" to "Kill, kill, kill, kill, kill, kill!" (*The Complete Pelican Shakespeare,* ed. Alfred Harbage [Baltimore: Penguin, 1969], 4.6.175, 183). Thomas's idea to walk on stilts as a method of outwitting the ants recalls Lear's "delicate strategem to shoe / A troop of horse with felt" (ll.181–82).

19. Cf. "a kind of light" (*LL,* 191). Marlow describes his experience as "sombre enough," "not very clear": "And yet it seemed to throw a kind of light" (Joseph

Conrad, *The Heart of Darkness: Norton Critical Edition* [New York: Norton, 1963], 7). Jerome Thale ("The Anatomy of the Mental Personality," *New Introductory Lectures on Psycho-Analysis, University of Toronto Quarterly* 25 [July 1955]: 82–112, rpt., *Norton Critical Edition,* 180–86), cites this line as evidence that Conrad's tale is a version of the Grail quest.

20. Like Anna and Saul in *The Golden Notebook,* Martha and Thomas "break down into one another," and, as in that relationship, it is the man who goes further in the process of disintegration.

21. Thomas's manuscript presents Martha with "a very different job of editing" (269) from that presented by Johnny's, though both documents make a contribution to the unwritten history of Africa.

22. Idries Shah, *Thinkers of the East: Teachings of the Dervishes* (Baltimore: Penguin Books, 1972), 194; quoted in Nancy Shields Hardin, "Doris Lessing and the Sufi Way," in *Doris Lessing: Critical Studies,* ed. Annis Pratt and L. S. Dembo (Madison: University of Wisconsin Press, 1974), 151.

23. Evelyn J. Hinz ("Hierogamy versus Wedlock: Types of Marriage Plots and Their Relationship to Genres of Prose Fiction," *PMLA* 91, no. 5 [1976]: 900–913), discusses Martha and Thomas's relationship as a hierogamic, or sacred, marriage. Their union takes place outside social structures—they are separated by social class, and each is married to someone else—and in a natural setting: "Hierogamous unions must take place in the open or in an elemental setting because their object is to evoke the primordial marriage of the elements"; "the object . . . the regeneration or rebirth of the cosmos . . . is less a matter of 'getting back to nature' than a matter of getting nature to come back" (909); such a union requires "that one abandon one's connection with history . . . or reverse the process of civilization" and "shed . . . the whole orientation toward rationalism and empiricism" (908). Hinz's description of hierogamy as characterizing mythic narrative rather than "prose fiction" or "the novel," and of "the mythic artist" as viewing "reality as that which is imbued with the divine, that which is eternally recurrent, that which is transmitted in history or myth" (905), corroborates my sense of *Landlocked* as the site of Lessing's shift from social realism to myth. Her reading confirms my sense of Thomas as a figure associated with fertility, like the "dying god" of the Grail legend.

24. Cf. the numerous "keys," "doors," and "gates" associated with love, marriage, books, Marxism, which promised a way out but provided only a way back into the system Martha was trying to escape. Like "the key [that] / Turn[s] in the door once and . . . once only" at the end of *The Waste Land,* such keys "confirm a prison" (ll. 411–14).

25. Ingrid Holmquist criticizes Lessing in these terms: "From having been forward-looking fighters for social change, her fictional characters have become introspective and enmeshed in the past, bent upon inner consciousness. . . . Lessing's thinking has passed into its opposite: from having been . . . progressive, rational, and atheistic, it has become what could be called regressive, irrational, and religious" (*From Society to Nature: A Study of Doris Lessing's Children of Violence,* Gothenburg Studies in English 47, Acta Universitatis Gothoburgensis [Gotebort Sweden, 1980], 8–9 and 168). Nicole Ward Jouve criticizes Lessing's "evolution towards a collective voice," a "detached trans-individual vision" ("Of Mud and Other Matter—the *Children of*

*Violence,"* in *Notebooks, Memoirs, Archives: Reading and Rereading Doris Lessing,* ed. Jenny Taylor [Boston: Routledge and Kegan Paul, 1982], 85, 124). John Leonard criticizes Lessing for losing "interest in people" ("The Spacing Out of Doris Lessing," *New York Times Book Review,* Feb. 7, 1982; rpt., Sprague and Tiger, *Small Personal Voice,* 201, 205); Barbara Elshtain says that the "compelling characters have faded from [Lessing's] fiction": her "millenarianism" has required her "to eliminate those passional cantankerous human beings who engaged with and against one another in history" ("The Post–*Golden Notebook* Fiction of Doris Lessing," *Salmagundi* [Winter-Spring 1980]: 96). But Lessing denies that her work has fundamentally "changed direction." "In reality I am the same person who wrote about the same things" ("Doris Lessing: Testimony to Mysticism: Interview by Nissa Torrents," *Doris Lessing Newsletter,* 4, no. 2, [Winter 1980]: 1); though she also admits that "since writing *The Golden Notebook* I've become less personal" ("Doris Lessing at Stony Brook: An Interview by Jonah Raskin," in Schlueter, *A Small Personal Voice,* 68). Actually—and I do see more of a continuum than a contradiction in her work—in a way she has never been very "personal"—"Martha could not bear that people tended to fall into types"—yet she is continually discovering that they do and is repeatedly behaving like one herself (*PM,* 15, 250, 279, 335; *RS,* 36). "One may imagine oneself as altogether unique and extraordinary . . . but one behaves incredibly, inexorably, exactly like everyone else" (*MQ,* 211). Early on, Martha's experience of oneness with the universe gives her knowledge of a reality that transcends the social; the powerful descriptions of October and January, of the African landscape, the light, stars, and sky, evoke a cosmic setting that dwarfs the human drama, and scenes in the early novels have archetypal as well as sociocultural resonances (see, e.g., *MQ,* 73).

26. Terry Eagleton, *Literary Theory: An Introduction* (Minneapolis: University of Minnesota Press, 1983), 110.

## Chapter 5

1. All references to the *Children of Violence* are to the New American Library editions and are referred to as *MQ* (*Martha Quest*), *PM* (*A Proper Marriage*), *RS* (*Ripple from the Storm*), *LL* (*Landlocked*), and *FGC* (*The Four-Gated City*).

2. *The Golden Notebook* (New York: Bantam, 1971), 4, 472.

3. This is one of several echoes of Woolf: "There she sat, herself" (215) and "there is it" (558) recall Woolf's *Mrs. Dalloway* and *To the Lighthouse,* respectively. During her breakdown Martha thinks of Septimus Smith: *"The young man in Virginia Woolf's story who was mad. He heard the birds talking in ancient Greek"* (521). Like Woolf's protagonists, Martha has moments of heightened awareness that transcend time, and Lessing's narrative form, like Woolf's, legitimizes such moments by delegitimizing linear time.

4. The term *growing point* recurs: "'That is freedom,'" says Lynda,'"that's mine. It's all they let me have,'" as she traces with her finger "a spiral that had once been a growing point in the wood" of the table in the kitchen at Radlett Street (118); Mark's growing point is his passion for Lynda (109), Frances's growing point is with Jill (430), Paul's is money (436), and the Coldridges become "growing places" for others (534). Martha generalizes her own growing point to the collective, realizing "that if

she was feeling something, in this particular way, with the authenticity, the irresistibility, of the growing point, then she was not alone, others were feeling the same, since the growing point was never, could never be, just Martha's" (485–86).

5. For an excellent discussion of Mark as novelist, see Melissa G. Walker, "Doris Lessing's *The Four-Gated City:* Consciousness and Community—a Different History," *Southern Review* 17, no. 1 (Jan. 1981): 102–6.

6. Adrienne Rich ("The Temptations of a Motherless Woman," *On Lies, Secrets, and Silence: Selected Prose, 1966–1978* [New York: Norton, 1979], 98) notes the parallel between *The Four-Gated City* and *Jane Eyre.* See also Barbara Hill Rigney, *Madness and Sexual Politics in the Feminist Novel: Studies in Bronte, Woolf, Lessing, and Atwood* (Madison: University of Wisconsin Press, 1978), 77. Joyce Carol Oates's response suggests something about the way the novel defeats expectation: "We keep waiting for Martha, the 'heroine,' to become central again and to move on to new adventures. We particularly wait for her to fall in love or to somehow shape her shapeless, peculiar life. She does not . . . this is a strangely undramatic novel" (*Saturday Review of Literature* 52 [May 17, 1969]: 48; rpt., Sprague and Tiger, *Critical Essays,* 176).

7. Frederick R. Karl suggests that Martha "uses Mark Coldridge's house as . . . an escape from a social and political world she cannot control" (20) ("Doris Lessing in the Sixties: The New Anatomy of Melancholy," *Contemporary Literature* 23 [Winter 1972]: 15–33).

8. Sydney Janet Kaplan, *Feminine Consciousness in the Modern British Novel* (Chicago: University of Illinois Press, 1975), 172.

9. "Doris Lessing at Stony Brook: An Interview by Jonah Raskin," in *A Small Personal Voice: Doris Lessing, Essay, Reviews, Interviews,* ed. Paul Schlueter (New York: Vintage, 1975), 65.

10. Mary Ann Singleton, *The City and the Veld: The Fiction of Doris Lessing* (Lewisburg: Bucknell University Press, 1977), 215.

11. Dagmar Barnouw, "Disorderly Company: From *The Golden Notebook* to *The Four-Gated City,*" in *Doris Lessing: Critical Studies,* ed. Annis Pratt and L. S. Dembo (Madison: University of Wisconsin Press, 1974), 75.

12. Paul Schlueter, *The Novels of Doris Lessing* (Carbondale: Southern University Illinois Press, 1973), 75; Roberta Rubenstein, *The Novelistic Vision of Doris Lessing: Breaking the Forms of Consciousness* (Urbana: University of Illinois Press, 1979), 168; Claire Sprague, "'Without Contraries Is No Progression': Lessing's *Four-Gated City,*" *Modern Fiction Studies* 26, no. 1 (Spring 1980): 116.

13. Elizabeth Dalton, *Commentary* 44, Jan. 1970, 31.

14. "Western society for the past three hundred years has been caught up in a fire storm of change . . . change sweeps through the highly industrialized countries with waves of ever accelerating speed and unprecedented impact" (Alvin Toffler, *Future Shock* [New York: Bantam, 1970], 9). This book was a big seller in the early 1970s.

15. Cf. T. S. Eliot, "East Coker," *Complete Poems,* 123:

> In succession
> Houses rise and fall, crumble, are extended,
> Are removed, destroyed, restored . . .

16. Doris Lessing, interview by Jonah Raskin, at Stony Brook; reprinted in Schlueter, *A Small Personal Voice,* 66.

17. DuPlessis describes Martha's progress as a "looping back motion" apparent "elsewhere in the female quest" (*Writing Beyond the Ending: Narrative Strategies of Twentieth-Century Women Writers* [Bloomington: Indiana University Press, 1985], 193). In "Martha Quest to Ambien II" Sprague notes that "the repetition that plagues Martha Quest is sacramental and desirable in the world of *Shikasta*" (*Rereading Doris Lessing: Narrative Patterns of Doubling and Repetition* [Chapel Hill: University of North Carolina Press, 1987], 168)—though I see it as becoming sacramental earlier, in *Four-Gated City*.

18. Another dimension of London is suggested when Martha scrapes the wallpaper off the wall and reads back in time: "Thirteen times had a man stood on trestles . . . and stretched new clean paper over the stains and dirts of the layer beneath" (74). As Christine W. Sizemore notes, the city "exists not only in three dimensions of space, but in three additional dimensions, perhaps of time: the *histories, lives,* and *loves* of people" ("Reading the City as Palimpsest: The Experiential Perception of the City in Doris Lessing's *Four-Gated City,*" in *Women Writers and the City: Essays in Feminist Literary Criticism,* ed. Susan M. Squier [Knoxville: University of Tennessee Press, 1984], 177). See also Sprague's discussion of "imagery of layering" and "imagery of stripping or peeling": "layering comes to represent Martha's ability to accept her past, present, and potential selves and to see these selves as co-existing with present events in time" ("Without Contraries," 102).

19. Stephen Jay Gould, *Time's Arrow, Time's Cycle: Myth and Metaphor in the Discovery of Geological Time* (Cambridge: Harvard University Press, 1987). For the association of the linear with the West and the cyclic with the East, see Samuel L. Macey, *Patriarchs of Time: Dualism in Saturn-Cronus, Father Time, the Watchmaker God, and Father Christmas* (Athens: University of Georgia Press, 1987), 165–66; for biblical history as linear, see M. H. Abrams, *Natural Supernaturalism* (New York: Norton, 1971), 32–37. Gould, like Richard Morris (*Time's Arrows* [New York: Simon and Schuster, 1984]) and Mircea Eliade (*The Myth of the Eternal Return* [Princeton, N.J.: Princeton University Press, 1954] and *Images and Symbols: Studies in Religious Symbolism* [New York: Sheed and Ward, 1961], 72–73), identifies the cyclic with archaic and the linear with the modern and Western. Rubenstein notes the centrality of both to Lessing's fiction:

> The linear mode is a metaphorical abstraction for the kind of mental activity associated with rational thinking, analysis, logic, the unidirectional unfoldings of history and of life through time. By contrast, the circular mode reverberates throughout myth and the nonrational, the suprarational and synthesizing levels of mental activity: symbol, dream, hallucination, madness, extrasensory perception, mystical vision. The contrast between these modes of cognition and the attempt to reconcile their often contrary orientations . . . produce a central tension and energy in Lessing's fiction. (*Novelistic Vision,* 8)

20. Lessing says "she had begun to use metaphor . . . because so many words had become inadequate for what she wanted to express" (interview with Malcolm Dean,

BBC Television, May 7, 1980; Ann Scott, "The More Recent Writings: Sufism, Mysticism and Politics," in Taylor, *Notebooks,* 167). Susan Kress makes a useful distinction between the cliché that contains an important truth but has simply been "dislocated from its root in experience" and the cliché that is a "trap laid by the culture, official phrases designed to freeze in official molds" ("Lessing's Responsibility," *Salmagundi* [Winter–Spring 1980]: 131, 114, 119).

21. So did Anna Wulf's mother die when she was a child, and though she retains "the image of somebody strong and dominating, whom Anna had had to fight" (42), and though characters such as "Mother Sugar" and Anna's friend Molly play mothering roles, Anna is without a biological mother in the novel—and this seems to be a requisite for the character to develop the mother in herself and risk openness to the experiences of others. The presence of a biological mother, Lessing seems to suggest, is too threatening to allow this risk. Martha also develops her nurturing side only after Mrs. Quest disappears from *The Four-Gated City.*

22. Elayne Antler Rapping, "Unfree Women: Feminism in Doris Lessing's Novels," *Women's Studies* 3 (1975): 33–34, 43–44.

## Chapter 6

1. Much of this chapter appeared in my book *Changing Stories: Feminist Fiction and the Tradition* (Bloomington: Indiana University Press, 1991), 105–29.

2. *The Golden Notebook* (New York: Bantam, 1973), x–xi. She felt that this put her in "a false position" because "The last thing I have wanted to do was to refuse to support women" (viii). "I got angry over the reviews of *The Golden Notebook.* They thought it was personal—it was, in parts. But it was also a highly structured book. . . . The point about that book was the relation of its parts to each other. But the book they wanted to turn it into was called *The Confessions of Doris Lessing"* (interview with Roy Newquist, in *Doris Lessing: A Small Personal Voice: Essays, Reviews, Interviews,* ed. Paul Schlueter [New York: Vintage, 1975], 51).

3. Rachel Blau DuPlessis, "For the Etruscans," in *The New Feminist Criticism: Essays on Women, Literature, and Theory,* ed. Elaine Showalter (New York: Pantheon, 1985), 279.

4. *A Proper Marriage,* 62. All references to the *Children of Violence* are to the New American Library editions and are referred to as *MQ* (*Martha Quest*), *PM* (*A Proper Marriage*), and *FGC* (*The Four-Gated City*).

5. Carey Kaplan and Ellen Cronan Rose, *The Canon and the Common Reader* (Knoxville: University of Tennessee Press, 1991).

6. John Leonard describes it as having changed his life (*Newsday,* Mar. 17, 1988, pt. 2, 8; rpt., "In Person," *Doris Lessing Newsletter* [*DLN*], 12, no. 2 [Fall 1989], 5. Louis Kampf (*On Modernism: The Prospects for Literature and Freedom* [Cambridge: M.I.T. Press, 1967]), describes "Lessing's massive novel" as "a significant, and exemplary, attempt to deal with" the central questions of modernism (322), "a very true—and very great—work of art" (326); and Robert Taubman ("Free Women," *New Statesman* [Apr. 20, 1962]; rpt., *On Contemporary Literature,* ed. Richard Kostelanetz [New York: Avon, 1964], 402–3), calls it "unique in its truthfulness and range . . . the sort of book that determines the way people think about themselves,"

though he slips in a snide comparison with de Beauvoir—Lessing "says far more of genuine interest, is less self-conscious and much less boring" (403). And Irving Howe calls it "the most absorbing and exciting piece of new fiction I have read in a decade," but he too gets in an invidious comparison: Lessing is "radically different from other women writers who have dealt with the problems of their sex . . . in that she has no use either for the quaverings of the feminist writers or the aggressions of those female novelists whose every sentence leads a charge in the war of the sexes. . . . And Miss Lessing is far too serious for those displays of virtuoso bitchiness which are the blood and joy of certain American lady writers" (*New Republic* 147, 15 Dec. 1962, 17–20; rpt., *Critical Essays on Doris Lessing,* ed. Claire Sprague and Virginia Tiger [Boston: G. K. Hall, 1988], 181, 178). Rose and Kaplan point out that the first Lessing scholarship was written by men—James Gindin, Frederick Karl, Frederick P. W. McDowell, John Carey, Paul Schlueter—but that after 1971, far more women than men wrote about her: "From 1971 to 1986, 78% of the articles, 88% of the books, 93% of the MLA presentations, and 95% of the dissertations on Lessing in this country were written by women" (13, 16–17).

7. Anthony Burgess, *The Novel Now: A Guide to Contemporary Fiction* (New York: Norton, 1967), 19.

8. P. W. Frederick McDowell, "The Fiction of Doris Lessing: An Interim View," *Arizona Quarterly* 21 (1965): 329–30. See Mona Knapp *"The Golden Notebook:* A Feminist Context for the Classroom," in *Approaches to Teaching Lessing's "The Golden Notebook,"* ed. Carey Kaplan and Ellen Cronan Rose (New York: Modern Language Association of America, 1989), 109–10, for a discussion of McDowell's essay and other sexist criticism of the novel.

9. Walter Allen, *The Modern Novel in Britain and the United States* (New York: Dutton, 1964), 277.

10. Patrick Parrinder, "Descents into Hell: The Later Novels of Doris Lessing," *Critical Quarterly* 22, no. 4 (Winter 1980): 14.

11. Frederick R. Karl, *A Reader's Guide to the Contemporary English Novel* (New York: Farrar, Straus and Giroux, 1971), 291.

12. James Gindin, *Postwar British Fiction: New Accents and Attitudes* (Berkeley: University of California Press, 1962), 86, 83–84.

13. Bernard Bergonzi, *The Situation of the Novel* (Pittsburgh: University of Pittsburgh Press, 1970), 200–202.

14. "The Small Personal Voice," in *A Small Personal Voice: Doris Lessing, Essay, Reviews, Interviews,* ed. Paul Schlueter (New York: Vintage, 1975), 3.

15. Mervyn Jones ("The State of Fiction: A Symposium," *New Review* 5 [Summer 1978], 1), expresses surprise that "over the last ten years, more novels haven't been written employing the *Golden Notebook* technique" and concludes that writers are "unable to take off from the groundwork which she had already attained" because they feel "daunted" (47). As my *Changing the Story* demonstrates, *The Golden Notebook* did inspire followers who employed its techniques (Bloomington: Indiana University Press, 1991).

16. John Holloway, "The Literary Scene"; and Gilbert Phelps, "The Post-War English Novel," both in *The New Pelican Guide to English Literature: The Present,* ed. Boris Ford (Harmondsworth: Penguin, 1983), 65–125, 417–49.

17. *British Novelists since 1900,* ed. Jack I. Biles (New York: AMS Press, 1987).

18. Lennard J. Davis, *Resisting Novels: Ideology and Fiction* (New York: Methuen, 1987), 157.

19. Alice Bradley Markos, "The Pathology of Feminine Failure in the Fiction of Doris Lessing," *Critique: Studies in Modern Fiction* 16 (1974): 92, 89–90.

20. Showalter refers to the novel's "aversion to the feminine sensibility" (*A Literature of Their Own: British Women Novelists from Brontë to Lessing* [London: Virago, 1978], 309). Also see Ellen Morgan "Alienation of the Woman Writer in *The Golden Notebook,*" in *Doris Lessing: Critical Studies,* ed. Annis Pratt and L. S. Dembo (Madison: University of Wisconsin Press, 1974), 63. Mona Knapp argues that Anna does not "make a breakthrough toward feminist self-consciousness." "She remains male-oriented and resents even the physical condition of femaleness" (*Doris Lessing* [New York: Ungar, 1984], 60).

21. Catharine R. Stimpson, "Doris Lessing and the Parables of Growth," in *The Voyage In: Fictions of Female Development,* ed. Elizabeth Abel, Marianne Hirsch, and Elizabeth Langland (Hanover, N.H.: University Press of New England, 1983), 193–94.

22. Jenny Taylor, "Introduction: Situating Reading," in *Notebooks, Memoirs, Archives: Reading and Rereading Doris Lessing,* ed. Jenny Taylor (Boston: Routledge, 1982), 9.

23. Joanne S. Frye, *Living Stories, Telling Lives: Women and the Novel in Contemporary Experience* (Ann Arbor: University of Michigan Press, 1986), 172.

24. I argue this point more fully in "Divided Selves: Women and Men in *The Golden Notebook*" (in *The [M]other Tongue: Essays in Feminist Psychoanalytic Criticism,* ed. Shirley Nelson Garner, Claire Kahane, and Madelon Sprengnether [Ithaca: Cornell University Press, 1985], 280–305). Judith Kegan Gardiner also describes empathy as a means to change in *The Golden Notebook:* "As the book progresses, Anna finds seeing from the other person's perspective and feeling as they do essential to her mental health and to her fiction" (*Rhys, Stead, Lessing and the Politics of Empathy* [Bloomington: Indiana University Press, 1989], 120, 151). Patricia Waugh similarly sees "the solubility of [Anna's] ego boundaries as . . . a source of utopian strength"; "for Lessing, salvation can come only through a profound and full recognition of our relational needs and desires and the attempts to construct a collective world which is not based on the competitive striving of the isolated ego" (*Feminine Fictions: Revisiting the Postmodern* [London: Routledge, 1989], 204, 208). See also Jean Wyatt's *Reconstructing Desire: The Role of the Unconscious in Women's Reading and Writing* (Chapel Hill: University of North Carolina Press, 1990), for a discussion of Anna's breakthrough in relation to theories of creativity powered by empathy—theories of Joanna Field, Evelyn Fox Keller, and Heinz Kohut (157–62).

25. Nancy Chodorow, *The Reproduction of Mothering: Psychoanalysis and the Sociology of Gender* (Berkeley: University of California Press, 1979), 103, 166–67. See also Carol Gilligan, *In a Different Voice: Psychological Theory and Women's Development* (Cambridge: Harvard University Press, 1982): "Men and women may perceive danger in different social situations and construe danger in different ways—men seeing danger more often in close personal affiliation than in achievement and

construing danger to arise from intimacy, women perceiving danger in impersonal achievement situations" (42).

26. They illustrate what Andrew Tolson terms "the limits of masculinity" (*The Limits of Masculinity* [London: Tavistock, 1977]) and what Warren Farrell terms "the confines of masculinity" (*The Liberated Man, or Beyond Masculinity: Freeing Men and Their Relationships with Women* [New York: Bantam, 1975], 29–31); see also Herb Goldberg, *The Hazards of Being Male* (New York: New American Library, 1976).

27. Jean Wyatt argues that as Anna and Saul break down into each other, Anna finds herself playing the parts in Saul's unconscious scenarios rather than discovering the unknown in herself. While Lessing's version of the unconscious proves, disappointingly, to be as ideologically programmed as the conscious mind, Wyatt concedes that playing out the social scripts is productive, since making the unconscious conscious frees Anna and Saul, at least temporarily, from fixed ideological responses (*Reconstructing Desire,* 149–54, 163).

28. Cf. Martha Lifson's discussion of the novel's "non-chronological treatment of time": "The novel works frequently to confuse one's sense of time by slowing it down or speeding it up, or to suggest, by juxtaposing sections of the notebooks, that disparate events occurred simultaneously" ("Structural Patterns in *The Golden Notebook,*" *Michigan Papers in Women's Studies* 2, no. 4 [1978]: 102). Anne Mulkeen similarly suggests that the novel's form allows a simultaneous movement back, forward, and within: "Free Women" "moves forward in present time," "but as we take each step forward, we are also asked to explore in depth: to go inward, into the world of Anna's mind . . . to go backwards, through the times and experiences those notebooks attempt to record" ("Twentieth-Century Realism: The 'Grid' Structure of *The Golden Notebook,*" *Studies in the Novel* 4, no. 2 [Summer 1972]: 264–65).

29. Roberta Rubenstein's Jungian reading stresses Anna's search for "personal wholeness" and sees Anna's "crackup" as ultimately resolved "into positive integration" (*The Novelistic Vision of Doris Lessing: Breaking the Forms of Consciousness* [Urbana: University of Illinois Press, 1979], 6, 89). See also Mary Cohen, "'Out of the Chaos a New Kind of Strength': Doris Lessing's *The Golden Notebook,*" in *The Authority of Experience: Essays in Feminist Criticism,* ed. Arlyn Diamond and Lee R. Edwards (Amherst: University of Massachusetts Press, 1977), 178–93. Mulkeen argues that "disintegration," which "seems the most all-inclusive movement in the book, [is] set against a structure which calls for unity and interrelationship" (270).

30. As Claire Sprague observes, "a few years ago we were all talking . . . about splits and divisions and fragmentation. . . . Now I'm hearing about diversity, about multiplicity, about protean selves, about incoherence as a potentially positive thing" (quoted in *DLN,* 11, no. 2 [Fall 87]: 12). Sprague's revisions of "Doubletalk and Doubles Talk in *The Golden Notebook*" (*Papers on Language and Literature* 18, no. 2 [Spring 1982]: 181–97) to "Doubles Talk in *The Golden Notebook*" (in Sprague and Tiger, *Critical Essays,* 44–60) illustrate this shift: in the latter she explores fragmentation as a means to multiplicity and suggests that "doubles and multiples force us to see at least double, force us to question any single view of personality or reality" (55). Frye argues that multiple selfhood offers a way beyond the either-or choice between femaleness and adulthood, autonomy and sexuality (92–93), and in both *The Golden*

*Notebook* and *The Waterfall* protagonists choose "an enabling self-fragmentation" (146). Hite suggests that, "despite a rhetoric of wholeness informing [Lessing's] encyclopedic novel, the emphasis throughout is on the complexity of experience, its intractability to integration"; "fragmentation, breakage, gaps, and lapses are precisely what allow possibility to emerge" (*The Other Side of the Story: Structures and Strategies of Contemporary Feminist Narratives* [Ithaca: Cornell University Press, 1989], 64).

31. Cora Kaplan describes her reassessment of subjectivity:

> In the early stages of thinking about women and writing I had, in common with other feminists, talked mostly about the ways in which women were denied access to something I have called "full" subjectivity. . . . In the last few years I have come round to a very different perspective on the problem, drawn from Marxist and feminist appropriations of psychoanalytic and structuralist theories. . . . Rather than approach women's difficulty in positioning themselves as writers as a question of barred access to some durable psychic state to which all humans should and can aspire, we might instead see their experience as foregrounding the inherently unstable and split character of all human subjectivity . . . The instability of "femininity" . . . points to . . . the impossibility of a . . . unified and cohered subject—
> and to a "potentially hopeful incoherence." ("Speaking/Writing/Feminism," in *On Gender and Writing*, ed. Michelene Wandor [London: Pandora Press, 1983], 57–59).

32. Roland Barthes, *S/Z* (New York: Hill and Wang, 1974); Julia Kristeva, "The Novel as Polylogue," *Desire and Language* (New York: Columbia University Press, 1980), 159–209; Catherine Belsey, *Critical Practice* (London: Methuen, 1980).

33. As Adrienne Rich says, "In order to change what is, we need to give speech to what *has been,* to imagine together what *might* be" ("The Contemporary Emergency and the Quantum Leap," *On Lies, Secrets, and Silence: Selected Prose, 1966–1978* [New York: Norton, 1979], 260). Cf. Mary Daly, *Beyond God the Father: Towards a Philosophy of Women's Liberation* (Boston: Beacon Press, 1973): "Women have had the power of naming stolen from us" (8).

34. Nissa Torrents, "Testimony to Mysticism: Interview with Lessing," *DLN* (Winter 1980): 12.

35. See Jenny Taylor, "Introduction: Situated Reading," in Taylor, *Notebooks,* 32, 34–35; and Claire Sprague, "Dialectic and Counter-Dialectic in the Martha Quest Novels," *Journal of Commonwealth Literature* 14, no. 1 (Aug. 1979): 40.

36. An early reviewer remarked that the "Chinese box" arrangement of *The Golden Notebook* is "similar to Brecht's 'alienation technique' on the stage" (Jeremy Brooks, "Doris Lessing's Chinese Box," *Sunday Times,* 15, Apr. 1962, 32; quoted in Taylor, *Notebooks,* 1), adding "The alienation technique and the use of montage, the way in which the novel 'lays bare the device' of the conditions of its own production, recall not only the work of Brecht but the debates of the Russian Formalists, and the writings of Walter Benjamin." Eagleton summarizes Walter Benjamin's *Understanding Brecht* (London: *NLB,* 1973) in a way that makes clear its relation to Lessing: "The task of theatre is not to 'reflect' a fixed reality, but to demonstrate how character and action are historically produced, and so how they could have been, and still can be, differ-

ent . . . Instead of appearing as a seamless whole, which suggests that its entire action is inexorably determined from the outset, the play presents itself as discontinuous, open-ended, internally contradictory, encouraging in the audience a 'complex seeing' "; the audience becomes "collaborator in an open-ended practice, rather than the consumer of a finished object" (*Marxism and Literary Criticism* [Berkeley: University of California Press, 1976], 65–66. See also Rosalind Coward and John Ellis, *Language and Materialism: Developments in Semiology and the Theory of the Subject* (London: Routledge, 1977), 36–37.

37. Georg Lukács, "The Ideology of Modernism," *The Meaning of Contemporary Realism* (1963), trans. John and Necke Mander (London: Merlin Press, 1969), 19; "1946 Preface," *Studies in European Realism* (New York: Universal Library, 1964), 9; "The Problems of a Philosophy of the History of Forms" (1920), *The Theory of the Novel* (Cambridge: MIT Press, 1971), 40–55.

38. For Gramsci on hegemony, see *The Modern Prince* (London: International Publishers, 1957); and Raymond Williams, *Marxism and Literature* (Oxford: Oxford University Press, 1977), 108–14. See also Walter L. Adamson, *Hegemony and Revolution: A Study of Antonio Gramsci's Political and Cultural Theory* (Berkeley and Los Angeles: University of California Press, 1980).

39. Louis Althusser, *For Marx,* trans. Ben Brewster (1969; reprint, London: New Left Books, 1977; first published in French, 1966); *Lenin and Philosophy and Other Essays,* trans. Ben Brewster (London: New Left Books, 1971; first published in French, 1968), esp. 231–36; see also Pierre Macherey, *A Theory of Literary Production,* trans. Geoffrey Wall (London: Routledge, 1978); first published in French, 1966).

40. In 1957 Roland Barthes described myth as "a conjuring trick" that "transforms history into nature" (*Mythologies,* trans. Annette Lavers [New York: Farrar, Straus, and Giroux, 1972], 142, 129).

41. Antonio Gramsci, "The Study of Philosophy," *Selections from the Prison Notebooks* (New York: International Publishers, 1976), 323.

42. The term is Frank Lentricchia's, *Criticism and Social Change* (Chicago: University of Chicago Press, 1983), 76.

43. Coward and Ellis, *Language and Materialism,* 74, 67–68; see also Althusser, "Ideology," 162; and *For Marx,* 233.

44. Fredric Jameson, *The Political Unconscious: Narrative as a Socially Symbolic Act* (Ithaca: Cornell University Press, 1982), 98–99.

45. Roland Barthes, *Writing Degree Zero,* trans. Annette Lavers and Colin Smith (New York: Hill and Wang, 1968), 13, 16.

46. Raymond Williams, *Marxism and Literature* (Oxford: Oxford University Press, 1977), 176.

47. Rachel Blau DuPlessis, *Writing beyond the Ending: Narrative Strategies of Twentieth-Century Women Writers* (Bloomington: Indiana University Press, 1985).

48. Lessing uses the same image Drabble will use (in *The Waterfall* [New York: Fawcett, 1977], 139) of a woman waiting at a window, to suggest female bereavement: "waiting, every night . . . staring out the window waiting for a man whom she knew, quite well, would never come to her again" (227).

49. Diana Trilling cites these discussions of "real" as opposed to clitoral orgasms approvingly (*Times Literary Supplement,* Oct. 1978, 1165) whereas Showalter cites them as evidence that Lessing has not "confronted the essential feminist implications of her own writing" (*Literature,* 311); but neither makes a distinction between Lessing and her protagonist. For Lessing's sense of all this, see chap. 2, n. 59.

50. "The right man" is associated with the "real story" by Rennie in Atwood's *Bodily Harm,* when Rennie looks back to a time when "she had ambitions, which she now thinks of as illusions: She believed there was a right man, not several and not almost right, and she believed there was a real story, not several and not almost real" (New York: Simon and Schuster, 1982), 62.

51. "One result of this tendency was the vacuousness of Soviet linguistics from the 1930s to the 1950s," with its view of language as "a superstructural form" (Coward and Ellis, *Language and Materialism,* 78–79).

52. As Rubenstein says, Lessing reveals that "objectivity is an aesthetic and epistemological convention" (*Boundaries,* 74). "All perception is interpretation; there is no single authoritative view of events" (102). Betsy Draine notes, "No longer bound to find *the* truth. . . . Anna is free to present *her* truth, with renewed conviction" (*Substance under Pressure: Artistic Coherence and Evolving Form in the Novels of Doris Lessing* [Madison: University of Wisconsin Press, 1983], 86).

53. Raymond Williams, *The Long Revolution* (London: Chatto and Windus, 1961), 20, 37–38.

54. Sprague suggests that *The Golden Notebook* is "steeped in an awareness of 'dark doubles'" ("Doubletalk," 197), that "doubles and multiples force us to see at least double, to question any single view of personality or reality," and that this is more than a revelation of the complexity at the heart of reality; it is a "burst[ing] of the boundaries of twoness" ("Doubles Talk," 55–56). See also Elizabeth Abel, "*The Golden Notebook:* 'Female Writing' and 'The Great Tradition'" (in Sprague and Tiger, *Critical Essays,* 101–7), who argues that, like the women's writing advocated by Hélène Cixous, the form of *The Golden Notebook* "dramatically challenges the structure of binary oppositions" (102, 104).

55. Caryn Fuoroli, "Doris Lessing's 'Game': Referential Language and Fictional Form," *Twentieth-Century Literature* 27, no. 2 (Summer 1981): 164. Fuoroli relates Lessing's "awareness of the problematic nature of language" to her "dissatisfaction with social realism" and suggests that Anna realizes the limits of referential language and comes "to define herself through an intuitive knowledge beyond the confines of social reference": "Yet, having done so, she also acknowledges and accepts referential language as a stabilizing force and as a means of communication. No matter how confining this language may be, it is necessary as a means of maintaining personal and social order" (146). Susan Kress notes that "the pressure to deny language is opposed by another, the necessity of forming, of shaping, of 'naming'" ("Lessing's Responsibility," *Salmagundi* [Winter–Spring 1980]: 118).

56. Sprague and Tiger, *Critical Essays,* 10. Nicole Ward Jouve points to the contradiction between Lessing's critiques of convention and her conservatism regarding language; she argues that nothing happens "from *inside* the language . . . the process of writing itself is excluded, except as a tool, from the operation that is taking place": "The prose never really confronts you with the experience of madness" ("Of

Mud and Other Matter—*The Children of Violence,*" in Taylor, *Notebooks,* 114–115). Jean Bethke Elshtain objects that, though Lessing's articulate characters discuss the limits of language, Lessing herself does not seek "new and innovative forms of expression" ("The Post-*Golden Notebook* Fiction of Doris Lessing," *Salmagundi* [Winter–Spring 1980]: 101).

57. He goes on to say, "Probably that sequence of words . . . is a definition of all literature, seen from a different perspective" (*Briefing for a Descent into Hell* [New York: Bantam, 1972], 112).

58. DuPlessis suggests that each notebook's "acts of containment are criticized by the presence of the others, for each constructs a reality that tries to exclude the others" (*Writing Beyond,* 101). Mulkeen describes *The Golden Notebook* as "completely self-questioning— . . . only its many juxtaposed, overlapping, and sometimes contradictory viewpoints, taken together, can approximate the 'density of our experience' now" ("Twentieth-Century Realism," 267). Draine describes the resolution of the novel as a "saving schizophrenia—a state that permits [Anna's] commitment to practical goals, visionary ideals, art, works, altruism, social reorganization, logic, and order, while at the same time allowing her to acknowledge and even honor all that accompanies chaos" ("Nostalgia and Irony: The Postmodern Order of *The Golden Notebook,*" *Modern Fiction Studies* [Spring 1980]: 48).

59. Contrary to Ruth Whittaker's assertion that "*The Golden Notebook* is not a treatise advocating autonomy for women; rather, it is a lament for its seeming impossibility" (*Modern Novelists: Doris Lessing* [New York: St. Martin's Press, 1988, 70–71), Anna does achieve autonomy, though she does so, paradoxically, by submerging herself in the experience of others. Phyllis Sternberg-Perrakis (*The Golden Notebook:* Separation and Symbiosis," *American Imago,* [Winter 1981]: 407–28) describes Anna's overcoming the "need to lose herself in symbiotic relationships with others, her massive separation anxiety," and learning "to be alone" (408). But Anna achieves this precisely *because* she first loses herself in a symbiotic relationship with Saul; it is her ability to break down into him that enables her to break away from him.

60. Neither can Anna; as she says of Saul during their breakdown, "I say *he,* taking for granted that I can pinpoint a personality. That there is a *he* who is the real man. Why should I assume that one of the persons he is is more himself than the others? But I do" (591).

61. John Fowles, *The French Lieutenant's Woman* (Boston: Little, Brown, 1969), 417.

62. Margaret Drabble, "Doris Lessing: Cassandra in a World under Siege," *Ramparts,* Feb. 1972, 52.

## Chapter 7

1. Doris Lessing, *The Summer Before the Dark* (New York: Bantam, 1974), 29, 1, 5.

2. Sydney Janet Kaplan, "Passionate Portrayal of Things to Come: Doris Lessing's Recent Fiction," in *Twentieth-Century Women Novelists,* ed. Thomas F. Staley (London: Macmillan, 1982), 5–6.

3. Betsy Draine, *Substance Under Pressure: Artistic Coherence and Evolving Form in the Novels of Doris Lessing* (Madison: University of Wisconsin Press, 1983), 112.

4. Draine discusses the ambiguity of the seal dream, which refers both "to Kate's motherliness, her need to be mothered, and her desire to reject the motherly role" (*Substance,* 121). She also discusses disagreements about whether the ending is "despairing" (129).

5. As Draine suggests, "Just as in her personal life Kate seeks to break the codes of conventional thought and false memory in order to think about her experience truthfully, so at the Global Foods conference Kate's job is to break the code of a foreign language": "Both in her private life and in her work, Kate is in search of what lies behind the veil—a once obscured meaning, a half-forgotten identity, a long-evaded truth" (*Substance,* 116–17). Language is described as a "veil," a pane of glass, a material that is variously transparent or semitransparent, "badly cleaned" or opaque, depending on Kate's expertise (*Summer,* 84, 107, 49).

6. Elizabeth Hardwick cannot forgive Lessing for not allowing Kate a meaningful career: "Why did Doris Lessing drop Kate Brown's work so quickly? Here at last is an exciting, very-well-paid job with attractive people, a propitious break with the domestic past. . . . Why is the love affair so cool and sexless?" (Review of *Summer, New York Times Magazine,* May 13, 1973, 1–2). But Lessing sets up such expectations precisely in order to show that they are beside the point.

7. Simone de Beauvoir, *The Second Sex* (New York: Vintage, 1952), 789.

8. I have found that this is the scene female readers are most likely to remember, the scene they can recall when they have forgotten everything else about *The Summer Before the Dark*—"Oh, that's the one where she walks in front of the construction workers!" It's a scene that epitomizes some central experience of women in this culture.

9. Margaret Drabble, *The Middle Ground* (New York: Bantam, 1980), 242. I've compared these mid-life identity crises novels in "Bleak Houses: Doris Lessing, Margaret Drabble, and the Condition of England," *Forum for Modern Language Studies* 28, no. 4 (1992): 304–19.

10. Lessing said in an interview, "We're very biological animals. . . . It's hard for many people to take, but 90 percent of our . . . thoughts are in fact expressions of whatever state or human stage we're in"; she describes young women who skip marriage and children as "trying to cheat on their biology" (J. Hendin, "Doris Lessing: The Phoenix 'Midst Her Fires," *Harper's Magazine* [June 1973]: 84–85; quoted in Kaplan, "Passionate Portrayal," 13).

11. Kate's remembering in response to the needs of Maureen recalls Sethe's and Denver's remembering in response to the needs of other people in Toni Morrison's *Beloved* and suggests a social dimension to memory (Gayle Greene, "Feminist Fiction and the Uses of Memory," *Signs* 16, no. 2 [Winter 1990]: 1–32).

12. For example, Lorelei Cederstrom, "Doris Lessing's Use of Satire in *The Summer Before the Dark, Modern Fiction Studies* [Spring 1980]: 144–45.

13. If the seal is Kate's "motherliness," as Draine (*Substance*) suggests, then letting it go is letting go of her children and relinquishing this stage of her life; Kate becomes—like Anna Wulf—"intelligent enough to let them go," to let go of the

significant others in her life. But if "the seal stands for the inner, nonmaternal self that Kate has been nursing back to life in the last few months" (as Draine also suggests [127], then letting it go requires a different level of interpretation—which Kaplan provides in reading the ending as a letting go of the burden of personality and joining others in the collective unconscious ("Passionate Portrayal," 7).

14. I disagree with Draine's view of the novel as rendering Kate's "recovery of selfhood and reintegration with the vital world" (*Substance,* 111) in a way that achieves a "perfect imaginative poise" of the parts (130). I see the parts, rather, as splitting off from one another in a way that makes Lessing's move to fantasy inevitable.

15. *Memoirs of a Survivor* (New York: Bantam, 1976), 217.

## Chapter 8

1. *The Memoirs of a Survivor* (New York: Bantam, 1976), 8.

2. For example, Michael L. Magie, "Doris Lessing and Romanticism," *College English* 38 (1977): 531–52.

3. Having read through thirty-five reviews of this novel, I have to say that most readers missed the point: "As a novel it is half-achieved, over-theoretic and under-imagined," says Ronald Bryden (review of *Memoirs, New Statesman* 88, Dec. 6, 1984, 826). It "include[s] too many disparate elements for its own good," according to Peter Ackroyd (review in *Spectator* 233, Dec. 21, 1974, 797). Christopher Lehmann-Haupt calls it "all heavy breathing and no vital images—all significance and no substance" (*New York Times* 124, June 2, 1975, 23). Alex Zwerdling refers to its "generic characters and situations unable to root in the soil of real fiction" ("Toward Prophetic Fiction," *Sewanee Revue* 2 [June 29, 1975]: xl). Rene Kuhn Bryant refers to its "fantasy that, although detailed, is devoid of color, of texture, of shape" ("Mrs. Lessing's Vanishing Point," *National Review* 28, Apr. 30, 1976, 462). Judith McPherson says, "While there are moments of intense imagining, they are dissipated and fragmented throughout, and Lessing's own genuine, intensely scrutinizing voice gets lost in the clutter. We are left instead with weariness and dissolution" (*Library Journal* 100, July 1975, 1346). The most intelligent misreading is Betsy Draine's, which I will discuss later.

4. *The Four-Gated City* (New York: New American Library, 1976), 584 (hereafter *FGC*). All references to the *Children of Violence* are to the New American Library editions and are referred to as *MQ* (*Martha Quest*), *PM* (*A Proper Marriage*), *RS* (*Ripple From the Storm*), and *LL* (*Landlocked*).

5. *The Golden Notebook* (New York: Bantam, 1971), ix.

6. Nancy Shields Hardin, "The Sufi Teaching Story and Doris Lessing," *Twentieth Century Literature* 23 (1977): 316. See also Roberta Rubenstein: "Increasingly, beginning with the breakthrough of *The Golden Notebook,* the author's focus evolves away from psychological realism altogether, taking shape in the symbolic, mythopoeic, and mystical dimensions of experience that go beyond language" (*The Novelistic Vision of Doris Lessing: Breaking the Forms of Consciousness* [Urbana: University of Illinois Press, 1979], 109).

7. "Like the games of children who can make playacting a way of keeping reality a long way from their weakness?" (20) The image of the game recurs (88, 107, 158) and is especially important in relation to the work on the carpet, which looks like a game "only it was not a game; it was serious, important . . . to everyone" (80).

8. Whereas "Martha or Anna actively struggled . . . Emily and the nameless narrator are no longer active; they sit passively in the empty city, waiting to be subsumed by a mystical force outside themselves" (Pamela McCallum, "Survival Gear," *Canadian Forum* 55 [Dec. 1975]: 57).

9. Draine, *Substance,* 133, 139.

10. At one point, after one of the gangs takes off on one of the many "migrations" (nearly persuading Emily to go with them, who stays, however, because of Hugo), the pavement is littered with waste: "It was about then I understood that the events on the pavements and what went on between me and Emily might have a connection with what I saw on my visits behind the wall" (40).

11. Roberta Rubenstein links this to "the evolving consciousness, [which] in its effort to retain new self-discoveries, inevitably repeats the cycle of recovering and then forgetting the knowledge housed in its own deep layers" (*Novelistic Vision,* 229). This implies that the narrator's "householding" is an analogue to her self-discovery.

12. "My Mother's Life," pt. 1, *Granta* 14 (Winter 1984): 52–68; "My Mother's Life," pt. 2, *Granta* 17 (1985): 227–38.

13. Betsy Draine, *Substance Under Pressure: Artistic Coherence and Evolving Form in the Novels of Doris Lessing* (Madison: University of Wisconsin Press, 1983), 138. Walter Clemons refers to the characters taking off "into an extrasensory realm where I'm unable to follow them" ("Things to Come," *Newsweek* 85, June 16, 1975, 76); Malcolm Cowley calls the ending a "cop-out" ("Future Notebook," *Saturday Review* 2, June 28, 1975, 23); so too does Victor Howes ("Biting a bullet with a marshmallow center," *Christian Science Monitor* 67, June 12, 1975, 22); Victoria Glendinning finds it "disappointing that all she and Emily found at the end of the road was a fairy godmother" ("The Return of She," *Times Literary Supplement,* Dec. 13, 1974, 1405). Victoria Middleton, on the 1978 MLA panel on Doris Lessing, called *Memoirs* a "consolatory escape from, rather than a confrontation with, contingent reality" and suggested that with it Lessing had "entered her dotage," affirming her "desire to 'remain a child for ever'" (quoted in *Doris Lessing: The Alchemy of Survival,* ed. Carey Kaplan and Ellen Cronan Rose [Athens: Ohio University Press, 1988], 28).

14. Katherine Fishburn suggests something like this when she says that the very "fact that we are reading [the] novel and attempting to solve its mysteries and resolve its paradoxes" "engages us in an inevitable process of change," and our "reward" is not in "finding answers to our questions" but rather in *"trying* to find them"—"our only reward is one of changed perceptions whereby we learn to see our own world quite differently" (*The Unexpected Universe of Doris Lessing: A Study in Narrative Technique* [Westport, Conn.: Greenwood Press, 1985], 38, 50).

15. Lessing describes *Memoirs of a Survivor* as "the direct result of my meditating about the inadequacy of language. I write as in legends or in fairy tales, by means of metaphors and analogies" ("Testimony to Mysticism: Interview by Nissa Torrents" *Doris Lessing Newsletter* [Winter 1980]: 4, 13).

16. Lessing describes the "birth experience" she had taking mescaline: "I was both giving birth and being given birth to . . . I was both [mother and baby] but neither." "This baby who was still in the womb did not want to be born. First, there was the war . . . and the smell of war and suffering was everywhere . . . the baby did not want to be born to those parents . . . and . . . it was bored. . . . This baby had been born many times before, and the mere idea of 'having to go through it all over again' (a phrase the baby kept using), exhausted it in advance." Lessing speculates, "I think that my very healthy psyche decided that my own birth, the one I actually had, was painful and bad . . . and so it gave itself a good birth—because the whole of this labor was a progress from misery, pain, unhappiness, toward happiness, acceptance" ("Doris Lessing at Stony Brook: An Interview by Jonah Raskin," in *A Small Personal Voice,* ed. Paul Schlueter [New York: Vintage, 1975], 58–59).

17. As Ellen Cronan Rose suggests, the ending "demands that we abandon our accustomed notion of what is real, enlarging our definition of reality by incorporating the contents of experience we cannot rationally understand" ("The End of the Game: New Directions in Doris Lessing's Fiction," *Journal of Narrative Technique* 6, no. 1 [Winter 1976]: 71). Rubenstein describes the ending as "a rendering into language and image of the essentially ineffable experience of transcendence—the state of elevated consciousness characteristic of the mystical experience, whether conceived as union with the deity, dissolution of ego boundaries, satori, enlightenment, illumination, or apotheosis" (*Novelistic Vision,* 237). Lee Edwards (*Psyche as Hero: Female Heroism and Fictional Form* [Middletown, Conn.: Wesleyan University Press, 1984]), describes "a new symbolic order that reflects a radicalized and feminist metaphysics" (284).

## Chapter 9

1. *Shikasta* (New York: Vintage, 1981), 3.

2. Mona Knapp, *Doris Lessing* (New York: Ungar, 1984), 131. She was not the only one to criticize the novel for being escapist. Karen Durbin describes Lessing's recent fiction as "retreat[ing] not merely from realism but from reality" ("Doris Lessing Inside Out," *Village Voice* 24, Nov. 12, 1979, 41); according to Anthony Burgess, "to posit cosmic aetiologies and galactic cures is an evasion of reality as well as a mockery of terrestrial suffering"; "Creeping towards Salvation," *Times Literary Supplement,* Nov. 23, 1979, 11).

3. John Milton, *Paradise Lost,* bk. 1, l. 3; *Complete Poems and Major Prose,* ed. Merritt Y. Hughes (New York: Odyssey Press, 1957), 211.

4. "The trouble for me," says Alex de Jonge, "was that the narrative is very dispersed" (review of *Shikasta, Spectator* 244, June 12, 1980, 22). According to Mark Ably, "The celestial machinery creaks and grumbles . . . a mosaic, a hodge-podge" ("In the Century of Destruction," *Maclean's* 92, Nov. 26, 1979, 62). Ursula Le Guin calls it "earnest and overambitious, badly constructed, badly edited," and refers to its "unshapeliness" and "aesthetic incoherence"—though she acknowledges that Lessing's "creative spirit" redeems "this lurching, lumbering, struggling book" (review, *New Republic* 181, Oct. 13, 1979, 32, 34). *Publishers' Weekly* found it "not so much a novel as a rather cumbersome literary device" whose characters "seem

more like ideas on legs than people" (216, Sept. 17, 1979, 140). Others criticized it for its failure to fulfill their expectations about character and plot: "Much of the book is pedantic, turgid, polemical, and lacking in the kind of novelistic tension found in character interaction" (*Choice* 17, Apr. 1980, 221); "There is little character development . . . and what characters there are prove difficult to care about" (Durbin, "Doris Lessing," 40). The most imaginative reading is Betsy Draine's, who calls it a writerly text that "provides material for the production of imaginative satisfaction, but leaves to the reader the task of 'writing' the constituent elements into a whole" (*Substance Under Pressure: Artistic Coherence and Evolving Form in the Novels of Doris Lessing* [Madison: University of Wisconsin Press, 1983], 144). Ruth Whittaker also finds its "temporal dislocation" challenging: "It is as if [Lessing] is determined that we should think in cosmic, rather than individual or national, or even merely human terms, and some of the difficulty of this novel lies in coming to terms with this gigantic canvas" (*Modern Novelists: Doris Lessing* [New York: St. Martin's Press, 1988], 100). Katherine Fishburn describes it as "challeng[ing] us not just emotionally but also intellectually and epistemologically" "to join it in redefining reality itself" (*The Unexpected Universe of Doris Lessing: A Study in Narrative Technique* [Westport, Conn.: Greenwood Press, 1985], 59). But generally, reviews of this novel were not welcoming: it was criticized as escapist, incoherent, and even immoral.

5. Interview with Christopher Bigsby, in *The Radical Imagination and the Liberal Tradition: Interviews with English and American Novelists,* ed. Heide Ziegler and Christopher Bigsby (London: Junction Books, 1982), 188–208; quoted in Whittaker, *Modern Novelists,* 103.

6. William Shakespeare, *The Complete Works,* ed. Alfred Harbage (Baltimore, Md.: Penguin, 1975), *As You Like It* (2.2.12, p. 252); *King Lear* (2.4.265, p. 1882).

7. Draine, *Substance,* Le Guin calls it "Calvinist" in its view of humanity as "incapable of doing good on its own" (review, 32). Knapp complains that Lessing's "requiring [the individual] to submit to the master plan" (*Doris Lessing,* 132), to the "religious . . . resignation to the will of the higher-ups," is reminiscent of "the dangers of the Fuhrer principle" (162–63).

8. Hyman Maccoby, "Heaven and *Shikasta,*" *Listener* 102, Nov. 22, 1979, 716. Edmund Fuller calls it "a pale shadow of the Judeo-Christian expression of the condition of man" ("Doris Lessing's Imaginative Flight through Time," *Wall Street Journal* 194, Nov. 19, 1979, 22).

9. So, too, apparently do critics have "other ideas" of themselves. George Stade, for example, bristles that "the new unearthly perspective reduces the size of her earthlings" ("Fantastic Lessing," *New York Times Book Review,* Nov. 4, 1979, 1).

10. Jeanette King, *Doris Lessing* (London: Edward Arnold, 1989), 73.

11. Draine objects that Zone Six is radically incongruous with the rest of *Shikasta,* that its fantasy is "out of alignment with the science fiction mode" (*Substance,* 156–57), but I see it as making sense in terms of the novel's intertextuality with *Paradise Lost.*

12. Draine, *Substance,* 158.

13. Stanley Fish, *Surprised by Sin: The Reader in Paradise Lost* (London: Macmillan, 1967).

14. King, *Doris Lessing,* 73.

15. Fishburn also describes a process by which we come to "accept the alien perspective as the normative perspective" and "to question the human perspective for being too limited" (*Unlimited Universe,* 79).

16. Even the messiah is a multiple event, as Draine points out, since there are in *Shikasta* numerous reincarnations rather than one: Johor's incarnation is not "the unique and all-important event in salvation-history" (*Unexpected Universe,* 155).

17. Irony in fact is the initial response of the Giants to learning that they will cease to exist and their work has come to nothing—"not protest," which would be "inappropriate," but "an acknowledgment of the existence of *irony*" (40). This is heroic in the Giants, though it quickly degenerates to self-important posturing, once they succumb to the degenerative disease.

## Chapter 10

1. Doris Lessing, *The Marriages Between Zones Three, Four, and Five (As Narrated by the Chroniclers of Zone Three)* (New York: Vintage, 1981).

2. Betsy Draine describes it as "an allegory of spiritual progress, loudly signaling its affinities with the grail legend and the Arthurian cycle by its medieval romance trappings—kings and queens, courts and palaces, magic shields, a noble steed, warriors in armor, women in long flowing dresses" (*Substance Under Pressure: Artistic Coherence and Evolving Form in the Novels of Doris Lessing* [Madison: University of Wisconsin Press, 1983], 162).

3. Minda Bikman, "A Talk with Doris Lessing," *New York Times Book Review* 85, Mar. 30, 1980, 24. This book was more favorably reviewed than *Shikasta:* "Lessing, 60, has written often about the struggles between men and woman and the dimensions of sex and love, but never with more sweetness, compassion and wisdom," says Paul Gray ("Soul Mates," *Time* 115, Apr. 21, 1980, 520). Eric Korn calls it "genial and humane" ("Al·Ith in Wonderland," *Times Literary Supplement,* May 9, 1980, 520); Ursula Le Guin calls it "finer-grained and stronger than *Shikasta* . . . unencumbered by metaphysical machinery . . . with a rising vein of humor uncommon in her work" (review of *Marriages, New Republic* 182, Mar. 29, 1980, 34). According to *Library Journal,* "Lessing will re-win those admirers . . . who were put off by the galactic scope of *Shikasta*" (105, Apr. 1, 1980, 878). Of course, it also had its detractors: *Publishers Weekly* described it as "inhibited by Lessing's determinedly simple narrative style from developing interest, force or momentum" (217, Feb. 8, 1980, 67); *Booklist* described it as "a wispy fable whose murky ideas supply only a dull, simplistic resonance and whose flashes of inspired writing are few and far between" (76, Mar. 15, 1980, 1030).

4. For the "work of the imagination" that went into the writing, see chap. 10, n.14.

5. Bikman, "A Talk," 24; and *Shikasta* (New York: Vintage, 1981), ix.

6. Marsha Rowe suggests a further complexity: though the novel is like "myth in the way it postulates a world above time, in components of its plot and in its gender archetypes," it also depicts a world immersed in time, in which change is a "dialectical . . . process . . . reaching resolution only to have to begin again at a new level" ("If

you mate a swan and a gender, who will ride?" in *Notebooks, Memoirs, Archives: Reading and Rereading Doris Lessing,* ed. Jenny Taylor [Boston: Routledge, 1982], 194).

7. Though in one sense the novel evokes gender types, even stereotypes—Al·Ith is quintessential woman as Ben Ata is quintessential male—it also offers a powerful demonstration of the way individual consciousness is structured by social values. As such, *Marriages* is an extremely effective tool for getting students to see the way gender is socially constructed.

8. Murti is able to remain fixed in her illusion, however, whereas Jarnti is stripped of his by Zone Four's changeover to peace. Like the men in *The Golden Notebook,* Jarnti is what he does and so is incapable of change: "I've been one thing all my life. That is what I am"; "My life—it's gone, cancelled, wiped out" (235). He cannot even accept Dabeeb's attempts to comfort him, since he now feels that she is patronizing him—and she is, since that is what women do in Zone Four: now "both their occupations were gone!" (235).

9. Lusik sounds very like Doris Lessing here: "It's been my experience again and again . . . that you only have to write something and what you write starts coming true in all kinds of direct and indirect ways. It's as if you bring something towards you if you imagine it and then write it" (letter to Roberta Rubenstein; quoted in *The Novelistic Vision of Doris Lessing: Breaking the Forms of Consciousness* [Urbana: University of Illinois Press, 1979], 198).

10. As Draine notes, the title of the novel echoes Blake's *Marriage of Heaven and Hell* and suggests, like Blake, "that 'Opposition is true friendship' and that the marriage of 'Contraries' is not only possible but necessary to human progress." Lessing "imagines not only the transformation of two enemies into a companionable couple, but also a continual stepping outward of the transformed mate to meet and embrace a new opposite. . . . There is therefore no permanent marriage in this novel; instead there is a process of loving and learning . . . [and] learning to ally oneself with the communal progress toward Gnosis" (*Substance,* 161).

11. Ruth Whittaker, *Modern Novelists: Doris Lessing* (New York: St. Martin's Press, 1988), 105.

12. I see *Marriages* as more than "the classically well-made text" that Draine describes. Draine says that, "because of its simplicity of moral vision, *Marriages* is able to be a singular, a readerly, and a pleasurable text" (*Substance,* 168); that unlike *Shikasta,* with its plurality and multiplicity, *Marriages* "moves continually to bring multiplicity into unity, difference into affinity, separateness into consolidation" (161). I see the novel as more complex than this. For a provocative discussion of the sense of art in the novel, see Katherine Fishburn, *The Unexpected Universe of Doris Lessing* (Westport, Conn.: Greenwood Press, 1985), 96–103. Fishburn also sees Lusik as a socially responsible artist who takes upon himself the burden of making change.

13. Raymond Williams, *The Long Revolution* (London: Chatto and Windus, 1961), 20, 37–38. See my discussion of Williams in relation to *The Golden Notebook,* chap. 5.

14. Interview with Christopher Bigsby, in *The Radical Imagination and the Liberal Tradition: Interviews with English and American Novelists* ed. Heide Ziegler and

Christopher Bigsby (London: Junction Books, 1982), 188–208; quoted in Whittaker, *Modern Novelists,* 104).

## Chapter 11

1. Ellen Goodman, "Doris Lessing as Jane Somers: The Media Response," *Doris Lessing Newsletter* 9, no. 1 (Spring 1985): 3.

2. Doris Lessing, *The Diary of a Good Neighbour* (hereafter *DGN*) and *If the Old Could* (hereafter *IOC*), published together as *The Diaries of Jane Somers* (New York: Vintage, 1984), vii.

3. A suggestion that comes as a bit of a surprise to those of us who quailed, as younger readers, at Mrs. Quest. Lessing reveals what might have been another personal factor behind *Diary of a Good Neighbor,* and another reason for the pseudonym, when, in the afterword to *The Making of the Representative for Planet 8,* the fourth novel in the Canopus series, she accounts for her interest in the freezing planet in terms of her lifelong fascination with the Antarctic expeditions of Robert Falcon Scott (an interest she shared with her mother), adding, almost as an afterthought: "Or perhaps something else was going on. I finished writing it the day after the death of someone I had known a long time; though it did not occur to me to make a connection until then. It took her a long cold time to die, and she was hungry too, for she was refusing to eat and drink, so as to hurry things along. She was ninety-two" (New York: Knopf, 1982, 144–45).

4. "My Mother's Life," 1, *Granta* 14 (Winter 1984): 59; see also "My Mother's Life," pt. 2, *Granta* 17 (Fall 1985): 227–38 (hereafter cited parenthetically in text).

5. *A Proper Marriage* (New York: New American Library, 1964), 151; (hereafter *PM*).

6. The essay "My Father" first appeared in the London *Sunday Telegraph* (Sept. 1, 1963); it was reprinted in *Vogue* (Feb. 15, 1964) and then in *A Small Personal Voice: Essays, Reviews, Interviews,* ed. Paul Schlueter (New York: Vintage, 1975), 83–93 (hereafter *SPV*); also *The Norton Reader*. *Shikasta* is dedicated to her father.

7. Bookshelf, "Profile of Doris Lessing," interviews produced by Abigail Appleton, BBC Radio, May 1, 1992.

8. *The Four-Gated City* (New York: New American Library, 1976), 223, 272.

9. Dustjacket, *The Memoirs of a Survivor* (New York: Knopf, 1974).

10. Ellen Cronan Rose, "A Lessing in Disguise," review of *The Diaries of Jane Somers, Women's Review of Books* 2, no. 5 (Feb. 1985): 7–8.

11. Simone de Beauvoir, *The Coming of Age* (New York: Putnam's, 1972), 2.

12. It is significant that Lessing's mother was a nurse. Lessing speculates on her mother's deprivations in relation to her determination to become a nurse: she had been close neither to her father, her stepmother, nor her sister—"whom, then, did she love, this poor girl brought up without affection?" Since "middle-class girls did not become nurses," she had to defy her father to become a nurse: "Why did she fight so hard to become a nurse, if not that she needed to care for and to nurture people and to be loved for it? I have only just had this thought: I could have had it before" (*G,* 1: 54–55).

13. Maudie and Jane are similar in their self-sufficiency, which is why Jane can take her on. Maudie also values "training. It stands between you and nothing. That,

and a place of your own" (p.18). "I have my thoughts," Maudie says more than once (36, 156, 165), and Jane finds herself reiterating this and saying other things Maudie might say (139, 165). At the end Jane incorporates not only Maudie's strength and pride but also her rage.

14. Mona Knapp, *Doris Lessing* (New York: Ungar, 1984), 26.

15. Rachel Blau DuPlessis describes alternative familial arrangements in twentieth-century women's fiction (*Writing Beyond the Ending: Narrative Strategies of Twentieth-Century Women Writers* [Bloomington: Indiana University Press, 1985], chap. 10 and 11). So too does Jean Wyatt, in *Reconstructing Desire: The Role of the Unconscious in Women's Reading and Writing* (Chapel Hill: University of North Carolina Press, 1990), chaps. 9 and 10.

16. *Changing the Story: Feminist Fiction and the Tradition* (Bloomington: Indiana University Press, 1991), 202–5; see also my essay "Doris Lessing, Feminism, and the Mother," in *Narrating Mothers: Theorizing Maternal Subjectivities,* ed. Brenda O. Daly and Maureen T. Reddy (Knoxville: University of Tennessee Press, 1991), 139–56.

17. Naomi Wolf points out that, though women's magazines "are trivialized, they represent something very important: women's mass culture": that they "are mostly written by women for women about women's issues" and "are the only place for women to go find out what's going on in the other world—the female reality so fleetingly acknowledged by 'serious' journals." She suggests that "they have popularized feminist ideas more widely than any other medium—certainly more widely than explicitly feminist journals," though she also describes their complicity with advertisers: "What editors are obliged to appear to say that *men* want from women is actually what their *advertisers* want from women" (*The Beauty Myth: How Images of Beauty are Used Against Women* [New York: Morrow, 1991], 70–73).

18. Other terms that are similarly used to dehumanize and distance old people are "these old things" (39) and "dear little children" (*IOC,* 346).

19. Quoted in Goodman, "Doris Lessing," 3.

**Chapter 12**

1. Cf. *Briefing for a Descent into Hell:* "There are people in the world all the time who know . . . But they keep quiet. They just move about quietly, saving the people who know they are in the trap" (New York: Bantam, 1972), 274.

2. Doris Lessing, *The Good Terrorist* (New York: Knopf, 1985), 35.

3. Jim is "genuine cockney, the real thing" (26), and "Jasper's tones were almost those of his origins," but Bert's "posh" "public school" "tones" are "roughened" with the intention of sounding working class (26–27), while Roberta reverts to working class under stress (237, 251–52). In Faye BBC alternates crazily with cockney (29, 105, 285): "Voices and laughs, we make them up" (125).

4. Jeannette King, *Doris Lessing* (London: Edward Arnold, 1989), 100.

5. Philip and Faye, "two of a kind, victims, born to be trampled over and cut down" (266), are both associated with eggs, chicks, and birds (275, 162, 104).

6. As Alison Lurie says, "Alice is strong, emotionally intuitive, and sympathetic, brave, warmhearted, hard-working, and generous—the sort of woman whose domestic

skills and maternal sympathy have traditionally held the world together." Lurie adds that she is "a personification of England itself": "She has the traditional English sense of fairness, acute awareness of class differences, humor, courage, capacity for hard work, love of domestic coziness, and unease about sex" ("Bad Housekeeping," *New York Review,* Dec. 19, 1985, 9, 10).

7. Judith Kegan Gardiner sees this as a betrayal and describes Lessing's relation to her protagonist as that of an angry rejecting mother ("Authorial Empathy in Lessing's Fiction," 1986 MLA panel on "Doris Lessing's Authorial Personae"; also in *Rhys, Stead, Lessing, and the Politics of Empathy* [Bloomington: Indiana University Press, 1989], 166). But I think Lessing is turning not so much on a daughter as on a former self, with the vehemence that only by one's former illusions are capable of provoking.

8. As King observes, "The reader is . . . drawn by the narrative method and the plot into identifying with a point of view which is itself ironicized and undermined. . . . There is no easy, comfortable position for the reader to adopt, either of detachment or of close identification with a point of view clearly presented as the authoritative one" (*Doris Lessing,* 104).

9. And as these same reviewers acknowledge. Susan Lardner admits to having "trouble deciphering the psychological message" ("A Kind of Dryness," *New Yorker,* Oct. 14, 1985, 140). Deirdre Levinson blames Lessing: Alice's memories "could have done something to account for Alice's ensuing immitigable rage. But while it seems to be the intention here to make psychological sense of Alice, the outcome is . . . a travesty," and she dismisses the novel as "devoid of inner coherence" ("Future Shocked," *Nation,* Nov. 23, 1985, 558).

10. "There was an empty place in her, a pit, a grave; she had been dreaming, she knew, of the house, now boarded up, with the 'For Sale' notice outside" (226). Alice never does excavate this pit, just as she never figures out what's in the pit in the yard next door.

11. In *A Retreat to Innocence* (1956) the protagonist's mother is similarly on her mind, but the meeting with her never takes place. This is the other political novel with which *The Good Terrorist* invites comparison, and the comparisons are suggestive: the protagonists are both smug, provincial, middle-class young women, though the political forces they get involved with are quite different—Jan Brod really is heroic, for the myth of Stalin and the Soviet Union is still intact. In *A Retreat to Innocence* the encounter with the mother that is promised, built to, anticipated, is finally eluded, whereas in *The Good Terrorist* the meeting takes place, the mother speaks, and the illusion of the "great man" is blasted.

12. Lurie points out the similarity in sound between the names Alice Mellings and Doris Lessing and suggests that "Alice stands in for her creator, and represents, in a distorted and exaggerated way, her own reactions to contemporary England" ("Bad Housekeeping," 10).

13. Denis Donoghue describes the style of this novel as "insistently drab, presumably in keeping with the dreariness of the life it depicts" ("Alice, the Radical Homemaker," *New York Times Book Review,* Sept 22, 1985, 3). In this instance I agree—in this novel, as in *A Ripple in the Storm,* Lessing's style is unlit by its usual brilliance, and in both novels the flatness is of a piece with disillusionment.

14. Margaret Drabble, *The Middle Ground* (New York: Bantam, 1980), 19. See my essay "Bleak Houses: Doris Lessing, Margaret Drabble, and the Condition of England," *Forum for Modern Language Studies* 28, no. 4 (1992): 304–19.

15. Margaret Drabble, *The Radiant Way* (London: Weidenfeld and Nicolson, 1987), 385.

16. Levinson suggests that "this book may come as a shock to those who remember Lessing as a champion of the radical young" ("Future Shocked," 55).

**Chapter 13**

1. *The Sense of an Ending* (London: Oxford University Press, 1975). See chap. 3, note 19.

2. Lorna Irvine, "No Sense of an Ending: Drabble's Continuous Fictions" (in *Critical Essays on Margaret Drabble,* ed. Ellen Cronan Rose [Boston: G. K. Hall, 1985], 75, 84–85).

3. *The Fifth Child* (New York: Knopf, 1988), 120.

4. As Carey Kaplan and Ellen Cronan Rose suggest, Lessing's work "is still in the process of becoming, still full of surprises, play, audacity, dogma, recantation, and grouchy dismissal of critical appraisal" (*Doris Lessing: The Alchemy of Survival* [Athens: Ohio University Press, 1988], 5).

5. *The Real Thing: Stories and Sketches* (New York: HarperCollins, 1992).

6. Bookshelf, "Profile of Doris Lessing," interview produced by Abigail Appleton, BBC Radio, May 1, 1992.

# Bibliography

Abel, Elizabeth. "*The Golden Notebook:* 'Female Writing' and 'The Great Tradition.'" In *Critical Essays on Doris Lessing,* ed. Claire Sprague and Virginia Tiger, pp. 101–7. Boston: G. K. Hall, 1986.

———, ed. *Writing and Sexual Difference. Critical Inquiry* 8, no. 2 (Winter 1981).

Abel, Elizabeth, Marianne Hirsch, and Elizabeth Langland, eds. *The Voyage In: Fictions of Female Development.* Hanover, N.H.: University Press of New England, 1983.

Ably, Mark. Review of *Shikasta.* "In the Century of Destruction." *Maclean's* 92 (Nov. 26, 1979): 62.

Abrams, M. H. *Natural Supernaturalism.* New York: Norton, 1971.

Ackroyd, Peter. Review of *Memoirs. Spectator* 233 (Dec. 21, 1974): 797.

Adamson, Walter L. *Hegemony and Revolution: A Study of Antonio Gramsci's Political and Cultural Theory.* Berkeley and Los Angeles: University of California Press, 1980.

Alexander, Flora. *Contemporary Women Novelists.* London: Edward Arnold, 1989.

Allen, Paula Gunn. *The Sacred Hoop: Recovering the Feminine in American Indian Traditions.* Boston: Beacon Press, 1986.

Allen, Walter. *The Modern Novel in Britain and the United States.* New York: Dutton, 1964.

Alther, Lisa. *Kinflicks.* New York: New American Library, 1975.

———. "The Writer and Her Critics." *Women's Review of Books* 6, no. 1 (Oct. 1988): 11.

Althusser, Louis. *For Marx.* Trans. Ben Brewster. Harmondsworth: Penguin, 1969 (first published in French 1966). Reprint. London: New Left Books, 1977.

———. *Lenin and Philosophy and Other Essays.* Trans. Ben Brewster. London: New Left Books, 1971 (first published in French, 1968).

Amis, Kingsley. Review of *Four-Gated City. Spectator,* Oct. 8, 1954. Reprinted in *Critical Essays on Doris Lessing,* ed. Claire Sprague and Virginia Tiger, 174. Boston: G. K. Hall, 1986.

Anderson, Linda. *Plotting Change: Contemporary Women's Fiction.* London: Edward Arnold, 1990.

Anzaldúa, Gloria, and Cherríe Moraga, eds. *This Bridge Called My Back: Writings of Radical Women of Color*. New York: Women of Color Press, 1981.

Ascher, Carol, Louise De Salvo, and Sara Ruddick, eds. *Between Women: Biographers, Novelists, Critics, Teachers, and Artists Write about Their Work on Women*. Boston: Beacon Press, 1984.

Atwood, Margaret. *Bodily Harm*. New York: Simon and Schuster, 1982.

Baker, Niamh. *Happily Ever After? Women's Fiction in Postwar Britain, 1945–1960*. New York: St. Martin's Press, 1989.

Bakhtin, M. M. "Discourse in the Novel." In *The Dialogic Imagination: Four Essays*, ed. Michael Holquist. Austin: University of Texas Press, 1981.

Ballantyne, Sheila. *Norma Jean the Termite Queen*. Harmondsworth: Penguin, 1986.

Banks, Olive M. *Faces of Feminism: A Study of Feminism as a Social Movement*. Oxford: Basil Blackwell, 1986.

Barnouw, Dagmar. "Disorderly Company: From *The Golden Notebook* to *The Four-Gated City*." In *Doris Lessing: Critical Essays*, ed. Annis Pratt and L. S. Dembo, 74–97. Madison: University of Wisconsin Press, 1974.

Barr, Marleen. *Alien to Femininity: Speculative Fiction and Feminist Theory*. Westport, Conn.: Greenwood Press, 1987.

Barthes, Roland. *S/Z*. Trans. Richard Miller. New York: Hill and Wang, 1974.

Belsey, Catherine. *Critical Practice*. London: Methuen, 1985.

Benjamin, Walter. *Understanding Brecht*. Trans. Anna Bostock. London: NLB, 1973.

Bergonzi, Bernard. *The Situation of the Novel*. Pittsburgh: University of Pittsburgh Press, 1970.

———. *Contemporary Novelists*, ed. James Vinson, 373–74. New York: St. Martin's Press. 1976.

Bertelson, Eva. "The Persistent Personal Voice: Lessing on Rhodesia and Marxism: Excerpts from an Interview with Doris Lessing," London, January 9, 1984. *Doris Lessing Newsletter* (Fall 1985): 9, no. 2: 8–10, 18.

Biles, Jack I., ed. *British Novelists since 1900*. New York: AMS Press, 1987.

Bookshelf. "Profile of Doris Lessing." Interview produced by Abigail Appleton, BBC Radio, May 1, 1992.

Boyers, Robert. *Atrocity and Amnesia: The Political Novel since 1945*. Oxford: Oxford University Press, 1985.

Bradbury, Malcolm, ed. *The Novel Today: Contemporary Writers on Modern Fiction*. Totowa, N.J.: Rowman and Littlefield, 1977.

Brooks, Ellen W. "The Image of Women in Lessing's *Golden Notebook*." *Critique: Studies in Modern Fiction* 15, no. 1 (1973): 101–9.

Brooks, Jeremy. "Doris Lessing's Chinese Box," *Sunday Times*, April 15, 1962, 32. Quoted in *Notebooks, Memoirs, Archives: Reading and Rereading Doris Lessing*, ed. Jenny Taylor, p. 1. Boston: Routledge, 1982.

Brooks, Peter. *Reading for the Plot: Design and Intention in Narrative*. New York: Vintage, 1984.

Bryant, Fanny. *Ella Price's Journal*. Berkeley: Ata Books, 1972.

Bryant, Rene Kuhn. Review of *Memoirs*. "Mrs. Lessing's Vanishing Point." *National Review* 28, Apr. 30, 1976, 462.

Bryden, Ronald. Review of *Memoirs. New Statesman* 88, Dec. 6, 1984, 826.

Burgess, Anthony. *The Novel Now: A Guide to Contemporary Fiction.* New York: Norton, 1967.

———. Review of *Shikasta.* "Creeping towards Salvation." *Times Literary Supplement,* Nov. 23, 1979.

Cederstrom, Lorelei. "Doris Lessing's Use of Satire in *The Summer before the Dark.*" *Modern Fiction Studies* (Spring 1980): 131–45.

Chodorow, Nancy. *The Reproduction of Mothering: Psychoanalysis and the Sociology of Gender.* Berkeley: University of California Press, 1978.

Clemons, Walter. Review of *Memoirs.* "Things to Come." *Newsweek* 85, June 16, 1975, 75–76.

Cohen, Mary. "'Out of the Chaos a New Kind of Strength': Doris Lessing's *The Golden Notebook.*" In *The Authority of Experience: Essays in Feminist Criticism,* ed. Arlyn Diamond and Lee R. Edwards, 178–93. Amherst: University of Massachusetts Press, 1977.

Collins, Patricia Hill. "Learning from the Outsider Within: The Sociological Significance of Black Feminist Thought." In *(En)Gendering Knowledge: Feminists in Academe,* ed. Joan E. Hartman and Ellen Messer-Davidow, 40–63. Knoxville: University of Tennessee Press, 1991.

Combahee River Collective. "A Black Feminist Statement." In *But Some of Us Are Brave: Black Women's Studies,* ed. Gloria T. Hull, Patricia Bell Scott, and Barbara Smith. Old Westbury, N.Y.: The Feminist Press, 1982.

Conrad, Joseph. *The Heart of Darkness: Norton Critical Edition.* New York: Norton, 1963.

Coward, Rosalind, and John Ellis. *Language and Materialism: Developments in Semiology and the Theory of the Subject.* London: Routledge, 1977.

Cowley, Malcolm. Review of *Memoirs.* "Future Notebook." *Saturday Review* 2, June 28, 1975, 23.

Daiches, David. *The Present Age in British Literature.* Bloomington: Indiana University Press, 1958.

Dalton, Elizabeth. "Doris Lessing." *Commentary* 44 (Jan. 1970): 31.

Daly, Mary. *Beyond God the Father: Towards a Philosophy of Women's Liberation.* Boston: Beacon Press, 1973.

Daniel, Robert L. *American Women in the Twentieth Century: The Festival of Life.* New York: Harcourt, 1987.

Davidson, Kathy, and E. M. Broner, eds. *The Lost Tradition: Mothers and Daughters in Literature.* New York: Ungar, 1980.

Davis, Lennard J. *Resisting Novels: Ideology and Fiction.* New York: Methuen, 1987.

de Beauvoir, Simone. *The Second Sex.* New York: Vintage, 1952.

———. *The Coming of Age.* New York: Putnam's, 1972.

de Jong, Alex. Review of *Shikasta. Spectator* 244, June 12, 1980, 22.

Deckard, Barbara Sinclair. *The Women's Movement: Political, Socioeconomic, and Psychological Issues.* New York: Harper and Row, 1983.

de Lauretis, Teresa. *Feminist Studies / Critical Studies.* Bloomington: Indiana University Press, 1986.

———. *Technologies of Gender*. Bloomington: University of Indiana Press, 1987.

Dembo, L. S. *Interviews with Contemporary Writers*. Madison: University of Wisconsin Press, 1983.

Diamond, Arlyn, and Lee R. Edwards, eds. *The Authority of Experience: Essays in Feminist Criticism*. Amherst: University of Massachusetts Press, 1977.

Dinnerstein, Dorothy. *The Mermaid and the Minotaur*. New York: Harper and Row, 1976.

Donoghue, Denis. Review of *The Good Terrorist*. "Alice, the Radical Homemaker." *New York Times Book Review*, Sept. 22, 1985, 3.

Drabble, Margaret. *The Middle Ground*. New York: Bantam, 1980.

———. *The Radiant Way*. London: Weidenfeld and Nicolson, 1987.

———. *The Waterfall*. New York: Fawcett, 1977.

———. "Doris Lessing: Cassandra in a World Under Siege." *Ramparts*, Feb. 1972, 50–55.

———. "Interview with Margaret Drabble." Iris Rozencwajg. *Women's Studies* 9 (1979): 335–47.

Draine, Betsy. "Nostalgia and Irony: The Postmodern Order of *The Golden Notebook*." *Modern Fiction Studies* 26, no. 1 (Spring 1980): 31–48.

———. *Substance under Pressure: Artistic Coherence and Evolving Form in the Novels of Doris Lessing*. Madison: University of Wisconsin Press, 1983.

DuPlessis, Rachel Blau. *Writing Beyond the Ending: Narrative Strategies of Twentieth-Century Women Writers*. Bloomington: University of Indiana Press, 1985.

———. DuPlessis, Rachel Blau, and Members of Workshop 9. "For the Etruscans: Sexual Difference and Artistic Production—The Debate Over a Female Aesthetic." In Eisenstein and Jardine, 128–56. Reprinted in *The New Feminist Criticism: Essays on Women, Literature, Theory*, ed. Elaine Showalter, 271–91. New York: Pantheon, 1985.

Durbin, Karen. Review of *Shikasta*. "Doris Lessing Inside Out," *Village Voice* 24, Nov. 12, 1979, 40ff.

Eagleton, Terry. *Marxism and Literary Criticism*. Berkeley: University of California Press, 1976.

———. *Literary Theory: An Introduction*. Minneapolis: University of Minnesota Press, 1983.

Eder, Richard. Review of Lessing's *The Fifth Child*. "An Allegory of One Child Too Many." *Los Angeles Times*, Mar. 27, 1988, 3.

Edwards, Lee. *Psyche as Hero: Female Heroism and Fictional Form*. Middletown, Conn.: Wesleyan University Press, 1984.

Eisenstein, Hester, and Alice Jardine. *The Future of Difference*. New Brunswick, N.J.: Rutgers University Press, 1985.

Eliade, Mercea. *Images and Symbols: Studies in Religious Symbolism*. New York: Sheed and Ward, 1961.

———. *The Myth of the Eternal Return*. Princeton: Princeton University Press, 1954.

Eliot, T. S. *The Complete Poems and Plays, 1909–1950*. New York: Harcourt, 1952.

Ellmann, Mary. *Thinking about Women*. New York: Harcourt, 1968.

Elshtain, Jean Bethke. "The Post–*Golden Notebook* Fiction of Doris Lessing." *Salmagundi* (Winter–Spring 1980): 95–114.

Evans, Sarah. *Personal Politics: The Roots of Women's Liberation in the Civil Rights Movement and the New Left*. New York: Vintage, 1980.

Farrell, Warren. *The Liberated Man, or Beyond Masculinity: Freeing Men and Their Relationships with Women*. New York: Bantam, 1975.

Felski, Rita. *Beyond Feminist Aesthetics: Feminist Literature and Social Change*. Cambridge: Harvard University Press, 1989.

Ferguson, Mary Anne, Marianne Hirsch, and Elizabeth Langland. "The Female Novel of Development and the Myth of Psyche." In *The Voyage In: Fictions of Female Development,* ed. Elizabeth Abel, 228–43. Hanover, N.H.: University Press of New England, 1983.

Ferree, Myra Marx, and Beth B. Hess. *Controversy and Coalition: The New Feminist Movement*. Boston: Twayne, 1985.

Firchow, Peter. Interview with Doris Lessing. *The Writer's Place: Interviews on the Literary Situation in Contemporary Britain*. Minneapolis: University of Minnesota Press, 1974.

Fish, Stanley. *Surprised by Sin: The Reader in Paradise Lost*. London: Macmillan, 1967.

Fishburn, Katherine. "The Nightmare Repetition: The Mother-Daughter Conflict in Doris Lessing's *Children of Violence*." In *The Lost Tradition: Mothers and Daughters in Literature,* ed. Kathy Davidson and E. M. Broner, 207–16. New York: Ungar, 1980.

———. *The Unexpected Universe of Doris Lessing*. Westport, Conn.: Greenwood Press, 1985.

Flax, Jane. "The Conflict Between Nurturance and Autonomy in Mother-Daughter Relationships and within Feminism." *Feminist Studies* 4 (1978): 171–89.

Fowles, John. *The French Lieutenant's Woman*. Boston: Little, Brown, 1969.

Freeman, Jo. *The Politics of Women's Liberation*. New York: David McKay, 1975.

Friedan, Betty. *The Feminine Mystique*. New York: Norton, 1983.

Frye, Joanne S. *Living Stories, Telling Lives: Women and the Novel in Contemporary Experience*. Ann Arbor: University of Michigan Press, 1986.

Fullbrook, Kate. *Free Women: Ethics and Aesthetics in Twentieth-Century Women's Fiction*. Philadelphia: Temple University Press, 1990.

Fuller, Edmund. Review of *Shikasta*. "Doris Lessing's Imaginative Flight through Time." *Wall Street Journal* 194, Nov. 19, 1979.

Fuoroli, Caryn. "Doris Lessing's 'Game': Referential Language and Fictional Form." *Twentieth-Century Literature* 27, no. 2 (Summer 1981): 146–65.

Gatlin, Rochelle. *American Women since 1945*. Jackson: University Press of Mississippi, 1987.

Gardiner, Judith Kegan. *Rhys, Stead, Lessing, and the Politics of Empathy*. Indiana University Press, 1989.

———. "Authorial Empathy in Lessing's Fiction." Paper presented at the Modern Language Association, 1986.

———. "On Female Identity and Writing by Women." In *Writing and Sexual Difference,* ed. Elizabeth Abel. *Critical Inquiry* 8, no. 1 (Winter 1981): 347–61.

———. "A Wake for Mother: The Maternal Deathbed in Women's Fiction." *Feminist Studies* 4, no. 2 (June 1978): 146–65.

Garner, Shirley Nelson, Claire Kahane, and Madelon Sprengnether, eds. *The (M)other Tongue: Essays in Feminist Psychoanalytic Interpretation,* 15–29. Ithaca: Cornell University Press, 1985.

Gilbert, Sandra M., and Susan Gubar. *The Madwoman in the Attic: The Woman Writer and the Nineteenth-Century Literary Imagination.* New Haven: Yale University Press, 1979.

———. *The Norton Anthology of Literature by Women: The Tradition in English.* New York: Norton, 1985.

———. *No Man's Land: The Place of the Woman Writer in the Twentieth Century.* Vol. 1: *The War of the Words.* New Haven: Yale University Press, 1988.

———. *No Man's Land: The Place of the Woman Writer in the Twentieth Century.* Vol. 2: *Sexchanges.* New Haven: Yale University Press, 1989.

Gilligan, Carol. *In a Different Voice: Psychological Theory and Women's Development.* Cambridge: Harvard University Press, 1982.

Gindin, James. *Postwar British Fiction: New Accents and Attitudes.* Berkeley: University of California Press, 1962.

Glendinning, Victoria. Review of *Memoirs.* "The Return of She." *Times Literary Supplement,* Dec. 13, 1974, 1405.

Godwin, Gail. *The Odd Woman.* New York: Warner, 1974.

Goldberg, Herb. *The Hazards of Being Male.* New York: New American Library, 1976.

Goodman, Ellen. "The Doris Lessing Hoax." *Washington Post,* Sept. 27, 1984, 31. Reprinted as "Doris Lessing as Jane Somers: The Media Response." *Doris Lessing Newsletter* 9, no. 1 (Spring 1985): 3.

Gould, Lois. *The Final Analysis.* New York: Avon, 1974.

Gould, Stephen Jay. *Time's Arrow, Time's Cycle: Myth and Metaphor in the Discovery of Geological Time.* Cambridge: Harvard University Press, 1987.

Gramsci, Antonio. *The Modern Prince.* London: International Publishers, 1957.

———. "The Study of Philosophy." *Selections from the Prison Notebooks.* New York: International Publishers, 1976.

Gray, Paul. Review of *Marriages.* "Soul Mates." *Time* 115, Apr. 21, 1980, 520.

Greene, Gayle. *Changing the Story.* Bloomington: Indiana University Press, 1991.

———. "Bleak Houses: Doris Lessing, Margaret Drabble, and the Condition of England." *Forum for Modern Language Studies* 28, no. 4 (1992): 304–19.

———. "Divided Selves: Women and Men in *The Golden Notebook.*" In *The (M)other Tongue: Essays in Feminist Psychoanalytic Interpretation,* ed. Shirley Nelson Garner, Claire Kahane, and Madelon Sprengnether, 280–305. Ithaca, N. Y.: Cornell University Press, 1985.

———. "Feminist Fiction and the Uses of Memory." *Signs* 16, no. 2 (Winter 1991): 1–32.

———. "Looking at History." In *Changing Subjects: The Making of Feminist Criticism,* ed. Gayle Greene and Coppélia Kahn, 4–27. London: Routledge, 1993.

———. "'A New Kind of Knowledge': Doris Lessing's *Landlocked.*" *Contemporary Literature* 28, no. 1 (Spring 1987): 82–103.

———. "Shakespeare's *Tempest* and Eliot's *Waste Land:* 'What the Thunder Said.'" *Orbis Litterarum* 34 (1979): 289–300.

Greene, Gayle, and Coppelia Kahn, eds. *Changing Subjects: The Making of Feminist Criticism*. London: Routledge, 1993.

Hardin, Nancy Shields. "Doris Lessing and the Sufi Way." In *Doris Lessing: Critical Studies,* ed. Annis Pratt and L. S. Dembo, 148–64.

———. "The Sufi Teaching Story and Doris Lessing." *Twentieth-Century Literature* 23 (1977): 314–26.

Hardwick, Elizabeth. Review of *Summer Before the Dark. New York Times Magazine,* May 13, 1973, 1–2.

Hartman, Joan E., and Ellen Messer-Davidow, eds. *(En)Gendering Knowledge: Feminists in Academe*. Knoxville: University of Tennessee Press, 1991.

Heilbrun, Carolyn. *Reinventing Womanhood*. New York: Norton, 1979.

———. *Toward a Recognition of Androgyny*. New York: Knopf, 1973.

———. *Writing a Woman's Life*. New York: Norton, 1988.

Hendin, J. "Doris Lessing: The Phoenix 'Midst Her Fires." *Harpers,* June 1973, 84–85.

Hinz, Evelyn J. "Hierogamy versus Wedlock: Types of Marriage Plots and Their Relationship to Genres of Prose Fiction." *PMLA* 91, no. 5 (1976): 900–913.

Hirsch, Marianne. *The Mother/Daughter Plot: Narrative, Psychoanalysis, Feminism*. Bloomington: Indiana University Press, 1989.

Hite, Molly. *The Other Side of the Story: Structures and Strategies of Contemporary Feminist Narratives*. Ithaca: Cornell University Press, 1989.

———. "Review of Claire Sprague's *Rereading Doris Lessing*." *Doris Lessing Newsletter* 11, no. 2 (Fall 1987): 12–13.

Hole, Judith, and Ellen Levine. *The Rebirth of Feminism*. New York: Quadrangle, 1971.

Holloway, John. "The Literary Scene." In *The New Pelican Guide to English Literature: The Present,* ed. Boris Ford, 417–49. Harmondsworth, 1983.

Holmquist, Ingrid. *From Society to Nature: A Study of Doris Lessing's Children of Violence*. Gothenburg Studies in English 47. Acta Universitatis Gothoburgensis, 1980.

Howe, Irving. Review of *The Golden Notebook. New Republic* 147, Dec. 15, 1962, 17–20. Reprinted in *Critical Essays on Doris Lessing,* ed. Claire Sprague and Virginia Tiger, 177–81. Boston: G. K. Hall, 1986.

Howes, Victor. Review of *Memoirs*. "Biting a Bullet with a Marshmallow Center." *Christian Science Monitor* 67, June 12, 1975, 22.

Irvine, Lorna. "No Sense of an Ending: Drabble's Continuous Fictions." In Ellen Cronan Rose, ed. *Critical Essays on Margaret Drabble,* 73–86. Boston: G. K. Hall, 1985.

Jacobus, Mary, ed. *Women Writing and Writing About Women*. New York: Barnes and Noble, 1979.

———. "The Difference of View." In Jacobus, *Women Writing,* 10–20.

Jameson, Fredric. *The Political Unconscious: Narrative as a Socially Symbolic Act*. Ithaca: Cornell University Press, 1982.

Jong, Erica. *Fear of Flying*. New York: Signet, 1973.

———. Review of *Summer before the Dark. Partisan Review* 40 (1973): 500–503.

Jouve, Nicole Ward. "Of Mud and Other Matter—*The Children of Violence*." In Jenny Taylor, 75–134. Boston: Routledge, 1982.

Jung, Carl. *Mandala Symbolism*. Princeton: Princeton University Press, 1972.

Kaminer, Wendy. *A Fearful Freedom: Women's Flight from Equality*. Reading, Mass: Addison-Wesley, 1980.

Kaplan, Carey, and Ellen Cronan Rose. *Doris Lessing: The Alchemy of Survival*. Athens: Ohio University Press, 1988.

———, eds. *Approaches to Teaching Lessing's "The Golden Notebook."* New York: Modern Language Association of America, 1989.

Kaplan, Sydney Janet. *Feminine Consciousness in the Modern British Novel*. Chicago: University of Illinois Press, 1975.

———. "Passionate Portrayal of Things to Come: Doris Lessing's Recent Fiction." In *Twentieth-Century Women Novelists,* ed. Thomas F. Staley, 1–15. London: Macmillan, 1982.

Karl, Frederick R. "Doris Lessing in the Sixties: The New Anatomy of Melancholy." *Contemporary Literature* 23 (Winter 1972): 15–33.

———. *A Reader's Guide to the Contemporary English Novel*. New York: Farrar, Straus and Giroux, 1971.

Kaufman, Sue. *Diary of a Mad Housewife*. New York: Bantam, 1970.

Kermode, Frank. *The Sense of an Ending: Studies in the Theory of Fiction*. London: Oxford University Press, 1975.

King, Jeannette. *Doris Lessing*. London: Edward Arnold, 1989.

King, Mary. *Freedom Song: A Personal Story of the 1960s Civil Rights Movement*. New York: Morrow, 1987.

Knapp, Mona. *Doris Lessing*. New York: Frederick Ungar, 1984.

———. *"The Golden Notebook:* A Feminist Context for the Classroom." In Carey Kaplan and Ellen Cronan Rose, 108–14, *Doris Lessing: The Alchemy of Survival,* ed. Athens: Ohio University Press, 1988.

Korn, Eric. Review of *Marriages*. "Al·Ith in Wonderland." *Times Literary Supplement,* May 9, 1980, 520.

Kostelanetz, Richard, ed. *On Contemporary Literature*. New York: Avon, 1964.

Kress, Susan. "Lessing's Responsibility." *Salmagundi* (Winter–Spring 1980): 95–131.

Kristeva, Julia. "The Novel as Polylogue." In *Desire in Language: A Semiotic Approach to Literature and Art,* ed. Leon S. Roudiez, 159–209. New York: Columbia University Press, 1980.

———. "Women's Time." *Signs* 7, no. 1 (1981): 13–35.

———. "Word, Dialogue, and Novel." In Roudiez, *Desire in Language,* 64–91.

Laing, R. D. *The Politics of Experience and the Bird of Paradise*. Harmondsworth: Penguin, 1970.

Lardner, Susan. "Angle on the Ordinary," *New Yorker,* Sept. 19, 1983, 140–54.

———. Review of *The Good Terrorist*. "A Kind of Dryness." *New Yorker,* Oct. 14, 1985, 136–40.

Laurence, Margaret. *The Fire-Dwellers*. Toronto: McClelland and Stewart, 1984.

Le Guin, Ursula K. Review of *Shikasta. New Republic* 181, Oct. 13, 1979, 32, 24.

———. Review of *Marriages. New Republic* 182, Mar. 29, 1980, 878.

Lehmann-Haupt, Christopher. Review of *Memoirs*. *New York Times* 124, June 2, 1975, 23.

Leonard, John. "In Person." *Newsday*, Mar. 17, 1988, 2:8. Reprinted in *Doris Lessing Newsletter* 12, no. 2 (Fall 1989): 5.

———. "The Spacing Out of Doris Lessing," *New York Times Book Review*, Feb. 7, 1982. Reprinted in *Critical Essays on Doris Lessing*, ed. Claire Sprague and Virginia Tiger, 204–9. Boston: G. K. Hall, 1986.

Lessing, Doris. *African Laughter*. New York: HarperCollins, 1992.

———. *Briefing for a Descent into Hell*. New York: Bantam, 1972.

———. *The Diaries of Jane Somers*. New York: Vintage, 1984.

———. *The Fifth Child*. New York: Knopf, 1988.

———. *The Four-Gated City*. New York: New American Library, 1976.

———. *The Good Terrorist*. New York: Knopf, 1985.

———. *The Golden Notebook*. New York: Bantam, 1973.

———. *The Grass Is Singing*. New York: New American Library, 1976.

———. "A Conversation with Doris Lessing," ed. Bernd Dietz and Fernando Galvan. *Doris Lessing Newsletter* 9, no. 1 (Spring 1985): 4–6.

———. Interview by Minda Bikman, *New York Times Book Review* 85, Mar. 30, 1980, 1ff.

———. Interview with Christopher Bigsby. *The Radical Imagination and the Liberal Tradition: Interviews with English and American Novelists*, ed. Heide Ziegler and Christopher Bigsby, 188–208. London: Junction Books, 1982.

———. Interview by Henryk Kellermann and Hans-Peter Rodenberg. *Doris Lessing Newsletter* 13, no. 1 (Summer 1989): 3–4.

———. Interview with Roy Newquist, Oct. 1963. *Counterpoint*. Chicago: Rand McNally, 1964. Reprinted in Schlueter, *A Small Personal Voice*, 45–60..

———. Interview by Jonah Raskin, at Stony Brook. In Schlueter, *A Small Personal Voice*, 61–76.

———. Interview by Nissa Torrents. "Testimony to Mysticism." *Doris Lessing Newsletter* 4, no. 2 (Winter 1980): 12–13.

———. *Landlocked*. New York: New American Library, 1966.

———. *The Making of the Representative for Planet 8*. New York: Knopf, 1982.

———. *The Marriages between Zones Three, Four, and Five*. New York: Vintage, 1981.

———. *Martha Quest*. New York: New American Library, 1964.

———. "Afterword to *The Story of an African Farm* by Olive Schreiner," in *A Small Personal Voice: Doris Lessing, Essays, Reviews, Interviews*, ed. Paul Schlueter, 97–120. New York: Vintage, 1972.

———. *A Proper Marriage*. New York: New American Library, 1970..

———. *Prisons We Choose to Live Inside*. New York: Harper and Row, 1987.

———. *The Real Thing: Stories and Sketches*. New York: HarperCollins, 1992.

———. *Retreat to Innocence*. London: Michael Joseph, 1959.

———. *A Ripple from the Storm*. New York: New American Library, 1966.

———. *Shikasta*. New York: Vintage, 1981.

———. *The Sirian Experiments: The Report by Ambien II, of the Five*. New York: Knopf, 1980.

———. *The Summer before the Dark.* New York: Bantam, 1974.

———. "The Small Personal Voice," In Schlueter, *A Small Personal Voice,* 3–21.

———. "My Father." In Schlueter, *A Small Personal Voice,* 83–93.

———. "My Mother's Life," pt. 1. *Granta* 14 (Winter 1984): 52–68.

———. "My Mother's Life," pt. 2. *Granta* 17 (Fall 1985): 227–38.

———. "Women's Quests." *Partisan Review* (May 1992).

Levinson, Deirdre. Review of *The Good Terrorist.* "Future Shocked." *Nation,* Nov. 23, 1985, 557–59.

Lifson, Martha. "Structural Patterns in *The Golden Notebook.*" *Michigan Papers in Women's Studies* 2, no. 4 (1978): 95–108.

Lorde, Audre. "The Master's Tools Will Never Dismantle the Master's House." In *This Bridge Called My Back: Writings of Radical Women of Color,* ed. Gloria Anzaldúa and Cherríe Moraga, 98–101. New York: Women of Color Press, 1981.

Lukács, George. "The Ideology of Modernism." In *The Meaning of Contemporary Realism* (1963). Trans. John and Necke Mander, 17–46. London: Merlin Press, 1969.

———. *Studies in European Realism.* 1–19. New York: Universal Library, 1964, 1946.

———. "The Problems of a Philosophy of the History of Forms" (1920). In *The Theory of the Novel,* 40–55. Cambridge: MIT Press, 1971.

Lurie, Alison. Review of *The Good Terrorist.* "Bad Housekeeping." *New York Review,* Dec. 19, 1985, 8–10.

Lydon, Susan. "Review of *Four-Gated City.*" *Ramparts,* Jan. 1970, 48–50.

McCallum, Pamela. Review of *Memoirs.* "Survival Gear." *Canadian Forum* 55 (Dec. 1975): 56–57.

Maccoby, Hyman. "Heaven and *Shikasta.*" *Listener* 102, Nov. 22, 1979, 715–16.

McDowell, P. W. Frederick. "The Fiction of Doris Lessing: An Interim View." *Arizona Quarterly* 21 (1965): 315–45.

Macey, Samuel L. *Patriarchs of Time: Dualism in Saturn-Cronus, Father Time, the Watchmaker God, and Father Christmas.* Athens: University of Georgia Press, 1987.

Macherey, Pierre. *A Theory of Literary Production.* Trans. Geoffrey Wall. London: Routledge, 1978.

McPheron, Judith. Review of *Memoirs. Library Journal* 100 (July 1975): 1346.

Magie, Michael L. "Doris Lessing and Romanticism." *College English* 38 (1977): 531–52.

Marcus, Jane. "Invisible Mending." In *Between Women: Biographers, Novelists, Critics, Teachers, and Artists Write about Their Work on Women,* ed. Carol Ascher, Louise De Salvo, and Sara Ruddick, 381–95. Boston: Beacon Press, 1984.

Margulies, Alfred. "Toward Empathy: The Uses of Wonder." *American Journal of Psychiatry* 141, no. 9 (1984): 1025–33.

Markos, Alice Bradley. "The Pathology of Feminine Failure in the Fiction of Doris Lessing." *Critique: Studies in Modern Fiction* 16 (1974): 88–99.

Miller, Jean Baker. *Toward a New Psychology of Women.* Boston: Beacon Press, 1976.

Miller, Jerome A. "Wonder as Hinge." *International Philosophical Quarterly* 29, no. 1 (Mar. 1989): 53–66.

Miller, Nancy K. *The Heroine's Text: Readings in the French and English Novel, 1722–1782*. New York: Columbia University Press, 1980.

———. "Arachnologies: The Woman, The Text, and the Critic." In Miller, *Heroine's Text,* 1986, 270–95.

———. "Emphasis Added: Plots and Plausibilities in Women's Fiction." *PMLA* 96, no. 1 (Jan. 1981): 36–48.

———. ed. *The Poetics of Gender*. New York: Columbia University Press, 1986.

Millett, Kate. *Flying*. New York: Simon and Schuster, 1990.

Milton, John. *Paradise Lost. Complete Poems and Major Prose*. Ed. Merritt Y. Hughes. New York: Odyssey Press, 1957.

Miner, Valerie. *Movement*. New York: Methuen, 1982.

Mitchell, W. J. T., ed. *On Narrative*. Chicago: University of Chicago Press, 1980.

Morgan, Ellen. "Alienation of the Woman Writer in *The Golden Notebook*." In *Doris Lessing: Critical Studies,* ed. Annis Pratt and L. S. Dembo, 54–63. Madison: University of Wisconsin Press, 1974.

Morris, Richard. *Time's Arrows*. New York: Simon and Schuster, 1984.

Morrison, Toni. *Beloved*. New York: Random House, 1987.

Mulkeen, Anne M. "Twentieth-Century Realism: The 'Grid' Structure of *The Golden Notebook*." *Studies in the Novel* 4, no. 2 (Summer 1972): 262–74.

Neumann, Erich. *The Great Mother: An Analysis of the Archetype*. Trans. Ralph Manheim. Princeton: Princeton University Press, 1972.

Newquist, Roy. "Interview with Doris Lessing." In *A Small Personal Voice,* ed. Paul Schlueter. Vintage: N.Y., 1975, 45–60.

Oakley, Anne. *The Men's Room*. New York: Ballantine, 1988.

Oates, Joyce Carol. Review of *Four-Gated City*. *Saturday Review of Literature* 52 (May 17, 1969): 48. Reprinted in *Critical Essays on Doris Lessing,* ed. Claire Sprague and Virginia Tiger, 174–76. Boston: G. K. Hall, 1986.

O'Rourke, Rebecca. "Doris Lessing: Exile and Exception." In *Notebooks, Memoirs, Archives: Reading and Rereading Doris Lessing,* ed. Jenny Taylor, 206–26. Boston: Routledge, 1982.

Parrinder, Patrick. "Descents into Hell: The Later Novels of Doris Lessing." *Critical Quarterly* 22, no. 4 (Winter 1980): 5–25.

Pearson, Carol, and Katherine Pope. *The Female Hero in American and British Literature*. New York: R. R. Bowker, 1981.

Piercy, Marge. *Small Changes*. New York: Fawcett Crest, 1973.

Plath, Sylvia. *The Bell Jar*. New York: Bantam, 1981.

Porter, Nancy. "Silenced History—*Children of Violence* and *The Golden Notebook*." *World Literature Written in English* 12 (Nov. 1973): 161–79.

Pratt, Annis. *Archetypal Patterns in Women's Fiction*. Bloomington: Indiana University Press, 1981.

Pratt, Annis, and L.S. Dembo, eds. *Doris Lessing: Critical Studies*. Madison: University of Wisconsin Press, 1974.

Preussner, Dee. "Talking with Margaret Drabble." *Modern Fiction Studies* 25, no. 4 (1989–90).

Rapping, Elayne Antler. "'Unfree Women': Feminism in Doris Lessing's Novels." *Women's Studies* 3 (1975).

Rich, Adrienne. "The Contemporary Emergency and the Quantum Leap." *On Lies.*

———. "Disloyal to Civilization: Feminism, Racism, Gynephobia." *On Lies,* 275–310.

———. "The Temptations of a Motherless Woman." *On Lies,* 89–106.

———. "When We Dead Awaken: Writing as Revision." *On Lies, Secrets, and Silence: Selected Prose, 1966–1978,* 259–73. New York: Norton, 1979.

Rose, Ellen Cronan. "The End of the Game: New Directions in Doris Lessing's Fiction." *Journal of Narrative Technique* 6, no. 1 (Winter 1976): 66–75.

———. Review of *The Diaries of Jane Somers.* "A Lessing in Disguise." *Women's Review of Books* 2, no. 5 (Feb. 1985): 7–8.

———. "Twenty Questions." *Doris Lessing Newsletter,* 4, no. 2 (Winter 1980): 5.

Rose, Ellen Cronan, and Carey Kaplan, eds. *Approaches to Teaching Lessing's "The Golden Notebook."* New York: Modern Language Association of America, 1989.

———. *The Canon and the Common Reader.* Knoxville: University of Tennessee Press, 1991.

Rosen, Ellen I. "Martha's 'Quest' in Lessing's *Children of Violence.*" *Frontiers* 3, no. 2 (1978): 54–59.

Rowe, Marsha. "If you mate a swan and a gander, who will ride?" In *Notebooks, Memoirs, Archives: Reading and Rereading Doris Lessing,* ed. Jenny Taylor, 191–205. Boston: Routledge, 1982.

Rozencwajg, Iris. "Interview with Margaret Drabble." *Women's Studies* 9 (1979): 335–47.

Rubenstein, Roberta. *Boundaries of the Self: Gender, Culture, Fiction.* Urbana and Chicago: University of Illinois Press, 1987.

———. *The Novelistic Vision of Doris Lessing: Breaking the Forms of Consciousness.* Urbana: University of Illinois Press, 1979.

Ruddick, Sara. "Maternal Thinking," *Feminist Studies* 6, no. 2 (Summer 1980): 342–67.

———. *Maternal Thinking: Toward a Politics of Peace.* Boston: Beacon Press, 1989.

Russ, Joanna. "What Can a Heroine Do? or Why Can't Women Write?" In *Woman as Writer,* ed. Jeanette L. Weber and Joan Grumman, 158–63. Boston: Houghton Mifflin, 1978.

Sage, Lorna. *Contemporary Writers: Doris Lessing.* London: Methuen, 1983.

Shafer, Roy. "Narrative in the Psychoanalytic Dialogue." In *On Narrative,* ed. W. J. T. Mitchell, 25–49. Chicago: University of Chicago Press, 1980.

Schlueter, Paul. *A Small Personal Voice: Doris Lessing, Essays, Reviews, Interviews.* New York: Vintage, 1972.

Shakespeare, William. *The Complete Pelican Shakespeare.* Ed. Alfred Harbage. Baltimore: Penguin, 1969.

Shah, Idries. *The Sufis.* New York: Doubleday, 1971.

———. *Thinkers of the East: Teachings of the Dervishes.* Baltimore: Penguin, 1972.

Showalter, Elaine. *A Literature of Their Own: British Women Novelists from Bronte to Lessing.* London: Virago, 1978.

———. *The New Feminist Criticism: Essays on Women, Literature, Theory*. New York: Pantheon, 1985.

Shulman, Alix Kates. *Memoirs of an Ex–Prom Queen*. New York: Bantam, 1972.

Singleton, Mary Ann. *The City and the Veld: The Fiction of Doris Lessing*. Lewisburg: Bucknell University Press, 1977.

Sizemore, Christine W. "Reading the City as Palimpsest: The Experiential Perception of the City in Doris Lessing's *Four-Gated City*." In *Women Writers and the City: Essays in Feminist Literary Criticism,* ed. Susan M. Squier, 176–90. Knoxville: University of Tennessee Press, 1984.

Squier, Susan M. *Women Writers and the City: Essays in Feminist Literary Criticism*. Knoxville: University of Tennessee Press, 1984.

Smith, Barbara. Introduction. *Home Girls—A Black Feminist Anthology,* ed. Barbara Smith. New York: Kitchen Table / Women of Color Press, 1983.

Smith, Harold L., ed. *British Feminism in the Twentieth Century*. Amherst: University of Massachusetts Press, 1990.

Snitow, Ann Barr. "A Vindication of Doris Lessing." *Voice Literary Supplement* 39, Oct. 1985, 6ff.

Spacks, Patricia Meyer. *The Female Imagination*. New York: Knopf, 1975.

Sprague, Claire. "Dialectic and Counter-Dialectic in the Martha Quest Novels." *Journal of Commonwealth Literature* 14, no. 1 (Aug. 1979): 39–52.

———. "Doubletalk and Doubles Talk in *The Golden Notebook*." *Papers on Language and Literature* 18, no. 2 (Spring 1982): 181–97.

———. "Doubles Talk in *The Golden Notebook*." In *Critical Essays on Doris Lessing,* ed. Claire Sprague and Virginia Tiger, 44–60. Boston: G. K. Hall, 1986.

———. *Rereading Doris Lessing: Narrative Patterns of Doubling and Repetition*. Chapel Hill: University of North Carolina Press, 1987.

Sprague, Claire, and Virginia Tiger. *Critical Essays on Doris Lessing*. Boston: G. K. Hall, 1986.

Stade, George. Review of *Shikasta*. "Fantastic Lessing." *New York Times Book Review,* Nov. 4, 1979, 1.

Stamberg, Susan. "An Interview with Doris Lessing." *Doris Lessing Newsletter* 8, no. 2 (1984): 3ff.

St. Andrews, Bonnie. *Forbidden Fruit: On the Relationship between Women and Knowledge in Doris Lessing, Selma Lagerlof, Kate Chopin, and Margaret Atwood*. Troy, N.Y.: Whiston, 1986.

Sternberg-Perrakis, Phyllis. "*The Golden Notebook:* Separation and Symbiosis." *American Imago* 38, no. 4 (Winter 1981): 407–28.

Stevenson, Randall. *The British Novel since the Thirties: An Introduction* Athens: University of Georgia Press, 1986.

Stewart, Grace. *A New Mythos: The Novel of the Artist as Heroine, 1877–1977* Montreal: Eden Press, 1981.

Stimpson, Catharine R. "Doris Lessing and the Parables of Growth." In *The Voyage In: Fictions of Female Development,* ed. Elizabeth Abel, Marianne Hirsch, and Elizabeth Langland, 186–205. Hanover, N.H.: University Press of New England, 1983.

Stitzel, Judith. "Reading Doris Lessing." *College English* 40, no. 5 (Jan. 1979): 458–504.

Stone, Laurie. *Ms.* July–Aug 1987, 29.

Sukenick, Lyn. "Feeling and Reason in Doris Lessing's Fiction." In *Doris Lessing: Critical Studies,* ed. Annis Pratt and L. S. Dembo, 98–118. Madison: University of Wisconsin Press, 1974.

Swinden, Patrick. *The English Novel of History and Society, 1940–1980.* London: Macmillan, 1984.

Taubman, Robert. "Free Women." *New Statesman,* Apr. 20, 1962. Reprinted in Kostelanetz, 402–3.

Taylor, Jenny, ed. *Notebooks, Memoirs, Archives: Reading and Rereading Doris Lessing.* Boston: Routledge, 1982.

———. "Introduction: Situated Reading." In Taylor, *Notebooks,* 1–42.

Thale, Jerome. "The Anatomy of the Mental Personality." *New Introductory Lectures on Psycho-Analysis. University of Toronto Quarterly* 25 (July 1955): 82–112. Reprinted *Norton Critical Heart of Darkness,* 180–86.

Thorpe, Michael. Reprinted in *Doris Lessing.* London: Longman, 1973.

Tobin, Patricia. *Time and the Novel: The Genealogical Imperative.* Princeton: Princeton University Press, 1978.

Todd, Janet, ed. *Feminist Literary History.* New York: Routledge, 1988.

———. *Women Writers Talking.* New York: Holmes and Meier, 1983.

Tolson, Andrew. *The Limits of Masculinity.* London: Tavistock, 1977.

Torrents, Nissa. "Testimony to Mysticism: Interview with Lessing." *Doris Lessing Newsletter* 4, no. 2 (Winter 1980): 12.

Trilling, Diana. Review of Doris Lessing. *Times Literary Supplement,* Oct. 1978, 1165.

Walker, Melissa G. "Doris Lessing's *The Four-Gated City:* Consciousness and Community—a Different History." *Southern Review* 17, no. 1 (Jan. 1981): 97–120.

Wandor, Michelene. *Once a Feminist: Stories of a Generation.* London: Virago, 1990.

Waugh, Patricia. *Feminine Fictions: Revisiting the Postmodern.* London: Routledge, 1989.

Webb, Marilyn. "Feminism and Doris Lessing: Becoming the Men We Wanted to Marry." *Village Voice,* Jan. 4, 1973, 1ff.

Webber, Jeannette L., and Joan Grumman, eds. *Woman as Writer.* Boston: Houghton Mifflin, 1978.

Weldon, Fay. *The Fat Woman's Joke.* Chicago: Academy, 1967.

Weston, Jesse L. *From Ritual to Romance.* Garden City, N.Y.: Doubleday Anchor, 1957.

Whittaker, Ruth. *Modern Novelists: Doris Lessing.* New York: St. Martin's Press, 1988.

Williams, Raymond. *The Long Revolution.* London: Chatto and Windus, 1961.

———. *Marxism and Literature.* Oxford: Oxford University Press, 1977.

Wilson, Elizabeth. *Only Halfway to Paradise.* New York: Tavistock, 1980.

———. "The British Women's Movement." In *Hidden Agendas: Theory, Politics, and Experience in the Women's Movement,* ed. Elizabeth Wilson and Angela Weir, 93–133. London: Tavistock, 1986.

———. "Yesterday's Heroines: On Rereading Lessing and de Beauvoir." In *Notebooks, Memoirs, Archives: Reading and Rereading Doris Lessing,* ed. Jenny Taylor, 57–74. Boston: Routledge, 1982.

Wilson, Elizabeth, and Angela Weir. *Hidden Agendas: Theory, Politics, and Experience in the Women's Movement.* London: Tavistock, 1986.

Wolf, Naomi. *The Beauty Myth: How Images of Beauty Are Used Against Women.* New York: William Morrow, 1991.

Woolf, Virginia. *Mrs. Dalloway.* New York: Harcourt, 1925.

Wyatt, Jean. *Reconstructing Desire: The Role of the Unconscious in Women's Reading and Writing.* Chapel Hill: University of North Carolina Press, 1990.

Zwerdling, Alex. Review of *Memoirs.* "Toward Prophetic Fiction." *Sewanee Revue* 2 (June 29, 1975): 36.

# Index